To CALEB
   BEST WISHES IN ALL YOUR
POSITIVE WORK TO BENEFIT MAN-
                     KIND!
      Oliver W. Hill
           12/2/2000

The Big Bang
<u>Brown vs Board of Education,</u>
                    and Beyond

To Caleb
   May God Guide your
Path as you chose the
work that will enliven
your great contribution
to Human Progress

              Best wishes
              John
              12/2/2000

Oliver W. Hill, Sr. Accepting the 1999 Presidential Medal of Freedom
from President William Clinton

The Big Bang
<u>Brown vs Board of Education</u>,
and Beyond:
The Autobiography of Oliver W. Hill, Sr.

by

Oliver W. Hill, Sr.

Edited by

Jonathan K. Stubbs

FOUR-G Publishers, Inc.
2000

FOUR-G Publishers Cataloging-in-Publication

Hill, Oliver, W. Sr.
   The Big Bang: Brown vs Board of Education, and Beyond; the autobiography of Oliver W. Hill, Sr., by Oliver W. Hill, Sr.; with Jonathan K. Stubbs, editor. Winter Park, FL., FOUR-G Publishers, Inc., 2000.

   400 p. 23 cm
   Hardcover -- ISBN: 1885066-79-1
   Paperback -- ISBN: 1885066-62-7

Copies of this book are available from:

Oliver W. Hill Book Fund
3108 Noble Avenue
Richmond, VA 23228
E-mail: owh999@aol.com

Published by
FOUR-G Publishers, Inc.
P.O. Box 2249
Winter Park, FL 32790
(407) 294-6446

Printed in the UNITED STATES OF AMERICA
Cover design by Mary Wismar-Davis

Cover credit: Bank of America
Cover credit: Richmond Free Press
Cover credit: Richmond Times Dispatch

iv

TABLE OF CONTENTS

Dedicated
to the memory
of my
beloved wife,
Beresenia Walker Hill

Mrs. Beresenia Walker Hill
1911-1993

AUTHOR'S ACKNOWLEDGMENTS

I join Brother Stubbs, the editor, in extending thanks to all who have helped us with this project. I especially thank the editor for accommodating the many changes that I required.

Commencing with the Virginia Commission on Women and Minorities in the Legal System Award presented to my law partner, S.W. Tucker and me in 1987 by Associate United States Supreme Court Justice, Lewis F. Powell, Jr., my life has been like a roller coaster. I have had a number of fantastic highs and some equally devastating lows. Starting in 1948 with the Chicago Defender Merit Award which was conferred upon me following my election to the Richmond City Council, I have received my share of positive recognition. Incidentally, the Chicago Defender Merit Award plaque, with a modest bit of hyperbole, referred to me as "fearless". Notwithstanding that description, I have not sought or been worried about stardom because all of my life, I have been a team player. In my early years, I played team sports like basketball, football, soccer, baseball; and in my legal, humanitarian and political activities I have been part of a large team of lawyers and activists dedicated to creating a more just and humane society for all human earthlings.

I have had tremendous support for my endeavors from my family and friends. I especially wish to acknowledge the efforts of innumerable NAACP members and supporters over the past seventy years. There are many names that I should call but records have been destroyed, my memory is not what it once was, and I cannot presently do justice to those whom I desire to honor as I would like to. However, to all those who are living and to those who have passed on I owe and acknowledge a great debt of thanks.

While in the last decade, I have been literally showered with honors, including the naming of the Richmond Juvenile and Domestic Relations Court Building in my honor; the naming of the Freedom Fighter Award of the Virginia State Conference of NAACP Branches in my honor; and more recently, I was awarded the Presidential Medal of Freedom. And, as I mentioned, I have also had some challenging lows during that same time. Accordingly, I wish to close these acknowledgments by pointing to the lives of several individuals who were close to me who have passed away during that time. At the beginning of the decade of the 1990's, S. W. Tucker, my long time partner and friend whom I met in my junior year of college, died. Tucker and I had planned to form a firm together in 1940 but before we could do so he received his military induction greetings from Uncle Sam.

Less than three years after Tucker's death, Thurgood Marshall, my law school classmate and compatriot in many civil rights struggles commencing in the 1930's and ending in the 1960's also passed away. Thurgood and I were life long friends.

An even more devastating loss which I suffered in the same year of Thurgood's death was the passing of my beloved wife, soul mate, companion and friend, of over sixty years, Beresenia Walker Hill. Without Bernie's invaluable sacrifices and support, much of what I have been able to accomplish would have been impossible. Bernie's passing has affected me in ways in which I am still coming to terms.

Not long after Bernie's death, Bernie's sister, Evalyn Walker Shaed who was a loyal and compassionate friend to me for over sixty years also died. Evalyn was a member of our household for nearly sixty years, the second mother for our son, Oliver, Jr., and the office manager of our law firm for many years.

In addition, I pay tribute to Harold Marsh who was one of

my law partners for approximately thirty years and whose recent assassination has been a great tragedy to our community. Moreover, Spotswood Robinson, III, my first law partner, long time friend and associate, and the godfather of my son passed away recently. About a month following Spot's death, my fellow activist and friend of nearly fifty years, A. Leon Higginbotham, Jr. died. These transitions, all happening within a short period of time, have caused me great pain.

In these circumstances, writing this book has been complicated. The challenges have been compounded because I have experienced a series of mini strokes, a heart attack, and the recent loss of my vision. I make these comments not by way of excuse but by way of explanation. Even though this book is approximately four hundred pages long, some people who should be acknowledged have not been explicitly and extensively recognized, and some matters of historical interest have not been included.

I am reminded of the adage that one's friends do not need explanations and one's enemies will not believe them. I am further reminded of another statement which is familiar, especially in Negro communities, in the United States, and which I will paraphrase here: "please charge any omissions or misstatements to my head, and not to my heart."

The August, 1999 *Richmond Times-Dispatch* coverage of the awarding of the 1999 Presidential Medal of Freedom to Oliver W. Hill, Sr.

The announcement of the Bank of America Salute to Oliver W. Hill, Sr., *"Richmond, VA Native and Civil Rights Pioneer"* in <u>The Richmond Free Press</u>, 1999

EDITOR'S PREFACE

In some respects, Mr. Oliver W. Hill, Sr., and I are very alike; in others we are quite different. For example, Mr. Hill has stated in the past that I may call him, Oliver. That is broad-minded, progressive and egalitarian. However, on some matters, I am more conventional in my approach; accordingly, I have been unable to refer to Mr. Hill as Oliver. In my southern "down home" African-American cultural tradition, you don't call a person twice your age, and infinitely more wise, by his first name. That said, (gentle reader) you may better understand the genesis of this collaborative effort by Mr. Hill and me.

I first met Mr. Hill briefly in 1986 while planning my move back from Washington, D.C. to Virginia. Elaine R. Jones, Esq. who now directs the Legal Defense Fund with which Mr. Hill has worked for over fifty years, gave me prescient advice: pay a courtesy call at the law firm of Hill, Tucker & Marsh.

Some months later, I met Mr. Hill in the Clerk's Office of the Circuit Court of Gloucester County, Virginia. Mr. Hill and his protégé, Randall Johnson, Sr. (now Chief Richmond Circuit Judge Randall Johnson) were conducting legal research. It struck me that Judge Johnson, Reuben Hill, Jr. (another African-American attorney in the Clerk's Office at that time) and I were all beneficiaries of the dedicated efforts of Mr. Hill which had spanned over half a century. I am convinced that subconsciously I decided that if an opportunity presented itself I would try to show my respect and appreciation for his work. After all, but for the efforts of Mr. Hill and others like him, I would not have been blessed with the opportunity to practice law or engage in numerous other personal and professional activities.

In 1989, I began to teach full-time at the University of Richmond School of Law, and early in 1992 decided to approach

xii

Mr. Hill with the idea of writing his autobiography. Mr. Hill readily agreed to a series of interviews (some lasting several hours) regarding his life and work. These interviews were painstakingly transcribed by Ms. Anne Smith, my legal assistant, and were subsequently edited into chapters by A. Pierre Jackson, one of my research assistants who has since become a member of the Virginia bar and a dynamic force for progressive change. Incidentally, Mr. Jackson is presently headquartered in Farmville, Virginia, the site of one of the five cases which was consolidated in the litigation which became known as <u>Brown v. Board of Education</u>.

Following this initial restructuring of the book, the manuscript has been edited and commented upon by a number of distinguished individuals. There is a great danger in naming names. Invariably, despite one's best efforts, someone is left out. To avoid this difficulty, I wish to thank ALL those individuals who read, conducted research for, encouraged and in any way supported the work on this book. I also thank God for life itself, which has lasted long enough to bring this project to fruition.

In my view, these thanks are neither gratuitous nor superfluous; for when Mr. Hill and I began working on this project in 1992, a number of individuals actively supported the endeavor; however, they are not physically present now to appreciate its conclusion. I mention specifically, Mr. Hill's wife, Bernie, whose judicious reading of the manuscript and sagacious counsel (particularly regarding sometimes colorful choices of words) added much to this version of the text. In addition, retired Chief Judge A. Leon Higginbotham, Jr., graciously consented to write the foreword for the autobiography; however, before he could complete this project, he passed away. Furthermore, retired Chief Judge Spottswood W. Robinson, III, readily agreed to be a sounding post and resource for the writing of the autobiography; however, he, too, has moved to higher ground. Finally, my beloved father, Calvin Kenneth Stubbs, was very interested in the project from its inception, and even as he recognized the imminence of his own departure, he encouraged me to persevere with "the book."

Having thanked all those who participated in any way to bring this book to fruition, and therefore hopefully having partially gotten myself off of the hook associated with being a forgetful professor, I nevertheless wish to thank specifically some individuals who have been involved in this work. First, I am grateful to the author himself, Mr. Hill, for putting up with me for seven years and going over the text of the manuscript word by word, sentence by sentence, line by line, paragraph by paragraph and page by page on at least half a dozen occasions. Mr. Hill's attention to detail, positive outlook upon life, and determination to continue struggling for justice for all has been an inspiration to me and an educational experience which has served as a capstone to my professional development in the law. Mr. Hill has persevered with this endeavor despite the deaths of loved ones and several significant health challenges.

Secondly, I wish to thank my legal assistant, Anne Smith, who has corrected the book too many times to be counted. Thirdly, I wish to express my gratitude to my colleagues at the University of Richmond School of Law, and especially Okianer Christian Dark, who provided mentorship and encouragement in this project, John Paul Jones, who likewise provided advice and encouragement and W. Hamilton Bryson, whose pioneering biographical work in Virginia legal history provided inspiration.

Further thanks are due to Professor Daryl Dance of the University of Richmond English Department, who read early and late drafts of the book manuscript and provided generously of her time and keen insights regarding the text; Adolphus L. Williams, Jr., Esq., my mentor and friend, who similarly provided comments on early and late versions of the manuscript; and A. Pierre Jackson, Esq., my former student and research assistant and now colleague at the Bar, who worked assiduously in bringing this project to its present state.

Ms. Esther Vassar volunteered to chair fundraising efforts for the publication of the book and provided expert editorial assistance as well. Through Ms. Vassar's efforts a number of individuals and corporate sponsors stepped forward to provide tangible financial support for this compelling cause. Specifically thanks are due to The Freddie Mac Corporation, which provided generous material support; Jim Ukrop, Chairman of the Ukrop Corporation for a substantial grant; Dominion Resources and its forward thinking Senior Vice President, Eva Teig; U.S. Senator Charles "Chuck" Robb whose unwavering support has been invaluable; and the judges of the Oliver W. Hill, Sr. Court Building, namely Chief Judge Angela Edwards Roberts, and Judges Harold W. Burgess, Jr., Audrey J. Franks, Kimberly B. O'Donnell, Richard D. Taylor, Jr. and Ann Holton.

Similarly, the American Bar Association Book Publishing Division furnished editorial support in the early stages of the manuscript development and extended itself in numerous other ways to further the prospects of publication. Within the legal academy, thanks are due colleagues too numerous to name, and while I thank them all I specifically wish to express gratitude to my supportive friends Linda S. Greene, Alice Gresham-Bullock, Steven W. Hobbs, Bryan Fair, Leland Ware, Warner Lawson, J. Clay Smith, Jr., Joseph D. Harbaugh, Taylor Reveley, Gregory Williams, Charles Ogletree, Jack Greenberg, Stephen Carter and John Pagan. For expert technical help, research assistance and collegial support, I am also deeply indebted to Allen Moye. Other present and former students whom I wish to thank are the following: A. Gray Collins, Esq., Melanie Shepherd, Esq., Elbert Mumphery, Esq., Deborah Hines, Esq., Carla Jean-McNeil Jackson, Connie L. McCalla, Ramona Taylor, Courtney Sydnor, Chris Bain, Esq., Rophenia Crawley, Terrance Deans, Carla Simmons, Esq., Randall Johnson, Jr., Esq., Dawn Johnson, Esq., Nadine Carter, Esq., Vanessa Wilson, and Tara Minter, Esq.

For encouragement and support additional thanks are due to the Old Dominion Bar Association and to members of Mr. Hill's firm, particularly Mr. Hill's law partners, especially Henry Marsh, Esq., Clarence Dunnaville, Esq., and the late Harold Marsh, Esq. Unfailing cheerfulness and assistance from the Hill, Tucker, and Marsh support staff is also greatly appreciated, especially that of Mr. Hill's legal assistant, Ms. Margaret Cosby and the irrepressible Dr. Diane Marsh.

This book benefitted from the expert photographic assistance and eagle eye of Herbert "Sonny" Rudlin of Adams Camera Shop in Richmond. Thanks is also due to Dr. Clifford Muse, Archivist of Howard University, for his generous assistance in obtaining photographs of Mr. Hill's longtime friends and mentors Dean Charles Hamilton Houston, Judge William H. Hastie and Professor Leon A. Ransom.

I acknowledge with deep gratitude the good cheer and thoughtfulness of Mr. Hill's immediate family, especially Oliver, Jr. and his wife, Renee, as well as Thomas Ferrell, Maia King, Jelani Ferrell, Jamaa Bickley-King, and Jananda Hill.

A few final personal notes. The support of my family, both personal, genetic, and spiritual has been invaluable. My wife, Pamela (Lovely One), our daughter, Amanda (Little Lovely One), my mother, E. P., my brother, M.A., and my new mom, Mom Lessie, as well as others, (you know who you are), thank you very much.

As a personal tribute to Mr. Hill, following the last chapter of the book and endnotes, I have written a short story on the human race and human rights.

As editor, while I have done my best to make the book as polished as possible, I readily accept the responsibility for flaws in the present text.

AUTHOR'S INTRODUCTION

In writing this book I had several objectives in mind. First, I wish to correct the mistaken notion that the African American civil rights movement started in the 1960's with the sit-ins or perhaps a bit earlier in Montgomery, Alabama with Dr. Martin Luther King, Jr. Contrary to popular belief, the African American civil rights struggle dates back to the mid-seventeenth century when an African American slave woman fought for the freedom of her child by bringing a lawsuit asserting that the child was free because the father was a free Negro. Contemporaneous with her action was a lawsuit initiated by a black slave for freedom from a black slaveholder. From those beginnings, Negroes have engaged in an unrelenting struggle for human freedom and dignity employing a variety of responses including, running away, nonviolent protests, and armed insurrections. In addition, Negroes have participated with courage and valor in all armed conflicts involving the United States from colonial days to the present.

In this book, I will discuss (among other things) the civil rights struggle in the twentieth century. For now, I wish to point out that Virginia is an example of the pervasive unremitting difficulties that Negroes have had in obtaining full protection of their constitutional rights. Here are a few examples of what I mean. In 1901 and 1902, a constitutional convention was held in Virginia for the express purpose of disenfranchising Virginia's Negro citizens and reestablishing segregation. Carter Glass, a leading segregationist politician, candidly addressed his fellow delegates at the convention about the primary purpose of the proceedings: "Discrimination! Why that is exactly what we propose; that exactly, is why this Convention was elected—to discriminate to the very extremity of permissible action...with a

xvii

view to the elimination of every Negro voter who could be gotten rid of, legally, without materially impairing the numerical strength of the white electorate."[1] Speaking candidly to his fellow segregationists, Senator Glass said: "This plan will eliminate the darkey as a political factor in this state in less than five years... [T]he article of suffrage which the convention will today adopt does not necessarily deprive a single white man of the ballot, but will inevitably cut from the existing electorate four fifths of the [N]egro voters."[2]

After making ample provision for disenfranchising Negro voters, and ensuring segregation in public education and transportation, the promulgators of this nefarious document became fearful that if it were submitted to the voters for approval that it would be defeated. Instead it was unlawfully rammed down the throats of the Virginia populace by proclamation. In <u>Jones v. Montague</u>,[3] the Supreme Court of the United States sustained this travesty.

In fact, within one hundred days of the promulgation of the Constitution, over one hundred and twenty-five thousand Negro voters were purged from the voting rolls.[4] Of the nearly one hundred and fifty thousand Negro voters in the state, by October 15, 1902, only twenty-one thousand remained on the rolls. When the poll tax became effective in 1903, this small remnant of Negro voting strength was reduced further.[5] The poll tax provided that to vote in an election, a voter had to pay one dollar and fifty cents per year for each of the three preceding years. The tax had to be fully paid at least six months before the election was held. The requirement that the poll tax must be paid six months prior to the election was one of many gimmicks designed to trap the unwitting prospective voter.

Despite such unconstitutional discrimination, Negroes fought back. For instance, in 1904, the local electric trolley company in Richmond adopted regulations which segregated Negroes who rode the trolleys. Negroes responded by boycotting the trolleys, and they walked for nearly a year. The boycott was organized in large part by John T. Mitchell, Jr., a local Negro journalist and publisher of a Negro paper called "The Planet." The boycott was well supported by all segments of the Negro community and caused the trolley company great financial difficulty. To help the company overcome the financial losses and break the strike, the segregated legislature passed legislation legalizing segregation in public transportation. That succeeded in breaking the boycott.

Another pre 1950s or 1960s Negro attempt to attain full constitutional protections of citizenship rights is reflected in City of Richmond v. Deans,[6] in which the United States Supreme Court upheld the ruling of the lower federal courts that a Richmond city zoning ordinance unconstitutionally sanctioned certain types of residential segregation. The Deans case relied on the earlier Supreme Court decision of Buchanan v. Worley,[7] which had held unconstitutional a Louisville ordinance prohibiting whites from moving into majority black blocks and vice versus. These rulings were not, however, effective in curbing the widespread and pernicious effects of residential apartheid.

It is an interesting historical footnote that in response to the segregationist positions of both the Democratic Party and the Republican Party, in 1921, Negroes in Virginia nominated an all black ticket to run in the general election for statewide offices. Leading the ticket were, John Mitchell, Jr., editor of the black newspaper, "The Planet," (gubernatorial nominee), Theodore Nash of Newport News (nominee for lieutenant governor), and J. Thomas Newsome, Esq. (nominee for attorney general). The ticket also included Maggie L. Walker (the first woman to become president of a bank in the United States) as nominee for superintendent of public instruction. Her place on the ticket was especially auspicious because women had just received the right to vote during the previous year. J. Z. Baccus ran on the ticket for secretary of the commonwealth, and J. L. Lee ran for commissioner of agriculture. Notwithstanding the unconstitutional disenfranchisement of nearly one hundred and fifty thousand blacks in Virginia, the all black ticket made a respectable showing.

In <u>West v. Bliley</u>, in 1930, the Fourth Circuit ruled that Negroes could participate in formerly all white Democratic primaries. The Democratic primary was tantamount to a general election because the Democrats were such a dominant party in Virginia politics. Joseph Pollard, a Negro lawyer, and Alfred E. Cohen, a Jewish lawyer brought this case, and in so doing helped open an electoral door for Negroes in the Fourth Circuit. Nevertheless, in many places the law was not enforced. Accordingly, as I will discuss later, another Negro lawyer named Thomas Hewin, Jr. and I had to go to Greensville County, Virginia in 1939 to ensure that Negroes could in fact exercise the voting rights that the courts previously had upheld.

In 1930, under the leadership of Charles Hamilton Houston and many corroborating lawyers of the NAACP, a strategy was planned and organized to overturn the infamous <u>Plessy v. Ferguson</u> decision. A public education and legal action program which spanned twenty-four years culminated in the landmark decision of <u>Brown v. Board of Education</u> in 1954. While <u>Brown</u> has had a profound impact upon American law and society on many levels, one of the most important effects of <u>Brown</u> regarding the civil rights movement of the 1950's and 1960's is that <u>Brown</u> destroyed both the legality of Negro segregation and substantially removed much of the stigma associated with it. Without the <u>Brown</u> precedent, the legal basis for the bus boycotts, sit-ins, and many other protests activities to affirm Negro rights would have been, at best, precarious.

To help facilitate understanding of some of the modern aspects of the civil rights movement, one cannot underestimate the significance of the politically risky action of President Harry S. Truman, in issuing an executive order to desegregate the military. Truman's actions helped create a moral climate and a practical example of how desegregation could work and represented the first time that a national political figure took a stand for the civil rights of Negroes and other oppressed people, even though such a stand could have cost Truman his political life.

A further catalyst for the civil rights movement which is too little appreciated is the passage of the Civil Rights Act of 1964 and more specifically the central role that President Lyndon Baines Johnson played in lobbying for, ensuring and facilitating that bill becoming law. In the early 1960's, Lyndon Johnson had stated to a meeting of governmental employees on intergroup relations, that a trip that Johnson had taken to underdeveloped countries made him more aware of the plight of Negroes in the United States. Johnson said that if he ever had an opportunity to do something about it, he would try to alleviate those conditions. Following Kennedy's assassination and despite the furious and united opposition of southern Democratic leaders, Johnson stood firm despite threats that he would be defeated in the general election of 1964. In my judgment both Truman and Johnson demonstrated a rare combination of moral and political courage in advocating and defending the rights of those who have traditionally been oppressed by the American social and legal system.

Turning to other aspects of the historical context in which I have been active, I was born on May 1, 1907 in Richmond, Virginia forty-two years after the end of the bloodiest war in American history: the American Civil War. Chattel slavery had existed in the United States for over two hundred years, and a few months after the Civil War ended, the United States finally abolished chattel slavery through adopting the Thirteenth Amendment to the Constitution. The following year (1866) Congress passed a Civil Rights Act giving Negroes many basic rights on the same plane as white people. Only thirty-nine years before my birth, people of color in the United States obtained legal equality under the Fourteenth Amendment. Just thirty-seven years before I was born men of color were allowed to vote under the Fifteenth Amendment.

The United States Supreme Court gave early indications that the new amendments to the federal constitution were directed toward protecting the rights of people of color in the United States. Thus, the Slaughterhouse Cases, Strauder v. West Virginia, and Ex Parte Virginia, specifically acknowledged that the post-Civil

War amendments were directed toward protection of the former slaves.[8] However, this relatively progressive attitude of the Supreme Court was short-lived. In 1883 (a quarter-century before my birth) the United States Supreme Court decided the infamous Civil Rights Cases. In those cases, the Supreme Court narrowly interpreted the Fourteenth Amendment to apply only to state action. The Court invalidated the attempt of the Civil Rights Act of 1875 to proscribe racial discrimination by private individuals in matters affecting the general public - like accommodations, transportation and theatres. The narrow and grudging interpretation given the Fourteenth Amendment by the 1883 Supreme Court, was one in a long line of destructive precedents which had the effect of pushing Negroes back towards slavery. In this regard the Supreme Court failed to not only protect the fundamental human rights of Negroes under the U.S. Constitution but also the Court abdicated its responsibility to follow the common law. The United States (including Virginia) is a common law jurisdiction, and under the English common law travelers have a right to food and lodging provided the traveler can pay for them. Rather than recognize the applicability of this well established common law doctrine to Negroes, the Court made new law effectively ghettoizing and segregating Negroes. Today we hear a lot of talk about activist courts but segregationists on the United States Supreme Court created activist judicial doctrines long before the desegregation doctrine (which is consistent with the Constitution) emerged during the Warren Court (1954-1969).

It is worthwhile noting that the Civil Rights Cases were decided toward the end of the so-called Reconstruction Period. That was one period in American history in which Negroes had an opportunity to participate more fully in the civil and political life of the community. For example, during the Reconstruction Period, (roughly 1866-1888) Negroes were elected to the Virginia State Legislature, Richmond and other City Councils, local Boards of Supervisors, and justices of the peace.[9] In 1867, twenty-five Negroes were elected as delegates to the Underwood Constitutional Convention to frame a constitution for Virginia.[10] This convention crafted a state constitution which allowed male

Negroes and most white males, including many of those allied with the Confederacy, to vote.

In 1869, the General Assembly totaling approximately two hundred members included nearly thirty Negroes. During Reconstruction, the Negro legislators introduced bills to enhance all citizens' opportunities for public education and to replace verbal voting in public elections with a paper ballot. They also sought to appoint a state geologist to help develop Virginia's mineral wealth; and tried to curb excesses in using corporal punishment in the criminal justice system (the infamous "whipping posts").[11] These legislators promoted Negro participation on juries and introduced legislation creating the first publicly supported institution of higher learning for blacks in Virginia, The Virginia Normal and Collegiate Institute (now called Virginia State University).[12] The efforts of these legislators were remarkable, and resulted in some successful legislation, though Negroes never held anywhere near a legislative majority in Virginia. Education and land ownership were primary objectives of the newly freed slaves.

On a personal note, during this time my maternal grandmother met a Semitic American man and became pregnant by him. My grandmother gave birth to their daughter, my mother, in 1888. My grandfather later became a doctor. My grandparents' all too human behavior was probably illegal and undoubtedly frowned upon. Under the law, my mother came into the world in the twilight zone of so-called illegitimacy. She was born seven years before Booker T. Washington's controversial "Atlanta Compromise" speech. Washington had proclaimed that Negroes and white people in the United States could, in common matters be like the hand, but on matters involving social issues they could be as separate as the fingers. This so-called compromise position really helped prepare the way for the advent of even more widespread Jim Crow segregation measures throughout the South. In fact, the year after Washington's speech, in <u>Plessy v. Ferguson</u>, the United States Supreme Court upheld the doctrine of separate but equal.

As previously mentioned, in 1901 and 1902, just a few years after <u>Plessy,</u> and five years before my birth, a constitutional convention was held in Virginia for the express purpose of disenfranchising Virginia's Negro citizens and reestablishing segregation. Segregationists succeeded in their nefarious purpose and, three years before my birth, in <u>Jones v. Montague</u>, the Supreme Court made a mockery of its motto of equal justice under law by upholding the segregationists' constitution.

The Supreme Court continued its narrow, stingy interpretation regarding the rights of African Americans in <u>Hodges v. The United States</u> which, in effect, held that the Thirteenth Amendment ought to be narrowly construed so as to in essence invalidate Congress enactment of Civil Rights legislation to protect Negroes from the terrorist activities of groups like the White Camellias and the Ku Klux Klan. These groups had terrorized the newly freed slaves throughout the South, and had in some cases assassinated, mutilated and raped Negroes, in addition to destroying their real and personal property.[13] The Klan employed violence against whites who occasionally allied themselves with Negroes. <u>Hodges</u> was decided one year before my birth.

At the beginning of the Twentieth Century, in a prophetic statement in <u>The Souls of Black Folk</u>, W.E.B. DuBois said that the problem of the Twentieth Century was the problem of the color line. Four years later I was born into the midst of this problematic human condition.

Chapter I

Early Years

I arrived at the conclusion that it was just as stupid for me to hate white people because they were white as it was for white people to hate me because I wasn't white. Consequently, I began to judge people as people on the basis of my experience with them.

As I look back over nine decades of life, I have a number of thoughts and emotions. One of my overriding concerns has been with progressive, evolutionary change. In the following pages, I will touch on a number of issues involving evolutionary change. I begin with my own life story, including childhood in Richmond and Roanoke, Virginia; my high school, college, and law school years in Washington, D.C. (during the 1920's and 1930's) and my activities as an advocate of social change over the past seven decades. In particular, I will talk about my work as a lawyer on the team of activists who planned the public education and legal strategy which led to the Supreme Court striking down state supported segregation in much of American life. I will also discuss some of my experiences in state and national politics, as well as some of the interesting facts about serving in a segregated military during the Second World War. Finally, I will return to one of the overriding themes of this book: the need for progressive evolutionary change.

My early childhood was in a period when segregation was at its height. Accordingly, I had very little association with white folks. I was fortunate in that respect. At an early point in my development I concluded that for white people to get a job at anything that brought them into contact with the public, a major prerequisite was to have a nasty attitude towards Negroes. Streetcar conductors, brakemen or conductors on railroad trains, policemen, foremen for laboring gangs, all seemed to have had one prerequisite: a nasty attitude towards

1

Negroes. It was a rare situation if you found a white person in those type jobs who was courteous or even pleasant to Negroes.

To complicate matters further, white people had their stereotypes about Negroes. I learned early about these stereotypical ideas. We were supposedly lazy, untrustworthy, stupid. . . . As I said, white folks often had a nasty attitude towards Negroes.

Of course, we had stereotypes about them, too. For example, some Negroes said the white man was so crooked that he would steal the pennies off his dead mother's eyes. Another stereotype was that two kinds of white folks existed: good ones and bad ones. You could always tell the good ones because they were buried at least six feet deep. At that time, I firmly believed these stereotypes.

Regarding the development of stereotypes, in my opinion few whites had personal life experiences with Negroes to justify their conclusions that, in essence, Negroes are inhuman or fulfilled the array of other negative stereotypes. Most white people never got close enough to Negroes to know what we really thought and felt, or how we lived. They saw us through eyes blinded by prejudice, biased newspaper reporting and film makers, as well as by their own personal hostile and unsympathetic attitude.

In contrast, practically all Negroes had been victimized personally by white folks in various aspects of their lives. White folks cheated them in business transactions. White people discriminated against them in diverse contexts: politics, education, economics, justice, health care. And white folks subjected Negroes to physical and mental abuse — running the gamut from lynchings, burning Negroes at the stake, and castration, to taunts and other personal insults.

When I was growing up, it was common to see the term "nigger" in the newspaper. In referring to Negroes charged with criminal offenses, the usual terminology was "big, black burly."

Racist attitudes were also reflected in language. For example, many white people refused to capitalize the <u>N</u> in spelling Negro. In fact a large segment of white people claimed they could not pronounce the word "Negro." They would say "Negra" and it was hard to tell whether they were saying "Nigger" or "Negra."

This practice continued until recent times. I was doing some

2

consulting with a company and the general counsel and I were on pretty good terms. I raised this issue with him and he said "Negra" was the best he could do. He swore he couldn't say the word "Negro".

I have learned at least one lesson in life based on my own experience and my own thinking about the situation. I concluded that it was just as stupid for me to hate white people because they were white as it was for white people to hate me because I wasn't white. Consequently, I began to judge people as people on the basis of my experience with them. My experiences taught me to look at all people, and judge them on an individual, human basis.

Challenging Beginnings

While I was born into a two parent family, our original family unit did not remain intact for long. My father, William Henry White, Jr., left our family shortly after I was born. He came back about six months later. He claimed that he wanted to do right by my mother and me. Within six months he not only left home, he also left Richmond. I learned some of these things through reading the depositions of my parents' divorce.

The divorce occurred in 1911. In those days, before you could even apply for a divorce you had to be separated three years. Aside from the separation period, there could not be any collusion, appearance of collusion, cohabiting or anything like that during the separation. It was actually an adversarial situation. An interesting aside is that many years ago during my legal career, the court refused to grant one of my clients a divorce because it claimed there was some impropriety notwithstanding the fact of the plaintiff living in Roanoke while the defendant resided in Richmond.

My mother's maiden name was Olivia Lewis, and as I said, her father was a white medical student. In those days it was illegal for blacks and whites to marry. In Virginia, and generally, illegitimate children take the mother's name.

In later years I learned that my maternal grandfather had obtained a degree in medicine at The Medical College of Virginia and had become a physician practicing in New York. I remember once my mother asked me if I wanted to go to New York to see him. I was in law school then. My reply was that if he had any interest in me he would come down to see me. At that time, I didn't have much use for white

3

people anyway.

I do have a paper containing a name which may well be my maternal grandfather's name.

During my early years, my mother worked at the Homestead Hotel in Hot Springs, Virginia to take care of herself and me. I lived with my great grandmother and a grand aunt in Richmond.

I have no recollection of my maternal great-grandfather. Because divorce was uncommon in those days, I assume that he was dead. My great-grandmother had three children: my grandmother, my grandaunt and a son, who also lived in Scranton, Pennsylvania. I have no

Mrs. Olivia W. Hill
(Mother of Oliver W. Hill, Sr.)
(Circa 1950)

recollection of meeting my maternal granduncle.

Later, when I returned to Richmond from Roanoke at the age of nine, my great-grandmother tried to tell me something about my family. The only thing that lingered with me was the fact that she was telling me that my forebears had lived in Chesterfield County before the Revolutionary War. I don't remember if they were free or slaves. I suspect they were slaves. She mentioned a lot of their names; but I never heard them again. Now the memory of their names has long since faded.

Joseph C. Hill
(Stepfather of Oliver W. Hill, Sr.)
(Circa 1951/52)

4

I don't know any of my family members who lived before my great-grandmother Lewis and details about my great grandmother are beyond my ability to recall. However, I have no unpleasant memories of her and her daughter, my grandaunt.

On the maternal side, we did not have a very large family. My mother was an only child. I was an only child and my son is an only child with only one child of his own and two stepchildren.

Regarding my father's side of the family, my paternal grandfather, William Henry White, Sr., was the founder and pastor of Mount Carmel Baptist Church in Richmond, Virginia. I have very little recollection of Kate Garnet White, my paternal grandmother. I know nothing about her except that she was reputed to be part Negro and part Indian, carried herself in a regal manner, and was haughty. By strange coincidence, she and Maggie Walker, about whom I will say more later, were close friends. Given this family background, I am a genetically well diversified individual.

While I was living with my great-grandmother and grand aunt, my maternal grandmother who lived in Scranton, Pennsylvania, moved back to Richmond and died shortly after returning. The proximity of her death to her return suggests that she was ill before she came back. For these reasons, I always assumed she came back to Richmond to die.

When she died I was six years old and grandmother's death brought my mother and my stepfather, Joseph C. Hill, to Richmond. This was the first time that I really recalled seeing my mother. She had left Richmond when I was very young; and came back earlier for her divorce. However, I was too young to remember.

My mother and stepfather were a recently married couple when they arrived for grandmother's funeral. At the time of their marriage, they both were working at the Homestead Hotel at Hot Springs. They first met each other at that hotel. She was employed as a maid who dipped drinking water from the springs for guests; and my stepfather was a bellman.

I don't have any present memory of how I felt when I first saw my mother. However, my relationship with my mother and stepfather jelled instantly.

In those days when people of ordinary means died they took them

(right)

William Henry White, Jr.
(Father of Oliver W. Hill, Sr.)
(Circa 1900)

(left)

Kate Garnet White, (center)
Grandmother of Oliver W.
Hill, Sr., with two of her
daughters, Lizzie White
Pollard (left) and Susie
Armistead (right)

6

to the funeral home, embalmed their remains, put them in the casket and then brought them back to the house. I remember grandmother lying in the casket in our little house. The custom was to put colored crepe on the front of the house to indicate that the remains were in the house. There were different colored crepes for different types of remains. As I recall it, pink and purple were used for young people, and black for adults; white crepe was used, too.

When my grandmother died they sent me to stay for a few days with a more affluent aunt who lived not far away on a paved street with sidewalks. Her son had a tricycle. It was the first time I had ever seen one. She insisted that I say prayers before I went to bed. I don't remember if I had been saying prayers prior to that time or not. I stayed there a couple of nights.

Early Recollections

My earliest recollection involves events which happened before I was five years old. I do not have a continuous recollection of anything in particular, but by sharing these reminiscences with you, I hope that you will sense what it was like to be a child in a southern city like Richmond over eighty-five years ago.

I remember my maternal great-grandmother and grandaunt raising me in a little house on the side of St. James Street hill leading down to the railroad tracks. As I recall it, the house had three rooms downstairs including the kitchen and a room upstairs that was just a loft. My bed was upstairs.

My great-grandmother and my aunt attended Mount Carmel Baptist Church. While I don't remember much about the worship services, I remember Sunday School — especially the process of them getting me off to Sunday School.

Another memorable aspect of our Sunday activities was that we usually had chicken and dumplings. Whether we had it for breakfast or dinner I don't remember. However, apparently food was no problem as I have no recollection as a child of ever being hungry.

I also recall that on one week day some kids in the neighborhood and I slipped into the church, and I proceeded to climb up on a chair in the pulpit and started to mimic my grandfather. Suddenly, I looked up at the other end of the sanctuary and there he was standing in the

7

door! Boy, I got down and flew out of there. He was one of those fire and brimstone preachers. He was a big man with a beard, and all he had to do was frown a little bit and he really looked fierce. I don't remember having too much of a relationship with him. However, I can remember one Sunday sitting on the upstairs porch of their house across the street from the church. That is my only recollection that I have of my paternal grandmother.

Later I learned that my paternal grandfather, Reverend White, came from Chesterfield County. There was a family named Friend who lived out there. The Whites and the Friends are related. When I first came back to

Oliver W. Hill, Sr., at early age
(Circa 1914)

Oliver W. Hill, Sr., at age 4
(Circa 1911)

Richmond in 1939, one of the Friends invited me to come out and see her so that she could tell me about my paternal family history. However, I was so busy fighting segregation that I never took advantage of her offer. Looking back, I regret not finding out more family historical facts.

On August 13, 1913, not long after my maternal grandmother came to live with us, Reverend White died.

When I was six I left Richmond and went to Roanoke. I will discuss that in more detail later.

8

Rev. William H. Hill
(Grandfather of Oliver Hill, Sr.)

The first time I remember seeing my father I was nine years old. I had come back from Roanoke to visit my great grandmother and grand aunt and stayed about a week. He heard I was in the city and came to see me.

One day he took me out for a streetcar ride. Unfortunately, it wasn't a very enjoyable ride. I became nauseated by the odors emitted by the electric trolley; it smelled like something burning. To make matters worse, my father had the nerve to ask me did I want to come live with him. That was a stupid question to ask a nine-year-old kid who had never seen him before.

When I next heard of my father's whereabouts he was supposed to be somewhere in New York City. Once when I was in New York, my wife, Bernie, and I visited a street location where he allegedly hung out. I couldn't find him. I have no idea if he is still living or if he died or of what he died. Since I am over ninety years old, I seriously doubt that he is alive.

As I think back, my childhood was really pleasant. I only remember getting one whipping prior to leaving Richmond for Roanoke. I'm sure I got others, but that's all I remember. It happened like this: there had been a picnic at Buckroe Beach and someone had bought me a hard-shell crab. My grandaunt wanted me to go downtown with her and I wanted to eat my crab. I insisted on eating my crab and she insisted that I get properly dressed to go downtown. After a while I remember getting a whipping, putting on proper attire and going downtown. I don't know if I ever ate my crab or not. Like any kid, I have those kinds of recollections.

At the top of St. James Street hill going north, was a cemetery. The area was called Burying Ground Hill. My grandfather first started his pastorate at a church on Fells Street near the top of the hill, about two blocks west of St. James Street. On the right side of the St. James

Street hill and a little beyond the railroad tracks going up towards North Avenue there was a big leather goods place with saddles and whips hanging outside the store.

In winter some of the older boys rode sleighs down St. James Street hill. While I have no recollection of sleigh-riding down the hill myself, I enjoyed watching those boys speeding down the hill with the momentum carrying them across the railroad tracks and partially up the other side of the hill. Some of the sleighs almost came up to our house.

At the intersection of St. James and Preston Streets, there was a railroad crossing of the main line railroad tracks that I believe was used by both the Atlantic Coastline Railroad and Seaboard Air Line Railroads. On the north-west side of the tracks there was a high tower from which the watchman raised and lowered the gates to stop traffic when a train was approaching. The watchman had to climb a ladder to get up there. He was a rather remarkable person: he had a peg leg, and had to climb up to the tower with that peg leg. He raised and lowered the gate by pumping a pump handle. He knew the train times. When a train came he clanged a loud bell. I believe that this man had been injured on the job, and as a result received this employment as a type of compensation for injuries. This arrangement was a common practice in those days.

I also vividly recall a family who lived next door moving out. The little boy in the family came and asked me if I wanted to ride on the wagon. Thinking that I was going to have an opportunity to ride on the real wagon, I ran in the house and asked my great-grandmother could I ride. She gave me permission. The movers had taken the seat off of the wagon and put it on the ground. The boy and I got on the seat on the ground and he called "get up" to the imaginary horse. Much to my disillusionment and disappointment, our imaginary horse failed to move the wagon seat.

As I look back on my life I recall another interesting event related to this horse story. I traveled and moved around a lot after this little boy left, and to my knowledge, I never saw him again for the next fifty years. One day after I came back to Richmond in the late 1960's, I became engaged in a conversation with an employee of the Southern Aid Life Insurance Company, and we started talking about our childhood. We discovered that at one time we lived on the same street. He said that once when his family moved, another child was living next door and that "I remember us getting on the seat of the wagon and imagining that we were riding." I replied, "Hell, that was me."

I also used to play on a big hill on a vacant lot across the street from our house. As a matter of fact, the vacant land is still there. On the corner, on the other side of Preston Street, there was a little grocery store. Even when I was a child, it was boarded up. One day some kids broke into the store through a window. Two or three of us small kids climbed in there with the bigger boys. We took some candy or something. I remember running down Preston Street. Preston Street had row houses and a continuous porch. On this occasion, we ran in and out of these houses. We ran into one house where a couple was having sexual relations. We got an eyeful, although I doubt that at that time I had the faintest idea what they were doing. When the male hollered at us, we flew out of there! Those houses are all torn down now.

Once I was carried to a studio down on Second Street (in a building that is still standing) and had my picture taken in my "Buster Brown" suit. I still have one of these pictures, which is reproduced herein.

While I don't have any continuous memory of anything in particular that happened before I was five or six, some events stand out in my mind. For example, I recall hearing a tremendous explosion at the gas works on Bacon Street going towards Chamberlayne Avenue. Shortly, I heard screaming, yelling and hollering. My grandaunt was crying and my great-grandmother was trying to console her. I think the explosion had killed my grandaunt's boyfriend.

To give you a fuller perspective on some social conditions over eighty years ago, I will tell you a bit more about the hotel service industry in which my mother and stepfather worked. In those days Hot Springs was a seasonal resort with a spring season and a fall season. They kept a skeleton staff during the summers and winters. Instead of going to Hot Springs in the summer, rich people went north to the Berkshires, Adirondacks, Catskills and places like that.

Interestingly, Jews were excluded from vacationing in many places in the Berkshires, though facilities existed in the Catskills that catered to them. In the winter affluent folks would go to Florida and Bermuda. In fact, my mother and stepfather worked down at the Hotel Hamilton in Bermuda in the winter. It's funny how you remember being told about something like that. I've seen pictures of the Hotel Hamilton, though I've never been there.

11

As I previously mentioned, I am more than ninety years old. I think my family has longevity genes. My mother died in 1980 at age ninety-two. Although my grandmother died early, my great-grandmother lived until 1928 when I was in college. When she passed away, she was ninety-eight.

In my ninety plus years, I have noticed that on a number of levels, the relationships between Negroes and white folks are interesting. For example, to look at her, my mother was as white as any white person. In the 1970's after my mother came back here to Richmond to live, one day she was over at our house in the back yard. One of my white neighbors called me on the telephone and said, "There is a little old white woman wandering around in your backyard." I said, "It's all right; that's my mother."

Roanoke Days

As I mentioned, after my mother's mother died, my mother and my stepfather came to Richmond to attend grandmother's funeral. My mother and stepfather decided to take me to Roanoke with them after the funeral.

When we went to Roanoke, we lived at 39 Gilmer Avenue Northwest, with a family named Pentecost. The family included Mr. and Mrs. Pentecost and Mrs. Pentecost's two brothers. One of Mrs. Pentecost's brothers was a full brother, Roy Hamilton, and one a half-brother, Wilbur Pettitt. Except for my stepfather, all of the men in the house worked in the dining car service for the Norfolk & Western Railroad Company.

Mr. Pentecost and Mrs. Pentecost married when she was a young girl. Mrs. Pentecost was a marvelous person. She used to take pride in the fact that she had never worked in any white folks' kitchen. In fact, she never worked outside her home.

Mr. Pentecost was an excellent chef on the Norfolk & Western Railroad and was recruited to upgrade the railroad's dining car service. Boy, he could make chili con carne! He had a special recipe and carried that recipe to his grave. Much later in life, I learned that even if people have the same recipe it doesn't necessarily mean that the dish will taste the same. It is like the situation where some people read music and play a piano; and someone else can read the same daggone music and produce an altogether different effect.

On the railroad, Mr. Pentecost cooked and the second cook assisted and helped to prepare the meals. The third cook also helped do whatever was necessary to prepare the meals, and washed the pots and pans. In those days the service and quality of meals in dining cars was equivalent to that found in first class restaurants.

Mr. Pentecost had become accustomed to not having to worry about utensils because when he cooked in the kitchen of the dining car someone washed things almost as fast as he used them. This was necessary because of a lack of space. At home, when he cooked, he used a number of utensils, and he expected someone else to clean up after him. Mrs. Pentecost loved to have him cook, but she hated the awful mess that he left.

There were several bedrooms in the Pentecost house. My mother and my stepfather had a room, and I also had a separate room. Both families shared the same kitchen.

When we went to Roanoke, my stepfather and I soon developed a close relationship. I can remember my stepfather playing on the floor

Lelia Pentecost
(Circa 1915)

Bradford Pentecost
(Circa 1915)

13

with me; he gave me a toy wind-up train. We shared numerous similar occasions. I even remember once when I was six or seven that he gave me a poodle dog. However, I told him that I did not want a dog: I wanted a little brother. But the poodle, "Snookins" sufficed for the next eighteen years. Shortly after Snookins died, a man on the street gave me a puppy. It was cold, the dog was tiny, and I took it home. She grew and grew until she was large enough to stand on her hind legs and put her paws on my shoulders. She had a wonderful intuitive sense of whenever I was coming home. As soon as I arrived in the neighborhood the dog began to bark, jump up and down, and run to the door indicating she knew I was coming. Regardless of whether I was gone for a few hours, or days, or even a year the dog knew when I was in the vicinity. She too lived to be over twenty years of age.

In Roanoke, my stepfather operated a pool parlor. He even built a little stand for me to stand upon so that I could see over the pool table. He started teaching me to play billiards and pocket pool.

Before he could teach me much about the art of playing billiards or shooting pool, Virginia went dry, and that closed the saloons and killed the neighborhood in which his pool parlor was located. He tried to find another location. Unfortunately, at that time in Roanoke, the locations where a Negro could operate a business were very limited. He didn't see anything he wanted to do in Roanoke. Accordingly, he decided to go back to Hot Springs to work. That terminated my career as a potential professional pool player. Who knows, that may have kept me from becoming a "Virginia Fats."

My mother had considered staying in Roanoke when my stepfather decided to return to Hot Springs because by that time I had entered school. There was no adequate school for Negroes in Bath County where Hot Springs is located. There were only some one-room "schools" which my mother deemed unacceptable. In those days, Negro children in Roanoke couldn't go to public school until they were seven years of age. I do not know what the ground rules were for white children.

At that same time, in what was called a "changing neighborhood", Mr. and Mrs. Pentecost bought a large house four blocks farther west on Gilmer Avenue. When my stepfather decided to go back to Hot Springs, they were remodeling their new home. From time to time, during the summer before we moved in, we would go up there and see what was happening with the renovations.

I didn't know anything about my stepfather planning to go back to Hot Springs. I just assumed that because we were all living together, and the Pentecosts were going to move, we would all continue living under the same roof. I was perfectly content to live with the Pentecosts. Because Mrs. Pentecost and I got along so well, my mother decided to allow me to stay in Roanoke while she accompanied my stepfather to Hot Springs.

After we moved to 401 Gilmer Avenue, all the men at our house worked in the railroad dining car service. They would have short runs and long runs. For example, the railroad's call boy would come by and awaken Mr. Pentecost about two o'clock in the morning on the day he was going on his run from Roanoke to Birmingham, Alabama. On this trip, he would lay over in Birmingham and reprovision the dining cars. They would then come back to Roanoke, arriving sometimes at one or two o'clock in the morning. So he would be gone three days at a time. Then he would follow the same routine on a trip to Columbus, Ohio. After returning from Columbus, he would come in and the next morning go out to Norfolk, Virginia. Then he would come back, and he would have a two or three day layover. (I cannot recall the precise length of the layover at the moment.) Then he would go through this routine again.

Occasionally he had an overnight trip up the Shenandoah Valley — going towards Harrisonburg, Virginia. He went up one night and came back the next day. That was the pattern of the railroad dining car personnel operating out of Roanoke who lived at our house. Whether they did it differently somewhere else, I don't know. Mr. Pentecost's principal runs were to Birmingham, Alabama; Columbus, Ohio; and Norfolk, Virginia. They found the work and compensation to be acceptable. The only worry was an occasional train wreck.

At times we had other young men whom the Pentecosts knew come and stay with us. Such individuals were college students who had left school for a while to work on the railroad and save money to resume their education. Once a fellow whose last name was Davenport came and lived with us for a year while working on the railroad. He used to play records like "Mother McCree," and the wedding song "Because" for long periods of time on his days off. He later graduated from college and became a high school principal in his hometown, Chattanooga, Tennessee.

Concerning other aspects of family life, we did not follow the

15

usual family routine. We might eat breakfast together today and dinner tomorrow. So sometimes two or three days would go by and Mrs. Pentecost and I were there together. There would be no other male in the house. In that respect, my situation has always been different. We didn't have the daily routine that most people have where everybody comes down to breakfast, and everybody is home for dinner at a certain time. Meals were important in the sense that we liked to eat and many times they were festive occasions. However, meals never had "routine importance." For instance, sometimes our breakfasts together had the same importance that other families attributed to dinners. We didn't have a regimented type family relationship. However, notwithstanding this rather unique style, we had very good family relationships.

In contrast, my wife, Bernie, was born in a large family. They had family prayer at breakfast and ate dinner at the same time every day. They had the advantage of family centered social and spiritual nurturing — all that sort of thing. At the Pentecosts' Mrs. Pentecost and I enjoyed one another's company when the men were running on the railroad. Our joy was amplified when the men came home.

Another salient memory that I have as a child involved the sale of household products. Such products were sold door to door by traveling salesmen. At that time all of the salespersons were white men. As was the social custom, when they came to Negro homes, they would find out the name of a family from their neighbors. The salesman would knock at the door and ask for the lady of the house by her first name. If permitted, the salesman would then proceed to walk into the house with his hat on. However, at the Pentecosts' home, the standard practice was that if a salesman came to the door and asked was "Lelia" home, the reply was, "Not to you!" The door would be summarily slammed in the salesman's face.

If, however, the salesman asked for the lady of the house, he was permitted to enter the house. Nevertheless, if he failed to take off his hat, he would be asked to remove it. If he failed to comply with this request, he was told to leave.

Word soon spread among door to door salesmen that when they came to the Pentecost household, they should ask for Mrs. Pentecost, not "Lelia". They also knew to remove their hats when entering. Accordingly, when they came to our home, they treated Mrs. Pentecost with the respect that they accorded white female customers. Consequently, from early childhood I developed personal esteem and expected white folks to treat me like they did one another in such settings.

On rare occasions, when I came home there was no one there. For example, when I left Roanoke to go to Washington for high school, Mrs. Pentecost was away. She had gone to Chattanooga, Tennessee on a visit and had planned to be away another week. I waited until I got to Washington to call her. She didn't know what had happened to me. She laid me out for not letting her know sooner where I had gone. However, we were good friends up until the time she died in 1943. Mrs. Pentecost lived long enough to see me launch my legal and community service career. By the time she died, we had won the Alston[1] case which resulted in equalizing the salaries of Negro and white teachers in Virginia; and I was also involved in many other cases which helped lay the legal foundation for dismantling state supported segregation policies in Virginia and nationwide.

An Early Brief Movie Career

Let me tell you briefly about my abbreviated movie career. In the early twentieth century, Oscar Michaux was a prominent Negro film producer. By the 1920's, Michaux came to Roanoke and persuaded a group of Negroes, including the Pentecosts, to invest in the film "House Behind the Cedars." In most films, in those days Negroes were only portrayed as servants or clowns. This film was about middle class Negroes. I don't remember too much about the plot.

The only name of any of my fellow actors that I can remember now is that of a man whose name was Lawrence Chenault. Chenault was the male lead in "House Behind the Cedars" which Michaux filmed in Roanoke. In the film, he used our home (corner of Gilmer Avenue and 4th Street), the home of Jimmy and Alma Sewell who lived in the middle of the three hundred block of Gilmer Avenue, and the streets located between the residences. I was just playing a role in one of the scenes filmed in our front yard. It was a planned shot: and they filmed me walking among the guests of the lawn party as if I was looking for someone. You might say I made my cameo appearance about 1921. I am not positive why Oscar Michaux selected me to appear in the picture. However, I feel confident that it was at the behest of Mrs. Pentecost who constantly sought opportunities for me to enjoy a wide variety of experiences.

A couple of years ago, it was interesting that the son of a friend of mine, University of Richmond Professor Bob Alley, was working in the State Library. His work was in a section where he was dealing with old movies. He told his father that he had run across this Negro film producer and director named Oscar Michaux. Professor Alley's son commented on the difficulties that Michaux had encountered in getting his films distributed in Virginia. During that period, Virginia had a state censorship board. Unlike some of the scandalous movies of that time, like "Birth of a Nation" which portrayed Negroes in an overtly racist manner, Michaux's films were both more accurate and positive presentations of Negroes' lives. It is perhaps for these reasons among others that many white movie censorship boards made it difficult for him to show his films.

Bob asked me whether I had ever heard of this Negro producer and director to which I replied, "Did I know him? Why, I appeared in one of his pictures!"

The next thing I knew I received a letter from the film festival people at the University of Virginia asking me to be their guest at their 1991 Virginia Festival of American Film, and to appear on a panel discussing Oscar Michaux. It was real funny. My wife, Bernie, and I went. We had a wonderful time. We stayed at the Boar's Head Inn. We had three or four days seeing old movies and enjoying a couple of elaborate dinners.

The film festival was real interesting. A number of celebrities were there like Tim and Daphne Maxwell Reid, Patricia Kluge and Charlton Heston. Tim and Daphne Reid and I appeared together on the Oscar Michaux panel.

<u>More on Roanoke Life</u>

There are some more things to tell you about growing up as an only child in Roanoke during the World War I years and shortly thereafter. When I was a child, people in our social circle used to call Roanoke "little New York". In addition, for a brief period of about six or seven months a young girl my age lived with us at the Pentecosts' home. We washed dishes together and did things like that. I can't remember now why this little girl was there.

At that time there was also a teenage girl named Elizabeth who came from somewhere in one of the rural counties. She lived with Mrs. Pentecost and went to school. Finally the teenager decided to leave. Later she became pregnant and had a child. Then she wanted to come back. However, Mrs. Pentecost wouldn't take her back. With these few exceptions, I was the only child in the house. I had no alternative childhood experience to compare with being an only child.

When I was a child I had every childhood disease that came down the pike: diphtheria, measles, whooping cough and something else that I cannot remember at the moment. However, I don't think I ever had the mumps. Back in those days when you had one of those contagious diseases, you were quarantined. They put a sign up on the house. You were supposed to stay in your room, and nobody but the family could come in and out of the house. The usual quarantine period was three weeks. The block of Fourth Street beside our house was a regular playground for neighborhood children. In all of my situations, after two or three days I would be hanging out the window and yelling at the kids playing in the street.

When I was in Roanoke growing up in the period just before, during and after World War I, they didn't have many cars in the Negro neighborhood. I noticed that each make of car had a different sound. Accordingly, because of the scarcity of cars and distinctive sounds, I knew everybody's car a block before I could see it.

Starting Work

My recollections and observations are contrary to white folks' stereotypes about the work ethic of Negroes. When I was growing up nearly eighty years ago, people were work oriented. At a very early age I had daily chores including bringing in coal and wood for the stoves and washing dishes. Once a week, I had the responsibility of dusting furniture, mopping the floor and cleaning the common areas of the house.

Starting when I was about nine years old, I had my first "job". I was helping at an ice cream parlor a half block from where I lived, and for the odd services that I performed I was basically paid in ice cream. I remember once walking home at night from the ice cream parlor when suddenly I felt something on the back of my neck. I looked around and did not see anything. I did not know what or who touched me: and I did not wait around to find out! I practically flew home as fast as I could run. In fact, I almost ran past the gate to the side entrance of our home. The gate was latched, and I skidded trying to stop. Then it happened. I saw the cause of my fright flutter harmlessly to the ground. It was a leaf! The leaf must have been blown by the wind and settled on

19

the back of my neck while I was walking home. Whether my tiny guest enjoyed the ride, I suppose I will never know.

When I told Mrs. Pentecost about this experience, she laughed. However, looking back, I see how I was taught neither to fear the dark nor to panic when confronted with a strange situation. For example, when I was nine or ten, sometimes we would be sitting in the kitchen on winter nights. Most of the house was dark. From time to time, Mrs. Pentecost would think of something she wanted or claimed that she needed from the attic. I would always volunteer to get it for her. To do this, I had to go up to the second floor and then upstairs into the attic. I had to then walk to the center of the pitch black attic and turn on the electric light to see what I was sent to get. Sometimes, it was a fruitless search, but often Mrs. Pentecost had previously planted the object. Later I learned that the real purpose of the search was to teach me not to be fearful of the dark. Of course, I did not know that at that time. Later in life when I learned the truth about the situation, I was delighted because it benefitted me.

My first job ended abruptly when the police gave the ice cream parlor establishment a citation for violating the child labor laws. When I was ten or eleven, I also obtained a job during the summer carrying a barber his lunch. The barber worked downtown in a barber shop operated by a Negro. There was nowhere for him to eat because the eating establishments excluded Negroes. It was not a matter of having separate facilities to eat in: there were no facilities. Accordingly, the barber's mother would fix his lunch so he would have a hot meal.

All of the barbershop's clientele were white. I did not know the price that white people paid for a haircut. The cost of a haircut for children in those days in Negro barbershops was twenty-five cents.

During World War I, when I was ten I used to get up at 3:00 a.m. on Sunday morning and deliver papers. Nobody forced me, in fact it was my idea. I wanted to get the morning paper as it came off the press and get an early start on the street. It was purely a Sunday morning paper route. I started off with the Roanoke paper and the *New York Examiner* which was a Hearst newspaper. I am sure that today if a parent allowed a ten year old child to go out at three in the morning, the parent would be charged with child abuse, or some other unlawful activity like violation of child labor laws.

There was no radio or television. All the news came from the newspapers. The papers often carried screaming headlines to attract attention. On top of that, if there was anything of a startling nature, they put out an Extra. For instance, who won the World Series was something for an Extra. Or if a big train wreck occurred, they put out an Extra! "Extra, Extra, read all about it!"

I could start selling the New York paper on Saturday afternoon. The Roanoke paper, however, was not available until Sunday morning. Most of the times I tried to do it in time to get home, change clothes and get to Sunday School punctually at 9:30 a.m. Sometimes in the winter I would be so cold when I came home they would have to thaw me out. I would have been out for five or six hours when I returned home. I paid for my papers in advance. If I didn't sell them I was just stuck. As I think back, perhaps only my newspaper supplier had that rule. I don't know whether I could have turned in my unsold papers and gotten a refund.

Selling papers was the first regular occupation I had. I think I got started at that because I wanted to buy a bicycle. Like many other young people of that day, if I wanted to buy something I saved my money and bought it. The Pentecosts, my mother and my stepfather all frowned upon buying ordinary items on credit. I have learned that all societal changes are really not necessarily synonymous with progress.

When I was going through white neighborhoods I knew that you had to be very, very careful that you didn't get caught as you might be cuffed around. For example, I started selling papers early; and the best place to sell newspapers on Sunday morning was in certain white neighborhoods. If white boys came along, I had to run like hell. They would cuff me, and when we would catch them in our neighborhood, we would cuff them, too. It was sort of tit for tat.

Except from white kids chasing me and that kind of stuff, when I was in white neighborhoods, I was never in any great danger. However, I remember one time there were six or seven of them after me. I was running as fast as I could when I looked back and saw one little kid about my size coming on. The rest of them had dropped off but he didn't know it. I saw that he was out there by himself. I slowed up and let him think that he was catching up. Then I turned around and he saw that all his friends were a block away. He screamed and went hightailing. I grabbed a rock and threw it at him to help him along.

I can remember once when I was about ten or eleven years old, a white kid came through our neighborhood on a bicycle. We cuffed him up and slapped him around a little bit. When riding a bicycle or walking, we either avoided white neighborhoods (especially in economically disadvantaged sections) or rode as fast as we could through them. But nobody shot anybody or broke their arm or anything like that. They let us know that they didn't care anything about us and we let them know that we didn't care anything about them. This was one of the unfortunate results of racial segregation.

We used to get in gangs and go look for white boys in residential areas where poor whites and poor Negroes adjoined. They'd congregate in gangs too, and we would have rock battles. We did not know each other: we just feared and fought each other.

I guess the rock throwing battle was more of a game. I never even thought about why we did that. Perhaps because segregation prevented us from competing in baseball or softball games against the white children, the only games that we felt that we could participate in was something combative like rock battles.

In Roanoke, there were certain spots where the guys would congregate in the afternoons. We chose teams and played baseball or football depending on the season. When I went to Washington you could always go to the playground and pick up teams and play baseball or basketball.

I remember when I was twelve I got a job that summer on an ice wagon. I came back to my neighborhood and proudly boasted to the other boys on the corner, "Man, I got a job paying me thirty-six dollars a month!"

There weren't any automatic refrigerators then. People had ice boxes. The fancy houses had ice boxes with ice containers that opened on the back porch. Accordingly, you could put the ice in from the back porch and not have to go into the kitchen. You were "up there" when you had those kinds of ice boxes. In most houses, to put ice in the ice box you had to go into the kitchen, lift the top of the box (which was secured by hinges) and put the block of ice inside. (Nearly all houses had somebody at home; most women were not working.)

Our routine on the ice wagon involved starting out before sunrise, getting down to the ice factory by about 5:00 a.m., loading up, getting to our route site, and beginning our deliveries. On Fridays, Saturdays, and Mondays we usually got to our route at about 6:00 o'clock in the morning and worked until 11:00 or 12:00 at night. Those were eighteen-hour days. Wednesday was often a fairly rough day and we got off in late afternoon while Tuesdays and Thursdays the business was relatively light. We worked only eight or nine hours on Tuesdays and Thursdays and probably got off at 2:00 or 3:00 o'clock in the afternoon.

The blocks of ice weighed three hundred pounds. The ice sellers all knew how to cut a three hundred pound block in a deceitful way to produce what the sellers claimed were three hundred and fifty pounds in smaller blocks. When sold these blocks still had a total weight of three hundred pounds. However, these blocks generated the monetary value of three hundred and fifty pounds. The public thought they were getting more ice than they actually received and paid for.

At age twelve, I soon learned that the ice sellers were not only cheating the public: they were also cheating me! They paid the white boys forty-eight dollars a month. They paid me and the other Negro boys thirty-six dollars for doing the same work. Of course, I soon learned how to even up the score. The ice blocks that we had to carry usually had the purported weight of twenty-five or fifty pounds. We carried the blocks with ice hooks. Twenty-five pound blocks cost fifteen cents. Fifty pound blocks cost twenty-five or thirty cents.

When I was about fifteen years old, the railroad employees launched a general strike — sometimes referred to as the Great Railroad Strike of 1922. The strike breaking workers were referred to as "Scabs". They slept out in the railroad yards at night and were fed en masse during the day. I obtained employment as a waiter serving food to the strike breakers (who today are euphemistically referred to as "replacement workers"). I felt no remorse at serving strike breakers because the railroad unions, known as Brotherhoods, had not only refused to accept Negroes as members, but they also actively sought to limit Negro railroad employment to hard labor—jobs like firemen and track layers, etc.

The railroad call boy would come by at 4:00 in the morning to awaken us. There was a song that we sometimes sang which had lyrics similar to this:

> Wake up brother and
> Piss on the rock
> It ain't quite day
> but it's four o'clock.

23

The white man's pushing me
and I am pushing you
So wake up brother
And piss on the rock!

I also had a hair-raising experience while working as an adolescent. The next summer when I was about sixteen years of age, I worked as a laborer in the Norfolk & Western railroad yards. The railroad had a labor force, and when they needed extra labor they got a gang off the labor force from what was known as the "scrap wharf." My compensation was twenty-five cents per hour.

That summer I had a wide range of jobs. For instance, I mixed concrete from scratch. That involved combining and stirring the sand, water and cement with a shovel. I also transferred files of shippers' claims against the railroad from an old office building to a new office building and guided rails to the frog shop. They called the holes where the rails were connected "frogs."

It was while working at the frog shop that I almost got killed. A crane would bring the rails and dump them in a pile. We would get on the piles with crow bars and try to pry the rails apart so that they could be moved along stationary rails to a series of rollers. We put them on the rollers and rolled them down to the frog shop.

Anyway, I was standing on the ground with a crowbar trying to pull and loosen some rails to slide down to the rollers. The rollers were fastened to a platform behind me. Suddenly, the whole pile of rails came crashing down. I was barely able to get out of the way of the steel avalanche that was coming my way. If I had been less agile, I would surely have been cut in half by the sliding rails as they slammed me against the platform holding the rollers. I could have been killed when I was sixteen years of age instead of living to my present ripe old age.

As one might expect, I got involved in the railroad work through being reared by Mr. and Mrs. Pentecost. The Pentecosts also had a contract with the Norfolk & Western dining car service to provide parsley. We regularly received calls for one hundred or two hundred bundles of parsley which Mrs. Pentecost and I picked from a patch in our backyard. In addition, we had three grape arbors (two blue and one white) and a large cherry tree. During the summer we made wine from the grapes. When I became twelve, I began to receive an annual allotment of the wine for my use for the year.

24

Mrs. Pentecost's brother had dropped out of Morehouse College and began working on the railroad as a waiter. As I mentioned before, students frequently dropped out and spent a year working to get more money to return to school. However, Mrs. Pentecost's brother never went back to college.

Mrs. Pentecost was greatly concerned that this would happen to me; and she endeavored to keep me off the railroad. However, these jobs paid the best money that uneducated people could expect to make. This made the jobs especially attractive. Roanoke was a railroad town. In our circle, practically everybody either ran on a railroad or worked for the Norfolk and Western or the Virginian Railroad in such capacities as cooks, waiters, porters, trainmen, brakemen, firemen and messengers at the main office.

On Saturdays and on some Friday evenings I would go to one of the shoe shine parlors and shine shoes. Shoeshines usually cost a nickel or a dime; however, a special shine might bring a quarter tip. The proprietors furnished shoe paste, brushes and rags. Our earnings were primarily tips. The railroad, ice wagon, and shoe shine jobs exemplify some of the employment available for kids like me.

Early School Memories

Going to school in those days was probably similar in some ways to school now. For example, most of the classes, including mine, were large--about twenty-five or thirty students. My class remained the same all the way through the eighth grade. However, there were differences, too. You did not hear about children bringing guns to school. That was unthinkable.

When I was going to the third grade, the school's administration asked Mrs. Pentecost for permission for me to skip the third grade. They wanted to put me in a smaller and more studious class of less than ten. However, Mrs. Pentecost refused. Her reasoning was that I needed to take each grade as it came. Upon reflection however, I believe my educational development would have been helped had I worked with the smaller more studious group. This experience demonstrates that even conscientious parents do not necessarily know what is in the child's best interest unless they have had some previous experience upon which to make the decision.

When I was growing up, some kids were classified as incorrigible. I was a member of such a class. We weren't incorrigible in the sense that we didn't get our lessons or did anything unlawful. We were mischievous and disruptive.

For example, in the fourth grade, our regular teacher got married. We were given a substitute teacher. We found it easy to frustrate her. And from this point on, we acted more devilish and reached new lows of ingenuity in disrupting the educational process.

In fact, we became such a problem to the school authorities that, though most of us lived in the northwest section of Roanoke, the school authorities decided to transfer the entire class to the Gregory School in northeast Roanoke. At Gregory School, there was a very strong teacher, Miss Sarah Brown. Miss Brown made some progress in controlling us; however, she was not completely successful. The class had a misguided sense of loyalty. Regardless of what happened, no one would tell on anyone else. That facilitated our continuing some of our prior mischievous activities.

For example, at that time I had a man's coat that had been altered so that I could wear it. It had a concealed change pocket on the right side. I had a little mechanical "cricket". I could squeeze this device and it would make a chirping noise. Miss Brown would notice the noise coming from my direction, come around and say "Turn out your pockets." I would turn out all of my pockets — except the small, hidden change pocket. After she had walked away, I sometimes squeezed it again.

Everybody knew who did it, but nobody would say anything. We took pride in the fact that the class stood together. We did all kinds of foolish things like that.

I also talked and I always got poor grades on the conduct section of the report card. Nevertheless, my class was a pretty good class. It just took a strong teacher to hold the class. With a weak teacher we probably wouldn't have gotten good grades. Miss Brown was a good teacher and most of us respected her and got our lessons.

We were always into devilment. I don't remember all of it. When I was twelve or thirteen, we wore sashes. We used to chase the girls around the room and kiss them on the cheek. This was during the days of Rudolph Valentino and the motion picture "The Sheik". There was

26

also a song from that motion picture which we used to sing; I believe it was entitled "The Song Of Arabia".

We also wore our hair slicked down. This was accomplished by a preparation called "Stay-combed."

As far as athletics were concerned, the side street next to our house was a favorite place for football, an abbreviated form of baseball, as well as marble shooting. Early on the older boys in the general area started playing football; and when I was about thirteen, I tried to play with them. I began my football career as a center and the next year when I went to Harrison High School in Roanoke, naturally I went out for football. Our manual training teacher (who taught us carpentry), also taught us how to play football and basketball.

By the time I reached the seventh grade, basketball was introduced into the so-called Negro high school in Roanoke. We got up at 5:00 in the morning to practice basketball in the public auditorium. If there had been an affair in the auditorium during the previous evening, we had to stack the chairs and clear the floor before we could practice. We played our games in that auditorium, too. I don't know what arrangements the school board made for us to play there. After practice, we would come back home and those who had showers took a shower. Fortunately, I had a shower but most of the kids didn't. Then we'd go on to school.

This produced my first resentment of discrimination. I knew that my white counterparts at Jefferson High School had a gymnasium, with a basketball court including all the accessories like lockers and showers. They could practice in the afternoons.

Of course, basketball was a different game in those days. It remained so until I left college. For instance, after each basket, play resumed with a jump ball at center court. The same was true after every successful free throw. If there were a question about control of the ball, there would be a jump ball and no such thing as arrows showing which team had the right of possession.

Another difference is that today, basketball players take a charge. Back then if the player ended up taking the charge, the official would call a double foul. Foul on one player for charging and foul on the other for blocking. I contend that they ought to go back to the double foul rule. Today kids risk an injury taking some fool charge. It doesn't

27

make sense.   Calling double fouls would be one way of helping stop some of this.

I also enjoyed tennis.   Sometimes in the morning before work and every evening in the summer, if I wasn't working I played tennis.   I was sometimes on the tennis court practically all day.   Early in my tennis career, the owner of a lot on Third Avenue in Roanoke told some of the neighborhood children, that if we fixed up a lot that he owned we could use it as a tennis court.   We did so, organized ourselves into a club, and called ourselves the "Puff Adders".   Soon after, we encouraged six girls to join our tennis club.   We taught them to play tennis.   We played singles, doubles and mixed doubles.   I remember the names of two of the girls who played with us.   One girl named Gertrude lived with the Dudleys in a house next door to me; the other girl whose last name was Wise lived in the east end of Roanoke.   Both of these young ladies became proficient tennis players.   I played tennis from about age nine until I left Roanoke in 1923.   In that year the Downing brothers, who had achieved national recognition in the Negro Tennis Association, were going to Bordentown, Delaware, where the National Tennis Tournament was held annually.   The Downings were going to carry me to Delaware with them.   However, I was so excited about the prospect of going to Washington and attending Dunbar High School, that I did not think about trying to work out the tennis trip too.

On a different note, this was also a transitional period for high school development in Roanoke.   For a number of years before I reached the seventh grade, seventh grade was the end of primary and secondary public education for Negro students in Roanoke.   When Negro students finished the seventh grade, those desiring to continue their education in Virginia went to the academy at Virginia Normal and Collegiate Institute in Petersburg; at Virginia Union University in Richmond; or at St. Paul's College in Lawrenceville.

When I reached the seventh grade, my slightly disruptive class and I went to Harrison High School.   By that time, the highest grade for Negroes was the eighth grade.   Consequently, why they called Harrison a high school was a mystery to me.

However, the school board apparently had some nebulous plans to add grades one year at a time. Accordingly, the class of eighth grade students ahead of us went through commencement.   The next year the school board added a ninth grade.   That class went through all the commencement process again.   The succeeding year they added a tenth grade, and the following year an eleventh grade. Each year the same class had a commencement exercise: it happened to that class about four times.

However, after finishing the eighth grade in Roanoke, I went to Washington, D.C., to attend Dunbar High School.

Even though I have graduated from high school, college and law school, I never experienced the senior year social activities associated with graduation. For instance, my high school prom at Dunbar was not available to me because I graduated in January. I then started college at Howard in the spring quarter. Similarly, I did not participate in the social functions in my college senior year. After completing one quarter of what would normally have been my senior year, I started law school. I had to wait until the end of the first year of law school to receive credit for the work done at the law school, and to have it applied towards satisfying my undergraduate degree requirements. I received my B.A. at the end of the first year of law school. I attended the baccalaureate services and commencement exercises to receive my earned degrees.

My Social Life in Roanoke

Children's socialization during those early years was interesting, too. We learned to play various games. Aside from playing tennis and basketball, I was a very good card player. I had an advantage over the other kids in my community because most of their parents frowned on card games while Mr. and Mrs. Pentecost played cards and were liberal thinking people. They taught me card games early, and depending on the game I was available as the third or fourth player. I not only could remember the cards, but I also had a feel for the different card games.

As an only child in a family which emphasized home life, I had numerous opportunities to play with the grown-ups. On the other hand, my young friends couldn't play cards or dance at home. Since they couldn't do these things at home, it made my home more attractive to them. All the kids felt free at my house. I stayed near home in part because the kids liked to come there to play.

I was always taught that your home was where you lived and where you functioned. At one time there was a little recreation room in a building on Wells Avenue. Someone came in and said they were talking about building a YMCA in Roanoke. I came home all excited. I told

29

Mrs. Pentecost they were going to build a YMCA in Roanoke. She replied that a YMCA was a place for folks that didn't have a home. That became my attitude about the YMCAs, and fortunately, it also became my attitude towards bars.

I used to read a whole lot — especially the Boy Scout series, the Merriwell Series, Horatio Alger, wild west stories, mystery novels, and biographies. In the westerns they always played poker. I learned to play poker reading about card games in the wild west stories and following it up by checking the rules in Hoyle. I then taught the other kids. We would play for matches.

When I was young, shooting marbles was also a popular pastime. I remember two principal types of marble games. In one game you drew a large ring; and each player put in an equal number of marbles. The players would then take turns shooting. You could continue to shoot as long as you successfully knocked a marble out of the ring and kept your shooter in the circle. We usually played these games on the unpaved sidewalks or on a level area in a vacant field.

The second marble game format involved drawing a bow-shaped ring. Each player put marbles at designated places on the bow. Then standing from a distance a player would shoot his marble toward the ring trying to knock one out. Once you started, each successful shot allowed you to continue shooting from the place where your shooter stopped.

Two other boys (Norvell Coles and Maynard Law) and I were real good at shooting marbles. We used to win all the kids' marbles and then sell them back to them. One means of facilitating the sales was making punch cards. To give you an idea of what a punch card was, imagine the cardboard back of a writing tablet. You could put numbers on the back of the tablet; then fold a piece of paper and put it over the written numbers. For a small fee, a player could "punch" one of the designated points on the paper. When the player looked under the paper, he would see the number written on the tablet. That was the number of marbles he won.

Our fees ranged from a penny, to two cents or a nickel. After making the required payment, a player always won at least one marble each time he played this game.

As far as dancing was concerned, there wasn't too much of that among my associates. Back in the southern cities in those times dancing was frowned on by the Baptists, Methodists and all the Protestant churches. When I was a kid in Roanoke I remember on two occasions they held trials and expelled members from church for dancing. When the congregation voted to put one of Mrs. Pentecost's friends out, that caused us to leave High Street Baptist Church where my mother sang in the choir. We started attending First Baptist. Although my people danced at home, I don't remember too many kids dancing.

Occasionally people had dances in which participants paid a small entrance fee. I never did go to one of those in Roanoke. I couldn't dance well anyway, but I could one-step. I remember when I got to Washington, periodically they used to have dances in the Armory at Dunbar High School. It was always a problem for me because I had to listen to the music to see whether it was going to be a waltz before I could ask a girl to dance with me. The bands used to play a lot of waltzes and I couldn't waltz. Because I had to wait for the music to start and then run and look for a girl, that put me at somewhat of a disadvantage. When I look back now, I believe that if I had been thinking more, I could have used a different strategy. I could have asked the girl(s) that I wanted to dance with ahead of time, but I would have needed to say to them, "I cannot dance with you if the dance is a waltz!" I suppose you could call that a conditional offer.

Let me make a brief point on the Negro class structure in Roanoke when I was a child. The structure then was more democratic in the sense that African American people from various social strata mingled freely. For instance, I mentioned that I interacted a lot with adults. One of my pastimes was occasionally to play the card game, whist, with the women who had a club. Some of the women were wives of physicians and railroad workers. There were also teachers, a nurse and a domestic. I observed no class distinction being made among these various women. Nevertheless, I do remember one of Mrs. Pentecost's friends talking with Mrs. Pentecost. This friend was a nurse who had persuaded her husband, a dining car employee, to take a job as secretary of the YMCA in Washington, D.C. In talking with other family members and me, Mrs. Pentecost said that her friend would find a significant difference in the social relationships in Washington, D.C. Mrs. Pentecost stated that in Washington there was more division: a kind of "pecking order" based upon skin color and economic status.

Another interesting anecdote involves a relative of Mrs. Pentecost who was a big Baptist preacher in Roanoke. He got caught with one of

31

the women in the choir, was forced to resign and left town. He subsequently obtained a pastorate in Homestead, Pennsylvania; and ultimately, he died there. We went up there to his funeral and spent about a week. During this week I had my first experience playing with white children.

In Homestead, they had a big playground. (At one time they had a black pro baseball team there: The Homestead Grays. They may have had a team there at the time of my visit in 1920.)

Anyway, I wandered down to the playground and there wasn't anyone there but white kids. Practically all of them were Eastern Europeans — Hungarians and all that. In those days they were called "hunkies".

A baseball game was going on and I was standing around looking. The pitcher of one team got hurt. Somebody asked me could I play baseball. I said yes. They inquired whether I could pitch. I said yes. So after a brief warmup I went in and pitched.

I never had any speed but as I said, I had a wide variety of slow dipsy doodles or "junk" balls. I'd throw them over hand, side arm, under arm. I pitched and we ended up winning the game. I went down to this playground every day after that. Usually there were pick up teams. Sometimes, when not pitching I would play second base. I had a fine time playing with these new associates. But that was my only experience with white folks outside of a work environment.

I had also been to Columbus, Ohio where Mr. Pentecost had a sister. In addition once in the early 1920's when I was about thirteen I went to Pittsburgh.

In my travels to Columbus, Pittsburgh and Pittsfield, I noticed some differences. For example, when we went to Columbus, a strike was going on involving the streetcars. The employees would not enforce the fares. Accordingly, if you gave them a fare they took it. However, if you didn't, they didn't require you to. I and a number of other people rode the transportation vehicles without paying. At the time, I considered it a great lark.

On another occasion, Mr. Pentecost took me to Columbus, Ohio so I could see the appearance and attend the performance of Bert Williams, a famous Negro comedian. Some way or another the show got

32

canceled before we arrived. However, we spent many enjoyable evenings at home listening to Williams' records.

For instance, Williams had a song where he was explaining to his wife why he was so late getting home. He said, "I got stuck on a bar and had to drink the ole Green River dry to get home to you." The Green River was the name of a whiskey.

Another one of Williams' favorite routines involved a preacher who was preaching and got all riled up. The preacher started talking about a member of the congregation who had been down by the chicken coop. The implication of the message was that the member had stolen a chicken. At the end of the sermon, the preacher said, "Now we'll have prayer by that certain gentleman we have been talking about."

An old deacon got up and said, "Who was it, Lord, down to Sister Mamie Parker's playing "Five Up." The prayer continued: "I said, who was it, Lord down to Sister Mamie Parker's playing "Five Up" and lost <u>all</u> the church's money"? At this point the preacher recognized that the deacon was implicating him in the prayer, and the preacher jumped up and shouted, "Doxology! Doxology! Use all the doors!"

Williams was one of the first big black stars on Broadway. According to reports, he could just come out on the stage and people in the audience would begin clapping and laughing. During the early part of this century, many comedians who used African American type humor performed in black face. Even though he was black, Williams used black face too. Williams was a really fantastic comedian.

Invariably, Williams had his wife traveling with him. It was especially easy in those days to frame Negro males by claiming they were involved in romantic encounters with white women.

Anyway, the aborted Columbus appearance was my only chance to see him. I missed it and I was really disappointed.

<u>A Narrow Escape</u>

While my childhood was pleasant for the most part, like Langston Hughes said, "Life for me ain't been no crystal stair." There is one scary and unforgettable childhood experience I had. I couldn't have been more than eight or nine. Virginia adopted prohibition prior to passage of the Eighteenth Amendment. That was the reason my mother and stepfather left Roanoke. One day I observed some older boys picking up whiskey bottles which I learned that they carried to a distillery and sold there for pennies. I decided to pick up bottles also so I could make a little extra change. I searched the alleys and anywhere that I thought a person might have thrown a bottle. Afterwards, I carried the bottles to the distillery to sell.

When I got to the distillery, a guy on the first floor told me to take them up to the second floor. When I got up on the second floor, someone yelled out, "Grab the little nigger and cut his balls out." I didn't know what was the function of "balls"; but I knew they were mine and I didn't have any desire to part with them. Several men chased me all around the second floor of the building. They could just have been trying to terrorize this little Negro kid or they could have actually intended to have done me some harm if they had caught me. Fortunately, I was agile enough to get away. I don't know whether they were sadistic, or just scaring the hell out of me, or whether they actually wanted to harm me. But one thing was sure: they didn't catch me. Finally, I got loose and ran out of the distillery as fast as I could. I never tried to sell any whiskey bottles again.

As I said, Mr. Pentecost worked on the railroad. He came in late that night. When we told him the story, the next morning Mr. Pentecost carried me back to this distillery. I don't know what he intended to do when he brought me down to this establishment. However, there was no question that he was mad as hell.

We got there close to noon. There was nobody in sight. We waited around for a while, but finally he had to go out on his railroad run. When he came home several days later the whole thing had passed over. Nobody bothered me and nothing came of that. Of course, I was fearful at the time of the incident. I have always remembered it.

I don't know whether that was the only time that Mr. Pentecost was in that kind of position. He was a mild-mannered, even-tempered man and I don't remember Mr. Pentecost ever attempting to correct me. When I got a whipping, Mrs. Pentecost gave it to me. Nevertheless, I was not surprised when he asked me to go down to the building where the men had threatened to castrate me.

Mr. Pentecost was one of these persons who didn't talk a whole lot about himself or even about his childhood. The only thing he would talk to me about sometimes was items of interest in newspapers.

Sometimes he would bring a half dozen newspapers home. I'd look at the comics and he would read the news and editorial pages. We talked enough for me to become familiar with a wide range of out of town papers like the Washington Evening Star, Cincinnati Inquirer, St. Louis Dispatch, the Hearst paper which I later sold on my paper route, and the New York Times which was published by the Ochs Family who came from Mrs. Pentecost's hometown, Chattanooga, Tennessee.

Regarding the assault in the warehouse, no thought was given to calling the police because we perceived the police to be just as bad as the people who were chasing me. If we had gone down and filed a complaint they may have done something. We will never know. For one thing, I don't know if I could have identified anybody. During those days we had no association with the white police and no confidence in their fairness.

Chapter II

High School and College Days

I don't remember any time ever thinking I was going to drop out of school ... For some reason, I always thought I was going to college.

In 1916 my mother and stepfather left Hot Springs and moved to Washington, D.C. When we got involved in World War I, my stepfather did his bit to aid the war effort by working in the United States Navy Yard. I got along well with Mr. and Mrs. Pentecost; accordingly I stayed in Roanoke until I was in sixth grade. I then went up to Washington, D.C. for a semester but did not like it. I was permitted to return to Roanoke where I stayed until the summer of 1923. When I left Roanoke in 1923, I went to Dunbar High School in Washington, D.C.

Two things influenced me to go to Dunbar. Firstly, I had heard of Dunbar and recognized it as one of the finest high schools in the country. Secondly, my mother and stepfather were in Washington and this afforded me an opportunity to live with them.

While I started in the first year of Dunbar's four year program, Dunbar didn't give me full credit for all the subjects I had taken in Roanoke. I ended up being a half term behind. This was not all the fault of the Dunbar school officials. I could have taken some extra course work and made up the subjects myself. However, I made bad matters worse with my lack of scholarly seriousness. I received less than a passing grade in one English course and in one math course. My problem with the English class was that we took English right after physical education break. Each day we inevitably played basketball. I would always be worn out by the time I got to class. This led to some personality conflicts with my instructor. Looking back on the situation,

36

it was unquestionably my fault. I got my other grades all right. For some reason or other I had trouble with that class.

Both the elementary and secondary schools for Negroes in the Washington, D.C. school system were vastly superior to the schools afforded to Negroes in Northern Virginia and adjoining parts of Maryland. Consequently, to attend the superior public schools in Washington, D.C., many Negro students from Northern Virginia and Maryland resorted to the ruse of claiming residence with relatives who lived in Washington, D.C.

Of course, segregation in the Washington, D.C. public schools worked to the disadvantage of Negro students in many ways. For example, Eastern, Central, Western, Business, and Technical were all high schools for white students. Only two high schools existed for Negroes - Dunbar and Armstrong. Central was located on 11th Street, between Fairmount and Florida Avenue. I lived on Gresham Place which was two blocks north of Fairmount and three blocks east of Eleventh Street. While walking to Dunbar High School, I usually passed within two blocks of Central and could have passed directly by Business and Technical high schools. I usually walked to Dunbar which in my estimation was two or three miles away from my home. To get to Dunbar, I passed within the proximity of three white high schools.

As far as the organization of Dunbar's academic program was concerned, we reported to our homerooms in the morning for attendance purposes. Then you had your first, second, third and fourth hours, going down the line, with the instructors offering the subjects you were taking. You might have different children in each of your classes. Basically, you had a homeroom teacher and during the rest of the day you attended other teachers' classes. You may or may not have any classes under your homeroom teacher.

Academic subjects offered included math, biology, chemistry, zoology, physics, English, Spanish and German. In addition, we had music, art, history, physical education, and the military cadet corps. Within the main building, Dunbar had a business department which offered courses in bookkeeping, shorthand, and typing.

I took physics in high school and mathematics through solid geometry. A high percentage of the graduating class from Dunbar went on to college. A number of students went to Williams, Amherst and other New England colleges, while others went to Negro colleges like

37

Howard, Lincoln, Hampton, Virginia Union and Morgan. It was a fortunate break for those who lived in Washington because we could live at home and attend Howard. When I went to Howard, I lived at home, and tuition was about forty dollars a quarter. Many of my Howard classmates whose parents were at the lower end of the economic scale were also from Dunbar.

I suppose for all students there are a few teachers from their public school days who stand out. For me, in Roanoke there was Ms. Sarah Brown who taught us in the sixth grade, Ms. Sadie Lawson, who taught seventh grade, and Ms. Raeford, who taught us in the eighth grade. All of these individuals were strong teachers. Despite our shenanigans, they forced us to learn something constructive and socially beneficial.

Similarly, at Dunbar, I had a number of very good teachers. Mr. Neville Thomas was my favorite teacher and he greatly influenced me. We called Neville Thomas, "Cat" Thomas. In our American history class, the text that we used was one authored by a man named David Mussey. That's the only text book I really remember. If a student recited some alleged historical fact that Neville Thomas disagreed with, he would say, "You must have read that in Mussey."

Thomas taught history, with emphasis upon Negro history. Of course there was virtually nothing in the high school history texts about Negro history.

During this time, Dr. Carter G. Woodson was in Washington and just starting his Negro history week program. Woodson and others soon developed the Association for the Study of Negro Life and History. This organization had an office and library in Washington on Vermont Avenue.

We did a lot of outside reading, and Thomas prescribed most of it. You read Mussey if you wanted to, but when you recited, if you wanted to capture Neville's attention, you needed to cite sources outside of Mussey.

Another outstanding Dunbar teacher was Professor Weatherless. He taught chemistry and patented a device used by the Reo Auto Company. The company furnished him a new car every year. I presume the car served as partial or total compensation for his invention.

In addition, Dr. Eva Dikes was an outstanding English teacher who taught at Dunbar and later went to Howard. It was reported that at that time the salary scale at Dunbar was higher than that of most Negro colleges and universities. All of our teachers were well educated and most had advanced degrees. They talked about and had contact with contemporary matters. For instance, I remember one time a group of Russians came to Washington and one of our instructors served as interpreter for them.

Dunbar often had prominent speakers. While many Dunbar students were cocky, they were also well-motivated. Oft times when walking down the street we sang a little song which went like this: "If anybody asks you, 'Who we are, who we are?' Tell them, "We are the Dunbar Boys!'" We sang this refrain over and over.

We also had a number of extra curricular activities. In addition to football, basketball, baseball, soccer, gymnastics and track and field we also had the cadet corps. For example, the cadet competition between Dunbar and Armstrong was at old Griffith Stadium where the Howard University Hospital is located now. We would practice all spring for this competition. It was a big rivalry between the schools as well as between the companies. Everybody wanted to be No. 1.

In the one year I drilled, we were favorites to win the competition. However, on the day of the competition, the second lieutenant who was the commanding officer of the second platoon in our company dropped his sabre. The competition was so keen that any mistake would drop that company to the bottom of the list of competing companies. So despite our team being favored, we finished out of the running for an award.

I didn't like to drill and I wasn't interested in studying to become a military officer. I was not military minded. By the end of the first year at Dunbar I learned that if you majored in physical education you didn't have to drill. So I ended up majoring in Physical Education. Like many things in life, if you make decisions based on wrong premises, you do yourself more harm than good.

Because even as a child in Roanoke I was often involved in sports activities, it is not surprising that when I came to Washington, D.C. and attended Dunbar High School, I continued participating in athletics. For example, I went out for football and basketball. In the Washington public school system, our athletic program only included competing against Armstrong High School in all sports. In addition, we played

39

against Minor Normal in basketball. The normal schools in those days provided two years of education beyond high school. We also played against Frederick Douglass in Baltimore, as well as some of the outlying schools in Virginia. We had academic contests against Bowie Normal School in Maryland, and on one occasion, we also played Booker T. Washington High School in Norfolk.

Furthermore, one year we played Addison High School from Roanoke as well as Dunbar from Lynchburg. While we had these types of athletic competitions with Negro schools in the surrounding areas and occasionally from relatively far away, we never played against any of the white schools.

Throughout my tenure in high school, we always had a great track and field team. During the first three years that I was at Dunbar, our basketball and football teams were excellent. However, during the interim between the end of the athletic seasons and the beginning of my fourth year at Dunbar, Coach Hurt, who was then a coach at Virginia Seminary, recruited so extensively among Washington, D.C. area athletes that the athletic resources at both Dunbar and Armstrong were diluted.

Virginia Seminary was a collegiate institution in Lynchburg, Virginia. As its name indicated, the Seminary was principally a theological school and was not particularly academically rigorous. The reason that I say Lynchburg Seminary was not especially rigorous academically was that I had listened to a number of students from the Seminary give their sermons in our churches in Roanoke. In many cases they seemed to have no regard for the king's English.

Had I been unaware of the academic standards at the Seminary, I might have followed many of my fellow student athletes who went down to Virginia Seminary. They frequently viewed it as an opportunity to get away from home and go to school somewhere else. But after a couple of years they often learned the error of their decision.

The football game between Armstrong and Dunbar was always played the Wednesday before Thanksgiving. Whether we won or lost that game determined whether the season was considered a great success or a dismal failure. During my tenure at Dunbar, we won three years and lost one of these football games against Armstrong.

In fact, in 1926 we won my last game in high school. I threw a forward pass to my right end and he ran for a touchdown. I then place-

40

kicked the extra point. I also got my shoulder dislocated in the last two or three minutes of the game. The doctors didn't have all of the refined technology that they have now and they suggested that I not try to play football for at least a couple of years. Interestingly, both in high school and as a college freshman, I threw winning touchdown passes and kicked the extra point; I also ended up in the hospital in each case.

Because of Hurt's heavy recruitment which diluted the athletic pool, during my senior year in high school I had to play quarterback and defensive fullback. Today the defensive fullback is often called the middle linebacker. The other three years I played end on defense and offense.

In my day, we did not have positions designated as linebackers and wide receivers, nor was there frequent substitution of players. As I mentioned, when I was in high school and college, players had to play both ways -- both offense and defense. When we did so, the fullback was the linebacker, the quarterback played safety, and the two halfbacks were the corners. The ends on offense played end on defense, too. It was up to the line and the defensive fullback to stop any running plays. The halfbacks were so far back that, by the time they came up to the line, the runner would have made a substantial gain.

I was also a place kicker and place kickers were a novelty when I was in high school. Extra points were scored by rushing, passing or drop kicking the ball. When the kicker drop kicked the ball, he would let it fall to the ground and kick it as it hit the ground. In those days, the goal posts were on the goal line, not ten yards back as they are now.

There are also a couple of other interesting changes that have occurred in the years intervening since I played football back in the 1920's. For example, the ball was put in play from the place closest to where the preceding in bounds play ended. Thus, if a person on offense had the ball and was tackled near the side line, on the next play the ball would be placed close to the sideline. In a situation like that, the center would be the end because the center would be snapping the ball almost on the sideline. He could snap it to the quarterback, or any other player in the backfield for whom the play had been called. Instead of "shotgun" formations, some plays were made from kick formation. In addition, if a player ran out of bounds, the next play would start at the hash mark nearest the sideline where the preceding play ended. Consequently good running backs attempted to run out of bounds so that their team could run the next play from the regular offensive formation.

41

Unlike football today, there were no free substitutions of players. Thus, for example, if a player was removed from the game during a quarter, he could not return to the game during the same quarter.

Furthermore, rules on passing were different. For example, if during a four-down series, you threw a forward pass and it was incomplete, there was no penalty. However, for any second or subsequent incomplete forward pass during that series, a team received a five yard penalty. This was an attempt to discourage passing. Thus, if you threw three incomplete forward passes, you received two five yard penalties.

On offense, the quarterback determined the plays, called the signals, and generally ran the team. In high school when I was playing football, a new innovation, huddles, came into widespread use. Interestingly, during those days, substitutes were not allowed to talk with the rest of the team until after at least one play had been made. Coaching from the sidelines during those days, would cost the team a fifteen yard penalty.

Concerning my experience with playing basketball, I considered myself to be better at football than at basketball. Even though I played offense and defense, in some respects football did not require quite as much wind stamina as basketball. I believe in those days the basketball was bigger. Unless you were dribbling in for a lay up, most of the time when I was in high school (as well as in college) the coach wanted us to pass the ball until we found an open person who could get set and shoot. The game was much slower. Rather than dribble up the court, we would make a series of passes to initiate a set play.

As I mentioned, all held balls and every score resulted in a jump ball. Accordingly, we went back to center jump, jumped the ball and started again after scores from the field and foul shots.

A strong Negro basketball team existed in those days, too. It was called the New York Renaissance Big Five. One of the players was named Eyre "Bruiser" Saitch, and a man named Tatum played center.[1]

In Washington in 1928 or so I saw the Renaissance Big Five play the Original Celtics who were in New York at that time. Because a number of teams used the name "Celtics", to distinguish itself from others with the Celtics name, this particular team called itself the "Original Celtics." The Renaissance Big Five kept the ball for five solid minutes; and the Original Celtics just couldn't break it up. Finally, a player isolated himself and they flipped the ball over the Celtics defense and the man scored. The Renaissance won that game going away. During those days, the final scores of basketball games ranged from low scoring affairs which had final tallies in the twenties, to high scoring games in which teams scored about forty-five points.

My first experience in seeing white basketball players involved the Original Celtics from New York who played the Palace Laundry, a Washington pro basketball team. These teams played at the Arcade at 14th and Park Avenue, Washington, D.C. Nat Holman was one of the first outstanding white players that I remember. He was a terrific scorer and played for the Original Celtics. Another Celtic player was Horse Haggerty who was about six feet six inches tall.

The Palace Laundry was owned by a man named George Marshall. His business had the same name — Palace Laundry. This was in the 1920's before the National Basketball Association was created.

The first man that I remember seeing who could handle the ball so as to dunk it was Lanky Jones who played collegiate ball with Morgan State.[2] Lanky used to hook the ball between his palm and his wrist. He would jump up and slam the ball through the rim. However, from my perspective, dunking did not come in as a big deal until Dr. J introduced it during the 1960's and 1970's.

By the way, Marshall who owned Palace Laundry was the same man who bought the Redskins and moved them to Washington from Boston. He was a segregationist and refused to sign any Negro players. As a consequence, Negroes would boycott his team or when they did attend games, the Negroes cheered against the Redskins. This was especially the case when the Cleveland Browns came to town because Cleveland had several outstanding Negro players. Frequently, in those days, the Browns defeated the Redskins.

As far as baseball was concerned, as an early teenager I was good at pitching, but like most kids with no training or guidance I soon threw my arm out. When I was a youngster prior to each pitch, I would wind up throw it overhand, or I could come down side arm. I also had a little ole ball that I could throw underhand. I could throw a ball up there slow; and throw one slower next time. In those days, many pitchers threw really hard, and my slow unpredictable pitches were disconcerting to the batters. Furthermore, I had very good control, so that I kept the ball away from, or in close on, the batters.

43

In the early 1920's and for a long time thereafter, the entire team did a whole lot of talking to the batters. You never saw a silent baseball game. I would have the opposing hitters batting at the ball before it got there.

My baseball experience was basically of the pick-up variety. We often played baseball on sand lots and met there sometimes by agreement and other times just by chance. When a group of us boys got together, two people would step forward as team captains. Someone would toss a bat in the air, and one of the captains would grab the bat. The other captain would put his hand just above the place where the first one grabbed the bat, and then the captains would alternate placing their hands above each other until they got to the very top of the bat. The one who got the last place at the very top of the bat would get the first choice of players to be on his team.

From that point forward, each captain would choose players until a team was chosen. Of course, one tried to get the best players available, bearing in mind the positions that the persons to be chosen would have to play. The next criterion was to select one's friends as teammates.

We batted in order of position, often starting with the catcher, then going to the pitcher, first baseman, second baseman, third baseman and the outfielders. I'm not sure when teams in organized baseball leagues began choosing to make the lineup based on batting ability. However, in our sand lot games, we often allowed other members of the team to bat for weak hitters when they had two strikes on them. This was called "taking a person's third strike." I suppose this, like most of our rules, was created on an ad hoc basis - we made it up as we went along.

I never was a heavy hitter; however, I had a knack for getting on base. I had a good eye for balls and strikes, I could bunt very well, and generally I kept the opposing players on their toes. They wondered whether I was going to hit away or bunt. I would switch hit on occasion and placed the ball well. When I say I wasn't a heavy hitter I mean that I hit mostly singles and it was a case of placing the ball in left field or right field over the head of the first baseman or the third baseman.

One time when I was about fourteen years old we played a double header and I pitched the first game. We won. The pitcher who was supposed to pitch the second game hadn't come so I started the second game. About the third inning he still hadn't shown up and by that time my arm was getting sore and I had to quit. I ruined my arm. Problems with my arm were so bad that I couldn't throw from second base to first. I used to play a little second base, but because of the injury to my arm, I had to give up playing that position as well.

I do not know what type of player I would have been if I had avoided ruining myself before I even tried playing with the high school team. By the time I got that age, during summer times, I was mainly playing tennis. When I got to Dunbar I went out for the baseball team only once. The infield was sewed up so the coach had me try out for outfield. I could not gauge fly balls very well. I used to enjoy baseball and played softball and basketball on the playground.

At Dunbar we didn't have a tennis team. Thus, my competitive tennis ended when I left Roanoke. One reason I stopped seriously playing tennis was that after moving to Washington I had jobs most summers. My working hours were not conducive to practice or playing tennis consistently. Every summer I worked in hotels and restaurants at various resorts.

I had reasonably good health, but I also used to suffer with sore throats and colds. Everyone had those. When I was in high school I had tonsillitis several times and the doctors suggested that I should have my tonsils removed. I was admitted to Freedman's Hospital the night before the operation. The next morning the operation started with them using ether as an anesthetic. I still remember feeling like I was going down a tunnel, there was a clanging sound and as I got deeper I fell asleep.

The next morning I woke up with my throat sore on one side and I was hungry. I was in a large ward with about ten beds on one side of the room, an aisle down the middle of the room, and ten beds on the other side. I looked around but couldn't find a nurse.

There was a station at the end of the ward and I remember walking to the station and rambling around trying to find something to eat. A nurse came back and caught me. I asked why was my throat sore on one side and not the other. She told me that I had bled so much that they had to stop the operation. Of course, later when the other tonsil was removed the operation was performed under a local anesthetic. I have had other operations but no ether since that experience.

In addition to academic and extra curricular activities, I also worked. When I was in high school I had a variety of jobs. For example, as I did in elementary school in Roanoke, while in high school in Washington DC, I shined shoes on some Saturdays at shoeshine parlors. I also helped my stepfather with his part time evening job racking balls at the Arcade which contained a large pool and billiards parlor.   As I mentioned, at the Arcade they held basketball games and other events.

My stepfather's regular employment was at the Racquet Club, now known as the University Club on 16th Street, N.W.   On special occasions, for example when a tournament was going on, I worked with my stepfather.   While I was in high school, my mother worked for a while at the Indian Springs Golf Club as a maid. Prior to going to New York, Arthur Godfrey performed there occasionally with his ukelele.

On special occasions, I worked at the Indian Springs Club. Later my mother gave up that job and became an Avon salesperson.

1924 was my first full summer in Washington, D.C., and my stepfather got me a job working at the American League baseball park in the refreshment stands. That year, the Senators won their first World Series. We served the customers soft drinks, hot dogs and beer. The beer, Bevo, contained 3.2 percent alcohol.

On one occasion while in high school, the football coach called me and said that they needed a busboy at Allies Inn. Allies Inn was renowned as an excellent cafeteria, and was located near the old State Department Building which is now called the Executive White House.   I went down to Allies Inn, was given a white coat, and immediately put to work. One entrance to the Inn was via outside stairs up to the second floor cafeteria. I used that entrance and as I got up to the top of the steps, some guy came running out of the cafeteria. He bumped against me and scampered down the steps. Later I discovered that he had robbed the cafeteria!

The police and a detective came to Allies and someone told them that I could give a description of the thief. The detective asked me to describe the robber. I told him that I saw a young white man about "so high". I held my hand out about forehead level to indicate the robber's height. I told the detective that he was wearing a white shirt and dark trousers.

The detective further inquired what the robber looked like, and I said "He's a white man." The detective asked me three or four times what he looked like and all I said was that he was a white man. At that time, practically all white people looked alike to me. It's like white people saying all Negroes look alike. Of course this is merely an example of how unobservant some people are. However, at least Negroes have all kinds of colorations.

It was real funny. In your first experiences where you haven't had any associations with white people and just think of them as white people, many of them do look a lot alike. The primary reason is that you are not observing them as individual human beings but as part of an identified group.

Another amusing incident involved a lady who asked me for a servette. At that time I had not the faintest idea what a servette was. I looked around but I did not see anything that struck me as such an object. Finally I asked a fellow employee and he pointed to a stack of napkins on the table. I got one and went looking for the lady. I never found her because in the crowd of white folks I could not identify her either. These experiences demonstrate some of the practical difficulties of living in a segregated society. I had all kinds of experiences like that when I was coming up.

While still in high school another boy named Sonny Robinson and I tried to get jobs at the site where they were building the Lincoln Memorial and the Memorial Bridge, but the foreman wouldn't employ us. He said we were too young. We resolved our employment problem by getting ourselves a couple of buckets and walking around the city looking for coal which needed to be stored in people's basements. In those days, trucks delivered coal to people's homes. Where there was no alley next to the home, the delivery man would deposit the coal in front of the house or in a private area between homes known as areaways. By a variety of means, coal was then carried to the basement of the purchaser. Sonny Robinson and I carried on this hustle to make money until a better job became available.

One summer I went away from home for the first time and worked at a place called Eaglesmere in Pennsylvania in the mountains up from Williamsport. A friend of mine had an aunt who was a pastry cook, and he had been up there the previous summer. He talked about how great it was. So he got me a job working in the kitchen — dishwashing. To get to Eaglesmere, we caught a railroad train. However, I cannot recall if the train was operated by the Baltimore and Ohio (B&O) or the Pennsylvania Railroad.

47

The Big Bang, Brown vs Board of Education and Beyond

A unique feature of this trip between Washington and Williamsport, Pennsylvania was that we had to go through what was known as the horseshoe tunnel. If you were on the observation car, you could see the engine coming out the other end of the tunnel. This experience was similar to one I later had riding the Canadian Pacific Railroad going up from Winnipeg to Banff Springs. The C & P train went through a series of tunnels on this journey and, from the observation car as one was leaving one tunnel, you could see the engine entering another tunnel. I've often thought of going back there to Lake Agnes which is high above sea level and Lake Louise which is at sea level.

Coming back to my experience at Eaglesmere, there were seven hotels around the lake. I worked at a hotel named the Rankin Hotel. There was another hotel called the Forest Glen which was at one end of the lake where there was a boathouse and wharf. Many canoes were moored there as well.

One Tuesday afternoon I had a somewhat amusing experience involving several employees from different hotels who were on the wharf. The group included both Negroes and whites. Somehow the conversation came to the subject of swimmers. One of the white guys made some very disparaging remarks about Negro swimmers.

At that time Johnny Weismuller was an Olympic swimming champion and the young white man made a big to do about there being no Negro who had been an Olympic swimming champion. In retrospect, the conversation probably came up because Charlie Drew, who later became famous for his work in blood plasma, had worked at Eaglesmere during a previous summer and was a terrific swimmer. Drew created quite a stir in his efforts to recover the body of a person who had drowned in the lake. The person's body was eventually recovered by a diver using deep sea diving equipment.

I don't know whether somebody booted this particular white guy into the water or whether he fell accidentally off the wharf into about three feet of water. Anyway, as you can imagine, the crowd on the wharf was laughing as he was scrambling in three feet of water.

Finally it dawned on another fellow and me at the same time, that this doggone fool was going to drown if someone did not pull him out. We jumped in, grabbed him, got him out of the water and back on the wharf. Some fellows skilled in artificial respiration administered treatment to him. He had gotten himself into serious trouble! I remember walking back through the woods, and spontaneously beginning to laugh. When asked why, I replied, "That damn fool was talking about how great white folks can swim, could not swim himself and did not even have sense enough to stand up and walk out of three feet of water!" Having pontificated on the racial superiority of white folks, this associate was unable to swim, and more importantly, lacked sufficient common sense or presence of mind to stand up in three feet of water so he would not drown. I could swim a little and I had sense enough to jump in and stand up in three feet of water to help get him out.

As a matter of fact at ten or eleven o'clock at night, I used to go down to the wharf and get canoes, and I would ride up and down the lake. It was beautiful. I never would ride with anybody because I wasn't a good swimmer. I didn't want to take a chance on someone else turning the canoe over.

This was a multi-purpose lake. In the summer, people used it for swimming and canoeing. In winter, the lake froze and hotel employees would cut and store the ice. Each of the hotels had its own big ice house and stored ice in sawdust in the ice houses. All summer we would go into our ice house and get large blocks of ice. In this way, all the needs for ice were met in our hotel.

Mother was disgusted at the news that I was going to take a dishwashing job at Eaglesmere rather than working at the ball park. I overheard my stepfather tell her, "Well, don't worry about it, he is not going to last at that job more than two weeks." In one respect my stepfather was right. At Eaglesmere I did put out some feelers to see if there was any work that I could get in Atlantic City; however, I never received any reports back. I was determined to prove him wrong and felt that I could not cut tail and come home. Probably, the only reason I stayed at Eaglesmere the whole summer was that I heard him make those comments.

When I look back on it, however, I realize that my decision was foolish and that I should have gone back to the baseball park. By doing that, I could have made much more money in helping work my way through school. However, the prospect of being away from home and more on my own, led me astray in the sense that I did not make a wise decision from an economic standpoint. As I look back now, it is interesting that while I was working my way through school, I never worked south of Washington, D.C.

The Big Bang, <u>Brown vs Board of Education</u> and Beyond

One summer I worked up at the Hotel Aspenwall in the Berkshires, in Massachusetts — as an elevator operator. My stepfather told me about this job. My parents had these type connections with hotel employees because as I mentioned previously, my parents had worked in the hotel service industry in Hot Springs, Virginia and in Bermuda.

At the Hotel Aspenwall, the chief of service was a black guy from Virginia named Williams. Incidentally, Mr. Williams had a son in dental school in Washington who also worked at the hotel that summer.

I traveled to the Hotel Aspenwall by train from Washington, D.C. to Pittsfield, Massachusetts. I had traveled by myself on trains from Roanoke to Washington, D.C. and from Roanoke to points in West Virginia. However, I had not traveled north of Washington, D.C. by myself.

My stepfather had given me detailed instructions on what to do once I got off the train in Penn Station in New York City. There I was planning to make connections for the train to Pittsfield, Massachusetts. In those days, Red Caps and freelance porters would meet passengers as they got off the train and offer to put their bags on the train to which they were transferring or to carry them to the cab stand.

I caught a subway to shuttle from Penn Station over to Grand Central Station so that I could take the train to Pittsfield, Massachusetts. When I arrived at Grand Central, a white freelance porter came up to me and asked me where I was going. I told him. He grabbed my bag and said, "Follow me."

He went through a subway turnstyle and was sailing along at a brisk clip with my bag. I followed him, but neglected to put any money in the turnstile. The turnstile wouldn't let me through; however, I simply jumped over it and continued in rapid pursuit of this man with my bag. When we got to the train to which I was transferring, the freelance porter put my bag down and held his hand out for some money. I was relieved simply to retrieve my bag and I ignored him. I grabbed my bag and proceeded to continue my journey to Pittsfield, Massachusetts.

When the train arrived at Pittsfield, I caught a trolley which took me on the six mile ride to Lenox, Massachusetts.

They used to have a cartoon in the Washington Evening Star

50

called the Toonerville Trolley. It was a little trolley with two or three seats in it and a big stove pipe. When I got to Pittsfield the trolley looked exactly like the Toonerville trolley I had seen in the cartoon. It was an electrical trolley. Just like the trolley in the comic strip, this trolley had a stove pipe which may have run down to a pot-bellied stove. Perhaps it provided heat in the winter time.

Lenox itself was a sleepy village in that at night, at 8:00 p.m., everything closed down. Wednesday night, however, was an exception. On that night, everyone in the village would go to a large gazebo in the town square. The band would play and folks would sit around and listen to it. During my entire stay that summer, this was the only exciting thing that I observed the town's people doing.

The Hotel Aspenwall was a very staid place. Hotel policy limited clientele to ultra-rich gentiles and other prominent people. Hotel policy specifically excluded Jews and of course Negroes were out of the question. I remember one time, I was on the elevator, and a female guest got on. She had never given me anything. She said, "Go on! Go on, before that Kike gets on here!" I didn't know what she was talking about. I looked out the door to see what a "Kike" was. Lo and behold, the only thing that I could see was Mr. Johnson, a big elderly man, walking down the hall. Mr. Johnson gave me a quarter every time he rode the elevator up or down. This particular lady never gave me a red nickel. Of course, I waited for Mr. Johnson. He got on the elevator. She reported me to the manager. I also reported the incident to Mr. Williams, the chief of service. As far as I was concerned, there never was any repercussion.

On another occasion, at night, during a terrible rain storm, a Jewish family stopped at the hotel. They were given accommodations for the night and the head of the family was very pleased with the accommodations. The next day, he tried to make reservations for future stays at the hotel. However, during the daylight, the hotel employees determined that the family was Jewish. The hotel employees swore that they were booked up for the foreseeable future. They simply would not let this family come back to stay.

Chauncey DePugh, a prominent official in the State Department often came there. I don't remember any Cabots or Lodges coming to stay. But they had a whole lot of renowned people. I remember the Fleishmans for several reasons. It sounded like they had a Jewish name and it was unusual for Jews to be allowed access to such retreats. In addition, the Fleishmans had a big and expensive suite. Mrs. Fleishman

51

and family members stayed in the suite all summer long.

One family member would come in on Thursday and leave Monday morning. Every time he came he brought a lot of bags and other personal belongings. He carried them away the next time he left. He never gave anybody a red nickel.

At the end of the season he had a satchel full of money. He obtained the payroll list of all the service help and went around everywhere (including the kitchen) giving everybody a sizable gratuity. However, I never went back to the Hotel Aspenwall, so I do not know whether in future years, he continued this practice.

Interestingly, as a general proposition even those well to do people had a favorite name for Negro males: "George." The Pullman Company played it up. "George" would take care of things. There was abundant reference to George. While I do not recall any situation like this occurring at the Hotel Aspenwall, in the public world generally, some fool would also call Negro service employees "darkies" or "Niggers".

I think that the same management operated the Hotel Aspenwall and the Hotel Hamilton which was in Bermuda. The Hotel Aspenwall was a summer resort, and at that time the Hotel Hamilton was a winter resort. Some of the service help worked at both hotels, and most of the service help, including maids, were Bermudians.

It is interesting that in Bermuda, there was a big soccer match involving opposite sides of the island. Accordingly, for weeks before the match occurred, the help talked constantly about the soccer match. There was a great rivalry regarding who was going to win and typically one chose sides depending upon which side of the island one lived on. The excitement continued several days after the match was over, as word was awaited regarding which side of the island had won the match.

While I was working at the Hotel Aspenwall, I also met a fellow who had a side job making fires in the cottages in the village. When I learned that he was leaving, I made arrangements for him to turn his customers over to me. I used to get up early in the morning and trot down to one end of the village to start making my fires. I would work my way to the other end of the village. Sometimes all I had to do was light a fire that had already been laid. Other times, I had to start from scratch. However, at each residence, materials were set aside for making the fire. I started fires for people who were mainly summer visitors.

Up there in the mountains during that summer, until about nine or ten o'clock in the morning, the ground looked like the sea. Fog was everywhere.

One evening a group of us drove down from Lenox to Pittsfield to see a movie. On the way back, the fog was so heavy that we took turns getting out of the car and walking in front of it to make sure that it stayed on the highway.

On another occasion, I remember a bunch of us went to Pittsfield to see a movie. We caught the streetcar down there and when we got out of the last show it was so late that despite our whooping and hollering, the trolley, which was leaving, left us. We had to walk six miles from Pittsfield back up to Lenox. By the time we arrived back, we were a tired and hungry bunch. We broke into the kitchen and couldn't find a thing to eat but a pan of fresh asparagus. Up until that time, I claimed that I never liked fresh asparagus. However, I dove into that fresh asparagus that night, and have been a strong advocate of fresh asparagus ever since.

Another interesting fact was that at night some guys working at the hotel gambled. I happened to be one who was involved in playing cards. I had a roommate that summer who was a card shark. He could surreptiously deal seconds (meaning deal the second card rather than the first) and stack the deck. He was ostensibly a chauffeur for one of the guests.

He was an expert on how card sharks take advantage of people and told me what to watch out for. He could easily tell if a person was cheating. He said, "You always learn to listen because you can't see the con man cheat when dealing the cards." Magicians, card sharks, and other con people distract you with their hands, talk, and other diversions so that you won't pay attention. Otherwise, you would catch on. However, as long as you concentrate and listen you can protect yourself.

I also knew card sharks have what they call a "clutch." It's the way you hold the cards so you have the freedom of movement to do your underhand stuff. Most card sharks that I encountered had long fingers. They would hold the cards in the "clutch." You never see a real smooth card shark deal dishonestly. The only way you can detect it is if you keep your ears open and hear the swish of the cards. I would pick up the cards and start dealing from the "clutch."

53

While I learned how to read the backs of the cards, I never tried to be a card cheat. However, I knew how to protect myself. For example, I noticed that people playing cards develop patterns of behavior. I learned how to turn down a lot of good cards waiting and watching till I learned enough about the other guy so I could protect myself. This way, my opponent and I were pretty much on the same basis.

At the hotel, a musical trio consisting of a violin, cello and bass played classical music each afternoon. I experienced a major culture shock one afternoon when I entered the lobby and saw a female guest sitting with her legs crossed and smoking a cigarette.

Another interesting occurrence involved an elderly millionaire and his sixteen year old wife who stopped at the hotel for a few days. When word circulated among hotel guests about their presence, a long line of guests strategically placed themselves in chairs so that they could see the newlyweds as they left the elevator headed to dinner.

<u>An Early Romance</u>

I remember clearly something else that happened during that summer in Massachusetts. A Spanish aristocrat came to the Berkshires from Spain and brought his wife, a young daughter, two other younger children, and a woman who chaperoned the young daughter. They planned to put the daughter in a finishing school. The daughter and I got to see each other on the elevator. From time to time, I would go to their apartment which was secluded behind an iron fence. We would touch hands through the fence. We thought we were in love with each other. She soon made plans for us to get married.

Looking back on it, I will never know whether she was in love with me or whether she just didn't like the surveillance she was under. Anyway, she proposed that when she got out of school for Thanksgiving, that I come back up to a town in Connecticut where the school was located and one of her friends lived. We would meet, run off and get married. While I liked her a lot, I tried to slow things down. I remember telling her that I hadn't finished high school. She said we didn't have to worry about it; her daddy would take care of everything. He would support us and I could continue my education.

In the end, she and her family left the resort first and afterwards, I left. I had given her my address. She wrote. I was supposed to go up there right after Thanksgiving. That Wednesday, the day before

54

Thanksgiving, was my last football game, Dunbar vs. Armstrong, at Griffith Stadium. As I stated previously, near the end of the game, I got injured and was taken to the hospital. This provided a sound rationale for delaying the wedding plans.

I wrote and explained why I had not appeared during the Thanksgiving holiday. This did not solve my problem. She set up our rendezvous for Christmas. But, by that time I had really arrived at the conclusion that I wasn't thinking about marriage.

To use a popular expression of that day, she was "as pretty as a speckled pup." The only reason that really caused me to be cool about marrying her was finances. I just couldn't imagine myself facing her father and when he asked how I was going to support his daughter, responding that it was my understanding that he was going to take care of us until I finished school. . .

When I went to Pittsfield, that was really the first time I had ever been away from home by myself. The previous year while in Eaglesmere, Pennsylvania, I was accompanied by a friend and his aunt.

During 1926 when I worked at the Hotel Aspenwall, Ford carried over from distributing the cars, realigned his factories and went over to a gear shift. Everything prior to that had been the "tin Lizzy." The spark and the accelerator and all were on the steering wheel.

Interesting life.

Another thing - I was always taught that you ought to leave a job so you can go back if you need to. However, I've quit jobs. For instance, when I was in elementary school, during the evenings, Saturdays and occasionally on Sunday, I shined shoes in shoeshine parlors. To the best of my recollection, for people like me, our compensation consisted solely of tips. The usual tip was a nickel or a dime and occasionally one might receive fifteen cents or a quarter. For us, no salary was involved.

I recall on one Saturday I was working at a shoeshine parlor in downtown Washington, when a particular customer came in requesting a deluxe shoe shine. When you gave him a deluxe shine, he might give you a fat tip of fifty cents. On that day, I was the one giving him the shine, but he had no change. Accordingly, he paid at the desk. The proprietor took an extra ten cents out of the fifty cent tip due to me.

A lively discussion ensued. I said that the customer left fifty cents and I demanded to have it. Because I had heard the customer say, "Give the change to the shoeshine boy", and because my boss refused to give me the correct change, I quit.

Several weeks later I just happened to be going down G Street and passed by the shop. The proprietor said, "Hey, come back here. Where you been? Why did you stop coming to work?" I said, "Because you took my dime." He said, "Come on back here. We're going to get along fine, blah, blah, blah." I felt good that although I had quit that job under adverse circumstances, he wanted to rehire me. However, I still did not go back to work for him.

As I mentioned, I did not participate in high school commencement activities because I finished high school in mid-term and I started college in the spring quarter.

College Experiences

I don't remember ever thinking I would drop out of school or not attend college. Prior to my entering college, I had no immediate history of others in my family attending college.

The fear of my elders was that like so many others working on the railroad, I might decide to do that permanently. That was a particular concern of Mrs. Pentecost, <u>not</u> me. In those days, many college guys did drop out of school. Nevertheless, I always assumed I would go to college. One of the things that made me decide to really buckle down and do my studies was the decision to go to law school.

As an undergraduate at Howard, I did not consider myself an outstanding student; and as a general rule, I never got very close to any of my professors. As a matter of fact, I do not recall asking any of them for outside help. For the most part, I got along well with the teachers there. For example, when I started, I took Municipal Government under Ralph Bunche who was in his first year of teaching at Howard University.

In addition, Abram Harris, a professor from Richmond, taught us economics. I had an Omega insignia on my textbook; and Harris was himself an Omega. He made a point of telling me not to think that the fact of my having an Omega insignia on my book would mean something special. In fact, the thought had not even crossed my mind. I also took courses from a somewhat eccentric psychology professor whose name, as I recall it, was Charles Somner. Furthermore, I took philosophy from Alain Locke. However, I have often wondered why I took philosophy. I had no interest in that course whatsoever. Accordingly, I was always unprepared. In these circumstances, it is not surprising that in Professor Locke's class I made an uninspiring grade.

As one might expect, while I got along well with the teachers, there was one exception. We had a trigonometry professor who gave frequent tests. One morning as we were entering the classroom, a good friend of mine who was a fine young lady, and had been out all night partying, spoke to me. She said that I would need to sit so that she could see my paper. In essence, she wanted to copy off of my paper in the event that we had a test. In fact we did have a test and I complied with her request.

On a particular day, the trigonometry professor read off all the grades. The young lady who had copied my answers got a higher grade than I did. This provoked me to speak up. I said to our trigonometry professor that it sure would be a nice thing if we could see our papers some time so that we might be able to ascertain where we made mistakes and do better in the future.

In reply, he made some off hand remark to the effect that it was his class and he knew how to run his class. Before you know it one word was leading to another, and from that point, my relations with him were all down hill. I got my final grades in his class while I was working in Oswegatchie, Connecticut. He had given me a D.

I also took courses in real estate, political science, English, and foreign languages. I had begun studying Spanish and German in high school, and when I entered Howard during the spring quarter, my foreign language studies included German. I wound up having to take an advanced level German course. That meant I really had to work extra hard because the rest of the students were upper classmen.

I also took two courses in sociology. Dean Kelly Miller, an imminent sociologist, offered the courses. Miller wrote a number of books; however, at the time I studied under him, he was advanced in years and beginning to slip mentally.

The first class that I took with Professor Miller was Sociology 126, which he offered in the spring quarter. Another friend and I, Piggy

57

Waites, took that course with the understanding that we would take the introductory course, Sociology 125, in the fall. Piggy was from Norfolk and we took the fall course as planned. At the end of the fall quarter, Professor Miller asked me to give his final quarter exam in Sociology 125 because he was going to attend a conference and was not going to be present at Howard on the day of the exam. I administered the exam, and delivered the papers to his home. Much to my surprise, I received a grade of C. Professor Miller had a couple of children who were attending Howard at that time. When I told his daughter what had happened she laughed and told me "You know how Daddy grades exam papers—He starts at the top of the list and gives the first person an A, the next one a B and so forth, just going down the list in that order putting the grade beside their names. Go talk to him and he'll change your grade." However, at that stage in my academic career I didn't really care about grades, and when I thought about it since he graded papers in that manner, any grade that he gave me would not have meant anything. Consequently, I made no effort to get the situation rectified.

When I decided to go to law school, I became more focused. As I will discuss in more detail later, in law school I got closer to my teachers, including Charles Hamilton Houston, William H. Hastie, and Leon Andy Ransom. Nevertheless, I still continued my outside employment, focused on my academic studies during the week and played hard on the weekends.

Coming back to the situation at Howard as an undergraduate, Howard had compulsory ROTC. Students were required to deposit approximately thirty-eight dollars for uniforms. At the end of every quarter a student had to turn the uniform in, draw his money down at the beginning of the quarter, make another deposit, and draw the uniform again. It didn't make sense. However, that was the bureaucratic procedure.

At the end of the quarter, all ROTC students had approximately thirty-eight dollars. In those days, that was a lot of money. I used to hang out at the dormitory even though I lived in the city. We would have big poker games and black jack games on the campus. If you were lucky you would win a lot of money. If you were unlucky, you lost your ROTC money.

During the fall of my freshman year one Saturday we had a black jack game, and Piggy Waites (my buddy) and I won a lot of money — over three hundred dollars! It so happened that we won the money

58

after the end of the collegiate football season and a week before the freshman/sophomore class intramural football classic. The game represented a longstanding Howard tradition. At that time, I was a freshman, and some way or other, at a blackjack game a group of students started "woofing" about who was going to win the game. It was not long before the, "Put your money where your mouth is!" challenge took over. I ended up betting all my winnings on the freshman team.

This happened on a Saturday; the freshman/sophomore game was the next Saturday. While I had followed my doctor's advice and had not gone out for the varsity football team, now I had a bet exceeding one hundred and fifty dollars and wanted to protect my money. On Monday morning I went out and started practicing.

I was playing quarterback on offense and fullback on defense, just like my last year in high school. I was real good on defense. On offense I was a fair passer. As long as I kept people in front of me, I could maneuver as a runner. However, I had no speed and someone always came from behind to tackle me.

On the day of the game, one of my ends caught my pass and made a touchdown. I place kicked the extra point. In the fourth quarter we were still hanging on, leading seven to zero. In those days, we had seven people on the line, and both teams were using the varsity signals. Their quarterback started calling the signals and I timed myself. When the center snapped the ball I was going across the line of scrimmage between the center and the guard. I dived for the guy who was supposed to have the ball. However, somebody's foot caught me and when I woke up I was in the hospital. I had a concussion. This was a really tough break. I wasn't supposed to be playing football and that ended my football career.

My team held on and our seven points stood up. We won the game, seven to nothing and I won my one hundred and fifty (plus) dollar bet, too! I was injured in the last game in high school and the first time I tried to play in college. If I hadn't gotten hurt I might have gone on to play collegiate football.

My mother was greatly opposed to my playing football. There was no way for me to play at Howard without her knowing about it. However, the urge to play football was so strong that I started to change schools. I thought of transferring up to Lincoln University in Pennsylvania, but in the end decided not to go.

59

The Big Bang, <u>Brown vs Board of Education</u> and Beyond

After I had completed six quarters of ROTC, I quit drilling. About two weeks after I stopped, one of the ROTC instructors ran into me one day on the campus and wanted to know why I had not been to class. I replied that I had completed my requirements for drilling and that as far as I was concerned, for me, that was the end of my military career. In fact, I was so uninterested in the military that at that time I didn't even know where the firing range was on the Howard campus.

If a student participated in the program and sought a commission as a second lieutenant, he had to go away to summer camp. That was another reason I wasn't interested in ROTC. I used to go away and work in a different place every summer. That wasn't a good idea for making money but it gave me exposure to diverse people, places and experiences.

I was a happy-go-lucky guy on campus. Nevertheless, I did not take any "crip" (relatively easy) subjects. Everything I took was required.

In the summer of 1928, I didn't have a job so I went to Roanoke to spend the summer. While I was down in Roanoke, Leon Smallwood, one of my classmates from Washington, D.C. called me. He said they had a job for a waiter at the resort where he was working; and also that the employees played a whole lot of poker.

I immediately caught the train and went to a place outside of New London, Connecticut called Oswegatchie. One interesting situation that I remember is that Al Smith was running against Herbert Hoover for president. Oswegatchie was Al Smith country.

The only thing there was a hotel and a large dance hall. All during the summer, there were big dances, Friday and Saturday nights. We served set-ups and sandwiches. People brought their own whiskey or bought some from the local bootleggers.

We made our money hustling sandwiches, set-ups and ice. Most of the dining room crew came from Danville, Virginia. The head waiter was the principal at a high school down there. It was a common thing in those days for Negro teachers and principals who worked in the southern public school systems to supplement their salaries by working in resorts in the summer. They didn't get paid much for the nine months of the school year and nothing at all during the summer.

It was also common for many young women to discontinue their full time education at the normal school level and start teaching. They would go to college during the summer and get a degree after several years.

I arrived at Oswegatchie on a Sunday morning. The hotel staff used to play draw poker, with a wild joker. Leon had told them I liked to play black jack. Accordingly, to accommodate me, on my first night there they had a black jack game. Fortunately I got real lucky. I won between three and four hundred dollars. On the next morning, I got up early and decided to take the money and put it in the bank. I wasn't scheduled to go to work until Tuesday.

I was hitchhiking to New London and a guy came along in a truck. He showed me all this stuff that he claimed that he had just taken off a boat (and which I wasn't thinking about buying). He offered to sell me some of it and finally pulled out a package of some kind of perfume with a price tag of twenty dollars. After haggling for a bit he finally agreed to let me have the perfume for ten dollars. I went to the bank and deposited my winnings and returned to the hotel.

Initially, I told the hotel staff that I knew very little about poker. While I really did know how to play poker, I just sat and watched the game the first two or three nights to see how it went. Gradually, I began to play along with the rest of the staff. Occasionally, when I thought the situation was right, I pretended to be very excited about my hand, bet out of turn, and performed my enthusiastic novice routine. I would play the cards pat, meaning I did not draw against my hand. I also tended to make large bets, and all the players would fold. From time to time, someone would call me, and on those occasions I actually had a pat hand. That added credibly to my act.

However, I was not careful. One night I pulled this act and one of the players sited out — that is, he bet all the money that he could on the main pot and the rest of the money was a side bet. At the end of the hand, pretending to be magnanimous, I told the person who sited out to take the main pot and I reached over and took the side pot. However, everyone insisted that I show my hand. I had nothing. The players were surprised that I had been making such bold bets with such little support in my hand for them. From that time forward, they were on to me and invariably played their hands out.

Additionally, I also ran into a period of real tough luck. In poker, full houses are usually a winning hand. I didn't lose successive hands,

61

but I lost twelve full houses over a period of about two weeks. Usually those are pretty good sized pots. During this period, once a guy had a royal flush; that is, he had all of the cards of the same suit, in sequence, from the ace to the ten.

Later when I got back to Washington, on one of my first nights in town I met a guy who used to sell all kinds of perfumes, jewelry, other junk, and condoms. He said, "Come here, I haven't seen you in a long time. Tell you what! I got something good for you. You are a good customer. Give me twenty-five cents." He handed me a package. In it was the identical perfume for which I had paid ten dollars. During the preceding summer in Oswegatchie I had pawned and redeemed that perfume a dozen times for ten dollars.

Names: "Peanuts" and "Turkey"

I have had the name "Peanuts" since about the time I was a sophomore in college. I used to eat peanut cookies. We were sitting up playing cards one night over in a place we used to call the House of the Seven Gables. A student named "Red Fox", whose real name was Louis Campbell, said, "Damn you're always eating peanuts; I'm going to call you Peanuts." It stuck. That was a name I was called around Howard.

After I left law school, just a small group of folks I knew in law school called me "Peanuts." It was not generally known outside of my campus crowd.

Later when I met Thurgood Marshall in law school, I discovered that his nickname was "Turkey." It was said that he strutted like a turkey. In one of my letters to him while he was working for the NAACP during the 1940's, I addressed him as "Turkey" and signed the letter "Peanuts." At a recent conference one of the University of Virginia professors was teasing me about how unusual it was for a man who became a Supreme Court Justice to receive a letter calling him a turkey by a man named "Peanuts."

It developed that the professor's wife had been doing some research at the Congressional Library on the NAACP. She had unearthed several items of correspondence between Thurgood and me in which I referred to him as "Turkey" and signed my name as "Peanuts." Of course, he wrote to me in a similar vein.

<u>Social Activities and Employment While in College</u>.

One time I ran into my old friend Red Fox at the race track in Baltimore and found that he worked for the owner of a stable of horses. He traveled with the owner from Kentucky to Baltimore to Saratoga. He tried to give me some good horses on which to bet. I declined. I thought that I knew enough ways to waste money without adding horses to my list.

However, one time when I was in school, I was working in O'Donnell's Restaurant and some men came through on their way to Florida. They told some of us who were waiting on them that they were going to tip us on some good races. We were told, "You can put your bottom dollar on them." They also informed us of the nights that they were going to call.

They followed through. On the first night that they called their tip came through on a good long shot. However, none of us bet on the designated horse.

The next couple of nights that they called, no one bet because we had missed the opportunity to win on the long shot. However, the tips still appeared to be reliable and after a couple of more nights having decided that those furnishing the tips knew what they were talking about, the guys began to bet on the horses. When they did so, you can imagine what happened: those who bet lost.

As far as other social activities were concerned, I never learned to waltz until I was a freshman in college. Once I went to a dance at Lincoln University. The dance was a fox trot and I was dancing with a girl from Philadelphia whose name was Sarah Strickland. The band switched over to a waltz. I said to her that I had never learned to waltz, so we would have to get off the floor. She said, "Aw, come on I'll lead and you follow me." After that I gained confidence and learned how to waltz.

When I was at Howard we had dances at the dining hall. It was a beautiful scene because you could look out over the reservoir. For Howardites, it was a "lake so blue." At those dances, we received dance programs which had listed the name of each dance, the music for each dance, and a space for the names of the girls with whom one had signed up for that dance. You'd get the girls you wanted to dance with to sign your cards. There were girls I wanted to dance with and girls who

63

always wanted to dance with me.   We used to always save each other spaces on the cards.

Upon arriving at a dance, you promptly tried to get your card filled up with your preferred dance partners. Otherwise, on a particular dance, you might get stuck. The only time I had a problem was if I took a girl to a dance who was not very well known. In situations like that, I had to make sure that my date's card was full even if I had to take up the vacancies myself. I would never allow my escort to play the role of a wall flower.

In addition, while I was in college and occasionally while in law school, I drove taxi cabs. In those days taxi cab fares in Washington, D.C. were twenty cents anywhere in the city. Later, the fare went up to thirty-five cents.

Two large Negro owned companies existed. One was Capitol Cab Company. The other one was called Right Away Cab Company operated by the Baker brothers who were from Richmond.

When we were preparing to start a shift driving a cab, the company representative would give you the cab and take down the mileage. Cab drivers worked on a percentage basis. The company managers were good at estimating what they thought you ought to have earned during a night's work. However, sometimes we were better hustlers than they thought we were. During the period in which fares were twenty or thirty-five cents, pedestrians had to keep a sharp lookout for cab drivers. Cabbies were hell bent on getting their passengers to their particular destination, depositing them and getting the next fare.

I remember one occasion I signed out a cab around four o'clock in the afternoon, hustled like mad until twelve midnight, rushed home, washed, dressed and got my girl friend. We used to go to dances at 12:30 a.m. and 1:00 a.m. in those days in Washington. When the dance let out we went to a place for breakfast and I reported back about 8:00 a.m. in the cab.

The guy said, "Great day, you must have been to Baltimore or someplace." If you go somewhere outside the city limits, you were expected to charge a much higher fare. He couldn't believe that I had made the money that I had, then gone out of service about 12:00 a.m. until about 4:00 or 5:00 in the morning. The amount of income I made reflected how hard I hustled. The company representative was gauging the mileage.

I didn't tell him precisely what I did. However, we would go down and get cabs, work them, and go to dances. I never will forget that.

Another college adventure I remember involved a friend of mine named John Day. John was non-fraternal and I was an Omega. During Christmas, Omega Psi Phi was holding its annual conclave in Baltimore. John and I had very little money but we borrowed his father's car and we scraped together enough money to get gas for our trip to Baltimore. We set out on our journey. Although we were in Baltimore three or four days, we never got a room. The Negro hotel where the conclave was held was crowded, so we managed to change clothes and wash at friends' houses. We didn't actually go to bed. In fact, we spent most of our waking hours managing parties and arranging for "refreshments." Even though we went to Baltimore penniless, by the time we were coming back that Sunday to go to a midnight dance, we had money in our pockets and we brought back two fine sisters from Vassar. One was Connie and the other one was named Vivian. Both of them ended up marrying E. Phillip Sims, a famous cartoonist for Esquire Magazine. One of them reportedly committed suicide and then he married the other one.

We came back to Washington using what we called a back road. Somewhere along the way the rim came off one of the wheels. Fortunately, this happened near an automobile service station. While a guy was trying to fix the wheel for us we went into a nearby country store. The girls played the one-armed bandits, commonly called slot machines. My friend, John, and I were not interested in this method of losing one's money. This is one of the two times in my life that I stayed up for nearly a week.

Working in Canada

During the summer of 1929 John Day and I worked in Canada for the Canadian Pacific Railroad. I had just finished my sophomore year in college. I worked out of Montreal as a porter on sleeping cars. For several summers during the 1920's the Canadian Pacific Railroad and the Canadian National Railroad came to Howard and employed students as sleeping car porters. I do not know about the situation with the Canadian National Railroad, but the Canadian Pacific Railroad used French Canadians as waiters and cooks in their dining cars.

During the summer that I was there, I learned that the Canadian Pacific Railroad was bringing in a group of about forty European industrialists in an attempt to induce them to invest in Canada. I immediately applied for a place working on this special train. I was assigned to a car which carried the dining car crew. It turned out to be a good deal for me.

I had very little association with the industrialists, but I got along quite well with the members of the crew. I had no problems with the Canadian personnel, even though many of them spoke French most of the time.

The French Canadian railroad crew played a crazy game of poker. The house rules were that a four card bob (four cards of the same suit) would beat two pair. I was lucky at holding four card bobs in addition to being a better poker player than most of them. When they were off duty, I was often off duty as well. On occasions when we were all off duty, after meals, we usually had a very lively poker game. Fortunately, I was not only lucky, but also popular with the Canadian crew.

The tour carried us all over Canada. We had an extended stay at Lake Louise in Alberta, Canada. We also spent a week in Vancouver, British Columbia. During these extended stays the industrialists were taken on bus tours. The railroad crews also had extended furloughs, including lodging and food, while the industrialists were touring.

In our travels, we had many interesting experiences. One such experience occurred in going through the Canadian Rockies. As I stated earlier, the train did a series of figure eights; and from the observation car, you could see the train coming out of the tunnel as you were entering it.

Lake Louise was a truly beautiful lake. Up in the mountains above Lake Louise there was another lake called Lake Agnes. Several of my friends who were with me had been there the year before. They told me about Lake Agnes, and every day somebody was supposedly going with me up to Lake Agnes. Finally, we got down to the last day and nobody wanted to go. I was determined to go up there and see the Lake in the Clouds, which is what they called Lake Agnes. While I was walking up the mountain to Lake Agnes, I heard this thumping noise. I discovered it was my heart pumping. However, I got to the top. From that position I could look down at Lake Louise. It looked like a mirror.

Finally, I looked at my watch and I found I had overstayed my time. So I decided that I was going to take a short cut down a trail that I had noticed on my trip up the mountain. However, to my dismay, this trail led to a gap between two cliffs. Well, it was a tantalizing distance. I believed that I could run, jump, and make this gap. There were two problems. The first problem was that I had to run down the hill and then jump. The other problem was that between these two cliffs that I would have to clear there was a drop of several hundred feet to the ground. Finally I concluded the risk was too great and I decided not to chance it.

Accordingly, I had to double back and go down the ordinary road. I knew from our schedule of events that we were supposed to leave from Lake Louise at 3:00 p.m. When I got within about a half mile of the departure point, I heard the tram whistle. The tram ran from Lake Louise down to the railroad tracks. I started running trying to get there. That darn thing went off and left me. As a consequence, I had to walk. I don't remember how many miles it was but it was several miles. I finally straggled in there. They were holding the train for me. When I arrived and got on board, the train pulled off.

I struggled and got into my bunk. A member of the dining car crew persuaded me that the chef had a fine piece of roast beef for me and wanted me to come and get it. He knew that I was hungry. I dressed and went into the dining car and saw the meal laid out on the table before me. It really did contain a fine looking piece of roast beef. However, all I could do was pour a cup of tea and take a few sips. I was so sore and exhausted that I had no appetite for any type of food. It was all I could do to get back to my sleeping car. I stretched out on the berth to get some rest. I stayed there for two days.

The Canadian railroad job was a good paying job. We made approximately one hundred dollars per month and had a liberal layover compensation (LOC) program. On top of that the Canadian railroad had their own dining cars on the trains and their own restaurants in specified stations. Trains that did not have dining cars could stop at these stations so that passengers could get meals.

At all times when we were in service, members of the railroad crew could eat in the dining car after the regular meals, or if there were no dining car, we were furnished meal tickets to eat in the station restaurants. In other words, whenever we were on the road, whether we were working or deadheading, we received free room and board.

"Deadheading" refers to circumstances in which sleeping car porters were not actually in service for the company. For example, suppose your home base was New York, you made a trip to Pittsburgh and instead of going back to New York, you were sent on to Washington, DC for your next work assignment. The trip from Pittsburgh to Washington would be considered deadheading because you would not be working but on the way to work or to your home station.

Our conditions were much superior to those of Pullman Porters for at least two reasons. First, the Pullman Porters did not receive as much base pay as we did. Secondly, when they were deadheading, they had to pay for their own meals. Because of these disparities in treatment on the job, when trains serviced by Pullman Porters hooked up to our trains, and the Pullman Porters were not in service, we always looked out for the Pullman Porters.

During the summer that I worked in Canada, travel was very heavy. Frequently when we arrived in the station at the end of a run, be it a run in Canada or the United States, the station master would ask you not to leave because he wanted you to go somewhere else. You could bargain whether you went on the trip. The bargain involved layover compensation, which was the equivalent to over time pay. They called layover compensation LOCs.

The sleeping car porters in Canada were not unionized. However, in the United States, sleeping car porters were being unionized under the direction of the dynamic and courageous Negro labor and civil rights leader, A. Phillip Randolph.

Several of us from Howard had secured rooms for the summer at the home of a Canadian Pacific sleeping car porter who ran on the Vancouver run. The trains were known as Number One and Number Two going from Vancouver to Montreal, Canada. The passage of seventy years has dimmed my memory; however, as I recall, this man's run carried him on a journey which took six days and seven nights to complete going just one way. It took the same amount of time to come back. After making that complete circuit, he might have several days off for a layover.

There was also a faster train known as the Trans Canada. This train had all first class accommodations and made the trip much more quickly; however, I'm not sure now exactly how long it took to make the trip. I think that it was about twenty four hours faster. Some porters had girlfriends or wives on both ends of their railroad runs. At the house where we stayed, when the husband's train pulled out of the station, one of the red caps who worked in the station moved in until he came back. I guess these affairs worked both ways.

I can only recall running into one incident of racism all summer. That incident did not involve the company, but happened in Three Rivers, Ontario where we were in the railroad yards and in the process of adding or taking cars from our train. I was talking to a member of our crew. He was at one end of his car on the steps and I was on the steps of my car. Some little kids were in an adjoining field playing baseball. One of them happened to look up and said, "Oh, look, niggers, niggers." This was in a little town way up in North Ontario.

Looking back at the overall summer experience on the Canadian Pacific Railroad, the railroad was a fine company to work for, and I had a wonderful summer.

As far as a work ethic was concerned, one thing I was taught early in life was never to raise so much hell over the weekend that I couldn't go to work on Monday morning. In fact, I worked at a large number of places and changed jobs from time to time. However, I always tried to leave a job so that I could go back to it if I wanted to. Only once was I fired from a job; and that did not involve my job performance. At the time I was working at O'Donnell's Restaurant in Washington, D.C. The girlfriend of the owner of that restaurant felt I had snubbed her and that resulted in my employment being terminated.

Most times, I functioned in a rather moderate and conventional manner. However, there were times when we played hard. There were occasions where I stayed up all night, went home, set the alarm, got in bed, slept for as short a period as half an hour, got up, got dressed, and went to work.

Regarding my athletic career at Howard, I played well enough to make the varsity basketball squad. I played guard and center. I was not a star nor a particularly outstanding player. However, we did win the C I A A championship during the 1929-1930 academic year. For a period of several seasons, that was Howard's last championship basketball team. As I recall, I had more opportunities to play when the team was on the road than when we were at home.

During those years there was no tournament. The CIAA champ

was the team that finished first in the conference for that season.

At that time, the game was vastly different than the way it is played today. For example, the guards did not participate in scoring as much then. If Michael Jordan had been playing basketball back during those times, he would not have been a guard: he would have been a forward. During my tenure at Howard, the quality of Howard's athletics was quite high.

While I was an undergraduate, an incident typical of the times occurred. One time the basketball team was going down to West Virginia. The captain of the basketball team, Lou Coats, had a girlfriend named Margaret Hueston. At a pep rally before the team departed, and under the excitement of the moment, Margaret "bussed" Lou on the cheek. Kissing him on the cheek is bussing somebody. That's not even serious kissing. The Dean of Women, Dean Slowe, observed Margaret's actions. She considered it an infraction of standards of proper conduct for a Howard coed.

This bussing incident occurred at about 7:30 or 8:00 o'clock at night. By six o'clock the next morning Margaret was on her way home. Fortunately for her, her father, William Carroll Hueston, was a prominent member of the Elks in Indiana, a local judge, and served as President of the National Negro Baseball League from 1925-1930.[3] Judge Hueston called Dr. Mordecai Johnson and Dr. Johnson reinstated her in school. This terminated efforts of students who had determined to launch a campus-wide strike to bring Margaret back.

In my day, this was not an unusual type situation for female students at predominantly black colleges. Female students were frequently sent home for what we would today regard as minor infractions. In many instances, an unforgiving attitude existed towards women who had committed some transgression.

For example, after I began practicing law, Charlie Houston called me and said he wanted me to get the transcript of a former student at Virginia Normal and Collegiate Institute, the predecessor of Virginia State University. A young woman had gone off campus, had an affair, and become pregnant. She had been expelled from Virginia N & I. A few years later she decided she wanted to go to Howard and complete her education. Dr. Gandy, the president of Virginia N & I, refused to send her transcript to Howard so that she could matriculate. (Incidentally, one of Gandy's daughters was in college with me.)

Before filing a suit, I decided to discuss matters with Dr. Gandy. I made an unannounced trip to the college and happened to get into a conversation with Dr. Foster who at that time was the business manager. (Later Foster became President).

I told Foster what I wanted. He said, "Hell, he isn't going to give it to you either." This was a Tuesday or Wednesday and Foster stated that they were having a Trustees' meeting on the following Sunday. Foster told me to be available to address the Trustees' meeting and that as secretary he would see that I got a chance to say something. That's what happened. At an appropriate time, I was invited in to talk with the trustees. They were more reasonable and flexible than Gandy. The trustees voted to release the transcript. Then, like now, you had all kinds of crazy things like that happening.

As I mentioned previously, my stepfather's brother, Sam, was a lawyer who practiced in Washington, D.C. He had what we used to call a "sundown practice" and clients would come by mostly for wills and real estate transactions. However, his main occupation was with the post office.

When I was a sophomore in college, Sam had a cerebral hemorrhage and died. His widow, Natalie, was a very artistic person and we were good friends. She gave me a 1924 United States Code Annotated and later some other of Sam's law books. The gift of the Code was significant in piquing my interest in law. Later upon reading the annotated Constitution which Natalie had given me, I learned that originally the Constitution didn't include Negroes, whether free or slave, in any positive fashion. We were merely regarded as three-fifths of a person for purposes of determining representation in the House of Representatives for the benefit of slaveholders.[4] In addition, the Constitution legalized American participation in the transatlantic slave trade until 1808.[5] Moreover, the Founding Fathers provided slaveholders constitutionally guaranteed federal support in capturing and returning escaped slaves, as well as militarily suppressing the captives' attempts to obtain freedom.[6]

The thing that made me determined to go to law school was actually learning that it was the Supreme Court that had taken away our rights; and I saw no hope of regaining them through the political process prevailing in the late 1920's. At that time, it was not even possible to get Congress to enact legislation to make lynching or murdering Negroes a crime. Therefore, I determined to go to law school, become trained as a lawyer, and endeavor to get the Court to reverse its previous error in <u>Plessy</u>.

The 1929-1930 academic year was my last year on Howard's campus. There was a combination program in place at Howard whereby Howard undergraduates could attend any Howard professional school. If you completed your basic requirements for graduation in your first three years you could use your first year of professional school to satisfy the grade point requirements for the last year in college. At the end of my sophomore year, I investigated this academic possibility. I had taken enough required subjects to pursue this course of study. When I looked at my record I found that I could continue my present course of study and the only special prerequisite I needed to meet my requirements for graduation was another quarter in foreign language. I had studied Spanish in high school and German in high school and college. Upon the recommendation that Latin would be helpful in practicing law, I decided to take a quarter of Latin.

In this Latin class I first met Samuel Wilbert Tucker who would later be my law partner for many years. He was a freshman and I was a junior. Four years later when I finished law school, Sam finished college. I'll go into more details later.

The next year in September, 1930 I entered law school. Howard undergraduate colleges were on the quarter system and the law school was on the semester system. When it came time to graduate, this created a predicament for me. At the end of my first year in law school, I took my last law school exam on Thursday. I waited to pick up my grades. I hand carried my grades over to the registrar's office and waited to be advised whether I would be able to graduate from college the next day. I had assumed that I would graduate and had already participated in the baccalaureate services held on the previous Sunday. Accordingly, in June, 1931, I received my A.B. from Howard University. When I finished law school, I went through the same type process.

I now will share some thoughts and experiences on my civil rights and human rights activities.

Chapter III

Civil Rights and Human Rights Activity

I believe that most white folks thought that segregation was right and proper, and apparently saw nothing wrong with unequal treatment of Negroes. However, the few whites who would discuss the situation talked as if the only reason that segregation existed was because the law required it. This type of talk led some Negroes to believe that if the segregation laws did not exist, segregation would vanish. In a back-handed way, this led many Negroes to believe that white folks had greater respect for the law than they in fact did. However, when the Supreme Court ruled the segregation laws unconstitutional, many Negroes experienced a rude awakening as white folks' reputed great respect for the law disappeared. Like many other people, segregationists only respect the law when they perceive it is favorable to them. Many white folks sought every conceivable means to circumvent the change that the law mandated.

Prior to 1930, Howard was an evening law school taught primarily by white adjunct professors. When we entered in 1930, the students in the evening program who had completed their first year of studies were permitted to enter the second year class as day students. The third year students were allowed to finish their senior year in the evening division. The evening division was discontinued at the end of my first academic year in the law school.

My first year class had an even number of students. It so happened that half of the class were members of the Alpha Phi Alpha fraternity. Early during the school year a non Alpha heard one of the Alphas boasting, "We can run this class."

I was a member of another fraternity, Omega Psi Phi. When the Alphas' comment came to our attention, I helped organize and became the leader of the Coalition of non-Alphas. Thurgood Marshall was the leader for the Alphas. So anything Thurgood and I could agree on happened. If we didn't agree, it didn't happen. This situation continued throughout our law school career. In fact, the Washington Post carried a little story about a law school class (ours!) that had no class officers. Neither Thurgood nor I ever complained about the other class members permitting us to run things.

In the next pages, I will share with you some experiences gained in over seventy years of civil and human rights activities.[1] I will include historical tidbits, background regarding the creation of Howard's full time day law school program, some law school experiences and some of my law related activities beginning in the 1930's. I will leave for later a more in depth discussion of the <u>Brown v. Board of Education</u> case.

<u>Some Early Foundations of the Modern Civil Rights Movement</u>

Segregation or American apartheid was called "Jim Crow" and was not like a jack-in-the-box: springing up at random. It was <u>always</u> there. Living under a regime of racial repression did not mean that you ran around all the time thinking someone was going to hit you on the head. However, on the other hand a negative situation could rapidly develop. For instance, a Negro could walk down a street and a white person might bump into him — accidentally or otherwise. What happened depended on the attitude of the white person involved, and the police. The police always favored the white folks. One could not predict what negative consequences, whether civil or criminal might follow an accident. These patterns of social behavior were more prevalent then. A potentially harrowing situation constantly prevailed. The situation was worse in southside Virginia and points further south.

An interesting and little known story involving segregation unfolded at the turn of the century. The Clay Street line in Richmond was the first electric trolley line in the United States. During the Reconstruction period in Virginia there was no legalized public segregation in transportation. However, in 1902, a state constitutional convention was held to revise the progressive Underwood Constitution which had been adopted during Reconstruction. U.S. Senator Carter Glass promoted this convention which resulted in legislation that disenfranchised most Negroes and enabled private companies to issue regulations providing for segregation in public transportation.[2] The privately owned electric trolley company in Richmond issued their segregated seating regulations.

In response to these Jim Crow regulations in 1904, Negroes in Richmond boycotted the trolleys and walked for nearly a year. The boycott was organized by a local Negro journalist named John T. Mitchell, Jr. and well supported by all segments of the Negro community. Because of the boycott, the trolley company suffered great financial difficulty. To help the company overcome its financial difficulties and break the boycott, the General Assembly passed legislation making segregation in public transportation the law of the state. That succeeded in breaking the boycott.[3]

As I mentioned previously, I think the first thing that got in my craw about Jim Crow involved my playing basketball in Roanoke in what was called a "high school", which in fact, ended with the eighth grade. We had to get up early in the morning and go down to the Roanoke Auditorium. If there had been an affair there the night before we had to remove and stack the chairs in piles against the walls. Only then could we practice. In contrast, my white counterparts had a gymnasium amply equipped for these types of activities, and they made full use of them.

I also remember an incident which occurred during Christmas holidays in 1928 involving a trip to Roanoke. I was in college then. While the train was in the station in Washington, D.C., some white train employees were sitting smoking cigarettes in the Jim Crow car assigned to Negroes. The car had limited seating space for passengers because a portion of the car's capacity was available for carrying baggage.

It so happened that three Negro ladies were seated in the car when I got on board. In those days except for very elderly Negro women who might smoke a clay pipe at home, very few if any Negro women smoked. Those women who did, did not do so in public. In fact, the only times I remember seeing Negro women smoking in public was occasionally when I passed a brothel on Henry Street in Roanoke, and some of the women of the house were hanging out of the second floor window calling to passing men to "come on in!"

In any event, the white railway employees smoking in the presence of these Negro women in the cramped Jim Crow car, immediately incensed me. Their behavior demonstrated no respect for the women. I told the two men that they had no business in the passenger car in the first place — much less smoking in it. I demanded that they get the heck out of it immediately.

The two men hesitated. They seemed taken aback and did not appear to know whether to respond verbally, or physically, or to leave. After hesitating briefly, they left. Although I may have appeared belligerent, I had no intention of engaging in physical combat with them. I had intended to get the conductor if they had refused to leave voluntarily. After they left, the ladies thanked me heartily.

All these things added up: they bothered me. Not long after my decision to go to law school, in the summer of 1930 at the corner of 11th and U Streets in Washington, D.C., I remember meeting Johnny Davis, a well-respected Rhodes scholar and activist. I was waiting for the streetcar and Davis saw me. He spoke to me and asked me what were my plans. I told him that I was going to law school. He asked me why. I told him I wanted to become a good lawyer and challenge the constitutionality of the Virginia segregation laws. He wished me much success. In the later 1930's, Davis helped organize the National Negro Congress, a group with which I participated in Washington.

Regarding the effort to develop a strategy to eliminate <u>Plessy v. Ferguson</u>, this was not a one person operation. A lot of people had the same ultimate objective in mind; however, we employed different approaches. It took years of planning and meticulous work. For example, in the late 1920's Dr. Mordecai Johnson, President of Howard University, talked with Justice Brandeis. Brandeis reportedly told Johnson that very frequently Negro lawyers would come up with meritorious cases, but too often the record was so inadequate that the Court could not take the case.[4]

As a result of their discussion, Dr. Johnson decided he was going to make Howard University Law School a first class law school. A primary focus of Howard's mission, as envisioned by Johnson, would be to train black lawyers to properly prepare cases and develop adequate records for achieving success in the Supreme Court.

Dr. Johnson selected Charles Hamilton Houston as the person to take charge of this law school project. Charlie had graduated from the well regarded "M Street" High School in Washington, D.C. (M Street High was the predecessor to Dunbar which I attended.) Charlie went on to Amherst College where he graduated Phi Beta Kappa. After graduating from Amherst, Charlie taught English in the Commercial Department at Howard University. He then helped pressure the War Department to create a military facility to train black officers to lead black troops in World War I. Houston became an army officer, suffered a number of indignities while fighting for this country (including being nearly lynched in France by some white enlisted men), and returned to the United States in 1919.[5]

Charlie was accepted as a student at Harvard Law School, became the first Negro admitted to the Law Review, and graduated with honors. He also studied at Harvard for his post graduate work on a doctorate in juridical science.[6]

Charlie had helped litigate <u>Corrigan v. Buckley</u>,[7] a suit challenging private discrimination against Negroes in real estate transactions. The case went to the United States Supreme Court; and the Court dismissed the appeal. The Court claimed that it lacked jurisdiction. By narrowly interpreting the Fifth, Thirteenth and Fourteenth Amendments, the Court in effect upheld the racially exclusive language. Charlie was active with the NAACP and was a good leader of the fight for positive change. I am sure that probably attracted him to Dr. Johnson.

Charlie Houston decided to convert the law school from a part time evening law school to a full time day program. This created quite a stir in the Washington, DC legal community (especially among adjuncts who were not retained). Charlie stuck to his guns and established a strong core of lawyers whose ideas and ideals coincided with his. They were dedicated to teaching and training the incoming Howard Law School students. For example, William H. Hastie, Jr., a graduate of Harvard Law School served as a member of the faculty.[8] Hastie subsequently had many other accomplishments, including helping to draft legislation for increased self government in the Virgin Islands, serving as governor of the Virgin Islands, becoming the first appointed Negro federal judge in the United States, and being appointed to the Third Circuit Court of Appeals. Incidentally, he was an Omega.

In addition, the faculty included Professor Leon A. ("Andy") Ransom who had earlier graduated from Ohio State University Law School where he received academic honors and was a member of the

Order of the Coif. He later received a doctorate in juridical science from Harvard.[9] Andy also litigated and won a number of important cases in the United States Supreme Court like <u>Hale v. Kentucky</u>[10] and <u>Chambers v. Florida</u>.[11] Andy was a member of Alpha Kappa Psi fraternity. Andy and I later became very close friends. Andy, his wife Willa, who was commonly called "Bill," Bernie who was my girlfriend in law school (and later became my wife) and I became a foursome for bridge.

<u>Law School Days</u>

As fate would have it, five or six students, independently motivated to challenge segregation, came to Howard at the same time. When I matriculated at the Howard Law School in 1930, we were the first full-time freshman class of the school. We had a three year law program.[12]

Eddie Lovett, who was very brilliant, was in the class ahead of us. Another student in Lovett's class was J. Byron Hopkins, Jr. Byron was the cousin of Claude Hopkins, a famous big band leader of that day. One of their relatives was a dormitory mother in the men's dormitory on campus and her husband operated the university post office.

In addition, one of my classmates was Henry Sweet whose brother was the well-known physician, Dr. O.H. Sweet of Detroit, Michigan. Henry's motivation for attending law school came about as a result of an experience involving his brother. In the late 1920's Dr. Sweet moved into what we called in those days a "changing neighborhood". After Sweet moved in, some white folks demanded that he move his residence and warned that if he did not, they would run him away. Dr. Sweet did not change his residence. Instead some of his friends joined him inside the home on the night that the mob was supposed to appear.

A mob of white people congregated as they threatened; and they loudly demanded that Dr. Sweet vacate his home. A bullet fired by a mobster struck the side of the house. However, a bullet fired from within the house in retaliation struck someone in the mob and killed him. The state indicted Dr. Sweet for the murder of this man. The case became a *cause celebré* and the NAACP obtained the services of the renowned lawyer, Clarence Darrow, to defend him.[13] Darrow obtained Dr. Sweet's acquittal. This experience helped galvanize Henry Sweet to do something to challenge segregation and other racist injustices.

Incidentally, later Darrow lectured to my class on several

occasions. On one occasion, Darrow recounted how he became involved in the Sweet case. Darrow stated that the NAACP had undertaken to procure legal counsel to defend Dr. Sweet, and they sent a delegation to meet with him to attempt to secure his legal services. The delegation included Walter White, the Executive Secretary of the NAACP, Roger Baldwin, the founder of the American Civil Liberties Union, and Oswald Garrison Villard, of an old New England family which published the "New York Post" at that time. During the course of the discussions, Darrow turned to Baldwin and stated words to the effect that Darrow had always been sympathetic to the problems of "your people." Baldwin stated that he was not a Negro.

In response to Baldwin's denial of African ancestry, Darrow turned to Villard and said, "I am sure you understand what I mean." Villard asserted that he was not a Negro either.

Darrow then looked across the table at blond-haired, blue-eyed, white complexioned Walter White and said, "At least I won't make the mistake of thinking you are a Negro." Whereupon, Walter White dryly replied, "But I am a Negro." Walter White was just as white as could be. So were his brother and sister. They were Negroes by choice because had they chosen to do so, they could easily have passed for whites. They never ceased to identify themselves with other Negroes. Interestingly, many years later when Ed Dudley and I were trying a teacher salary case in Atlanta, we were invited to a social event at the family home of the Whites.

Howard's senior evening class included Belford Lawson from Roanoke and Henry Lincoln Johnson, whose father was a Republican committeeman from Atlanta, Georgia. Johnson's father was a big shot politically because Republicans were in control of things in those days. As a class, we first-year students had very little physical contact with the senior class. We were there in the morning, and gone by late afternoon. They came in the evenings.

Regarding our law school routine, classes started at 8:00 a.m. and ended at 11:30 a.m. During my first year, although we were leaders of rival factions, Thurgood and I became close friends and studied together.

During the first year, every day Thurgood and I would go to lunch. Our favorite place was one of Father Divine's restaurants. They sold down home soul food. The servings were ample and the price was right.

All you had to do was enter the restaurant, wave your hand in the air and say, "Peace. It's truly wonderful." In return, you got a great big meal for a quarter.

After lunch, we started researching cases and about 4:30 p.m. I had to go to my job. Thurgood would catch the train to Baltimore. I am sure that Thurgood studied more than I did. However, this disciplined schedule and sense of shared purpose kept us very close.

During the course of my law school career, in all our classes, we were fortunate to have bright and interesting professors. Charlie Houston taught evidence. We used Wigmore's evidence text. When the final exams were given, Charlie told us that if we thought it would help, we could use any books, notes, or even the kitchen stove. However, Charlie gave so many essay questions that your initial reaction was that you would be lucky to read all the questions much less answer them. Other than your brains, extensively using reference materials was not a viable option.

Professor Walter Wheeler Cook taught another memorable class in Conflict of Laws. Cook was a visiting Professor from the University of Chicago and was the premier Conflict of Laws authority of his day. I vividly remember Cook posing questions, leaning way back after doing so, and animatedly gesturing to us for our response.

George E. C. Hayes taught an interesting course on the English common law. Hayes was one of the best trial lawyers in the District of Columbia. In addition, William Houston, Charlie's father, presented some engaging classes. Occasionally, he seemed a bit eccentric.

As I mentioned earlier, from the upper grades of elementary school, I usually had a job. During my first year in law school, I obtained employment as a waiter working seven evenings per week at Stoneleigh Courts apartment complex. This was a fashionable apartment complex with conservative residents.

During my second year of law school the Negro waiters at Stoneleigh Courts were replaced by white waitresses. However, despite the changed circumstances, I obtained employment elsewhere. I worked as a waiter for dinner parties, conventions and receptions.

We got jobs principally by word of mouth. For example, during the latter part of my second year in law school, I had some friends who were working down at the Capitol when a vacancy occurred. They told me about it, and I went down there and got the job.

I worked at the Capitol, as an employee of the House of Representatives in the lunch room which was part of the public Dining Room complex. On the House side of the Capitol, they had a public dining room and lunch counter. At the House of Representatives lunch counter, lunch began at noon. Several of us worked in the dining room department of the House. We arranged for a cab to meet us at 11:30 a.m. at the conclusion of our classes and rush us over to the Capitol. When the House of Representatives was not in session, we didn't work.

I was working there at the termination of President Hoover's term and I witnessed President Roosevelt's inauguration. It was a really interesting time. Incidentally, the last year that the Republicans were in power before the Roosevelt era, the report was that the House restaurant lost twenty-eight thousand dollars. The first year that the Democrats were in, it was reported that the House Restaurant made ten dollars.

When in the 1980's the House scandal erupted regarding the failure of House members to pay their bills, I laughed. Failure to pay restaurant bills up to that time was a non partisan congressional characteristic. In that regard, things had not changed in the half century between the time I left the Capitol and the scandal of the 1980's.

When working there we served sandwiches and soup and desserts. Bean soup was a favorite delicacy among a number of congressmen and members of the general public.

As I mentioned previously, I entered law school under a joint degree program which allowed me to obtain my bachelor's degree upon successfully completing my first year law school course work. At the end of my third year in law school, we took our final law exams on Wednesday and graduated two days later on Friday. By prior arrangement, after completing our final exams, Thurgood and I celebrated exuberantly.

When we started in 1930, Howard was not accredited by the American Bar Association or the American Association of Law Schools. During our orientation, Charlie pointed this fact out. He stated that we would accomplish the objective of obtaining law school accreditation and membership in the AALS. That took hard work on the part of the

Charles H. Houston, Dean
Howard University Law School

Leon Andrew Ransom
Professor of Law
Howard University Law School

Class of 1933 Moot Court
Seated first row: Oliver W. Hill, Sr. (2nd from left)
Thurgood Marshall (5th from left)

faculty and students.

Most members of the law school community were highly motivated people. Under the leadership of Dean Houston, Howard Law School significantly improved its academic program. The ABA accredited the Law School at the end of 1931; and in December of that year, Howard became a member of the AALS.

During their senior year, the Howard law students of the evening class began preparing themselves to engage in different civil rights activities. The class of highly motivated young Negroes was small but aggressive.

Soon after their graduation, with the guidance and assistance of William H. Hastie, they developed an organization, The New Negro Alliance, and began picketing the Sanitary Grocery Stores. The activists sought to persuade the management to hire Negroes. Their picketing activities were resisted and some of them were arrested for picketing. The New Negro Alliance brought suit against the Sanitary Grocery Stores seeking to establish the right of peaceful picketing to secure employment.

These picketing activities resulted in a Supreme Court decision establishing the right to peaceful picketing to overcome employment discrimination.[14]   The Sanitary Grocery Stores later became Safeway Stores.

Following the picketing of the Sanitary Grocery Stores, members of the New Negro Alliance also picketed the People's Drug Stores in the mid-1930's. Among the Howard students engaged in the picketing of People's Drug Stores was one of Frederick Douglass's grandsons. On one occasion, we marched from northwest Washington, D.C. to Frederick Douglass's home in Anacostia in the southeast section of the city.

Once started, these activities continued throughout the decade of the 1930's. I remember vividly one of the pickets was a very assertive and seemingly fearless African American woman. However, one evening when she turned on the radio and heard the broadcast of Orson Welles' "War of the Worlds" she panicked and called her mother in New York City. She left Washington by motor car saying that she was going to New York to get her mom. Her reaction typified many people's terror at Welles' story. She demonstrated her fearlessness by heading to New York--the supposed focus of the Martian invasion--to rescue her mother.

(right)
William H. Hastie, Chief Judge
U.S. Court of Appeal
Third Circuit

(below)
National Bar Association
Convention, Baltimore, Maryland
(circa 1934)

This was quite a time of political and societal ferment. I think my activity in some of this protest related work may have caused domestic law enforcement organizations like the F.B.I. to watch my movements with more than passing interest. I'll say a bit more about that later.

When I was in law school, we used to call Dean Charlie Houston "Iron Pants". Charlie mentored both Thurgood Marshall and me and was the one who took us to our first National Bar Association meeting.

That National Bar Association meeting was held in Baltimore on a hot summer's day and the windows of the meeting house were up. As Charlie, Thurgood and I approached the building, we could hear the fiery oratory of J. Thomas Newsome, a brilliant criminal trial lawyer from Tidwater, Virginia. Newsome had a large clientele of Negro and white clients. Charlie, Thurgood and I sat down outside the window and listened as Newsome regaled the assembly of lawyers.

Getting Started

In 1933, I finished law school. At that time, I was living in Washington, D.C. but since I intended to practice in Virginia, I re-established Roanoke as my legal residence. In my application to take the Virginia bar, I set forth these facts.

While preparing for the bar, I was working as a waiter at O'Donnell's Seafood Restaurant down at 12th and E Streets, Northwest, Washington, D.C. One day I ran into Sam Tucker who had finished college in 1933. Tucker and I had first met in a Latin class in his freshman year at Howard. As we talked, law inevitably came up, and we discovered that we both were studying for the bar.

Sam Tucker was about 12 when he started working in the office of his father who was in the real estate and insurance business in Alexandria, Virginia. Tucker's dad had joint office space with a lawyer named Thomas Watson. Apparently, even as a child, Tucker was very precocious and a voracious reader. Tucker's interest in the legal profession sort of evolved. Mr. Watson took a great interest in him. Early in his office work, Tucker learned how to type, and he served as clerk for Watson. From that point until he took the Bar, Tucker was reading and studying law under Watson's supervision.

Although it was 1933, we studied Watson's copy of the 1924 Virginia Code. The law didn't change as rapidly in those days as it does

85

now. The Code was part of Tucker's contribution to our studies; I furnished a set of Professor Dudley Warner Woodbridge's Notes. Woodbridge taught law at William and Mary Law School, and was considered a Virginia bar exam guru back in the 1930's. His Notes were part of an established bar preparation course. After hearing of his reputation, I contacted him and purchased his notes.

I had Thursday afternoons off so on those afternoons I would take my set of Professor Woodbridge's Notes over to Alexandria, Virginia. Tucker read the Notes and I studied Watson's Virginia Code. Of course, we discussed what we had read and its meaning. I left in time to catch the last streetcar departing Alexandria at midnight on the way back to D.C.

When I took the Virginia bar exam, several other members of my law school class had already taken the D.C. exam. Two or three of them had passed. Thurgood had taken the Maryland bar exam in June of 1933 and passed. Consequently, in December when I took the bar, I felt some pressure.

I remember several remarkable things about the bar exam experience. The night before the exam, I went to Richmond, and stayed at the Slaughter's Hotel. Slaughter's was a famous hotel for Negroes in those days. When I registered, I asked the clerk to call me at 7:00 o'clock the next morning. After making that request, I went to bed.

I woke up early the next morning. It was a dark, dreary, rainy, day. I stayed in bed reading my notes and thinking about the bar exam. Finally I reached over and got my watch to see what time it was. I felt like it should be time for me to get up. In fact, it was past 8:30 a.m. The exam was scheduled to start at 9:00 a.m.

I was mad as hell because I had relied upon the hotel staff to call me. I jumped up, got dressed and went to the lobby. I was not only late but I also had no idea where the State Capitol Building was.

A hotel employee told me I should go down to Broad Street and get a cab. I went running and hailed a Yellow Cab. The cab driver wanted to know how to get into the Capitol grounds and I said, "Hell, I don't know where it is much less how to get into it." Anyway, he rode around and got there. I went running into the building.

I located the Assembly Room of the House of Delegates Room

where the exam was being administered. When I got there, all I saw was a sea of people. The only thing on my mind was trying to locate a vacant seat. I spotted one all the way down on the front row. I went directly to it and sat down. Mr. Watts, the clerk, came by and gave me my examination papers.

Like everything else, segregated seating may have been the order of the day (even for taking the bar!) However, I was late, excited and focused on finding any available seat. I did not see or think about the racial seating pattern. When I entered the House of Delegates chamber, I was looking forward and moving to the front. I sat down in the only vacant seat I saw. The rest of the Negroes were in the back of the room. Since I had entered the room from the rear I had passed the row where they were seated before I even got a good look.

Furthermore, I had been living in Washington for a decade. Social and employment segregation was rampant in Washington. However, Washington had sufficient non-segregated public places so that in a public place I had become unaccustomed to looking for an area set aside for Negroes. Examples of non-segregated public places included street cars, public libraries, parks, and museums. However, other public places denied Negroes admission including hotels, restaurants, theaters and churches.

Mr. Watts, the Clerk for the Virginia Court of Appeals, came by picking up the cards. I was already reading the examination. When he picked up my card, he put it behind one of his fingers. He kept my card separate from the others. I noticed this maneuver, however, I did not let it bother me. At that point, that was the least of my worries. I just went on reading.

I looked at the first question: and it involved federal procedure. During my tenure in law school we were not taught federal procedure. Fortunately, I had enough sense to say to myself, "Well, I don't know this so I'll go on to the next question." I went to the other questions. Afterwards I came back to the federal procedure question: and used my imagination.

At the end of the first morning session, we had a break. I went out into the hall and one of the examiners, Stuart Campbell, was talking to a group of white applicants. Campbell was from Wytheville and served as an examiner for many years.

I waited until he finished talking to the other bar applicants and asked him what was his experience regarding applicants who did not do well on the first section but did very well on the subsequent sections of the exam. His reply was to the effect that, "Oh, nah, it is a common experience. If they don't do well the first session they might as well forget it."

I went back to the exam and that afternoon I didn't have too much difficulty with any of the questions. The exam had a number of sections. I don't remember the exact number.

The next day we continued the examination. I did not feel much anxiety about any of the questions after my federal procedure problem. However, I was really worried about my examination performance on that first morning. Due to the examiner's remarks I was sure that I had flunked the dad-blamed thing. He really scared me.

Having sat in the front row initially by happenstance, I retained my same seat throughout both days of the examination. I did not say anything to anyone about the seating situation and no one said anything to me. Due to this seating arrangement, I did not have much contact with the other Negroes taking the bar examination.

On the second day of the exam, the last section contained something like two hundred and fifty or three hundred true/false questions - I checked those off quickly and got out of there early. Since I had checked my bag at the bus station while I was on the way to the Capitol, I went straight to the station.

After leaving the Capitol, I thought very little about the examination. By about 5:00 p.m. when the exam was ending, I was almost in Washington.

Sometime in early February, I was at a dance and really feeling no pain. A guy came up to me and said, "Congratulations, Counselor." I said, "Congratulations on what?" He said, "You don't pass a damn bar every day, do you?" I asked him how he knew because I hadn't heard anything. He said he had seen it in the newspapers at the end of December. That sobered me up in a hurry.

The Library of Congress opened very early in the morning. When it opened I was there. I got the Roanoke paper for the last week in December, and there in one of the editions was an account of the

December Bar Exam results. A certain name stood out among the successful applicants in what appeared to me to be bold letters: OLIVER WHITE HILL.

I called Mrs. Pentecost in Roanoke and asked whether she had heard anything from the State Bar. She replied affirmatively stating that something had come from the examiners. What had happened was that the bar examiners had sent to my Roanoke address the customary card requesting my poll tax receipts for the previous three years. The examiners wanted evidence that I had paid those taxes. Mrs. Pentecost had sent the card to Attorney Jacob Reid. Reid had piddled around and was late sending back the receipts. In those days, Virginia required poll tax payment for a variety of things. The problem revolved around Mrs. Pentecost's lack of knowledge about the card's significance.

She then told me that something had just come in the mail saying I had passed the bar exam. She stated that she was going to call me; however, people were slow in making long distance telephone calls in those days. Usually when people wanted to transmit messages in a hurry, they used telegrams. For example, folks used telegrams to give death notices as well as train arrivals. Men or boys riding bicycles usually delivered such telegrams. Commonly, you would see Western Union or Postal Telegraph employees riding through the streets making deliveries on their bikes. People in our community did not rush to make long distance telephone calls. This helps account for why I had not learned that I had passed the bar until I attended a dance in February.

Incidentally, Jacob Reid was the great uncle of William Ferguson Reid — the first black legislator in the Virginia General Assembly in modern times. William Reid's sister, Mrs. Alice Reid Calloway, was also a member of the Richmond School Board. Among a host of professionals, this family of Reids includes the very knowledgeable, beautiful and quite articulate former Secretary of Energy, Mrs. Hazel Reid-O'Leary.

Coming back to the bar examination itself, three hundred people took it and exactly one hundred and fifty passed and one hundred fifty failed. I remember seeing that in the newspaper. It was the largest class that had ever taken the examination up to that time. Tucker and two or three other Negroes also passed.

At that time, it was customary to appear and be sworn in before every court in which you sought to practice. Although I was in

Washington, only a streetcar ride away, it did not occur to me to go to Alexandria and be sworn in.

Tucker's father had taken the bar exam four or five times but he didn't study with us. While Tucker and I took the bar exam in December of 1933 and passed, unfortunately, Tucker's father did not pass. After Tucker passed, I don't think that his father ever took the exam again.

In September 1934, I got married and went to Roanoke to begin my law practice. I had waited until I returned to Roanoke to be sworn in. The court clerk told me that it was a good thing that I had been sworn in when I did. If I had not been sworn in before December, he said that I would have had to retake the bar exam. I never checked the Virginia Code to see whether he was pulling my leg or not.

I lived with the Pentecosts while I practiced in Roanoke. My wife, Bernie, was teaching in the Washington, D.C. public schools. She would come down from D.C. to visit on weekends and holidays.

In those days people in Washington never really experienced the Depression that one found in the states. The federal government continued to function with relatively minor apparent changes. The New Deal brought a lot of hustle and bustle to Washington, and many people received employment as lobbyists and employees of new agencies. Some federal employees might have had their salary reduced.

The New Deal also brought a whole lot of new people to Washington. Unlike the previous Hoover administration, the Roosevelt administration was active in creating new agencies and experimenting with different approaches to revitalize the economy. Accordingly, as I started my practice in Roanoke, I was really surprised when I saw the contrast in living conditions.

My first office in Roanoke was in a building with a drugstore on the first floor and professional offices on the second floor. There were two physicians, two dentists, and including me, two lawyers, in the building. J. Henry Clayter, a lawyer, Dr. Brown, a physician, and Gardiner Downing, a dentist, all had offices in the rear of the building. I had a desk and chair in their reception room. Whenever I had a client come in, which was very seldom, I used Clayter's office. Gardiner Downing was one of three brothers in the building: E. D. Downing was also a dentist, and L.C. Downing, a physician. E.D. and L.C. Downing had offices in the front of the building.

Clayter was not a Howard graduate. He had studied at a correspondence school, LaSalle, in Chicago. As a matter of fact I think he served for a period in the District Attorney's office in Chicago prior to coming to Roanoke.

In any event, after I arrived, Clayter ordered new stationery. I awaited the arrival of this stationery with great anticipation. When the stationery arrived, across the top of the letterhead, it read: "J. Henry Clayter, Attorney at Law". On one side under a line in small print, appeared my name. When I first saw the stationary, it is difficult to express how disappointed I was. I had imagined both our names would be in large letters. "CLAYTER & HILL" or vice versus. That was probably the first time I had ever paid close attention to the heading of legal stationery.

I wish you could have seen Clayter's desk when I first went there. The desk was covered with papers. Papers all over it. It was a regular replica of the desk in "Shoe", like that depicted by the comic strip creator, Jeff MacNelly.

One time Clayter had gone to Baltimore and was gone for a couple of days. I thought I would do him a favor and straighten things up a little. Accordingly, by the time he came back I had put all his papers on his desk in orderly piles. When Clayter came in and saw this, he hit the ceiling, crying out, "How am I going to find anything now?"

Concerning resources for doing legal research, they were sparse. In his library Clayter had a Virginia Code and a few other books. Aside from the Code, Clayter had little other reference material.

I wanted to establish a strong client base; however, Clayter was very little help to me. He did a few positive things to assist me. For instance, he introduced me to the courts in Roanoke and carried me over to Salem to introduce me to the judge there. However, after that I was on my own except that he allowed me to help him on two civil cases. In addition, once he had a case in West Virginia and I accompanied him.

By prior arrangement, we agreed to work with an outstanding West Virginia Negro law firm named Capehart & Miller. Leon Miller, one of the firm members was originally from Roanoke, Virginia and was a prominent Democrat. Harry Theopart Capehart was a Republican, active with the national Republican Party.[15]   I was told that depending on which party was in office, the appropriate member of the firm would become the Assistant U.S. District Attorney for that district.

In those days, most Negro lawyers had a solo general practice. Like general medical practice, our general legal practice required us to make house calls. People in real serious condition needed you to visit them at home. I frequently went to clients' homes to talk to them.

Clayter didn't have many clients that came to the office. Clayter had a small civil practice including very infrequent personal injury cases. However, his principal practice seemed to be in police court. Police Court was equivalent to our present General District Court (criminal division). Like our present General District Court, the Police Court was not a court of record. When cases were appealed from the Police Court, they were tried <u>de novo</u> (over from the beginning) in Circuit Court or in the Hustings Court.

In the early days of my practice, most of the cities also had "Hustings Courts." Hustings Courts had statutory jurisdiction over specified matters, depending on the locality, and sometimes included condemnation of lands for public use, divorce and criminal matters. The difference between Hustings Court and Police Court was that Hustings Court was a court of record similar to present day Circuit Courts.

The courts of record that handled civil and equity cases were labeled either Law and Equity, Law and Chancery, or Circuit Courts. In counties, the courts of record were the circuit court which had full jurisdiction over civil, criminal and equity matters.

Virginia was also in the forefront in the movement to create juvenile courts. In Virginia, in 1914 the Juvenile and Domestic Relations Court was created. Thomas C. Walker, a Negro lawyer from Gloucester, Virginia was one of the early participants in helping to develop the juvenile courts system in Richmond.[16]

As I recollect, I never went to Police Court in Roanoke. I think it was because I did not feel comfortable competing with Clayter for business. However, looking back on that situation, I regret not going to Police Court. I would have gained valuable experience and probably improved my financial situation.

As a part of his general practice of law, Clayter had divorce cases.

However, during the 1930's divorce cases were both infrequent and quite adversarial situations. Few people had money necessary to get a divorce. Accordingly, folks just separated.

Another impediment to divorce was that the law required the person to wait for six months to file for a legal separation, and for three years to file for a final decree of divorce. A further example of the difficulty in obtaining a divorce in Virginia involved the strict proof of all of one's material reasons for seeking divorce. Thus, you had not only to establish your case but also eliminate any appearance of connivance with the defendant or condoning of the activity of which the plaintiff complained.

In Northern Virginia and in the Tidewater areas, local practice required litigants to take depositions before a Commissioner in Chancery. In Richmond and other parts of the state, deposition practice was not so strict. Secretaries served as scriveners of testimony and notaries for the swearing in of witnesses. Unless a matter was strongly contested, the use of legal secretaries eliminated the need for a court reporter to take the deposition in ordinary cases.

This period in history covered the height of the Depression. Most Negroes had very little money. Leaving aside an occasional divorce case, unless Negroes were sued in civil justice courts, little litigation existed in the Negro community. In those civil suits, local merchants sued Negroes for non payment of debts.

While in Roanoke, I also remember being appointed by Judge J. Lindsay Almond on several occasions to represent criminal defendants pro bono. (Almond later became Congressman, Attorney General and Governor of Virginia.) During those days in capital cases, the compensation was twenty-five dollars. For felonies where the penalty was less than ten years, for court appointed lawyers, neither the statute nor the court provided any compensation. Indeed, until recent years, in run of the mill type federal criminal cases, the Eastern District of Virginia provided no compensation for court appointed lawyers. Both the federal government and the states took a very stingy posture when it came to funding lawyers to represent poor people charged with committing crimes.

To give you a further sense of the depressed state of lawyer fees at that time, we only charged fifty dollars, including costs of court, for uncontested divorces.

On one occasion that I still remember quite well, Judge Almond appointed Jacob Reid and me to represent an indigent criminal defendant who had been charged with murder. This was the same Jacob Reid whom my foster parents had gotten to file the poll tax receipt so that I could become admitted to the Virginia bar. In any event, Reid had been practicing law since I was a little boy. He was accordingly quite seasoned. In contrast, I had not been practicing very long. This was my third or fourth case overall, and my first murder case.

In advising the client whether to seek a jury trial or a judge trial, Reid and I could not agree. With a judge there was only one person involved. Accordingly, Reid argued that a judge trial would be better.

Normally, in Roanoke, in those days, I would have preferred a judge rather than a jury. However, in this case, I thought that the wiser course of action would be to take a jury. I had two reasons for this suggestion. First, you cannot predict the outcome of a jury's behavior. Twelve people must agree upon a verdict not just one. Therefore, I believed that we had a better chance to sway the jury to see things our way. The facts were such that we were sure that the defendant would likely be convicted. If they convicted him, I hoped that at least one juror would hold out for a sentence other than death.

My second reason for suggesting a jury trial was not because I was enamored with juries. Rather, as I pointed out to Reid and the defendant, in the past three weeks, in similar type cases, two juries had convicted defendants: and sentenced them to the electric chair. I was sure that if after hearing the evidence, Judge Almond decided to convict our client, the judge would say that two recent juries had expressed the community's sentiment. Thus, I was sure that the judge would follow the juries' lead and in our case also sentence our client to death.

We went back and forth on this and our client really couldn't decide what he wanted to do. As a matter of fact, when we got to the court we were sitting in the judge's chambers for quite a long time trying to help the client figure out which way to go. Finally, he decided to follow Jake's advice. After all, Jake was the older and more experienced lawyer.

We tried the case before Judge Almond and the judge found him guilty. The evidence showed that the defendant had been in town for only about an hour and had gotten involved in a gambling enterprise. An argument ensued and he killed the victim in cold blood. In the circumstances, the judge decided to give the defendant the electric chair. While sentencing the defendant, the judge noted that in the recently preceding weeks, two juries had given defendants the electric chair. He decided to do the same thing, for according to the judge, the jury had spoken the community's sentiment. My "prophecy" had come true. For some reason, however, I do not believe the defendant actually died in the electric chair. I believe that he was killed in a jail break.

A few other interesting matters relating to the practice of law include my first personal injury case which arose in the early 1940's. I represented the estate of a man who had been struck and killed by an automobile. At issue, was whether my client was jaywalking. Rather than risk a verdict for the defendant, which was quite likely, with the family's consent, we obtained a small settlement.

Another curious historical fact involved many lawyers having sofas in their offices. I inquired why that was and later heard people talk about how lawyers occasionally got "paid": sometimes the client celebrated her freedom on the sofa ... .

Initial Practice Experiences

The first time I went outside of my jurisdiction to handle a case was in 1935. Late one night I received a telephone call from a Negro in Wytheville, Virginia, stating that Negroes in the county feared that a Negro in that county was going to be lynched because the accused was charged with shooting a deputy sheriff. The informant had called the NAACP in New York, and he had been told to call me in Roanoke. The fear of a lynching was not unfounded because, according to one authority, less than a decade earlier, about fifty men wearing hoods and masks had broken into the Wytheville jail and lynched a Negro accused of raping a white woman. Similarly, in 1900 a Negro named Daniel Long had been lynched there.[17]

The next morning I borrowed the Pentecosts' automobile. On my way to Wytheville I wondered what I would do if in fact I discovered that a lynching was about to or had taken place. I had decided to carefully "case" the situation and take appropriate action. That meant, if I deemed it necessary, I had planned to get out of there quickly and go to Bristol, Virginia to get some help.

When I arrived in Wytheville, I discovered that the situation was tense. However, I did not feel that a lynching was likely.

That night, along with the person who called me, I visited a white family in the town. They extensively briefed me on the public officials and many prominent white folks in the community. They offered to help in any way possible short of testifying in court or being otherwise identified.

This turned out to be a frequent pattern that I encountered in many counties in the state. I received much valuable information through this practice. Besides, I empathized with people who wanted to do right, but did not feel that they could afford to go public. In those days, one of the most disparaging and distressing things that could happen to white people was to be labeled a "nigger lover." Even today, this is true in many communities.

I agreed to represent this defendant. The preliminary hearing had already been held in police court and the trial date set. I returned to Roanoke. On the trial date, I went back to Wytheville and appeared in the Circuit Court. Only one person was in the courtroom at the time that I arrived. I inquired whether he was the commonwealth's attorney. After being advised that he was, I told him I was a lawyer from Roanoke who had come to represent the defendant in the case scheduled for trial that day. I offered him my card and asked him to move my admission to practice in that court.

As I have previously stated, in those days you had to be admitted in every court in which you practiced. He looked at me and said, "I don't know you." I replied, "You are just as right as you can be." I put my card in my pocket, went to a seat and sat down.

The courtroom later filled up. When the judge came in and the bailiff called for motions, I got up and said, "May it please the Court, I'm Oliver Hill of Roanoke, Virginia, a member of the Virginia Bar. I'm here to represent the defendant in this case; and I would like to move my admission to your bar." The judge instructed the clerk to swear me in and enrolled me in the Order Book.

That became my established practice when appearing in jurisdictions outside of my home base. After that experience without saying anything to anyone I would walk up to the bench and move my own admission. The only time that a comparative stranger moved my admission to the bar occurred in federal district court in Richmond. I will say more about the circumstances surrounding that situation later.

Fortunately, a more enlightened practice exists today. The bar examiners, some Virginia State Supreme Court Justices, other members of the bench and bar, and the successful applicants meet in a large hotel or courtroom and the new lawyers are sworn in en masse. This procedure has eliminated individual swearing in ceremonies in every jurisdiction, and entitles lawyers to practice in any Virginia state court.

Coming back to the Wytheville unlawful wounding case, on the second day of the trial, a local paper came out with a headline, "Negro Lawyer Appears in the Circuit Court of Wytheville County". Apparently this was the first time a Negro lawyer had been there in a long time. I assume that back in the earlier days there may have been a black lawyer in that court. However, it may be that I was the first one ever to appear. I do not know.

The defendant in the Wytheville case was convicted by a jury and sentenced to four years in the penitentiary. While the jury was out, the trial judge, Judge Sutherland, said that had the case been tried by him without a jury, he would have acquitted the defendant. The commonwealth attorney had probably insisted on a jury trial for just this reason. There was sufficient evidence to conclude that the deputy sheriff had been the instigator of the violence.

In this case, this judge acted in typical fashion. He did not intervene to right what he acknowledged was a possible miscarriage of justice. Accordingly, the judge's first mistake was his failure to grant my motion to set aside the jury verdict. Too many judges refused to set aside such verdicts and free Negro defendants in situations where they had a different opinion and knew justice had been denied. However, Judge Sutherland assisted me in obtaining an early release for this defendant.

Interestingly, Charlie Houston and J. Byron Hopkins were passing through Wytheville, heard that a Negro lawyer was trying a case there, and found me in the local law library on the evening of the first day of the trial. As part of the NAACP's education program, they were headed further south to investigate the deplorable academic conditions of Negroes in the south. I invited them to stay and participate in the trial but Charlie declined explaining that it might be perceived as grandstanding.

Charlie Houston was at that time special counsel for the NAACP. The Garland Fund had given the NAACP a grant consisting of a block of stocks to fund activities challenging segregation of Negroes in the United States. Houston had left his position at Howard Law School to develop and carry out the NAACP's educational program in the south. He started the educational program and published a number of articles informing the public regarding societal conditions and the activities of the NAACP to furnish equal educational opportunities for Negroes.

Unfortunately, the Garland Fund had been principally composed of securities; and the 1929 stock crash severely depleted the value of these financial resources. Accordingly, the monies that would have been used to fund the NAACP's educational program were significantly decreased.[18] During the mid 1930's, the case load for the NAACP became so heavy that Charlie Houston engaged Thurgood Marshall as his assistant. When the Garland funds became depleted, Houston turned the special counsel position over to Thurgood and returned to private practice in Washington, D.C. Because Charlie was more experienced than Thurgood, it was cheaper to pay for Thurgood's services than for Charlie's. Houston continued to actively participate in selected NAACP cases.

In 1935, we organized the Virginia State Conference of NAACP branches. There had been preliminary meetings in Richmond and Norfolk; however, the organizational meeting was held in Roanoke. One of my former law professors, Leon A. Ransom (known by most of his friends as Andy), had been deputized by the National Office to be the official representative of the National Office. I was the chairperson on the nominating committee.

We organized formally and elected as President of the Virginia State Conference of NAACP Branches, W.P. Milner, who was active in the labor movement. Milner worked as a printer for the *Norfolk Journal and Guide Newspaper*, a Negro owned and operated newspaper. Dr. Jesse Tinsley was elected Vice-President. Tinsley had graduated from Meharry Medical College in the 1920's with a degree in dentistry and since the early 1930's had been president of the Richmond branch of the NAACP.

Within a few weeks and before any substantial organizational activities began, Dr. Tinsley became President of the Virginia State Conference, succeeding Milner who had been fired from his job because of his union-related activities. Dr. Tinsley served in the capacity of president and did a superb job for nearly thirty years.

98

As far as the numbers of black lawyers in Virginia was concerned, in the mid 1930's there were four or five black lawyers up in Alexandria, five in Roanoke, between five and eight in Norfolk, two or three in Newport News and two in Portsmouth. In Richmond there were about fifteen and then there was one in Lexington, one in Lynchburg, and one in Gloucester. That was about it.

While in Roanoke, during the mid 1930's, I was accustomed to looking for creative ways to generate income. For example, I made some money by typing chain letters. I also represented a number of workers who gave me wage assignments. I filed wage assignments with the railroads' personnel office and made agreements with creditors to forestall garnishment. I collected my clients' pay and doled it out to their creditors, to my clients, and I retained a small bit for me. As I stated previously, my criminal practice was almost entirely pro bono. From time to time, I would visit the jails and prisoners would engage me to petition the judge for early release. By rendering these services, I successfully generated a small amount of income. Some Negro professionals gave me their unpaid debts to collect, and I wrote to their debtors but collected very little money.

However, these various and sundry activities failed to produce sufficient funds for me to pay what I considered a reasonable amount for my upkeep. Accordingly, in June of 1936 I discontinued my law practice and went back to Washington, D.C.

Before I left Virginia in 1936, I had gone around in Roanoke County in 1934-35 and taken a lot of pictures of the interior and exterior of the one-room schools. I knew we were going to use that type of evidence for community education and for litigation. I returned to Washington, D.C. because I knew that there I could find employment, and I missed my wife. I was glad that we could share each other's company on a daily basis. Bernie was still living in Washington and working as a school teacher when I returned from Roanoke.

Of course, in considering employment options, the first thing I thought about was something that I knew and had contact with. In Washington, I joined one of my old friends from high school and college, William T. Whitehead, and we started organizing a labor union of waiters and cooks in the hotels, clubs and restaurants in Washington and vicinity. At that time, the Congress of Industrial Organizations ("C.I.O.") was organizing on a non-segregated basis. Whitehead and I attended a lot of those sessions with the idea of trying to get the C.I.O. to accept our organization as an affiliate.

However, the C.I.O. was seeking to get the A.F.L. Waiters, Cooks and Bartenders Union to become affiliated with it. In those days, most of the A.F.L.'s unions were all white, or had segregated affiliates. The C.I.O. wanted to persuade the existing A.F.L. union of waiters, cooks and bartenders to join with the C.I.O. To the best of my recollection the C.I.O. refused to negotiate with us on this phase of the organizing activities.

As an alternative, the C.I.O. offered us a proposal whereby we would organize the railroad waiters and cooks. Neither Whitehead nor I was interested, principally because it required a lot of traveling and long absences from home. That ended our association with the C.I.O.

While trying to establish the C.I.O. affiliate during the summer, both Whitehead and I frequently took jobs as waiters. I ran from Washington to St. Petersburg on the Seaboard Railroad, and Washington to Jacksonville on the Atlantic Coastline Railroad as a waiter. At the beginning of the winter season, both of the railroads offered me a job. I refused the offers. At that time my wife wasn't well. Besides, as the boys say, I was a lawyer "in between engagements." I was trying to get some more money to resume practice.

Coming Back to Old Virginny

When I resumed my practice, I had always planned to return to Roanoke, Virginia. The switch to returning to Richmond in 1939 is an interesting story. J. Byron Hopkins, Jr. and J. Thomas Hewin, Jr., were individual practitioners in Richmond. The younger Hewin was the son of J. Thomas Hewin, Sr., who was an old practitioner in the city. As I mentioned earlier, Byron was in the class ahead of me in law school.

Byron and Hewin had a murder case which involved an issue that they wanted to discuss with Andy Ransom, one of our law school professors. They contacted Andy and made an appointment. Andy and I were still very close, and since this matter involved Virginia law, Andy contacted me. He said, "Why don't you come to my office and sit in on this session with Hopkins and another lawyer?" I did so.

When we got through talking about their legal problem, Byron asked me what I planned to do. This was about February, 1939. I said that I thought that sometime in 1939 I would go back to Roanoke. He said, "Why don't you come to Richmond and we will form the firm of Hopkins, Hewin & Hill?" This sounded great to me because I had always wanted to be part of a law firm. I agreed to come down during the Easter holidays to discuss matters. When I came down to Richmond during the holidays, we agreed orally to form the firm. Our understanding was that they would find suitable office space and I would arrive on May 1, 1939.

On May 1st, my thirty-second birthday, I showed up with the idea of becoming a member of the firm of Hopkins, Hewin & Hill. However, before I arrived in Richmond, Hopkins and Hewin had agreed to disagree at least temporarily on formation of a law firm. When I arrived and discovered these new facts, I had to put my expectations on hold.

After waiting awhile, I began to make other arrangements. I contacted Dr. Everett White, one of my old friends who had attended the Howard Medical School when I was in the law school. Everett had his office in two front rooms in a house at 117 East Leigh Street. In the back, beyond his office rooms, was a bathroom and a vacant room. We agreed that I would rent the back room as an office and have joint use of the reception area. I agreed to pay the magnificent weekly rent of five dollars.

I painted the room, rented or borrowed a truck, and drove over to Roanoke, where I secured my desk, my set of Corpus Juris, and some other books that I had left there. After purchasing a few other pieces of furniture, I opened my office. I paid my legal assistant five dollars weekly as her salary. My library consisted initially of the set of Corpus Juris and some text books. To supplement these resources and stay abreast of developments in the law, I went to the state law library occasionally and got half a dozen books or so to study over the weekend. I would bring them back on Monday morning.

Byron had offices on the second floor next door. For the first several weeks, I used Byron's Virginia Code and form books. I was still hoping that shortly we would get together and form a firm.

Unfortunately, Tom Hewin, Jr. who had the potential to be an excellent lawyer, was addicted to beer. Periodically, he disappeared. No one knew where he went. He sometimes was missing for extended periods of time. This did not help the formation of a law firm among the three of us. While the firm did not develop, during the balance of that

101

year Byron and I worked together loosely. On several occasions, Tom Hewin, Jr. and I did likewise.

Before my arrival in Richmond in 1939, Tom Hewin, Jr., had gone off on a beer drinking binge. On this occasion, Tom finally came back just before a trial he had scheduled down in Middlesex County, Virginia. The trial was supposed to start on a Monday morning.

On Saturday night before the trial, Dr. Toney, a physician in Middlesex and active in the NAACP, came down to Richmond to see about the scheduled trial. Dr. Toney had not heard anything from Hewin. Byron and I agreed to represent the defendant and returned to Middlesex with Dr. Toney.

At that time Hopkins did not have a car and neither did I. But that created no problem because Dr. Toney took us back to Middlesex with him. It was one of those stormy, rainy nights. We got down to West Point, Virginia, but they didn't have the bridges they have now. The cars during those days had running boards on the side upon which you stepped as you got into the car. At one point in crossing the lowlands near West Point, the water came up to and covered the running boards of the car.

We returned with Dr. Toney on Saturday night so that we could talk to the witnesses on Sunday. We stayed at Dr. Toney's home.

On Sunday we worked with the witnesses to prepare for the Monday trial. Bright and early on Monday, Tom showed up for the trial. It was a case in which the defendant was charged with arson.

The Commonwealth's Attorney had laid the indictment and the scene of the crime as running along highways going through Saluda, continuing through several places in the county, and through the town of Urbanna, and back to Saluda. We contended that this layout around the highways of the county constituted the scene of the crime. At that time under the relevant statute, anyone who lived within two miles of the scene was ineligible to serve as a juror. We went over the juror list. We were able to raise an objection for cause against everyone that they listed. The court sustained our objections and they had to empanel a new venire.

That took two or three days. After empaneling a new jury, we had what was regarded as a long drawn out trial of a couple days. The trial ended with a hung jury. The double jury and other expenses of the trial were regarded as a serious financial crisis by the local officials. We finally agreed that the defendant would pay the court costs provided charges were dismissed.

One interesting event arising during the trial was that after being subjected to four or five hours of cross examination by Tom Hewin the insurance investigator came down from the stand, walked out of the courtroom and fainted. In subsequent years, we had other such interesting experiences.

After that experience, Tom Hewin remained in Richmond for several months. However, early in 1940, Tom Hewin and his girlfriend vanished from Richmond. For several years their whereabouts were unknown . . .

By the time I returned to Richmond in 1939, a Joint Committee of representatives of the Virginia Teachers Association (V.T.A.) and the NAACP State Conference had been established. The V.T.A. represented the Negro teachers in Virginia. The Virginia Education Association (V.E.A.) represented white teachers.

I became the legal representative for the Joint Committee. The Committee's function was to actively promote teachers' salary equalization. While operating in my capacity as attorney for the Joint Committee of the NAACP and the Virginia Teachers Association, I was the only local lawyer involved in attempting to equalize the teachers' salaries.

While I was getting my practice started, I also rode around the state drumming up support in the local communities for the salary equalization project. I told people in each county what we were trying to do, especially that we planned to address the question of equal pay first. I informed them that after we got the teacher salary issue underway, then we were going to launch a broad based challenge against the segregated and unequal public schools.

On Sundays, Dr. Jesse Tinsley and I would visit churches in the outlying counties. We talked about the NAACP and its programs. Sometimes in the same county we would visit two churches on the same day. Occasionally, we spent the day visiting churches in different counties. Our efforts to educate the communities were highly successful.

I also attempted to negotiate with some school boards to resolve the salary and school bus transportation issues without litigation. Many rural systems had publicly funded school bus transportation for white students. However, the black students had to walk to school or pay private individuals to take them. While I tried the negotiated settlement approach, at that time I made no progress with school officials regarding issues of salary equalization or school bus transportation. We met this issue by filing suits to compel such school systems to provide equal salaries for Negro teachers and school bus transportation for Negro students.

One of the cases that Byron and I worked together on is an excellent illustration of southern justice involving Negroes during this period. A group of Negroes had been involved in a crap game out in the woods in Louisa County, Virginia. A deputy sheriff testified that when he came up, the men and boys saw him, ran and scattered. Some of them even left their money at the scene. In his zeal to catch them, the deputy shot at and hit one of the young men in the back of his thigh.

The injured young man had only been an onlooker. However, when the deputy arrived, this individual ran like the rest of those involved. His mother employed us to represent him.

The deputy recognized and swore out warrants against five or six of those involved. All of the defendants were charged with gambling. None of the defendants were represented by counsel in the general district court. They all were convicted. The mother of the wounded defendant contacted us and Bryron agreed to represent her son. We noted appeals for all defendants. The matter was tried de novo in the circuit court. Perceiving it to be in our clients' best interests, we agreed to represent all of his codefendants.

When we became involved, we had all of the defendants appeal the general district court conviction to the circuit court. At the trial in circuit court, after the deputy testified, the Commonwealth Attorney called one of the defendants to take the stand. When he started to question the defendant, we objected. Our client invoked the Fifth Amendment on the grounds that the testimony might be incriminating. The court sustained our objection. The Commonwealth's Attorney called another defendant with the same result. He complained to the court asking how could he prove his case. Finally, he saw that he could not prevail, and dismissed the cases against all the defendants.

We then filed a civil suit against the sheriff and his deputy for injuries our client had sustained. At trial, we established that the men and the boys were in the woods and that when they saw the deputy they ran. We also established that the deputy fired at the fleeing men and shot the plaintiff in the back of his leg.

In those days the Commonwealth's Attorney frequently appeared in criminal and civil matters involving government officials. In this case the Commonwealth's Attorney represented the defendants. At the beginning of the trial, the Commonwealth's Attorney referred to our client and witnesses as "darkies". We objected. The judge pretended that he did not hear the remark but said that no such expression would be tolerated in his court.[19]

The defense claimed that the deputy did not fire directly at the fleeing men but fired in the air. The court decided we should go to the scene and see what happened. The judge adjourned court and we all (including jurors) went out into the woods to look at the scene. When we arrived at the site the deputy again claimed that he fired in the air in the direction of the men as they were running. Following the deputy's assertions and after looking around for awhile, the judge exclaimed as follows: "I see what happened! The deputy shot up in the air, and the bullet ricocheted off that tree, and came down off that tree and struck another tree." Pointing at another tree, he continued, "Then the [magic] bullet ricocheted off that third tree so that it struck the plaintiff in the rear of his thigh."

Based on these suppositions, the judge ruled for the defendants. We recommended that the client appeal this decision. The client declined to do so. The client's mother was afraid that in the Virginia Supreme Court of Appeals he would obtain the same sort of justice. Had this case arisen later in my career, I am sure that instead of filing a tort action in state court, we would have filed in the federal courts, claiming civil rights violations under section 1983 of the United States Code. We would have had a better chance of recovery there.

Since she had no confidence in further litigation, our client's mother decided to drop the case. She paid our fee entirely in coins, some of which were so old and tarnished, they looked moldy. The coins appeared not to have been touched in years.

When I returned to Virginia in 1939, Martin A. Martin was practicing in Danville. Martin had graduated from Howard Law School

105

a few years earlier. Martin and I were both active with the NAACP and soon worked out an arrangement whereby we would associate with each other, particularly in cases in outlying counties.

Another interesting case early in my career, involved an assault in northern Virginia. Martin and I had a client who was reluctant to bring the action because the defendant was employed by the Duponts. At the behest of relatives and friends, he talked with us about his case. We convinced him that he had a good case and that we could obtain a verdict in his favor. This ultimately occurred as we won a verdict of five hundred dollars which in those days was a big deal. Our client was both surprised and delighted. One of his relatives recently identified herself at the Virginia State NAACP Conference Reception held on May 21, 1999 and reminded me of the occasion of these discussions.

Another lawyer nearby was named Sherwood "Shingee" Duigiud from Lynchburg. In the early 1940's, Duiguid had a client, Dr. Robert W. Johnson, who had attended Lincoln University and excelled in football. He had the sobriquet of "Whirlwind Johnson". In addition to his medical practice, Dr. Johnson operated a recreational area outside of Lynchburg in Campbell County. A clubhouse existed on the property, and the club had an ABC license.

On one occasion, during an altercation, one of Dr. Johnson's employees shot and wounded an obstreperous customer. The victim filed charges and the employee was prosecuted for unlawful wounding. Duigiud got Martin and me to help try the case.

The presiding judge, Judge Burks, was quite talkative. We tried the case on Friday, and I tried to expedite matters because the jury seemed receptive to our version of what had happened. I did not want to risk having the matter carried over the weekend. One could not predict what might transpire since the jurors lived in the same community as the victim's family and friends. Even though the jurors were not supposed to discuss the case, I remained skeptical about them obeying the court's instructions in this regard. Further, I did not feel comfortable with the prospect that for whatever reason, including having second thoughts during the weekend recess, the jury might decide the case adversely to our client.

Despite our efforts to expedite the trial and conclude it in one day, and even though we worked through the evening, we could not persuade the judge to give the jury the case that night. He insisted on carrying it over. On Monday, the judge submitted the case to the jury. Our worst fears came to pass: they convicted our client and sentenced him to the penitentiary. As I recall, I entered military service shortly thereafter and am not sure of the result of appeals, if any.

It should be noted that, not only was Dr. Johnson an excellent physician, he also helped train both Althea Gibson and Arthur Ashe in their brilliant tennis careers.[20] Ashe and Gibson became world ranked players, who emerged victorious at Wimbledon and Forest Hills.

Memorable Criminal Law Cases

During my legal career, I worked on a number of criminal law cases which raised issues of guilt and procedural fairness. When the clients were Negroes and the alleged victims white, the defendants' guilt seemed presumed and their punishment was severe. Accordingly, criminal law cases frequently raised significant concerns about fundamental justice.

For example, a celebrated case developed over in Martin's territory involving a defendant named Odell Waller. The defendant was a Negro tenant farmer who was charged with killing the white farm owner. An argument had developed between them because the white farmer allegedly had been cheating the tenant sharecropper. The white farmer produced a gun, and in an ensuring struggle was shot and killed.

In these circumstances, the Negro defendant was tried by a jury, convicted and sentenced to the electric chair. Waller was represented by an organization known as the Workers' Defense League that associated Martin as local counsel. After the trials and legal appeals were over, defense counsel appealed to Governor Colgate Darden for executive clemency.

The Workers' Defense League secured the services of a nationally known labor lawyer and of Edmund Preston, a liberal member of the Virginia law firm now known as Hunton & Williams. A petition was filed with Governor Darden and he agreed to hold hearings to determine whether he should intervene and grant clemency. He put on a big show by holding hearings as I remember it in the auditorium section of the library in the old Supreme Court building in Richmond. As a result of these public trappings and the array of evidence that was presented, we had high expectations that Darden would grant clemency. This was especially our perception of the situation since Darden fancied himself as being a liberal. But after the extensive hearing, Darden refused to intervene.[21] Ultimately, soon thereafter, Waller was electrocuted.

As a result of Martin's association with the WDL and his involvement in the Waller murder case, Martin made political contacts that enabled him to obtain a position in the Department of Justice. His assignment was to prosecute German sympathizers in California. Martin went out there in 1942. Late in 1942 or early in 1943, Martin wrote me and said, "You better come on in the government with me. I can get you in the Justice Department. Otherwise, you will end up being drafted, put into the Engineers, and sent down to a camp in Louisiana." Ironically, that is precisely what happened.

However, later Martin didn't like his assignments and in the summer of 1943 he resigned. He returned to Richmond and joined Spotswood W. Robinson, III who was called "Spot" by many of his friends. I will say more about that later.

Another memorable criminal law case that we had began before I returned to Virginia in 1939. Martin had a case in Halifax, Virginia where a Negro named Bradshaw had shot and killed a white deputy sheriff. They convicted the defendant and gave him the electric chair.

Martin appealed challenging improper jury instructions. The judge failed to tell the jury all of the possible verdicts. The Virginia Court of Appeals ruled with Martin that the instructions as given were prejudicial, and the court remanded the case for a new trial.[22] I hadn't been back but a couple of months then. At that time, Hewin and I went over to help Martin try the case. The case was retried but the result was the same. Once again, the jury sentenced him to the chair. This time they executed him.

This was a section of the state in which racial tension was high. Normally, a situation in which a Negro had killed a white deputy sheriff, exacerbated an already explosive societal condition. Because of the great tension a large number of state troopers had been stationed at the courthouse that day. As a matter of fact, we were happy to see the state troopers. Their presence provided a measure of calm to a volatile situation. Preventing a lynching was the idea because in those days you couldn't tell what a crowd of whites in a situation like that might do.

However, the presence of the troopers could be regarded primarily as window dressing because as Governor Harry Byrd, Sr., was reported to have said at the time that he proposed the Virginia anti-lynching law: "we don't need to lynch the niggers. We can try them and then hang them." At that time, Byrd's remark expressed the prevailing sentiment in that section of Virginia.

Virginia's anti-lynching legislation flowed from a lynching in Sussex County, Virginia in the late 1920's. Following this lynching of a Negro, the white mob continued its berserk behavior and destroyed a number of houses in which Negroes were living. It happened that the houses, which were not much more than shacks, actually belonged to state Senator Garland Gray, a stalwart of the Byrd organization. The objective of the anti-lynch law was not to protect the lives of Negroes, but to protect the property of white folks against the unruly actions of white lynch mobs.

We also had a number of rape cases. For example, I participated as local counsel in a case in 1941 in which Charlie Houston represented a man charged with rape. The defendant, Samuel Legions, looked just like Joe Louis, and seemed to greatly attract and be attracted to women of all colors.

In this case, the defendant spent the afternoon with his girlfriend. After leaving her, he remembered that earlier that day he happened to meet a white woman whom he had known for sometime. They had grown up in the same section of the county. He had made a date with this woman and was supposed to meet her in the back yard of her home.

That evening when he arrived at her residence, she persuaded him to come into her house stating that her husband was asleep. She assured him that he would not wake up. They got on the kitchen table and started to have sexual relations. She complained that there was something in his pocket that hurt her. It was a knife which he pulled out of his pocket and put on the same table.

Before they could resume, the baby started crying in the adjoining room. She went in the next room where her husband and the baby were. She changed the baby's diaper and brought the diaper back to the kitchen. She placed it on the same table with the knife. Then they proceeded to have relations on the same table. The husband woke up and they heard him coming that way! So the boyfriend jumped up and ran. Remembering that he had left something on the table, as he began his flight, the defendant grabbed the diaper instead of the knife. He

109

hightailed it out the back door and ran away from the neighborhood.

Later that evening, on the other side of town, he was apprehended. He had the soiled diaper in his hip pocket.

At trial, the prosecuting witnesses claimed that Sammy, the defendant, a person whom they knew, had smashed the sash, raised the window, and entered their bedroom window, knife in hand. The husband testified that Sammy told both of them to keep quiet or he would kill them. Sammy then allegedly went around to the wife's side of the bed and told her to slide over. Then Sammy attempted to get into bed with the wife, husband and baby and found it to be too crowded.

Accordingly, the prosecution alleged that Sammy had the wife get up out of bed, and he took her into the kitchen. While this was going on, the baby started crying and Sammy and the wife stopped their activities. The wife came back into the bedroom and changed the diaper with Sammy standing in the kitchen door watching. As Sammy and the wife prepared to go back to the kitchen and resume where they left off, Sammy said to the husband, "Keep the damn baby quiet!" The husband supposedly asked Sammy would it be all right to get out of bed and sit in the chair to rock the baby. Sammy consented. The husband got up and sat a few feet from the front door rocking in the rocking chair to keep the baby quiet. While doing so the husband allegedly said he could hear the kitchen table squeaking as the defendant and his wife were having sexual relations. Finally, the husband got up enough nerve to run out of the house, cross the street, and into a Negro tavern. He asked for help claiming that some man was raping his wife. He then went running back with a crowd from the tavern, looking for Sammy.

The alleged victim's house contained two rooms including the bedroom which was about ten feet square and a kitchen about half the size of the bedroom. The house also had a loft over the bedroom which could be reached by a ladder. The victim's residence was across the street from a Negro restaurant, in a densely crowded neighborhood.

As I mentioned earlier, Charlie Houston was back in private practice in Washington, D.C.: and he handled the case at the trial level, along with Joe Waddy and me. Waddy was the junior partner in the firm of Houston and Houston, and I was local co-counsel. While Charlie consulted with us during preparation and conduct of the trial, Charlie made all the final decisions of trial management. Early on, because we did not wish the prosecution to be able to produce material evidence that the defendant was actually at the scene, we decided to keep the defendant off the stand. As previously stated, at the time that defendant was arrested on the other side of town, he had a soiled diaper in his pocket.

The trial lasted three or four days. Every evening, Charlie, Joe and I would drive back twenty-five miles to D.C.; and then leave early the next morning, return to the courthouse, and resume the trial. When the all white jury first got the case on the night that the trial ended, they deliberated for a number of hours until about 12:15 a.m. At that point, they returned to the courtroom and the foreman told the court that they were hopelessly deadlocked. The judge further instructed them and insisted that they return to their deliberations. Fifteen minutes later they came back, found our client guilty and sentenced him to die in the electric chair.

On appeal, the Virginia Supreme Court reversed the jury's verdict. In its opinion, the Virginia State Supreme Court said:

> Here is the picture and setting. A [N]egro man enters a white man's dwelling, unarmed, save a pocket knife, which was never opened or brandished, in a thickly settled neighborhood, at an hour when people were accustomed to be up and about, and assembling particularly at a [N]egro restaurant. He attempts to force his way into the bed in which the man and his wife were sleeping with their child. Foiled in that, he compels the wife to go into another room where he accomplishes his nefarious purpose. This in a house affording quick and easy access to the outside where aid and help were readily at hand. But no alarm is given – no protest – no attempt to rescue – no resistance from either the prosecutrix or her husband, except the ineffectual and feeble efforts of the latter, which have been referred to, and which were not followed up - nothing but a shameful surrender and capitulation descending almost to complacence. The whole thing does such shocking violence to any righteous conception of human conduct as to be unbelievable even to the most credulous and naïve. [23]

On this basis the court reversed the jury's verdict because it was "unbelievable".

On remand, the Commonwealth's Attorney had no further evidence to present in any subsequent trial. Notwithstanding the

111

absence of evidence the Commonwealth's Attorney would not release the defendant. Under the law at that time, a defendant charged with a criminal offense who had not been tried within three terms of court was automatically entitled to release. So I waited for three court terms and filed a writ of habeas corpus demanding his release. The writ was granted and the defendant released.

The Richmond Afro Newspaper's photographer took a picture of the defendant and me coming out of the penitentiary. In the next edition of the paper in bold headlines, the caption of the story was, "Prisoner Goes Free: Lawyer Goes to the Army".

Joe Waddy and I worked on several cases arising out of his work as a member of Charlie Houston's law firm. Joe and his wife Elizabeth were very close to my wife, Bernie, and me. Later, Joe was appointed to the federal bench in Washington, D.C.

In addition, before I went into the army during World War II, I once represented five Negro defendants in the Richmond area who were accused of raping a white woman. The woman worked at a restaurant on West Broad Street, got off from work late at night and her boyfriend picked her up. He later sought to have sexual relations with her in a wooded section of Henrico County on Westwood Avenue. When she refused he put her out of the car and left her.

She walked back towards town, came to the vicinity of a defense plant, and flagged down the defendants who had gotten off from the midnight shift. The defendants took the complainant to an after hours establishment where they purchased a bottle of whiskey and some of them had drinks. They then went on the Richmond/Henrico Turnpike leading up to Dove Street in a secluded area near the cemetery. Several of the defendants had sexual relations with the victim while several other defendants allegedly held her down. Defendants got into the car and the victim tried to get in with them. They left her and drove off.

The victim then went to a house not too far from the crime scene. According to the first witness who saw her, she appeared disheveled and hysterical, with mud on the back of her clothes. The victim reported the crime.

I agreed to represent the defendants and, with my secretary, went to the jail and took statements from each of them. Not all of them had relations with the victim, but they were all charged with criminal activity growing out of the events of that night.

One of the defendants said that after some of his cohorts and the victim had finished their encounter, the victim tried to get back in the car with the men. That's when they drove off and left her.

After the trial date had been set, I called Professor Andy Ransom one of my former professors at the Howard University Law School and asked him to come down to the trial. I wanted him to sit at the counsel table with me and to consult on trial strategy. I requested that Andy make reservations from Washington, D.C. and stay at the Hotel John Marshall.

By our prior arrangement, he called me on the afternoon before the trial and said that he was at the Hotel John Marshall. He asked what should we do now, and I told him to sit tight and wait until I got there.

The Hotel John Marshall had lower and upper lobbies. When I got to the hotel, I went to the lower lobby and pressed the elevator button. The elevator operator arrived in the elevator and when he opened the door and saw me he said to me that I had to use the freight elevator. With that he slammed the elevator door in my face and proceeded to another floor. I put my hand on the elevator button and held it there. The bell rang, rang, and rang. When the elevator operator returned, I pushed my way on the elevator and told him that I wanted to go to the sixth floor. The operator hesitated but took me to the sixth floor where I met Andy Ransom.

I wanted to test for myself the rumor that I had heard concerning the John Marshall's alleged discriminatory policy of making Negroes ride the freight elevator. Based on my own personal experience, I told other Negroes to refuse to ride the freight elevator and insist on riding the regular elevator.

Later that evening, I received an urgent message from the defendants to come to jail. That night I went down to find out the nature of their concern. Several of them confessed that they had failed to tell me that they had purchased the alcoholic beverages illegally. Their thought was that if this evidence were discovered by the prosecution and disclosed at trial, this illegal purchase would reflect badly on them.

Andy Ransom and I discussed the rape case, and he sat with me

113

at the counsel table during proceedings. I tried the case without a jury in part because I felt that the facts of this case might lead a jury to give a harsher verdict than a judge might.

At the trial, as its first witness the prosecution called the woman to whom the victim reported the rape. Early in the testimony, before the witness had an opportunity to describe the circumstances under which she first observed the victim, I successfully objected to a question addressed to this witness. Fortunately for my clients, the prosecutor took her off the stand and called someone else. While he undoubtedly intended to call her back to testify again, he did not put her back on the stand. Consequently, much damaging testimony was kept out of the record.

When the victim testified, I cross examined her and asked her, "Isn't it true that you tried to get back in the car after these events that you alleged?" She said that she had. With that, I concluded my cross examination. I wanted the judge to draw the inference that after the alleged crime, the victim felt comfortable enough with the assailants to resume riding in the car with them. That bolstered our position that all the parties consented to whatever happened.

The judge did not totally accept our argument. He found defendants guilty and sentenced them to seven years in the penitentiary. Given the nature of the offense, his sentence manifested some doubt of their guilt.

In 1942 Martin A. Martin, another lawyer named William Alexander, and I went up to Bath County, Warm Springs to try a rape case. Alexander and I were in high school together at Dunbar High, and all three of us attended Howard University. Alexander had recently passed the bar and opened an office in Martinsville, Virginia.

Unquestionably, this rape case was the nastiest one I ever had to defend. On top of one of the mountains in Bath County in the winter, the defendant had encountered two little girls. One was a girl eight or nine years old, and the other about twelve. The little girls were going across the mountain to visit one of their relatives. The defendant grabbed the older girl, stripped her and raped her on top of the mountain in the snow. The other little kid ran back home.

The Commonwealth's Attorney asked the father, "What did you do when your child came in and gave you this report?" The father replied, "I ratched up over the door and got my gun and went a-huntin'."

The defendant's trail led back from the crime site to the vicinity of the house where he lived. The snow made the defendant's tracks easy to follow. This was another case in which the authorities had all kinds of state troopers present at the trial.

The case was tried by Judge Earl Abbott who resided in Covington, Virginia and we had an interesting experience with him. He was a very good judge, and conducted the case fairly. We raised issues of Negro exclusion from the grand and petit juries in Bath County. The judge said, "Oh no." He knew there wasn't "any discrimination" in jury selection because he had done much of it himself.

I challenged him to come down and take the stand: "I think we can convince you there was discrimination," I argued. He said, "You got any authority for that?" I said, "Well, when I was in law school I remember reading something about a case in which a judge took the stand and testified." (I have forgotten the name of the case now.) I also told the judge that for a precedent to exist, someone must act. Judge Abbott accepted my challenge and took the stand. Martin and I both questioned him, and he ended up agreeing that his actions were not as fair and non discriminatory as he had originally concluded. What had happened was that he simply had not thought of Negroes as competent jurors.

For example, the judge asserted that he knew and was friends with many prominent local Negroes. In response to that assertion, I asked, "How many of those Negroes did you think about at the time you were selecting the grand jury?" He admitted that he had not thought of any. He dismissed the grand jury panel and the petit jury and empaneled new ones. The new grand jury and petit jury met the technical requirements of the law.

We had not anticipated that we would be up there so long. We were on a financial shoestring because our client's wife had not produced the balance of the fee as she had promised. The possibility of obtaining the remainder of the fees was slim. Going to Richmond and coming back was unappealing. As the lesser of two evils, we decided to hang around a couple of more days.

While we were waiting for the new grand jury to reindict our client, the head waiter of the Homestead Hotel sent us an invitation to come visit his home. We were happy to accept because we thought it would be a good opportunity to get a free meal. When we arrived, he was not there.

His wife invited us in. She served us homemade wine and then asked us, "Could I fix you some lunch?" Someone stupidly said, "Oh, don't go to any bother." He was trying to be super polite. The wife clammed up and said nothing further about lunch. We all regretted this unfortunate remark. We could have all used the meal. We were hungry and consuming the potent home brew had not helped our famished conditions.

As I mentioned, the wife of the defendant was supposed to come up with some money but she was short of cash and hadn't quite raised it; accordingly, that day we had no money. The next day however, she made a partial payment.

The grand jury met and reindicted our client. We went to trial again. It lasted only one day. The case went to the jury early that evening. Around ten or eleven that night, the jury returned with a verdict of guilty. They sentenced him to thirty five years in the penitentiary.

This courthouse had an unusual feature in that it had a porch. As the trial ended, and we started out, there were a number of white men on the porch standing around. I heard one of them say, "The state troopers are here so thick that a man can't even do a little shootin' if he wanted to."

As a matter of fact, earlier that day, the head waiter had invited us to a party that night after the trial. However, after all that had happened, we got in our car, and since I was driving, we hightailed it straight down the mountain. We didn't think about stopping nor did we stop until we got to Lexington. I suppose they had a good time at the party but we were not interested.

The next time I saw my client he was in the penitentiary in Richmond. He wanted to know when I was going to get him out. I said, "Man, you're lucky as all hell."

I went into the Army shortly after that. I don't know what happened to him subsequently.

In early 1947 when the Martinsville rape case came up, the people supporting the defendants elected to go with a radical organization rather than the NAACP. Considering the alleged facts and the locale, the lawyers representing the defendants made many glaring mistakes. Rather than attempting to create an atmosphere of calm, as a consequence of their pretrial statements, they riled up the community. The white community exhibited a greater hostility towards the defendants than they might have otherwise. In this inflammatory context, the trials occurred early. With passions running high, each defendant stood trial one after the other, on successive days. The all white juries convicted each defendant and sentenced each one to die in the electric chair.[24]

After the prosecution obtained convictions and death sentences for the defendants, the defendants' relatives belatedly sought NAACP assistance. Martin and Tucker appealed the cases to the Virginia Supreme Court of Appeals. The defendants' trial lawyers had created a trial record that was so poor, that Martin and Tucker had little to work with on the appeal. After the appeals were exhausted in the Virginia courts and the authorities had set dates for executing the defendants, Martin and Tucker worked feverishly attempting to get a further stay of the executions.

Trying to get executive clemency, Spot Robinson and I went to see Governor Battle. However, we got nowhere. Martin and Tucker even went to Washington late on the night of the execution to talk with Chief Justice Vinson. As Chief Justice of the United States, Vinson was also Supreme Court Justice for this circuit. They tried to get him to do something but he wouldn't. Despite their heroic efforts, all of the Martinsville seven defendants were electrocuted.

In the late 1940's or early 1950's Martin and I tried another interesting rape case over in Harrisonburg. A teacher at a local college, Madison College, the predecessor of James Madison University, took a group of girls on a field trip. A stranger came up with a knife and grabbed one of the girls and threatened to rape her. The teacher said, "Let the girls go and take me." He agreed to that and the girls left. He had sexual relations with the teacher and he released her.

We spent two or three days up there trying this case. As I recall, his defense was that the relations were consensual. He got twenty or twenty-five years. Considering the kind of sentences that Negroes generally received in rape cases, we regarded this as a victory. After full discussion with the defendant, he decided not to seek reversal.

117

Tucker and I had another rape case up in Burkeville. However, in fact, this was like some other cases that we tried; namely a case of consensual sexual behavior. The alleged victim could not explain her absence from home to her irate husband. She tried to cover up her absence by alleging that the defendant had raped her. The all white jury found the defendant guilty and gave him thirty five years. The Court of Appeals denied our petition for writ of error.

In the early 1950's, we also had an interesting case down in Lunenburg, Virginia. What had happened was two brothers had built houses from the same plans. One was at the top of the hill and the other at the bottom, slightly to the rear of the first house. The brother who built the house at the bottom of the hill had died. After his death, the Negro family who worked for the decedent's family moved into his house. This Negro family consisted of the defendant and his parents.

On the night of the alleged crime, the defendant had gone across the road to a neighboring farm house to see his girlfriend. They drank some moonshine together and the defendant had sexual relations with her. The defendant consumed enough alcohol to become drunk. Accordingly, perhaps feeling no pain, he came staggering back across the road towards his house. When he got to what he believed to be his house, he couldn't find his key. Since he had no key, he climbed in the window, and went down the hall to what he thought was his room. When he started climbing into the bed he found it was already occupied by someone who grabbed him by his private parts. This sobered him enough so he knew he was in the wrong house! He ran and jumped out the window, and hightailed it to his own house.

Our client's story was that he was not the person who attempted to rape the alleged victim. He said he had never entered her dwelling that night. When the alleged crime took place, he was at home. His mother and father supported his alibi.

The Commonwealth's Attorney put the alleged victim on the stand and asked her to describe what happened. The old lady said that she had gotten into bed and hadn't quite gone to sleep. Then she felt this "Negra" climbing in the bed with her. The Commonwealth's Attorney asked her how she knew it was a Negro. She said because "I felt his ole nappy hair". The prosecutor then said, "What did you do?" She said, "Well, I reached down and grabbed his old thing and tried to break it off."

118

As she stated this, our client was sitting at counsel's table between Tucker and me. He shivered and mumbled, "She sure did." Tucker and I heard our client's comment; however, we sat expressionless. As was stated earlier, when she grabbed him, that sobered him enough that he realized that he was in the wrong place.

The old lady was confused regarding when the event happened. When she reported the incident she claimed the alleged attempted rape took place an hour later than the incident actually occurred. The defendant's parents testified that the defendant was home at the time that the victim alleged that the incident occurred. The parents were telling the truth about where he was when the victim claimed the crime occurred.

In addition, his girlfriend testified that they had just had sexual relations. As I stated, everybody liked him. We were able to get the sheriff and the clerk of the court to testify to his good character previous to this incident. Although we had all these white folks testifying to his good character, everyone was still mystified regarding his presence in the victim's house.

However, the jury found him guilty and gave him a minimum sentence – five years. The people who had employed us – his sisters, nephews, and other relatives from New Jersey – wanted us to appeal the case. I explained to them that we had raised some legal questions involving jury discrimination and we probably could bring it back for a new trial. We said that we would have to speak to the defendant and discuss the full situation. The defendant didn't want to retry it. He was tickled to death to just get the minimum sentence.

After the trial ended, despite conflicting evidence, we knew that he had been there in the old lady's house. I asked him what the hell he was after, and why he had not told us. I wanted to know the truth. He finally admitted that he had not told us or the court the truth. He said he was just drunk and thought he was going to his own house. He had no intention of fooling with that old lady. If he had told the truth at first, I am convinced that we could have gotten him off on a plea of guilty to trespass, a misdemeanor, probably with a suspended sentence. As I mentioned, the defendant was highly regarded by his employers in the community and had very good relations with the public officials. He meant no harm.

In these cases all the women were white and the men were

119

Negroes. I think the worst sentence that any of our clients received was thirty-five years. I can't say we got every rape or sexual assault case; or that there weren't some white lawyers who represented black men. However, during that period, our firm had the majority of these cases.

In the 1950's I also had another interesting criminal law case involving a Negro defendant. However, in this particular case a white teenage male had attempted to rape the defendant, an extremely attractive fifteen or sixteen year old Negro female. She had been invited by the young white boy to take a ride in his car. He took her into the woods, whereupon he suggested that they have sexual relations. She refused to have sex with him.

At that point he told her that he knew that she had slept with a number of white men in the town and that she had to have relations with him as well. Again, she refused to do so. He continued to insist and tried to force her to have sex.

A fight ensued. At this time I am not positive which person possessed the knife. However, during the fight, the young white boy received a stab wound in the abdomen from which he died. She quickly reported the incident to the local authorities. They promptly arrested her and charged her with murder.

I was contacted by some of the Negroes down in Nottoway County and asked to represent her. When I went to see her I asked her to give me the full story of what had happened. During the course of the interview, I learned of the allegations regarding her alleged sexual activities with some prominent white men in the community. I inquired whether these allegations were accurate. She said that they were true. I returned to Richmond and called the Commonwealth Attorney and asked him when was the preliminary hearing. He said he did not plan to have a preliminary hearing. Instead he had asked for a special grand jury. That grand jury was going to indict her the following day.

I suggested to him that perhaps he would want to wait a little while before doing that and discuss the case further. He insisted that he would do no such thing, and accordingly the grand jury was empaneled. They met and indicted my client.

After they indicted my client I went to the Commonwealth attorney's office and told him what my client's defense would be. I said that my client had defended herself from being raped. To bolster her credibility concerning the way in which the homicide occurred, I stated that we planned to introduce evidence that the decedent had alleged that my client had had sexual relations with a number of prominent white men in the town: and had named them. I told the Commonwealth Attorney that I was going to call each one of my client's alleged white sexual partners to testify regarding the veracity of these statements. We were prepared to present evidence of these men's whereabouts on specific dates and at specific times and places.

A few days after I discussed my client's defense with the prosecution, I was called and asked if she were released, would my client leave the county. I presume that the prosecutor investigated my client's story and discovered it sufficiently convincing that he concluded that he would do well not to prosecute her. My client, her family and I had already discussed the matter and decided that upon her release it was in my client's best interest to leave Nottoway and go to New York City to live with an aunt. Accordingly, I had no problem agreeing to the Commonwealth Attorney's suggestion. I went to Nottoway, and the authorities released her into my custody. I brought her to Richmond, Virginia and put her on a bus going to New York City. We feared that had she stayed in Nottoway, someone may have subjected her to physical violence.

We permitted the Commonwealth Attorney to believe that we went along with his proposal. However, in my mind I never doubted that my client was not guilty. Under Virginia law she had the right to protect herself from any assault—sexual or otherwise.

Despite a favorable overall record in defending felony criminal cases, there is one case in which I feel that I definitely did not meet the appropriate standard of competency in representing the accused. Partially because of a lack of time for trial preparation and partially because I had suffered ptomaine poisoning and been ill in South Hill for several days, I was inadequately prepared to defend the accused, Joseph R. Mickens, a fifteen or sixteen year old Negro boy who was alleged to have raped a white woman. Even though I was visibly ill at the time of trial, the judge, Floridus S. Crosby, pressured me into going to trial, and while I should not have allowed that to happen, it did. Judge Crosby convicted Mickens and sentenced him to death.

Fortunately, George Little, a lawyer who still practices in Richmond came to our rescue and persuaded Governor Price to commute the sentence. Later Little obtained Mickens' parole from incarceration.

Looking back on the situation, I should have insisted on not going to trial because the defendant's life was on the line and I was sick. Even if I were held to be in contempt and went to jail, at least on that day, Mickens would not have been convicted. Of course, later he might still have been convicted, sentenced and electrocuted . . .

Like many lawyers I have been asked the question, "How can you represent a client whom you know is guilty of a crime?" Basically, my response has been that the law presumes that each person is innocent until proven guilty beyond a reasonable doubt. Regardless of what the person may have done, he is entitled to that presumption and degree of proof. Furthermore, I defended many individuals because I wanted to prevent the state from killing them. While I did not uphold their criminal activity, I do not think that they should be killed, even in horrible situations like the Bath County case, the worst rape case I ever defended. The electric chair is not the answer.

As an advocate, it was, and still is, my responsibility to use all lawful means to provide my client with full protection.

Alston and Teacher Salaries

In the following pages I resume discussing another part of my life experiences upon returning to Richmond in 1939. That involves the struggle for equality in education.

When I returned to Richmond, I discovered that during the preceding year, Tom Hewin, Jr. and Byron Hopkins, Jr. had filed a suit in Norfolk in the state court challenging the gross inequality of pay between black and white teachers. The defendants had maneuvered to delay the proceedings. Finally, the case came up for a hearing on June 7 in the Norfolk Circuit Court. The court sustained the School Board's motion to dismiss, holding in effect, that the teachers waived their constitutional rights when they signed the contract.

Well, in the meantime, Aline Black, who was the plaintiff, had not been offered a contract for the upcoming year. So when the court dismissed her suit, she could not pursue her case any further because she was no longer employed as a teacher in the Norfolk school system. Her contract was not renewed despite her having had an eleven year record as an excellent school teacher.

At that time, the prevailing employment practice for teaching

122

personnel in Virginia was that the local school boards employed educators on annual contracts. Legally, this made it impossible for the educators to develop tenure. To terminate the teacher's employment, the superintendent simply refrained from recommending her reappointment. Failure to reappoint put the teacher out of a job.

In addition, many outlying counties placed numerous other restrictions on school teachers. For example, some counties did not allow teachers to continue employment after they married. Others did not let married couples teach in the same system. Moreover, some school systems required Negro teachers to live in and pay rent for dormitories provided by local school officials or influential citizens in the local community.

Furthermore, the teachers' social lives received close scrutiny. Many educators, especially the women, had to be very discreet about dating. In short, the local, typically male dominated school systems tried to maintain maximum control over the activities of their employees most of whom were women.

As I mentioned earlier, when I returned to Virginia in 1939, one of the first things that I did was to resume my work with the NAACP and the Virginia Teachers' Association. I became counsel to the Joint Committee and immediately devoted my time and effort to the teacher salary problem.

In Virginia, the cities and counties had established separate salary scales for Negro and white teachers. To use a concrete situation, in Richmond in 1940 when I filed suit, the beginning salary for Negro teachers ranged from three hundred and fifty to three hundred and ninety nine dollars ($399.00) per year and provided for increases to a maximum salary of nine hundred and ninety six dollars ($996.00).

I remember examining the Mathews County teacher salary program and discovering that Mathews County paid Negro teachers forty four dollars ($44.00) per month for nine months.

In most cases, the school boards only entered nine month contracts with their teachers. A few teachers had ten month contracts.

Accordingly, during the summer months many teachers had to supplement their income by engaging in other employment activities. As I have noted, when I was in high school and college, in some of the summer resorts where I worked, teachers and principals also worked as waiters, waitresses, cooks, bellhops, taxi drivers, and railroad personnel. When I resumed law practice in 1939, some of these well trained individuals were still persevering in diverse seasonal employment.

For white teachers, the salary range began where the salary range for black teachers left off. That is, for white teachers, the salaries ranged from one thousand dollars per year to eighteen hundred dollars per year.

I was running all over the state developing support for our program and bringing the teacher salary disparity to the forefront. We raised equal protection questions. The school authorities' defense was that it was a contract arrangement, that the black teachers had waived their rights when they signed the contract, and that consequently the teachers were bound by the terms of the contract.

In the wake of the legal setback in the <u>Black</u> case, we immediately set out to find another appropriate plaintiff for a test case. The teachers' association produced another plaintiff named Melvin O. Alston from the local Norfolk high school.

In the meantime, I studied the situation and read Borchard's text entitled <u>Declaratory Judgments.</u> Thurgood Marshall and I discussed our new case and its prospects for success in the courts. I suggested that we initiate a class action in federal court and sue on behalf of the class as well as the individual teacher. Thurgood readily agreed. We both thought that we would benefit from his experience in filing a similar successful suit in Maryland.[25]

In anticipation of filing the complaint, I had applied for admission to practice in the United States District Court for the Eastern District of Virginia. As I recall, my application had to lie in the Clerk's office for ten days before I could be admitted. I had planned to file the complaint on a Thursday; despite the fact it would be another five days before I could become a member of the Federal Bar in the Eastern District of Virginia. Part of the reason for filing the complaint on Thursday was we wanted to get our work well publicized in the Norfolk area, and the local Negro newspaper, The Norfolk Journal and Guide, came out on Friday.

Accordingly, I went down to Norfolk on a Thursday in August, 1939. I presented the complaint to the Clerk of the Court and requested that he file it. Since I had not been admitted to the bar of the Eastern

District court, I told the Clerk that Mr. Thomas Hewin, Sr., had also signed the complaint as local counsel. I said to the Clerk that Mr. Hewin was the only one of the signatories currently enrolled in the Eastern District and that I would be admitted the following Tuesday. I am not sure whether the younger Hewin had signed it or not.

Following the custom that we had developed at that time, the complaint also named as co-counsel Thurgood Marshall of New York, Andy Ransom and William Hastie from Washington, D.C. and Robert Ming of Chicago.

After this conversation, the Clerk went back into his office and stayed a long time. He finally returned and said that he couldn't find Mr. Hewin's name on the roll. This could have been due to several things. One was that this was 1939, about forty years after Mr. Hewin was admitted to practice, and I do not know whether Mr. Hewin had not signed the roll or whether the Clerk's Office had misplaced it.

But anyway, I said to the Clerk, "Well that doesn't matter. William Hastie is a former federal judge in the Virgin Islands and accordingly is a member of all federal bars." I stressed this point so seriously about Hastie, that the Clerk was uncertain what to do. Finally, he said, "I'm not sure about this but I tell you what I am going to do. I'm going to let you file the papers with the understanding that on Tuesday you will be admitted in Richmond."

We did it that way. I had been vehement about Bill Hastie's name being on the document as sufficient grounds to allow our filing. However, I often wondered later whether I was right or not. But at that time it just sounded reasonable to me. In the end, we filed the <u>Alston</u> case as a class action on behalf of Alston as a member of the Norfolk Teachers' Association. We alleged violation of the Civil Rights Acts and the Equal Protection clause of the Fourteenth Amendment.

On the following Tuesday, I appeared in the federal district court in Richmond. In the interim I had talked to James D. Carter, Esq., the general counsel and president of the Southern Aid Society of Virginia. Mr. Carter stated that he was a member of the bar of the federal district court for the eastern district of Virginia and promised to move my admission. Incidentally, for eight years before we moved to our present offices, I had the office Mr. Carter had used in the Southern Aid Building at Third and Clay Streets. The Southern Aid Society started out as a fraternal society and was the oldest African American insurance company in the United States.   In the 1980s, Atlanta Life Insurance took over the Southern Aid Society.

Coming back to my admission to the district court bar, the court was scheduled to convene at 10:00 a.m. I arrived early and when 9:30 a.m. had come and gone, and Mr. Carter had not shown up, I started to get nervous. I finally saw a man walking up and down the hall and I asked him if he was a member of the federal bar. He said that he was and he asked me, "What is your problem?" So I told him that Mr. Carter had promised to move my admission but he had not arrived. The man with whom I spoke was Thomas Williams, Sr., a prominent member of the Richmond bar. Mr. Williams said that he would be happy to move my admission. We immediately went to the clerk's office, and he examined my papers. In due course, he requested that the court admit me to practice before it.

In that regard, a funny thing occurred recently in court here in Richmond. I was over in Southside traffic court and the son of Thomas Williams, Sr. was sitting as traffic court judge there. In 1939 when his father moved my admission, the son was a younger lawyer practicing with his father. The son now is a retired traffic court judge. I told the son about the situation and we laughed about the incident.

Returning to the Norfolk teachers' salary case, after we filed suit, the defendants managed to get some postponements. We finally got to a hearing down in Norfolk on Abraham Lincoln's birthday in 1940. Our team of lawyers present at that time were William Hastie, Andy Ransom, Thurgood Marshall and me. We had agreed that Thurgood would introduce the case. Because I was the local lawyer, we also agreed that I would argue the main part of the motion. This was to be my initial appearance before a federal court.

But Judge Luther P. Way, the federal district judge, gave Thurgood such a hard time that Bill Hastie asked me if I minded if he took over. I agreed. However, I might as well have argued myself. Judge Way gave Bill Hastie as hard a time as he had given Thurgood or could have given me. At the conclusion of Bill Hastie's argument, Judge Way immediately ruled against us on the same basis as the state court. Judge Way asserted that upon signing the contract, the black teachers waived their constitutional rights.

We left the courtroom quite perturbed and greatly dejected. However, the day was partially saved as we heard on the automobile's

126

radio that the Supreme Court had reversed the lower court's judgement in <u>Chambers v. Florida</u>,[26] a case that Andy Ransom had argued before the Supreme Court. Chambers and several other defendants had been brutally tortured into giving confessions to crimes that they did not commit. They were convicted, and sentenced to die in the electric chair. After the rough treatment that we had received in Judge Way's court, Ransom's winning the <u>Chambers</u> case was some consolation.

One of the reasons for our great dejection was that the next term for the Fourth Circuit Court of Appeals was in April. That short time frame made it impossible for us to get our appeal filed, our briefs prepared, and our record printed so that we could be heard at the April term. After April the next term of court would be June. We were stuck. It seemed that the same thing was happening to Alston that had happened to Aline Black.

Nevertheless, we went forward with the preparation of our appeal. Later, we agreed to meet one Sunday evening at the Howard Law School in a last minute desperate effort to seek a way to accelerate our hearing. This Sunday happened to be the beginning of the last week of the court's April term.

Present at our Sunday conference in addition to me were Bill Hastie, Andy Ransom, Thurgood Marshall, Howard Jenkins and Bob Johnson. Bill Hastie was Howard's Law School dean at that time. Jenkins was a member of the law faculty who occasionally worked with us. President Eisenhower later appointed Jenkins as a member of the National Labor Relations Board. Bob Johnson was also a member of the faculty and later succeeded Hastie as law school dean. When the former British colony of Nigeria obtained independence, Johnson helped set up Nigeria's educational system. Later, when Kenya obtained independence, Thurgood Marshall drafted Kenya's constitution and worked assiduously to ensure that the legal system would be fair to the native Africans and the European settlers.

Ever since Judge Way's decision, we had been racking our individual minds regarding the solution to our dilemma. Now we were at the final hour. We had discussed the case from a variety of possible angles, considering every conceivable procedure. We were unable to come up with any workable solution.

Finally, about 10:00 p.m. I said, "Well, suppose I go back to Richmond and ask the court to hold a special session and hear our case before the school term ends?" I never will forget, Bill Hastie said, "Are you willing to do it?" I said, "Yeah, I'll do it." He said, "That settles it!"

So I drove back to Richmond. Little did I realize the ramifications of what I had just agreed to do.

In those days I was practically living in my office. I typed up the motion and notice, and early Monday morning, put it in the mail. After mailing the documents, I also called the Norfolk City Attorney and told a member of his staff that I had put the notice in the mail and that the matter would come up on the following Thursday. The last day of the term was Friday. I did not want to wait until the last day of the term.

On Thursday, I appeared. The court was where it is now in the old Post Office Building which is on East Main Street down the hill across Bank Street from the present Capitol grounds.

There was only one court room for the federal district court during those days. It was located on the third floor. Likewise, as I recall, there was one court room for the Fourth Circuit which was located on the fourth floor. However, since the early 1940's, the court's facilities have expanded and taken over what was then known as the Postal Annex Building as well as the upper floors of the old main post office.

Immediately before my case, the court called a motion presented by a lawyer named Leon Bazile. Bazile had been a former assistant attorney general and was one of the most prominent lawyers in the state at that time. Bazile was quite a powerful political figure in the state legislature. He later became a circuit court judge and made several bizarre decisions. For example, he tried the Loving[27] case challenging Virginia's anti-miscegenation statutes. He found the couple guilty of violating the statute and suspended imposition of sentence on condition that they leave Virginia and not return as husband and wife for twenty-five years. His order effectively banned them. Anyway, that's another story.

The Clerk of Court called Bazile's motion. Bazile was asking the court to reinstate a case that had been dismissed because he had failed to timely apply for an extension to file a responsive pleading. At that time, there were only three judges in the Fourth Circuit. Chief Judge John Parker was a man over six feet tall, heavy set with a booming voice. Judge Dobie was a former dean of the University of Virginia Law School who also wrote a treatise on evidence widely used in Virginia.

128

On the bench he was quite eccentric and often quoted statements in Greek. Judge Soper was from Maryland. Soper was a short, white-haired man, and an excellent judge.

The Fourth Circuit held hearings in different jurisdictions. They had a term in Baltimore, a term in Charlotte, and a term in Asheville, North Carolina. On one occasion we even met in Charlottesville, Virginia. However, the court heard the majority of its cases in Richmond.

When the court was not in session and you had a motion or other matter that you wanted to present to a judge, you often had to go to the home site of the judge whom you wanted to see. Parker's home was Charlotte, North Carolina; Judge Dobie was headquartered in Charlottesville; and Judge Soper had chambers in Baltimore. Otherwise, you simply had to wait for a term of court and bring your motion when and where the court convened.

An interesting piece of history is in 1930 the NAACP was one of the objectors to Chief Judge Parker when he was nominated to be an Associate Justice of the U.S. Supreme Court. Principally because of opposition from organized labor and the NAACP and despite President Herbert Hoover's strong support of Parker, Judge Parker's nomination was rejected.[28]

Coming back to the court scene, Bazile was standing before the court presenting his petition. Judge Parker looked out the window at the Capitol which was across the street and up the hill. Parker said, "Mr. Bazile, you were really up there in the Legislature! And you couldn't find time to come down here and file papers with the clerk requesting an extension of time?" Then he barked, "Your petition is denied!"

That was the first time I really felt apprehensive. I fully realized the enormity of my asking the court for a special term. Additional stress factors were that I had only been admitted to practice in the Fourth Circuit for a few months and I had never appeared before the court. In fact, this was my first case in which I appeared in any appellate court.

The clerk then called my case, Alston v. the School Board of Norfolk. Despite Mr. Bazile's experience with the bench that day, generally the court was very cordial. I got right to the point and started with my motion for a special term. Parker barked out, "Wait a minute. You mean to say that you want the United States government to go to all the expense, bring this entire entourage back, just to hear your case? What's so special about your case?"

Well, that gave me an opportunity: and I seized it! I immediately explained to the court what had happened with Aline Black's case, that we had filed our complaint in August, that the defendants had finagled with us, and delayed the hearing. When the district court ruled against us, we couldn't possibly get ready for this term.

The entire court got interested then. Soper seemed especially interested. While I do not remember his specific words, in effect he finally said, "suppose we give you an injunction?" I immediately agreed. Anything they did would have been all right with me provided they kept our case alive.

The Norfolk City Attorney who until this point had continued to sit out in the audience got nervous, jumped up, and came running up to the bar. He said it would not be necessary to enter an injunction. The court asked him if what I had said was true. He had to admit that it was. So he assured them that nothing was going to happen to Alston. The court then told me if anything adverse happened to my client to come back and they would do something about it. So as a consequence, no teaching personnel in the school system in the city of Norfolk got a contract until after our case was heard and decided in late August of 1940.

In the June term, in 1940, we had the hearing in Asheville, North Carolina. An amusing thing happened during the hearing. Instead of arguing his position, the City Attorney was reading his brief word for word. Judge Soper politely said, "We have read your brief, counselor, go on and present your argument." But the City Attorney continued to read. Soper then repeated, "Counselor, we have read your brief." The attorney kept on reading. Soper swung his swivel chair around so that his back was facing the attorney and looked out the window. That was the only time I have ever seen anything like that happen in the Fourth Circuit. As I mentioned previously, regardless of whether they ruled with or against you, it was a most cordial and genteel court.

After we got the reversal from the Fourth Circuit, the School Board applied to the United States Supreme Court for a writ of certiorari. After the Court's denial of certiorari, the City Attorney and School Board attempted to set up a meeting with the teachers one afternoon without notifying us. One of the teachers called Andy Ransom in Washington, D.C. Andy called me and immediately drove down to Richmond and met me. At this point, I became the driver on the trip to Norfolk. In those days, the stretch of the highway between, Suffolk and Norfolk was about the widest expanse of highway in that section of the state. As I remember the road had only three lanes.

In any event, I was driving Andy's car and I was doing better than ninety-five miles per hour—just cruising along! I saw a car fast approaching in my rear view mirror. I said to Andy, "Either that is a state trooper or that's some damn fool who thinks he's on a race track." Andy said, "That's the state police. I saw them when we passed." I said, "Well, why didn't you say something?" He replied, "I thought you looked at them and they looked at you and everything was all right . . ."

In the meantime, I belatedly started to slow down. The trooper put on his siren; I pulled over and the trooper got out of his car. He walked over to our car and said, "You know you were exceeding seventy-five miles per hour?" He asked to see my driver's license, and I showed it to him. Then he said, "We are going to carry you back to Suffolk." I said, "Why?" He said, "Because you have District of Columbia tags." I said, "The reason I was driving so fast was I am trying to get to Norfolk by five o'clock for a meeting with the City Attorney." We were trying to get there before the school officials could hold this meeting with our clients in our absence!

We argued and argued. He was adamant; so was I. He wanted to carry me back to Suffolk before the judge. I said, "Hell no, just give me a ticket. I have a Virginia driver's permit." There were two state troopers in their car. Finally, the other one said, "Go ahead and give him a ticket." So he gave me a ticket for exceeding seventy-five miles per hour.

By the time they caught up with me, we had reached the town limits of South Norfolk. But then they sat on my tail and I had to drive within the twenty-five mile per hour speed limit the rest of the way. It seemed like eternity. I guess they wanted to make sure I was going where I had said.

Fortunately, we finally got to the meeting place just as the meeting was starting. We walked in and the superintendent tried to say that the meeting was only with the teachers. I pointed out that their attorney was there and we had a right to be here, too. I stated that the matter was still being litigated. So, that broke up the meeting. Another set of motions was filed.

131

When the motions came up for a hearing, the school officials tried to make it appear that we were obstructing a peaceful settlement of the case. When my time came to speak Judge Way said, "I want to ask you one question, and I want an answer, yes or no." Well, it wasn't a yes or no situation. I was young then and the fact that he demanded a yes or no answer angered me. I started and later someone in the court told me I talked for twenty minutes. I think there was some hyperbole in his remark, but I was going over all the things that we had been subjected to.

Anyway, Judge Way sat there and listened to me. After I concluded, Judge Way said, "You all go on out and settle this thing." We finally resolved the matter by consent decree allowing the Norfolk defendants to equalize the pay within three years.

In the <u>Alston</u> case, we were confident that ultimately we were going to prevail. We thought we were going to win in the district court but we did not. After the hearing before the Fourth Circuit in Asheville, we thought the court would rule for us. It did.

However, one can't tell how the court will rule from the questions asked. You couldn't tell anymore then than you can tell now. With some judges you can pretty well tell how they will rule, but with the majority of judges you can't.

After we won the <u>Alston</u> decision, we did not celebrate. It was too early in the fight. Besides, the local school boards across the state did not "cave in." As I mentioned previously, after the Fourth Circuit's ruling, the Norfolk School Board applied for certiorari to the U.S. Supreme Court. While awaiting the Supreme Court's decision on whether to hear the case, I continued seeking negotiations with school superintendents. I was unsuccessful in reaching any settlements. Later, the Supreme Court denied certiorari in <u>Alston</u>. However, even after the court refused to review <u>Alston</u>, my negotiations remained unproductive.

The next teacher salary case that came up for trial was the <u>Roles</u> case in Newport News. That case also came before Judge Way.[29] The Newport News city attorneys filed motions to dismiss and started presenting the same arguments as the Norfolk defendants made. They argued that the teachers had waived their rights.

Judge Way said, "Wait a minute. I listened to that same malarkey before and they carried me up to the Court of Appeals: and I got spanked.

132

And I'm not going to be spanked anymore. So you present something else. We are going to trial on this case, right now!" We went to trial and they had no real defense, except "make believe" stuff.

Anyway, Judge Way indicated that the court intended to rule in favor of plaintiffs, and we worked out a consent decree on the same terms as were worked out in the Norfolk case. From that point forward, Judge Way and I became good friends. For some reason, Judge Barksdale actually entered the decree. Barksdale was a federal district court judge in the Western District of Virginia, whose home base was Lynchburg.

In the 1940's we were pressing school boards around the state to negotiate. For example, in the wake of the <u>Alston</u> decision, we finally settled the teacher salary case in Richmond without a trial.

On the other hand, if local school authorities refused a negotiated solution, as soon as we could locate teacher/plaintiffs who indicated a willingness to vindicate their constitutional rights, we filed suit. For instance we had teacher salary suits in numerous jurisdictions including Newport News, Sussex County, Chesterfield and Richmond.

Flowing from the teacher salary cases, many side issues evolved. For example, when we filed suit in Newport News they fired the principal of the elementary school and the principal of the high school. Similarly, in the Sussex case, the school board fired the teacher before we got to trial. She went to Washington, D.C. and got a better job in the federal government. In an attempt to discourage us and slow us down, several teachers were fired. However, I do not know a single one who did not manage to do better financially.

We also filed suit in Norfolk County. The local school officials fired the elementary school principals. The school officials made the principal of the white school the principal of the Negro schools. They set up a system of head teachers. Two of the young Negro men who were fired, James "Slim" Overton and Hugo Madison, decided to go to law school. As I recall, Slim became a substitute judge in Portsmouth, and Madison became a lawyer and successful businessman as well. As these facts indicate, there was never a quiet moment.

I also represented a man who refused to send his daughter to school in Fauquier County because she had to walk down Route 29. My client said it was too dangerous to have his child walking on the highway. There was no bus transportation for the black students, but they had

133

public transportation for the whites. This parent was arrested and convicted of violating the truancy law. He was tried in the police court and fined twenty-five dollars.

The father came down to Richmond and asked if I could do something about it.

I took the case, and we appealed to the circuit court. Adding insult to injury, in the circuit court, the judge found him guilty and fined him fifty dollars.

We appealed to the Virginia Court of Appeals. There we finally prevailed. The court reversed the circuit court's judgment; however, for a time, I did not hear anything about our victory. By then, I had been inducted into the Army.

Another interesting teacher salary controversy occurred down in Mecklenburg County, Virginia. My secretary, who was exceptionally efficient, reached me by telephone at 3:00 a.m. Monday morning in Lynchburg. It so happened that I was enjoying a rare poker game when she informed me that a teacher in Mecklenburg, Virginia had called concerning a meeting that was being held later that morning. Fortunately, a train was coming through in about half an hour. While I had been doing quite well at the game, you might say I received a higher "call." I left, caught the train and returned to Richmond. Because I had no car at the time, I took a taxicab to Clarksville, Virginia where they were having the meeting.

I had previously filed a petition with the school board. In response to the petition, the Mecklenburg school superintendent had called a morning meeting of the Negro school teachers and the school principal.

I arrived before the superintendent, and when he joined the gathering, he saw me and said that he had called a meeting of his Negro teachers. According to him, no one else would be allowed to be present. I rose and stated that I recognized the right of the Superintendent to have a meeting of his teachers. However, I indicated that I would like to make a few remarks to the teachers about the teacher salary situation before I left. I talked about some things they should consider.

After his initial attempt to eliminate me from participating in the meeting, following my comments, the school superintendent decided to make me the "moderator" of the meeting. In my role as moderator, I recognized potential speakers in the room whom I knew and whom I expected to make strong appeals for an equalization of teacher salary.

One older teacher had had her hand up for a long time. Because I thought she would likely present an Uncle Tom type of position, I avoided calling upon her as long as I could. Finally, I called on her. She started off by saying that she had been a supervisor for many years and had been a teacher in the schools for over thirty years. She had looked forward to the day when she would have the same salary as white teachers. She concluded by saying, "I want my salary equalized right now!" I was pleasantly surprised, indeed, shocked, and regretted that I had not called on her earlier. She gave a very eloquent presentation.

An interesting side note is that after I returned from military service in World War II, the superintendent of the Mecklenburg schools telephoned me to come out and see their new high school facility. The county authorities had engaged in a building program to make the black schools somewhat better, while keeping them separate from the white ones.

We entered the new high school. I noticed that no adequate science facilities existed. The gymnasium and the auditorium were in the same room. The library also served a combination role with some other educational activity. In fact, the more I saw, the less impressed I became.

Finally, we came to one of the superintendent's most prized accomplishments: Mecklenburg County now had brick outhouses for the Negro students. The more he showed me the more I fumed. The superintendent pointed out that outhouses were what the Negro children were used to. I retorted that we were trying to get people to expect and become accustomed to better conditions than the ones they were used to. Needless to say, he was disappointed with my reaction to this so-called progress. I was equally disappointed with his perception of what constituted progress.

In the Chesterfield teacher salary case, as was our frequent custom, I called the school superintendent as an adverse witness. In many cases, the state superintendent of education's annual report set forth most of the facts demonstrating that the separate but equal law had been violated. In this case, after having had the local school superintendent upon the stand all day, the judge asked me late in the afternoon how much longer did I think that my cross examination would last. I said, "I do not know. I imagine another four or five hours."

The Chesterfield school superintendent said glumly, "Four or five hours." We won that case.[30]

We also had an equalization of facilities case in King George County. That was interesting. I had an old school superintendent on the stand and I asked him, "You know, I noticed that you call the secondary school facility for the white children a "high school" and for the Negro children you call the facility a "training school." Why this difference in name?" The superintendent of schools said, "Well, high school is secondary education. With the Negroes we try to train them in something they could get a job doing." For the King George superintendent, it was as simple as that: he wasn't thinking about sending Negroes to college.

In many Virginia localities, white students were being taught electronics, chemistry and physics. In none of the Negro schools was any advanced technology taught. In the Negro schools, students were taught courses like home economics, beauty culture, carpentry and some brick laying.

<u>Other Civil Rights Related Activities</u>
<u>Transportation Matters</u>

Aside from the criminal litigation and teacher salary cases, we worked on a diverse variety of other legal problems. For example, one day in 1936 or 1937, I was down in Charlie Houston's D.C. office working on transportation matters. Things were especially bad then — politically, economically and otherwise. Charlie suggested that I go over to the House of Representatives Office Building and talk to Congressman Arthur W. Mitchell, a Negro whose district was in Chicago. Accordingly, I called Mitchell's office and made an appointment. In 1934, Mitchell defeated Oscar DePriest who had been the first black congressman since Reconstruction. DePriest was also the first black elected to the Congress from a northern state.

Mitchell was the first Negro elected to Congress from the Democratic Party. Before he went to Chicago to run against DePriest, Mitchell practiced law in Washington. I don't know whether he was ever admitted to the Virginia bar. In 1942, Mitchell himself was followed by Congressman William Dawson. That too is a story to be told presently.

136

However, returning to my meeting with Mitchell, one important reason for talking with him was that he had filed an action alleging discriminatory treatment similar to the case on which we were working. Mitchell was going from Chicago down to Hot Springs, Arkansas. As the train left Memphis, Tennessee, the conductor ordered Mitchell to move to the Jim Crow car. Mitchell initially refused and stated that he was a member of Congress. The conductor replied that it did not "make a damn bit of difference who [Mitchell] was that as long as [he] was a nigger [he] could not ride in that car."[31] Mitchell reluctantly moved to the Jim Crow car rather than risking being jailed and perhaps lynched. Understandably, to avoid the prevailing Jim Crow practices, some Negroes made reservations on Pullman cars.

I went to Mitchell's office in the middle of the afternoon. He was out when I got there. His secretary was friendly, and when Mitchell returned I told him who I was and that I had called and made an appointment. He wanted to know what I wanted with him. I told him we were doing private civil actions against the Railroad Commission. Like him, we were dealing with discrimination in transportation matters.

Boy, he went into a tirade. He exclaimed that he was damn tired of Negro lawyers riding on his coattails.

We never got to his private office. All of this "venting" occurred in his outer office where his secretary worked. I told him I was sorry that I had disturbed him and got the hell out of there. Charlie was furious when I told him about it. Charlie thought as I did that Mitchell ought to have been tickled to death that someone else was interested in litigation similar to his own. Furthermore, we were both convinced that Mitchell had missed a golden opportunity to help mentor a young lawyer.

Anyway, I never saw him again until years later. It was in Richmond in the early 1940s. Before 9:00 a.m. one Saturday morning (we worked Saturdays, too!), this man came into my office unannounced and without an appointment.

Without saying "Hello" or "May I take up your time?", Mitchell started telling me what his plans were. He said that he had bought a farm down in Dinwiddie County, Virginia, and planned to run for Congress in the same district that John Mercer Langston had represented in the late 1880's. An interesting historical fact is that Langston, a Negro, after having been elected confronted a challenge from the Democratic party which contested his election. He had to fight for his

137

seat for most of his two year term. In fact, he served less than six months.[32] In the next congressional campaign, through legal and illegal means, the Democrats succeeded in blocking blacks from voting. Consequently, Langston wasn't re-elected.

Coming back to the surprise visit of former Congressman Mitchell, I didn't say anything to him about our earlier meeting. Even though I was greatly tempted, I did not tell Mitchell what a skunk I thought he was.   Mitchell never developed sufficient support to initiate a congressional campaign. I doubt that Mitchell would have done anything constructive had he been elected.

Fortunately, we presently have a progressive congressman, Norman Sisisky, representing the Fourth District. In addition, we also have a brilliant, dynamic and erudite Negro congressman, Bobby Scott, in the Third district.

Regarding segregation in public transportation, after 1940 whenever I took public transportation I made it a practice not to ride Jim Crow. Whether I was riding buses or on railroads I always sat in areas reserved for white people. I simply hoped that I would be arrested so that I would have an opportunity to make a test case and challenge the segregation laws.

In the early 1940's, I also had an interesting experience regarding segregation in public transportation. I was representing a man named Mr. Boyd who was a relative of my step-uncle's wife. The wife had called me and told me that the local authorities were levying on Boyd's farm, and were about to take it. She asked me to intercede on Boyd's behalf.

By way of background on this case, Mr. Boyd was a school bus driver. A student had gotten off the bus and Mr. Boyd accidentally struck and killed her with the bus. (I was never certain whether in fact Mr. Boyd had been negligent.) To compensate the parents, the court had entered judgment against Boyd in the amount of three thousand dollars. To collect on the judgment, the creditor had levied both against Boyd's farm and his equipment. By the time the judgment came to my attention, the period for further judicial review or appeal had expired. I managed, however, to get the Farmers Home Administration to make him a loan so that he could pay off the levy and save his farm.

One night as I was coming home from Mr. Boyd's farm, at about

10:00 p.m., I got on a bus. The bus stop was known as Boyd's Tavern, and was located on Route 250 about twenty five miles south of Charlottesville, Virginia. Aside from the bus driver, I was the only one on the bus.

I sat about half way back in the bus on a seat next to the emergency exit door. These aisle seats had more leg room, and as a fairly tall individual, such seats were my favorite place to sit. We hadn't been riding too long when the bus driver looked up in the mirror and called out, "Get on the back seat." I didn't say anything in response to his request.

A few minutes later he said again, "I said, you'll have to get on the back seat." At that time I responded, "Get on the back seat for what?" The driver responded to the effect that I should get on the back seat because he "said so."

The bus driver then said, "Either you get on the back seat or I'll come back there and put you on the back seat."

I replied, "I'll be here." The bus driver didn't say anything for awhile and then he spoke again. He said, "If you don't get on the back seat I'm going to stop and call the sheriff." I replied, "You can do anything you please." I was kind of hoping that he would stop and get a sheriff. I was the only one on the bus and he wanted to have me arrested for refusing to sit on the back seat. This seemed an ideal case because it expressed the ridiculous nature of the segregation laws.

However, this was not to be. The driver kept on driving and no one else got on the bus. Accordingly, when we got to Richmond, he got off the bus and stood at the door. I got off the bus and as I got off he glared at me and I in turn glared at him.

Another interesting experience riding public transportation occurred in 1943, after I became a member of the military. I was stationed in Fort Claiborne in Louisiana and I had furlough coming up. I was eagerly anticipating the trip to Washington to visit, Bernie, my wife. In addition, we were nearly done with our basic training, and around the camp it was understood that we would be shipping out soon. Accordingly, I made arrangements through the transportation section of the camp to make reservations on "The Southerner" (an all Pullman through train) from New Orleans to Washington, D.C. To make my connections, I had to take a train from Alexandria, Louisiana to New

139

Orleans.

However, the person who made my reservations booked me on a train that got to New Orleans an hour <u>after</u> The Southerner had departed for Washington. I was disappointed and angry. I had a choice of waiting until the next morning or taking a regular train with Jim Crow coaches. Rather than lose that much time waiting at the station, I took a regular day coach train.

Had I been in Virginia or in another area of the South where I knew people, I would have followed my usual custom. I would have sat in the white part of the train to get arrested so that I might challenge the segregation laws. However, here I was in the Deep South in a soldier's uniform. The uniform gave me less protection than I would have had if I had been a civilian. Many whites resented and feared Negro soldiers. Often such white folks perceived Negroes as threats because we had guns and knew how to use them. Historically, many segregationists had opposed Negroes serving in the military in combat situations. They were not comfortable with Negroes having any semblance of authority or power. Accordingly, such individuals would go out of their way to make life for Negro servicemen miserable. Similar circumstances had prevailed in World War I in which Negroes confronted the irony of risking life and limb for a country that treated one like at best a second class citizen, and at worst, like an enemy. [33]

To make matters more complicated for me, this was my first trip back to Washington to see Bernie since June. I also recognized that if I were arrested, it was impossible to predict how long I might be tied up with officials down in Louisiana. I also knew that we were going to be shipping out soon. Taking all these matters into account, I decided that as much as I detested it, I would ride in the Jim Crow cars.

By the time the train reached Atlanta, the dining car had made the third call for dinner. I had been sitting on the train all day with nothing to eat. I got up, went into the dining car, and sat in the middle of the car waiting to be served. The steward told me that I could not sit there. In fact, he told me that I would have to get out and wait. I protested. I informed the steward that the crew had issued the third call for dining service, and I was entitled to come in and eat if I wanted to. However, the steward insisted that I leave. Of course, that provoked a very heated argument. He was threatening to have the train stopped and me arrested.

The only other passengers in the car were a white couple already sitting at one end of the dining car. They had not finished eating their meal. The steward thought that I could not sit and eat in the dining car until they had finished. At that point, the male member of the couple said that, "If our presence is keeping this soldier from eating, we will leave." By that time, I frankly did not care if the steward had the train stopped or not. I was very angry and had no intention of voluntarily leaving the dining car.

Just then a group of Negro officers from the Tuskeegee Air Corps came into the car. One of them was Dr. Brown Singleton who was from Richmond. He recognized me and spoke. We greeted each other and the three officers sat down.

The steward and I continued to argue. The officers recognized what was happening, and invited me to come and sit down and eat with them. When the steward recognized that the officers knew me, he said that I should go and eat with them. I told the steward that it was against military regulations for officers and enlisted men to eat together. Even though enlisted men and officers were not normally supposed to eat together, I finally relented. I sat at the table with them.

I felt at that point if I continued to insist on staying where I was in the car, it would make the case more difficult in the event that matters were taken further and I was arrested. I recognized that I might be charged with disorderly conduct. If that occurred, we might not reach the issue of challenging the segregation laws.

I had some experience in Virginia with a similar situation. In 1940, Pauli Murray and her cousin were arrested on a bus for refusing to get up and give their seats to white people. They were convicted and appealed to the Petersburg, Virginia Circuit Court. I, along with Lincoln Johnson, helped Robert Cooley, a well-known Negro lawyer in Petersburg try the case. The bus driver claimed that Murray had cursed him. Suspecting that we were intending to challenge the segregation laws Judge Wilson dismissed the segregation charges, convicted the defendants of disorderly conduct and fined them each ten dollars. That killed the case; we did not want to raise a constitutional issue tangentially.

As a result of this experience, Pauli Murray applied to Howard University Law School from where later she graduated with Honors. Subsequently, Murray sought admission to Harvard Law School for a

141

graduate degree. At that time, Harvard Law School did not admit women. The faculty met, voted, and split 50/50. While the controversy was raging about what to do about Murray's Harvard application, she was admitted to the University of California Law School at Berkeley. Murray subsequently came back east, practiced law for a while, wrote several books and later continued her pioneering activities for justice as an Episcopal priest.

We had a lot of litigation arising from public transportation matters because Negroes frequently refused to ride Jim Crow as they traveled south in trains or buses. They were often arrested and tried in Virginia state courts in Richmond. The usual pattern was that police court Judge Maurice would convict and fine defendants. We would then appeal the case to the Hustings Court.

In Hustings Court, Judge Ingram would "continue the case to ..." This meant continued indefinitely.

One day after a large number of cases had been "continued to," I challenged Judge Ingram and asked why he had not decided the cases. He said, "Oliver, you know that one day the Supreme Court will overrule the segregation statutes. But they are not going to overrule me!" We knew what he was doing and told the defendants to go home and forget it when their case was "continued to."

Fortunately, two cases arose that were beyond the jurisdiction of state courts in Richmond. One involved Irene Morgan in Middlesex County, and about eight or nine years later the Chance case arose in Greensville County.

In Morgan v. Virginia, in 1945, the Court ruled that segregation of passengers in interstate transportation was unconstitutional as a burden on interstate commerce. It did so, however, without overrulling Plessy. The Court seemed to view Plessy as a judicial sacred cow. Accordingly, despite many Negroes and whites viewing segregation as a societal badge of inferiority, the Court sought ways to avoid overruling the separate but equal doctrine.

I was still in the Army while Morgan was being litigated, and Spot Robinson handled the matter in the Virginia courts. Because Spot had not been practicing long enough to be admitted to the U. S. Supreme Court Bar, Thurgood Marshall arugued the case in the Supreme Court.

Another important transportation case was <u>Chance v. Atlantic Coastline</u>. Chance was principal of a school in North Carolina and on his way home. The police arrested Chance because he refused to move to the Jim Crow car in Richmond. When the train arrived in Emporia, Virginia, the conductor had the police arrest our client, charging him with violating the segregation laws. Prior to trial, the railroad withdrew the charge and paid the court costs.

My partner, Martin A. Martin, subsequently filed suit for false arrest and imprisonment and wrongful ejectment. For some reason, according to him, the case was scheduled for a hearing on a procedural matter. Martin asked me would I go to federal district court in Richmond and argue the issue because he had another matter scheduled outside the city.

On the day in question, Spot Robinson decided to go with me to the hearing. Judge Hutcheson ruled with us on the motion. However, the judge wanted to start the trial immediately. This caught us by surprise. It was about 11:00 a.m. at that time. We asked for a continuance until 2:00 that afternoon. The judge granted our request. We promptly called our office, asked them to call our client in North Carolina and tell him to come to Richmond immediately.

At 2:00 p.m. we were back in court! We started our case by calling the conductor of the train as an adverse witness. I kept the conductor on the stand until 5:00 p.m. The court adjourned for the day. We were delighted to see our client come into the court about 4:30 p.m. The case lasted for four or five days. Judge Hutcheson ruled against us on the validity of the railroad regulation mandating segregation. On appeal, the Fourth Circuit reversed and ordered a new trial. The Fourth Circuit held the railway regulation invalid. On remand, we won, but the jury only gave us fifty dollars in damages.[34] We were nevertheless satisfied because we had obtained a civil judgment against the railroad company and vindicated our client's constitutional rights.

<u>Organizing Resistance to Segregation: Additional Examples</u>

In the early 1940's, I helped organize the Old Dominion Bar Association in Virginia. The Old Dominion Bar Association initially included nearly all of the Negro lawyers in the state of Virginia. When the Old Dominion Bar Association was created, there were about thirty such individuals. I went around the state and personally spoke to each one of them, inviting them to join the association. Nearly all of them

Civil Rights Activists involved with desegregating University of Virginia Graduate Programs via the <u>Swanson</u> case. (Circa 1950) Left to right (front row only) Dr. Jesse Tinsley, Martin A. Martin, Spotswood Robinson, III, Gregory Swanson, Oliver W. Hill, Sr., Thurgood Marshall, Hale Thompson, and Robert Cooley.

agreed.

While I cannot remember now all of the names of the individuals who joined, I do recall that Lavinia Marian Fleming-Poe was the only woman lawyer to join the organization at that time, and she became the organization's first secretary.[35] Poe was the first Negro woman to pass the Virginia state bar; that happened in 1926, about six years after the state of Virginia permitted women to practice law without restriction. There were also two other Negro women who were lawyers in the Tidewater area of Virginia about that time, namely Bertha L. Douglass who practiced in Norfolk and Inez C. Fields who practiced in Hampton with her father, George Washington Fields. At its inception, neither Douglass nor Fields joined the organization.

Some of our members were quite elderly and two or three of them were born during or shortly after slavery. For example, Thomas C. Walker of Gloucester, Virginia was born in slavery in 1862 and in the late 1800's was elected to the board of supervisors in Gloucester. Walker was very active, and had a following of whites and Negroes. He was also a Justice of the Peace, appointed as a collector of Customs at Tappahanock, and was the first Negro in that area to become a member of the Virginia bar. Walker was a founder in the Negro Organization Society, a service organization that continued its activities well into the twentieth century. The Society's objectives included improving Negro schools, encouraging Negro home and land ownership, stimulating Negro business development (especially farming), and improving the physical and moral health of Negroes.

Walker was an important figure in his era. However, by the time my generation arrived on the scene, we used to call him "Uncle Tom." We called him that because we believed that some of his methods were a hindrance to our programs to eliminate segregation and because we did not have a complete knowledge of his former activities. I got along very well with Uncle Tom. My only objection to him was that Walker, like a lot of folks who had a major financial stake in maintaining the status quo, tried to impede progressive change. In Walker's case, it was his reluctance to challenge segregated schools. In many rural areas in those days, public school teachers lived in boarding houses run by some prominent local figure, sometimes white, and sometimes Negro. In Gloucester, Tom Walker had one such boarding house. Most public school teachers were single folks. If they married during the school year, they often lost their jobs. In most places, that was the practice. It was a racket.

145

Walker was quite a character. By the time I came along he was very elderly. However, he was still quite an orator.

I never actually had a case with or against him. He had an active litigation practice but I never saw him try a case. His cases were often down in the Gloucester area. Judging from the results, he was a very good lawyer during his hey day.

Walker had a lot of clout with the legislature and used it constructively. Through the Negro Organization Society, he operated a lot of programs beneficial to people living in rural areas.[36] He just never challenged segregation by seeking to end it. Apparently he challenged white folks to make them improve conditions in many respects for Negroes. When we organized the Old Dominion Bar Association, Walker joined and came to the meetings.

In addition, Tom Hewin, Sr. was another older lawyer who joined. Hewin was quite active until the middle of this century when he was fatally injured in an automobile accident. We also had another Old Dominion Bar member who was an old lawyer over in Lexington. He was up in his eighties.

After organizing the Old Dominion Bar Association, because of the overwhelming work load, we then created what was known as the Virginia State Conference Legal Staff. The staff included Martin A. Martin, R. Wendel Walker, Victor Ashe, Roland Eley, Robert Cooley and me. Martin A. Martin was initially headquartered in Danville, and Roland Eley worked out of Richmond. R. Wendel Walker of Portsmouth, Victor Ashe of Norfolk, and Robert Cooley of Petersberg were often active staff members. Local lawyers affiliated with the staff to provide services in civil rights cases so that a few of us would not have to run all over the state. Later, when Spotswood Robinson passed the bar, he became a member of the staff. Hale Thompson of Newport News, S.W. Tucker initially located in Emporia, and Reuben Lawson who worked in Roanoke subsequently became members as well. Thompson and Lawson worked in the Hill, Martin and Robinson law firm before branching out to work in Newport News and Roanoke, respectively.

In 1943 we organized the law firm of Hill, Martin and Robinson. After people got in trouble, they called the NAACP and the NAACP called us. We handled the bulk of the litigation for many years.

During the segregation era, many white folks made a big to-do

146

about the law. They claimed that they had to obey the segregation laws as much as they detested them. So we thought that once segregation laws were eliminated, the majority of white people would freely accept Negroes as human beings. We believed we would peacefully pass through a period of desegregation.

When the Court struck down segregation in areas of public education at the graduate school level,[37] transportation,[38] and labor relations,[39] one would have thought that the states would have voluntarily removed segregation laws on local buses and streetcars, and even in public schools and state employment. However, there were no such voluntary actions to desegregate. As a matter of fact, progress in what was supposed to have been the non sensitive areas only made some racists fight even harder to uphold segregation. This was paradoxical. Some white folks claimed to detest segregation laws so much, and yet when the courts struck the laws down, they found other reasons to maintain segregation.

Looking back, I guess that I should have known better and not been surprised. I came up during Prohibition. During that period, I observed what little respect people had for laws prohibiting the sale of alcoholic beverages. Folks were also disrespectful of tax laws and even made jokes about their disregard for traffic laws. For example, I recall that when I was in elementary school, we had one joke about some character who had a racy name and motored into town. The cops arrested him for speeding (most traffic cops were motorcycle policemen in those days). They carried him to court. The judge found him guilty and fined him twenty-five dollars. He said, "Judge, here's fifty dollars." The judge said, "What is that for?" He said, "That's to pay for the other fine because I'm going out the same way I came in."

Chapter IV

Working Towards
Brown and Beyond

> *Even though we initially sought enforcement of the separate but equal rule, I once argued before the Court of Appeals that if a school board built two schools side by side, brick for brick, room for room, with identical materials, curricula, and furnishings and limited Negro children to attending one school and white children to attending the other, I would still say it was discriminatory against the Negroes. As long as Negroes are excluded from the societal mainstream, they will continue to be relegated to a form of second-class citizenship. When the government excludes a person through segregation laws, and the general society by custom, that exclusion places the excluded person in a position where there are too many things that happen that the person doesn't know anything about. White children going to school have parents who are involved in various functions in the political, business and social affairs of the community. Those children bring experiences, perspectives, and other things to the schools that black children have had no opportunity to become familiar with.*

Taking Aim at Jim Crow

On April 23, 1951, Barbara Johns, a senior at Robert Moton High School in Prince Edward County, Virginia, led her class on strike to procure better school facilities and publicize the deplorable conditions of Prince Edward's Negro public schools. Barbara Johns was the niece of the Reverend Vernon Johns, a nationally known orator, civil rights protagonist, and minister.

148

On the afternoon of the first day of the strike, Barbara Johns called our office at about 5:00 p.m. At the time of the call, Spot, Martin and I were working on a motion for further judicial relief in <u>Corbin v. Pulaski</u>.[1] We were planning to go to Christiansburg, Virginia that week in preparation for our hearing in the case. The plaintiff in that case, Mathama Corbin, was the son of a dentist and had to ride approximately sixty miles daily to a consolidated school serving all of the Negro students for a number of communities including the counties of Pulaski and Montgomery and the town of Radford.

Regarding the Prince Edward situation, Barbara Johns told us that they were on strike; however, I stated that they didn't need to continue to strike because they had made their point. I said to her besides, "We've already filed a suit in Clarendon County, South Carolina challenging the constitutionality of separate schools there." I added that one case was enough to establish the legal principle. For these reasons I urged her to lead the students back to school. Having appeared before the school authorities in Prince Edward County on a number of occasions during the ten year period before the initiation of the Prince Edward suit, I was familiar with the deplorable school system about which they were complaining.

Law Firm of Hill, Martin and Robinson (Circa 1951)
Seated l-r: Martin A Martin, Oliver W. Hill, Sr.,
Spotwood Robinson, III

Nevertheless, Barbara Johns pleaded their cause so strongly, and I did not feel comfortable terminating our discussion on the telephone, that I said, "All right. We are coming through Farmville Wednesday morning. We will leave Richmond a little earlier and we will stop by and talk to you." She said, "All right." She told me that they would be at Reverend Griffin's church. Reverend Griffin was an outstanding leader in the turbulent years leading to, during and after the closure of the Prince Edward County Public Schools. In the <u>Davis</u> case, Griffin participated as an activist, and assumed a similar role in a suit involving his own children.

On Wednesday, Martin, Spot, Dean Thomas H. Henderson of Virginia Union University (one of our expert witnesses on educational matters), Allen Broadnax (our photographer) and I stopped by to talk to the class. On our way to Farmville, we had anticipated telling the class to go back to school. When we arrived we found these students had such fine morale and were so well disciplined that we didn't have the heart to break their spirit. We said to them that we were going to Christiansburg and we would return on Thursday night. We told them that there had been a change in NAACP policy. We were no longer taking cases to make separate facilities equal. Now we sought to challenge segregation <u>per se</u> and have the Court declare racial segregation in public schools unconstitutional.

Accordingly, we instructed the students that they first needed to talk with their parents. If their parents agreed to support them in a suit challenging segregation <u>per se</u>, we would take the case. We instructed them to ask their parents to be present on Thursday night to discuss the matter.

The offensive Negro high school in Prince Edward County consisted of a small building which was overcrowded the day that it was opened in 1939, plus a number of separate tar paper shacks. The shacks had tin stove pipes running from room to room. These pathetic rooms were heated through use of oil drums which acted as "stoves." I think coal was burned in the drums. During inclement weather the children were exposed to the elements -- rain, mud, cold, and ice as they made their way from the main building or one or more of the shacks located on the campus.

On the appointed Thursday night, we came back and met the children and their parents. We reiterated that we were not accepting

150

separate but equal cases any more. From now on, we were seeking to overturn __Plessy__. The parents agreed to stand behind the students. Someone suggested that since this action had county-wide ramifications, we needed to hold a county-wide meeting. The group reached consensus on this course of action and we scheduled another meeting for a week from the following Friday.

On that Friday night, the meeting was held. The church was packed to the rafters. The citizens had a long, serious, vigorous debate. Finally when the issue was put to the group whether to attack segregation per se, the group voted nearly unanimously to challenge segregation. Folks were fed up with the existing situation. They knew that something had to be done for their children, as well as subsequent generations.

Of course, as one would expect in such a large and diverse group of people there were some dissenting and doubtful voices. For example, a principal of a school in Cumberland County living in Prince Edward County argued that the better strategy was to attempt to make the schools equal. Some Negroes were also afraid that a direct challenge to segregation would make the white folks in the community mad. When looking at the types of schools the local authorities furnished the Negro population, you would have been tempted to say that the white folks were already acting like they were angry. Be that as it may, after a thoughtful and thorough debate, the overwhelming majority agreed that we must do something. They voted to seek an end to segregation.

We promptly filed a petition with the school board. When the board failed to grant the relief requested, we filed a petition requesting a three judge federal district court challenging the constitutionality of segregation per se. That was how the Prince Edward case (one of the five cases consolidated and heard by the Court in __Brown)__ got started.

Having previously discussed my reasons for becoming a lawyer, some law school experiences, and memorable events in my early career, I will now tell you more about the events leading up to and persons involved in the __Brown__ case.

In the early 1920's, a young man, Charles Garland, was left a very sizable estate, and being a public spirited person, Garland decided to establish a trust fund to benefit the NAACP. The trust helped to further the NAACP's work in seeking to end segregation--whether by law or custom.

As a result of the grant from the Garland Fund, and at the suggestion of Charlie Houston, Professor Nathan Margold of Harvard Law School was selected to conduct a study to determine the best course for the NAACP to pursue to achieve its civil rights goals. Margold suggested that we challenge the segregated public school systems and that suits be filed simultaneously throughout the South.[2]

Charlie Houston accepted Margold's recommendation on challenging unequal educational opportunities. However, he determined that filing multiple suits was infeasible and accordingly he modified the plan by suggesting that we initially attack segregation within the bounds of the existing law. Charlie argued that we should make the local officials live up to the holding that Plessy dictated not only separateness, but also equality. We were convinced that this would compel the white governmental officials to recognize that the public could not afford to maintain equal dual school systems. Some of us thought that public school officials would (eventually) recognize that dual equal public schools were financially infeasible and move to desegregate the schools. This was a tactical decision because even in the 1930's our ultimate goal was eliminating racial segregation -- root and branch.

The first case to present itself occurred while I was in law school. In North Carolina, two Negro lawyers, Conrad Pearson and Cecil McCoy, filed a suit which involved a Negro student at the North Carolina College for Negroes which is now North Carolina Central University in Durham. Interestingly, Conrad Pearson graduated from Howard Law School a year before I did.

The plaintiff, Thomas Hocutt, was denied admission to the School of Pharmacy at the all white University of North Carolina. Hocutt was unable to prevail in court in part because Dr. J. E. Shepard, the president of North Carolina College for Negroes, refused to release Hocutt's transcripts. By the time the court decided the petition for mandamus to compel Shepard to release the transcript, Hocutt was either no longer able or willing to proceed. I do not recall the specific details regarding what Hocutt's circumstances were at that time.[3]

Nevertheless, despite this minor setback, the NAACP continued its campaign in challenging segregation. Two years after our class graduated, Charlie left Howard Law School to become special counsel for the NAACP. In addition, shortly after graduating from law school, Thurgood took and passed the Maryland bar.

152

Even though he was a very effective civil rights lawyer, because of the Depression, Thurgood found it difficult to secure sufficient income to maintain an independent private practice. To alleviate the situation, Charlie selected Thurgood as his assistant. In 1935 Charlie and Thurgood filed one of their first important test cases, <u>Murray v. University of Maryland</u>.[4] The <u>Murray</u> case was initiated to desegregate the law school in Baltimore. The question was whether Murray was going to go to Maryland's law school or be forced to accept a grant from the state to study outside of Maryland. The state provided a fund to pay Negroes to leave the state to pursue graduate study. Maryland did not pay their transportation or living expenses out of state.

There was a slight competition between Charlie Houston and Belford Lawson revolving around which of these Alpha fraternity brothers was going to file the <u>Murray</u> case. Belford, who had graduated from Howard Law School in 1931, Charlie and Thurgood were all Alphas. Whichever of them filed the suit would have insisted on being in charge of case management. However, since Murray had sought the assistance of Thurgood, Thurgood and Charlie had "the inside track". They wound up filing the suit.

Incidentally, Belford was from a prominent Roanoke family. His sister, Sadie Lawson, was one of my seventh-grade teachers. When I was in the seventh and eight grades at the so-called Harrison High School, one of his brothers, Fred Lawson, was my coach of football and basketball. Fred also taught manual training.

Later, while I was in college, Belford helped to organize the inter fraternal council at Howard and became the first president. I remember a meeting at which I was very much impressed with him: though not impressed enough to become an Alpha. By then I was already an Omega anyway. He finished at the University of Michigan. Belford's wife, Margorie, was also a lawyer and became a domestic relations judge in the District of Columbia.

As I previously stated, in planning our anti-segregation strategy, we knew we had to educate the public and the courts including the Supreme Court. We didn't expect any positive action until we got to the Supreme Court. We planned to get to the Supreme Court by choosing good cases and making good records. We didn't want another Plessy <u>v. Ferguson</u> decision. We were careful that the Supreme Court would be without any basis for not deciding in our favor.

153

Initially our goal was to have <u>Plessy v. Ferguson</u> declared unconstitutional. However, Charlie's conclusion in the 1930's was that attacking segregation <u>per se</u> would have been tantamount to beating our heads against a brick wall. Our perception was validated by subsequent events. For example, following the Supreme Court's decision in <u>Brown</u>, segregationists were still maneuvering by hook and crook to defeat the Court's desegregation mandate. Even now, over forty years after Brown, there is only partial acceptance of full civil rights for persons of color.

<u>Missouri ex rel. Gaines v. Canada</u>[5] reflected the difficult battle that we faced in the late 1930's. <u>Gaines</u> was the first major NAACP litigation victory at the Supreme Court level in the school cases. In <u>Gaines</u> the issue involved enforcing the separate but equal doctrine where a Negro student, Lloyd Gaines, was denied admission to the all white University of Missouri Law School. Speaking for a divided Court, Chief Justice Hughes stated, "it was as an individual that he was entitled to the equal protection of the laws, and the State was bound to furnish him within its borders facilities for legal education substantially equal to those... afforded for persons of the white race."[6]

Plaintiff, Lloyd Gaines, mysteriously disappeared after the case was decided. While we were never able to confirm or deny foul play, it was strongly suspected.

Looking at the historical context, after World War II, President Truman ran into substantial congressional resistance from the Dixiecrats in his effort to promote civil rights for Negroes. President Truman had appointed a committee to study the United States' racial situation. In 1948, the committee came back with their well known report "To Secure These Rights".[7] The committee made numerous specific recommendations for alleviating the circumstances of those oppressed by the American social and political structures. These recommendations included the creation of a civil rights division in the Justice Department to protect the rights of all citizens, the establishment of analogous agencies at the state level, passage of a federal anti-lynching law, a review of the nation's wartime detention policy, and the grant of suffrage to Native Americans in New Mexico and Arizona. Furthermore, the Committee recommended abolition of the poll tax, protection of the right to vote in primaries, the termination of segregation in the Panama Canal Zone, and the creation of a permanent Civil Rights Commission to propose measures for continuing change.[8]

Truman endorsed the committee recommendations and sent them to the National Democratic Convention urging that the Democratic Party adopt them and include them in the party's platform. This aroused the ire of the segregationists especially those of the southern Democratic contingent led by J. Strom Thurmond of South Carolina. Thurmond threatened to organize a Dixiecrat Party in opposition to Truman's election unless Truman desisted from these democratic activities. When Truman stood firm and refused to withdraw the twelve points for adoption by the National Convention, the Dixiecrats followed through on their threat, walked out of the convention, organized the Dixiecrat party and nominated Strom Thurmond as their candidate for president. By splitting the Democratic Party's base in the South, it was anticipated that Thurmond's maneuver would make it easier for Dewey to defeat Truman.

Undaunted, and over the objection of General Eisenhower and others, Truman later issued an executive order integrating the armed forces. These actions took place against the backdrop of dynamic changes in human history. For example, in 1948, the United Nations adopted the Universal Declaration on Human Rights, and that made the United States look ridiculous with many of its segregationist policies. Colonialism was in the process of being dismantled. However, even with two world wars to "make the world safe for democracy," democracy seemed to be progressing faster nearly everywhere except in the United States.

We knew that it would be economically too costly to maintain separate and equal public facilities in such areas as schools, transportation, and recreation facilities. We hoped that by making it prohibitively expensive that would cause more white citizens to challenge segregation. We expected to reach the point where the white public would wholeheartedly join us in the fight to achieve a color blind society. Although we secured some cooperation from many broad-minded white persons, we never secured widespread support from the rank and file of the white community. That remains true even until today.

In planning a strategy to deal with the segregation of the public school children, we had to establish a body of law to substantiate our position. However, in analyzing the post World War II situation, we soon realized that our program of separate but equal was resulting in newer inferior school facilities for Negroes.

To ensure that they gave us inferior new schools, the white school boards constructed schools with wide ranging ridiculous combinations

155

of rooms. For example, some schools had one room used for cafeteria and gymnasium, or one room used for cafeteria, gymnasium, and the auditorium. Frequently, there existed a non-existent science department to boot. Indeed even when authorities purported to have a science department, the equipment was meager and facilities totally inadequate to study basic science like chemistry and physics. They did not pretend to study biology and botany. In the white communities, the schools had separate children's libraries, cafeterias and science facilities.

While progress at the secondary school level was discouraging, in the undergraduate and graduate school cases we had made some strides. For example, in <u>Sipuel v. Oklahoma</u> and <u>McLaurin v. Board of Regents of Oklahoma</u>, the NAACP won victories.[9] Those cases established the right of Negroes at the graduate level to participate fully in the educational process.

We also witnessed progress in the labor area as for instance in the cases of <u>Steele v. Louisiana and Nashville Railroads</u> and <u>Tunstall v. Brotherhood of Locomotive Firemen and Engineers</u>.[10] These cases involved the white railroad unions which called themselves Brotherhoods and which denied membership to Negroes. Under the relevant railroad labor legislation, the Brotherhoods were allowed to be the bargaining agent for the railway workers. <u>Steele</u> and <u>Tunstall</u> held that the Brotherhoods had to fairly represent non-member Negroes.

In our struggle to obtain equal rights in the area of employment discrimination, Charlie Houston conceived the idea of having congressional hearings to obtain relevant data. Congressman Adam Clayton Powell, Jr. helped us. For example, he held hearings involving discriminatory practices in the railroad industry. He also subpoenaed relevant information.

In dealing with the discriminatory labor practices of the Brotherhoods and management, the Congressional hearings enabled us to establish that there was a pattern of collusive decisions going back to the beginning of the twentieth century between the lily white unions and lily white management to eliminate all of the black railroad workers involved in operating the trains. Such workers included engineers, brakemen, and trainmen. When the firemen's jobs were considered especially difficult, dangerous, and degrading, the white railroad workers shied away from them. However, with advances in technology and the advent of the diesel engine, such jobs became more attractive. Instead of frantically shoveling coal with a raging fire and smoke all around,

156

diesel engines allowed firemen to sit serenely in the cabs of the locomotives with nothing more difficult to handle than a small oil can.

As you can see, much was happening nationally, and even internationally at the same time. In fact, after Sweatt v. Painter, [11] the Texas law school case, we thought we had a majority of the Supreme Court. It appeared that Chief Justice Vinson and the Associate Justices had adopted our theory on segregation and were prepared to overrule Plessy. For example, in Sweatt, the Court had accepted our argument regarding the makeshift law school and the criteria for a good law school. In the Sweatt case, Chief Justice Vinson said:

> Whether the University of Texas Law School is compared with the original or the new law school for Negroes, we cannot find substantial equality in the educational opportunities offered white and Negro law students by the state. In terms of number of the faculty, variety of courses and opportunity for specialization, size of the student body, scope of the library, availability of law review and similar activities, the University of Texas Law School is superior. What is more important, the University of Texas Law School possesses to a far greater degree, those qualities which are incapable of objective measurement but which make for greatness in a law school. Such qualities, to name but a few, include reputation of the faculty, experience of the administration, position and influence of the alumni, standing in the community, tradition and prestige. It is difficult to believe that one who had a free choice between these law schools would consider the question close. [12]

We had started with the graduate schools, teacher salaries and a wide-ranging attack on segregation, including Negro exclusion from grand and petit juries and the covenant cases as well as transportation matters. We thought that in higher education we would encounter less resistance because students would probably be more mature and the school officials would likely be more liberal minded. As a matter of fact, it did not work out that way.

Segregationist politicians were able to politicize the situation; and we ran into all kinds of bizarre and foolish tactics. These antics included having a lone Negro graduate student sitting outside the regular classroom to obtain instruction, [13] outside the dining room to eat and

157

outside the library to study. In planning our approach that culminated in <u>Brown</u>, we constructed our legal strategy working from the graduate school down.

In <u>Sweatt</u>, Chief Justice Vinson had talked about the intangibles. Those were some of the questions that we raised. Vinson seemed to be on our side and that persuaded us that it was time to ask the Court to rule regarding elementary and secondary schools like it had done with professional schools. We felt our strategy had succeeded and we were in the position to achieve our primary objective.

Accordingly, at the NAACP convention held in Boston in the summer of 1950, it was decided that we would challenge segregation <u>per se</u>. I was not at the convention because, when the convention met, Martin and I were trying <u>Blue v. Durham Public School District</u>, a case in Durham, North Carolina.[14] The case started in the late 1940's and involved a suit to equalize school facilities between Negro and white students. This was our last separate but equal case.

In 1950, Charlie Houston died. Charlie had been litigating the District of Columbia school case. However, he became too ill to handle it and he turned the reins over to James Nabrit and George E. C. Hayes. James Nabrit had a great career at Howard University. He was a professor and dean of the law school, as well as a vice-president and finally the president of the university. Nabrit also developed a remarkable civil rights course. George E.C. Hayes was a professor of law at the law school and one of the best trial lawyers in D.C.

Charlie had developed such an excellent, adaptable strategy, that even after he died the momentum went right on. In carrying out the objectives of the 1950 NAACP National Convention, Thurgood filed the <u>Clarendon County</u> case in South Carolina. The case challenged the segregated public schools in that county and represented a frontal attack on segregation. The case first appeared before Judge J. Waties Waring, a federal district judge in South Carolina. The case raised federal constitutional issues, and a special three judge federal court was empaneled to hear the case.

In the South Carolina case, Spot Robinson from our office joined the team that tried the case. The three-judge district court, over Judge Waring's dissent, ruled against us. The case was appealed to the United States Supreme Court. The Supreme Court remanded the case to the three judge court on a technicality.

Of course, as we conducted the litigation, we added some things to Charlie Houston's earlier plans. For example, Robert Carter, Thurgood's assistant, thought that sociological evidence would help our litigation strategy. However, I'm not sure whether the idea originated with Carter or with Johnny Davis who was a prominent Negro social scientist who taught political science at Lincoln. Davis was very active with Carter in developing this idea. As a result of their collaboration, they decided to devise a plan using sociological and psychological research as part of our litigation strategy.

We used this interdisciplinary strategy prominently in the Clarendon County, South Carolina, Topeka, Kansas, and Prince Edward County, Virginia cases. In the South Carolina case, Dr. Kenneth Clark testified. Both Dr. Kenneth Clark and his wife, Dr. Mamie Clark, testified in the Virginia case which I discussed briefly earlier, and will return to in a moment. Their testimony convincingly demonstrated the damaging effect of segregation on Negro school children.

For example, Dr. Kenneth Clark had several dolls - some were black and others were white. Clark asked Negro school children a number of questions, for instance to choose the dolls which they liked best, or the ones that were the prettiest, or the good dolls. Overwhelmingly, the children chose the white dolls. However, when the same children were asked to identify the bad dolls, the ugly dolls, the worst dolls, they chose the ones that most resembled themselves. These tests were further developed by Marian Radke and Helen Trager, and helped to illuminate the devastating impact upon Negro children of an educational system and society that was thoroughly segregated and racist.

An interesting aside is that there were two Johnny Davises. One, John P. Davis, was an activist and organizer of the National Negro Congress. He is the one who asked me why I was going to law school. He also founded and edited "Our World", a magazine in the 1930's. That publication was a forerunner of magazines like Ebony and Jet. Davis's son recently co-authored a biographical account on Justice Thurgood Marshall. This Johnny Davis was also a Rhodes Scholar. The second Johnny Davis, Professor John A. Davis of Lincoln University in Pennsylvania, was a prominent social scientist. Davis assembled the team of social scientists that we used as expert witnesses.

This background information may help you better understand the historical and individual human drama leading to the decision that

159

became known as <u>Brown v. Board of Education</u>.

As I mentioned earlier, the Prince Edward case was one of five cases which the Court consolidated and heard as a unit in <u>Brown</u>. The Prince Edward case came from nearby rural Southside Virginia whereas most of the other cases in Virginia came from both the cities and the counties.

In fact, we were often accused of choosing the places where suits were filed. However, the Prince Edward case is evidence of the untruth of those charges. If we had any choice in the matter, we would have never picked Prince Edward as a community for a test case. If we were going to pick a case, we would have worked with parents who wanted to improve their children's educational opportunities by challenging public school segregation in Richmond, or Norfolk or some other metropolitan center. Besides being in a more enlightened area, we would have done so for convenience both to our clients and to ourselves as lawyers. Regardless of where we filed the suit, the result in the district court would have been the same: the same three judges would have heard the case. In fact, when the matter was tried, Judges Hutcheson and Dobie voted against our position, but Judge Soper supported us.

I do not believe that local officials in Richmond or Norfolk would have closed their schools. The schools would have remained accessible, and the students would have still had some place to go. Only in the heartland of segregation, some place like Southside Virginia, would they have shut down all the public schools and let the children suffer rather than desegregate.

We certainly did not anticipate local officials shutting down all the schools. Still, we knew that Prince Edward wasn't the most wholesome atmosphere for a big test case.

Like I said, we didn't pick the Prince Edward case. The case, or more accurately the students and parents of that community, picked us. That notwithstanding, lawyers must take cases where they find them.

Nevertheless, a more pervasive silliness than we thought existed in the state, and as I will discuss in more detail later, the General Assembly passed legislation allowing the governor to close schools wherever courts ordered them desegregated. This statewide mania was in part attributable to the backward leadership of people like Senator

160

Harry Byrd, Sr. and the infamous Byrd political machine.

At the time that we instituted the Prince Edward County case, we had tried several other cases which had gone to the Fourth Circuit Court of Appeals. They included, for instance, Alston v. City of Norfolk School Board, Corbin v. Pulaski, the Arlington County School Board case,[15] and the Chesterfield County School Board case.

Corbin is an interesting example of what we confronted in those days. After the district court ruled against us, we appealed to the Fourth Circuit court of appeals which reversed the district court's judgment. We filed a motion for further relief and with several other lawyers I went over to Judge Barksdale's chambers in Lynchburg.

Opposing our motion was Alton Crowell who represented Pulaski County. Crowell associated Armistead Boothe of Alexandria, Virginia to assist him on the motion.

At our meeting in Lynchburg, Boothe, Crowell, Spot, Martin and I were there. I pointed out to Judge Barksdale that the circuit court had overruled the district court's judgment and that the school authorities had done nothing to equalize educational opportunity for the Negro students. Judge Barksdale said in reply, "Well, there isn't anything I can do."

I replied, "There most certainly is something you can do! You can order the school board to let these Negro children go to the white schools." Judge Barksdale got red in the face and began banging both his fists on the desk so that at one point I thought he was going to have a stroke.

He replied angrily, "I will not do it! I will not do it! I will not do it!" That ended the conference.

After the conference, Boothe and I caught the train together. For some reason I was going to Washington from Lynchburg; he was destined for Alexandria. We had a reasonable conversation even though we were on opposite sides of this case. At one point, the conversation drifted into a discussion of racial stereotypes. I told him about stereotypes I had to overcome that existed in the neighborhood when I was a child. For example, I shared with Boothe the two stereotypical stories that I told you about earlier, the first being that two classes of white people existed: good white folks and bad ones. "You could always

161

tell a good white man from the others because the good one was always buried at least six feet deep." The second tale was that you should never, never trust a white person because "they were so crooked they would steal the pennies off their dead mother's eyes." There were many others but I remembered those.

Interestingly, at the same time we had a case in Arlington County involving the truck company that Boothe's firm represented. A company truck stopped on the highway, and my client came down the highway in a touring car. My client couldn't stop fast enough and ran underneath the truck. The collision decapitated my client. Another member of Boothe's firm handled the case. We settled it before trial.

In those days Boothe was what we called a liberal white person. In 1961, he ran for lieutenant governor of Virginia in the Democratic primary on a slate with A.E.S. Stephens (gubernatorial candidate) and T. Mumford Boyd (attorney general candidate). The Stephens/Boothe/Boyd ticket opposed Byrd machine candidates led by former attorney general Harrison. The anti-Byrd forces received a considerable number of votes cast by Negroes and white liberals. However, these two groups seldom could muster enough votes to nominate candidates in the Democratic primary who opposed the Byrd organization. Boothe also ran unsuccessfully against Harry Byrd, Jr. for the U.S. Senate. Harry Byrd, Jr. succeeded Harry Byrd, Sr., founder of the Byrd machine.

Coming back to the <u>Brown</u> litigation, following the Supreme Court's remand of the South Carolina case, the Topeka, Wilmington, and Prince Edward cases came up for Supreme Court review. The Clarendon County case came back to the Supreme Court as well as the District of Columbia case. With all five cases before it, the Supreme Court consolidated the litigation with Brown as the lead case. Of course, if the cases had been decided in the order that they were filed, the Supreme Court would have first decided the Clarendon County case. Clarendon County rather than <u>Brown</u> would have been the leading precedent on public school segregation.

In each of the <u>Brown</u> litigation cases, the constitutionality of the separate but equal doctrine was challenged. All these cases were brought under the auspices of the NAACP and NAACP Legal Defense Fund. The Topeka, Prince Edward, and Clarendon County cases were filed under the Fourteenth Amendment challenging the separate but equal precedents. In the Wilmington case, the state court had ruled in favor of the plaintiffs and the school board appealed. The situation in the

162

Lawyers Representing Plaintiffs in <u>Brown</u> v. Board of Education (Local counsel for Topeka plaintiffs not pictured) (Circa 1953/54) Standing left to right: Louis Redding, Robert Carter, Oliver W. Hill, Sr., Thurgood Marshall, Spotswood Robinson, III, Jack Greenberg, James Nabrit, Jr., and George E. C. Hayes.

Delaware case was the reverse of that in the other cases in that plaintiff had won; however, the issue was fundamentally the same: and that was whether segregation in the public schools was constitutional.

Furthermore, under the existing judicial interpretations, the Fourteenth Amendment did not apply to the District of Columbia because the District of Columbia was not a state. Accordingly, the suit had been instituted in the District of Columbia federal district court under the Fifth Amendment Due Process Clause. Those were, however, legal distinctions. All of the cases challenged segregation in the public schools. We asked the Court to hold the separate but equal doctrine unconstitutional.

When the Supreme Court granted certiorari on these cases, we prepared and developed arguments viewing all five of the cases as a single unit. Thurgood argued strenuously for the abolition of segregation per se in all of these cases. His was the general argument attacking segregation at its constitutional roots. In addition, the other members of the team argued the specific facts and circumstances of the individual cases.

After the first argument of the consolidated cases, the Supreme Court could not agree on what to do about segregation per se in the public schools. Based on my perception and information subsequently unearthed, it appears that the delay was a judicial attempt to avoid overruling the Plessy doctrine. Chief Justice Vinson agreed to Frankfurter's suggestion that the Court delay a decision.

The official reason given for the re-argument, however, was for the Court to obtain further information regarding the views of the Reconstruction Congress on non-segregated public schools. In that regard, the Court submitted wide-ranging questions relating to the views and circumstances of the Congress concerning segregation in public education. The Court asked the lawyers to address these questions to guide the Court.[16]

As a result of the questions that the Supreme Court asked us on reargument of the Brown cases, we had to bring in historians and other academics. We conducted substantial historical, sociological and psychological research.

From my perspective, the net result was a waste of time. First, the Reconstruction Congress probably never thought of the public school

164

segregation issue when they promulgated the Thirteenth, Fourteenth and Fifteenth Amendments. Interestingly, however, in that period in establishing the District of Columbia schools, separate schools for whites and Negroes were created.

From our perspective, one of the crucial points was how the Court chose to interpret the Constitution. We believed that the appropriate method for interpreting the Constitution was to view and treat it as a living document. In short, the Court needed to interpret the Constitution to meet existing needs. This could be done by determining what general principles underlie constitutional provisions and then applying those principles to specific facts. Thus, for example, a fundamental objective of the Fourteenth Amendment was to establish equality of civil rights among citizens of the United States. When applied to the specific situation of public schools, the equality principle would lead to a desegregated school system, especially where history and practice had taught us that segregated schools were inherently unequal. In addition, personally I believed that the Supreme Court in Plessy was just plain wrong.

With all the adaptations that we used to effectively litigate, we still didn't digress from Charlie Houston's basic plan. That was, you use whatever techniques, knowledge, strategies and insights that circumstances required.

During the year of the re-argument, Chief Justice Vinson died. To fulfill a political obligation, President Eisenhower appointed Earl Warren as Chief Justice of the United States.

We knew that Earl Warren was an important figure in California politics, but we did not know how he would likely vote or how persuasive he would be as Chief Justice. However, he succeeded in his primary objective, of overruling Plessy v. Ferguson and doing this through a unanimous Supreme Court opinion. Warren's approach was both objective and positive. Without his perseverance in achieving an unanimous opinion, the decision would likely have been that of a divided court, perhaps six to three or five to four. Nevertheless, from our perspective, the overwhelming verdict was that Warren turned out to be a real gem. Segregationists were, and still are, critical of Chief Justice Warren.

Looking back, it is also interesting to note that in 1950 we thought Chief Justice Fred Vinson was in our judicial corner. However, later

165

research indicates that Vinson had not moved as far from traditional southern segregationist views as we had been led to believe by his decision in <u>Sweatt v. Painter</u>. As I had some personal knowledge of Chief Justice Vinson outside the judicial system, Vinson appeared more enlightened than many typical southern segregationists. Frequently, it is difficult to pinpoint the thinking of people who were not ardent segregationists. However, no question existed that Vinson opposed the overruling of <u>Plessy</u>. This was demonstrated by the research of Professor Bernard Schwartz at Tulsa University, who wrote a book discussing a number of the landmark Supreme Court cases, including <u>Brown.</u> The evidence which Schwartz uncovered revealed some of the behind-the-scenes complexity of judicial decision making. Schwartz's work demonstrated that Vinson opposed us on outlawing segregation <u>per se</u> in the public schools at the primary and secondary level.[17] It could have been that Vinson, like so many of his contemporaries, believed that the "the time just was not right."

Moreover, in those days, many white people supported segregation for political, social or economic reasons. In fact, most racial segregationists not only maintained their malicious personal attitudes towards Negroes, but also insisted that other white people publicly demonstrate a similar attitude.

Additional concerns in preparing our litigation strategy in <u>Brown</u> included a need to be sensitive to the position of Justice Frankfurter, the so-called "swing man." When Frankfurter was first appointed to the Supreme Court he was hailed as being a great liberal. However, as time passed, he became more conservative in his decisions.

The first problem that came to my attention emanating from Frankfurter's judicial decisions involved the so-called Pullman Doctrine.[18] That doctrine required a party to exhaust administrative remedies before seeking judicial review of the constitutionality of state statutes and regulations.

In civil rights cases, the <u>Pullman</u> Doctrine became in fact a futile, time-consuming and resource draining judicial delaying tactic. Faced with decades of segregationist rulings by an all white judiciary and bureaucrats, I did not see any reason for us to waste time and valuable resources engaging in fruitless activities.

Reaching a decision in the <u>Brown</u> case was a great problem for Frankfurter. He did not want to vote against Negroes. On the other hand, being a Jewish person, he did not want to be in the position of having voted to disrupt what was called "the southern way of life." Frankfurter seemed to feel that segregationists would retaliate against Jews, although throughout the South, many Jewish people were, in fact, segregationists.

In essence, I viewed Frankfurter as a wishy-washy prospect for overruling the doctrine in public schools. However, in terms of crafting our arguments, we felt that we needed to go to some lengths not to alienate him or lose his vote.

Following the rearguments in the __Brown__ case, we felt optimistic. Indeed, we believed that a majority of the Court now shared our views. For example, we were confident that Justices Douglas and Black would rule in our favor. Nevertheless, we also perceived Justices Jackson and Reed as presenting definite problems regarding obtaining their support to overturn __Plessy__.

An interesting historical footnote is that for the entire week before the Court handed down the __Brown__ decision, the Southern Regional Council assembled a task force consisting of a number of political, business and academic leaders from around the South to help plan the transition from a segregated to a desegregated society. I was a member of the task force and attended the conference held in Williamsburg. It was underwritten by a grant from the Fund For The Republic.

Prior to the announcement of the decision in __Brown__, we knew that a ruling in that case was going to come down on a Monday because in those days, the court always issued its rulings on Mondays. On several occasions Spot and I had gone to Washington, D.C. when we thought the case would be decided. However, on each of these occasions the Court did not hand down its ruling. As it would happen, on this particular Monday, May 17, 1954, both Spot and I had obligations which required us to remain in Richmond. I remember starting downtown and I got to the corner of Fourth and Leigh Streets when a bulletin came over the radio in my automobile saying that the Supreme Court was announcing its decision in the school segregation cases. Chief Justice Warren started talking. I turned the car around in the middle of the street and hightailed it back to the office. I ran upstairs yelling, "Turn on the radio, turn on the radio!" The radio was promptly turned on and everyone listened intently. Soon there was much hurrahing in our office as we were celebrating. We did no more work that day.

Reactions to Brown

Regarding the <u>Brown </u>decision, Virginia Governor Stanley initially made a comment to the effect that the world would not come to an end. At that time, Senator Harry F. Byrd, Sr. was out of the country. When Byrd came back, he rallied the segregationists to fight against the law of the land. In Virginia, the segregationists announced their so-called campaign of "massive resistance." Two years later, a majority of Senators and House members of the U.S. Congress from the southern states issued their infamous "Southern Manifesto" calling upon all southerners to resist any effort to desegregate public schools by "any and all lawful means." (As if one could lawfully violate someone else's constitutional rights.)

At a prior national NAACP conference, it was agreed that whenever the Supreme Court decided <u>Brown </u>a selected group of individuals would meet the following Saturday to discuss it and to issue a statement. Accordingly, following the Supreme Court's historic decision in <u>Brown v. Board of Education</u>, Dr. Tinsley, President of the Virginia NAACP, W. Lester Banks, Executive Director of the state NAACP, and I went to Atlanta as the Virginia delegation to discuss with other NAACP officials the appropriate response to the decision. The statement we issued was generally positive regarding the Court's decision because we recognized that we had won a major legal victory in overturning the nefarious <u>Plessy</u> decision.

After completing our business around 2:30 p.m. on Sunday, May 23, 1954, Banks, Tinsley and I had an interesting adventure. We went to the Atlanta Airport. This was during the days when you had to confirm your reservations. While we had confirmed reservations for a later flight, we decided to try to get an earlier one. We obtained the standby badges and waited patiently to see whether we would be able to get an earlier plane.

We were not able to do so. Accordingly, when our flight was announced, we were the first in line for the flight on which we were already booked. Nevertheless, the airport officials would not allow us on the flight because we still had standby badges on. We tried to explain to an airlines employee that the badges were for a previous flight. He refused to listen. Banks went back into the airport to get the airport manager; and by the time they returned all the seats on the plane had been filled except two.

168

They offered us those two seats. We refused the seats, stating that there were three of us and that we had confirmed reservations for the flight. Accordingly, we were not willing to fly unless all three of us were flying on the same plane together.

The airlines officials recognized the very real probability that they would be confronted with a lawsuit if we were not allowed on the plane. They raised the ante. They offered to allow us to stay in the best hotels in Atlanta and leave first thing in the morning for Richmond. We refused, stating that we had a meeting with Virginia's Governor Stanley the next morning and we needed to leave Atlanta on Sunday night.

The airline then attempted to find out which passenger was not confirmed on the flight. At first no one would confess. The plane was still sitting on the ground and the airlines officials turned off the engine, thus shutting off the air conditioning. It was a hot evening in May and finally after sitting there for nearly an hour and a half the culprit confessed. The individual acknowledged that he had not confirmed his reservation. That person got off and Dr. Tinsley, Mr. Banks and I boarded the plane. As we got on board, we confronted some sweltering, disgruntled, and downright angry passengers. The flight was over an hour and one half late leaving Atlanta.

Part of Virginia's Civil Right Leadership Team (mid. 1950's)
Seated left to right: Dr. Jesse Tinsley, Spotswood Robinson, III, Oliver W. Hill, Sr., and W. Lester Banks

Unfortunately for us, by the time we reached the Richmond area, weather conditions did not allow us to land. We flew to Washington and the airline bussed us back to Richmond. When we arrived at about 3:00 a.m., our families and friends were quite concerned.

Later that morning we had a very interesting meeting with Governor Stanley. The purpose of this meeting was to discuss the proper action to take following the Supreme Court's decision in Brown. Governor Stanley argued that we had made our point and had Plessy overruled. Stanley suggested that "Now, we should just let it ride." The group of nine African-Americans who met with Stanley included people from varying backgrounds and beliefs. However, even the most conservative of them viewed Stanley's proposal as absurd. All of us knew that if we accepted his proposal, the whites would say that Negroes did not want desegregation. No progress in desegregation could come in this way. We rejected the Governor's proposal.

On one hand, the Supreme Court performed an outstanding service to the American public by overruling Plessy v. Ferguson and declaring that racial segregation in public schools was unconstitutional. On the other hand, despite this courageous action, the Court's decision was fundamentally flawed in its failure to pursue the normal process that customarily prevailed in similar litigation situations. The school boards had unconstitutionally deprived Negro children of their rights. Instead of ordering these state officials to desegregate the school systems, the Court withheld any remedy for these constitutional violations. Rather, the Court set the case down for another hearing on what remedies to grant.

This required re-briefing and re-arguing along with the issuance of another opinion during the next term. In that opinion the Court embraced the infamous weasel words, "All deliberate speed." On remand, this terminology was supposed to guide the trial courts in working out the elements of the desegregation decision.

Unfortunately, the nefarious and fundamentally inadequate "all deliberate speed" doctrine constituted an abject failure in the attempt to accomplish a desegregated public school system. This noble objective was undermined as the Supreme Court sent out conflicting signals. Time has demonstrated that Frankfurter's alleged insertion of the all-deliberate speed requirement into the Brown desegregation remedies, turned out to promote a travesty of justice. Indeed, as is often stated, "justice delayed is justice denied." Some have said the Court talked out of both sides of its judicial mouth.

In response to the attempt by segregationists to develop legislative obstacles to __Brown__, I appeared before the Virginia General Assembly on November 30, 1955, approximately six months after __Brown II's__ unfortunate embrace of all deliberate speed. I made the following statement:

> Gentlemen:
>
> I appear before you today in a dual capacity. I represent the Virginia State Conference of NAACP Branches and, more importantly, I appear as an individual American citizen, resident of and domiciled in the Commonwealth of Virginia.
>
> The Association which I represent, and I as an individual, fervently believe in, and have striven and will continue to strive to bring about the development of, the concept of individual liberty and human dignity exemplified and expressed in the American Declaration of Independence. The action under consideration, coupled with the proposals which are to follow, constitutes a negation of those principles of individual liberty and human dignity. It is for these reasons we add our voice to those of the other good and responsible citizens of this Commonwealth who may appear before you in opposition to the course of action under consideration.
>
> You have been convened to consider a resolution changing a salutary provision of our State Constitution which, up until this very day, has served to bulwark, strengthen and materially aid in the development of the free public schools the cornerstone of American Democracy.
>
> It is common knowledge that the present proposal is simply an initial step in a series of proposals which, we believe, promulgated into law, can only serve to create a condition of strife, turmoil and confusion in the days immediately ahead until corrected by some future Legislature, the people of this Commonwealth, or by the United States Government. This course of action - designed to circumvent the ruling of the United States Supreme Court and to continue to deny citizens of the United States their constitutional rights because they are Negroes - if taken, conceived as it is in iniquity, can produce only harmful results.

Many good and responsible citizens of this Commonwealth will urge you to refrain from proposing that Section 141 of the Constitution of Virginia be repealed or in anywise tampered with on the grounds that the overall and underlying proposals are illegal, unchristian and un-American.

We believe that anyone who objectively considers the basic premise underlying the Report of the Gray Commission and the convening of this special session of the Legislature - that is, the maintenance of a system of racial segregation in the elementary, secondary and collegiate schools of this Commonwealth, fostered by law - will be compelled to conclude that this premise is wrong irrespective of whether it is considered from the viewpoint of science, religion, politics or historical facts.

The limitations of time will not permit an exhaustive presentation of any of these phases of the matter, thus I will limit myself to one small, but highly important, consideration which may not otherwise be urged.

The opponents of desegregation and of integration protest long and loudly about the Tenth Amendment to the Constitution of the United States as if no further amendments had been enacted. It is interesting to observe -- and I believe a comprehensive study would demonstrate - that, in their treatment of Negroes, commencing with the inclusion of the third paragraph of Section 2 of Article IV of the Constitution of the United States, which reads as follows-

"No Person held to Service or Labour in one State, under the Laws thereof, escaping into another, shall, in Consequence of any Law or Regulation therein, be discharged from such Service or Labour, but shall be delivered up on Claim of the Party to whom such Service or Labour may be due."

And continuing down to the matter which has given rise to the present state of affairs, the ruling oligarchies of the several southern states have done more to destroy the power of the individual states than any other factor in American history.

The adherents of racial segregation ignore entirely the virtual revolution created in the Federal-State relationship by the people of the United States, of which Virginia is still a part, when the people enacted the 14th Amendment in 1868. Prior to the enactment of the 14th Amendment, citizens of the several states derived their rights, privileges and immunities from the state in which they held legal residence. Unquestionably each citizen owed primary allegiance to his state. This condition of affairs was changed by the people of the United States. The sovereignty of the states was reduced. Section 1 of the 14th Amendment provides:

"All persons born or naturalized in the United States, and subject to the jurisdiction thereof, are citizens of the United States and of the State wherein they reside."

Today, gentlemen, all loyal persons subject to the jurisdiction of the United States, irrespective of whether they reside in Oregon or Florida, Texas or Maine, California or Virginia, or even Mississippi, owe their primary allegiance to the United States. It is time that we pause and consider this fact and stop this irresponsible talking and irrational action now taking place in Virginia and elsewhere in the South.

The Supreme Court simply gave recognition to the fact that all American citizens are entitled to be treated with the individual respect and dignity set forth in the Declaration of Independence, guaranteed by the Constitution of the United States, and consistent with the principles of a sovereign democratic power.

The action presently urged upon you by persons, many of whom are racial fanatics, is predicated upon superstitious myths having no basis in reality or fact. If it is your wish to hasten the increase of federal power and further reduce the prerogatives of local government over the affairs of the people of this Commonwealth, then carry out the bidding of the racial fanatics - for which purpose you have been convened. But we do not believe that the most powerful government ever to exist on the face of the earth, which gives succor to those made destitute by the ravages of nature, will find itself impotent to protect its citizens from the ravages of a handful of officeholders who, when afforded an opportunity to rise to the role of statesmen, either from lack of vision or moral courage, degenerate into mere politicians.

It does not take any great vision to recognize the fact that if the present devices could be successfully maintained, the final outcome would result only in a continued deterioration in the structure of our free public schools with resulting chaos and damage to all persons in the lower economic strata - white as well as Negro. This would be inevitable because a large portion of the state's finances would go into the development of private schools. It is a well known fact that the per pupil cost of education of students in private schools is considerably higher than that of students in public schools. It is also a matter of common knowledge that, with the public schools receiving the entire appropriation made available for the education of school children, our public schools are woefully deficient when compared with the public schools in the more progressive sections of this country. It is significant to note that Virginia is now almost at the bottom of the list in terms of facilities and educational content offered to our children. With the draining off of a large portion of the public funds into private schools, the progress made in recent years in the public school system will cease and, actually and comparatively, our public schools will decline.

I tell you with all the earnestness at my command that, if you succumb to the hue and cry raised in certain quarters of this Commonwealth, principally by those who have no faith in democracy, public education, or anything else that makes democracy meaningful to the ordinary person, then you shall have cast the die characterizing yourselves as petty politicians.

This appeal to common sense and justice was unavailing. Accordingly, we mobilized against the Court's wishy-washy position regarding remedies which had encouraged segregationists to organize resistance to the <u>Brown</u> decision. For example, here in Virginia the General Assembly created a Pupil Placement Board which took the authority from the local school boards to make pupil assignments. The Placement Board had the sole authority throughout the state to place local public school students. Accordingly, any Negro students who wanted to go to previously all white schools had to apply through the Pupil Placement Board. Of course, their petitions were denied. This was an artifice to avoid the Supreme Court's decision in <u>Brown</u>.

Similarly, many of the white citizens in Prince Edward County had demanded that the schools be closed if a single Negro student attended the white schools, and the local Board of Supervisors decided to appropriate public school funding in Prince Edward on a monthly basis so that if the courts ordered desegregation, the supervisors could cut off funding and close the schools. The supervisors had kept the schools open, but segregated, and when the Prince Edward School case came back from the Supreme Court on remand, the district court ruled against the plaintiffs. The court in effect held that by keeping the segregated schools open, the school board was in compliance with the Constitution.

We appealed to the Fourth Circuit and the Fourth Circuit ruled in our favor. By that time, Prince Edward had built a big new high school. They had planned to build a private academy for the white students.

In addition, at the same time, white citizens' councils and other organizations advocating massive resistance including violence, were formed in Virginia and throughout the south to resist <u>Brown</u>. Simultaneously, the Virginia General Assembly continued churning out anti-desegregation legislation. For example, the General Assembly passed statutes allowing the governor to close any school that the courts ordered desegregated. Because of the Pupil Placement Board's activities in sending Negroes to all Negro schools, we filed suits against school boards in Norfolk,[19] Warren County,[20] Charlottesville,[21] and Richmond. An interesting aside is that the local Richmond newspaper displayed a picture of members of the state pupil placement board who were kneeling

Lawyers defending public school segregation laws of the
Commonwealth of Virginia (circa mid-1950's)

175

on the ground with a ruler. The Pupil Placement Board claimed that the Calloway children who were Negroes bringing the suit lived several inches closer to the Negro school than to the white one.

Reporters and others constantly questioned us regarding when we thought schools would be desegregated. I consistently replied that desegregated schools would exist when we got judges who would order that Negro children attend white schools. I knew that in this crucial area of civic life, no elected white public officials would take the initiative and provide positive leadership. They put their political self interest in getting elected over the community's interest in progressive change and healing segregation's many wounds. Even the few who might have done something feared social ostracism of their wives and children, as well as possible physical harm to themselves. These fears were bourne out nearly two decades later in the ordeal of federal district Judge Mehrige, of Richmond, following his opinion allowing busing across city or county lines to desegregate schools in the same way that busing had been used for decades to maintain segregated schools.

This massive resistance to the Court's <u>Brown</u> desegregation ruling drew worldwide media coverage. I recall interviewers coming from the BBC to my home to interview me regarding the governmental officials' response to the Supreme Court's ruling. While an interviewer was asking me questions, I was sweating profusely because the interview occurred during the days when TV producers used big, hot lamps which generated as much heat as light.

That brings me to the Charlottesville school case. That case stands out in my mind in that the federal district judge was Judge John Paul. Former governor John S. Battle was representing the Charlottesville school authorities in the lawsuit that we had filed to desegregate the Charlottesville schools. Battle telephoned me at my offices on Leigh Street and asked me for an extension of time to file an answer to the Charlottesville complaint. I asked him how much time did he need, three or five days? In response he told me that he needed a thirty day extension to file an answer. I told him that I could not agree to an extension for that period of time. I pointed out that the rules allowed only twenty-one days for answering a complaint, and that if he insisted on such a long extension, we would have to just take it before the judge. I anticipated that the judge would grant Battle's request; however, I wanted the record to show that I had resisted the request. Accordingly, that was the route that we took.

By that time we had broken up the law firm of Hill, Martin & Robinson, but Spot and I continued to work together on school cases. One day Spot and I were talking on the phone, and I told him about Governor Battle's unreasonable request. After we talked about it a while, Spot said that he would ride up to Harrisonburg with me and meet Judge Paul too, because he had never met Paul.

The two of us rode up to Judge Paul's chambers in Harrisonburg for the hearing. There we met former governor Battle. As we entered Judge Paul's chambers and after Spot and I had introduced ourselves, Judge Paul asked us what brought us to the court. I'm not quite sure why I took the initiative but I told the judge that Governor Battle had requested an extension of time to file a response to our petition. Before I could say more, Judge Paul turned to Battle and asked him how much time he needed . ... three, four, or five days? At the judge's response, I brightened up. I knew the judge was thinking along the same lines that I was.

In reply to the judge's questions, Battle said that he needed thirty days. The judge said in essence that Battle did not need that much time. Judge Paul stated that one of Battle's law clerks could answer the complaint in little or no time. All Battle was going to do was deny the allegations in the complaint. So Paul denied the request for a thirty day extension to file an answer and gave a much shorter period of time, something like five days.

When I walked out of the judge's chambers I turned to Spot and said, "Spot, I think we got ourselves a real judge." Immediately upon returning to Richmond, I filed a motion for an order requiring the school board to admit Negro children to the previously all-white Warren County High School. Judge Paul signed the order. Later, at the appropriate time in the litigation in Charlottesville, he also ordered the local officials to desegregate the schools.

Immediately after Judge Paul ruled in Warren County, we filed a petition before Judge Hoffman requesting that he order the local officials to desegregate the Norfolk schools. Judge Hoffman issued the order to desegregate.

Promptly after Judge Paul's and Judge Hoffman's rulings, Governor Almond closed the schools in all the affected communities. Shortly thereafter, some white parents in Norfolk filed suit in the state court seeking to have the courts declare unconstitutional the Virginia statutes which allowed the governor to close the schools in the event of desegregation. The local state judge held the statute to be constitutional and his ruling was appealed to the Virginia State Supreme Court.[22] A suit raising the same issue was filed in the federal court. [23]

On the same day, January 19, 1959, both the three-judge federal district court and the Virginia State Supreme Court ruled that the Virginia statutes were unconstitutional. Almond then publicly began ranting and raving about closing all of the schools that were being desegregated and said that he was prepared to go to jail rather than to see the schools desegregated.

Almond intensified the rhetorical static by going on radio and making a speech denouncing the courts' decisions to desegregate the schools. Through Mr. W. Lester Banks, Executive Secretary of the Virginia State NAACP, I requested equal time to respond to Almond's speech.

Channel 8, the local ABC affiliate, gave me a prime time spot to respond to the speech. On the following Sunday evening, I went on the air and lambasted Almond's position. The next day Almond caved in. He decided and said that he was no longer going to go to jail. Later it was reported that along with some other business people Lewis Powell, Jr., and J. Harvie Wilkinson, Sr. had gone to see the governor. Purportedly, they told the governor that the opposition to the Court's decision <u>in Brown v. Board of Education</u> was making Virginia look ridiculous and was bad for business. I am told that that was the real reason that the governor caved in.

However, I believe and still contend that my speech also helped to move the process along in a positive direction. Incidentally, Powell later became an associate justice of the Supreme Court, and Wilkinson founded Crestar Bank. Wilkinson's son is currently chief judge for the United States Court of Appeals for the Fourth Circuit.

The TV movie and two documentaries on <u>Brown</u> were excellently done.

Another interesting bit of background involves W. Lester Banks, who served as NAACP Executive Secretary for the State of Virginia for many years. At Mr. Banks' request, I went to Charles City County in late 1942 or early 1943 to talk with him about the possibility of filing a teachers' salary lawsuit in Charles City County. Banks was a principal at the Negro high school in Charles City County at the time. However, by the time the moment had come to file suit, Banks had been drafted into the armed services. In addition, I was also drafted, and interestingly enough, the next time that we met we were both at Camp Claiborne in Louisiana.

After I returned to Virginia from the armed services, Dr. Tinsley and I resumed our practice of visiting counties and promoting the NAACP. At the same time we had gotten authorization from the Virginia State Conference to employ an Executive Secretary. Tinsley and I were appointed as a two man committee. I began to work with Dr. Tinsley to try to find an Executive Secretary who would go around the state to discuss the NAACP's program with interested individuals. Dr. Tinsley had a dental practice and I had a law practice. In those circumstances it was crucial to have someone else involved on a day to day basis in the organizational activities of the NAACP.

One day another member of the Executive Committee informed me that he had met someone whom he thought would be a fine Executive Director. Upon discovering that the prospective candidate was W. Lester Banks, and based on my prior experience with Banks, I readily agreed. Having heard that Banks was coming out of the army, we promptly arranged an interview and as a result thereof offered him the job of Executive Director of the Virginia State NAACP. He did a fine job. Coincidentally, the Virginia State NAACP during the 1940's and 1950's was the strongest and most active conference in the country and had the most extensive program challenging unlawful racial discrimination.

We were fighting civil rights litigation battles on many fronts. For instance, in addition to passing legislation allowing the governor to shut schools which the courts ordered to be desegregated, the General Assembly passed statutes to prevent so-called solicitation. The statutes were attempts to undermine the efforts of the NAACP to initiate and maintain legal challenges to segregationist practices in the state. The Virginia General Assembly's House of Delegates set up the Boatwright Committee and the Virginia State Senate established the Thompson Committee. These Commonwealth legislative committees attempted to get the membership list of the NAACP to intimidate and retaliate against its members for their civil rights activities. It was also at this time that S.W. Tucker took an increasingly aggressive stand in confronting massive resistance.

The NAACP and the NAACP Legal Defense Fund (also known in

house as the "Ink Fund") decided to challenge the constitutionality of the massive resistance statutes that declared the activities of the Ink Fund and the NAACP to be unlawful. Bob Carter, (who later became a federal district judge in New York) and I filed suit representing the NAACP. Spot Robinson as Regional Director of the Ink Fund and Thurgood Marshall sued representing the Ink Fund. The three judge federal district court consolidated these massive resistance cases and set them down for hearing. The three judge panel ruled in our favor on several issues and abstained from deciding others until the state courts had an opportunity to adjudicate them.

On appeal, by a divided vote, the Supreme Court vacated and remanded. The majority said that the three judge court should have abstained on each of the issues involving the state laws until the state courts could pass on them. When the cases came back, we litigated these matters in the state court -- and won a partial victory in the state supreme court. At this point, Thurgood and Spot decided to go back to the federal district court seeking judicial relief.

Bob and I thought that this was a waste of time and decided to apply for cert to the Supreme Court. An interesting aside is that in both the state and federal courts, by the time the litigation ended in the U.S. Supreme Court the case had carried the names of Attorney Generals Harrison, Patty, Gray, and Button.

Our appeal back to the U.S. Supreme Court progressed more quickly. During the course of the litigation, I wound up accepting a position in the Kennedy Administration. Bob Carter argued the case in the United States Supreme Court. We obtained a favorable decision (NAACP v. Button) while the Ink Fund case was still pending before the federal trial court.[24]

There were some personal costs for those plaintiffs courageous enough to file suits to vindicate their constitutional rights. For example, after they initiated lawsuits in Charlottesville, several plaintiffs lost their jobs. Some of them were lower wage workers like domestics. They had the fortitude to litigate in the courts but they paid a terrific economic price. In fact, if we had not been able to successfully resist the state government's attempt to get NAACP membership lists, many more people would have suffered economic and other forms of retaliation.

Furthermore, in numerous cities in response to the courts' desegregation decisions, many white residents fled to the surrounding

180

counties to avoid desegregation. This mid twentieth century example of white flight was repeated not only in Virginia and other parts of the South but nationwide. At the same time, some cities like Richmond attempted to annex surrounding predominantly white counties to maintain a white electoral majority.

Thus, for instance, in the early 1960's Richmond City Council tried to annex portions of Henrico and Chesterfield Counties. The court ruled in favor of the city allowing it to annex part of Henrico County. The court ruled that the city would have to pay the county forty million dollars in compensation.

The city decided this price was too expensive. City officials concluded that they should focus their energies on pursuing an annexation lawsuit against Chesterfield County. During subsequent litigation, evidence obtained in discovery revealed that former Mayor Bagley conspired with Chesterfield officials to dilute Negro voting strength. Bagley agreed to annex Chesterfield County property containing a number of white voters rather than annex a more sparsely populated area of county property. The more lightly settled part of the county included property owned by the DuPont Company and had a better tax base. Bagley's actions demonstrated that maintaining the political power of white folks outweighed the community's interest in economic development and in a fair resolution of issues presented by evolving social conditions.

A suit was also filed during the early 1970's to allow the school boards to ignore county district lines in carrying out the Supreme Court's mandate to desegregate schools. Judge Robert Merhige ruled in favor of the plaintiffs but the Fourth Circuit reversed. During this period Justice Powell along with Justice Rehnquist had been nominated to the Supreme Court and when the case got there Powell decided not to participate in the case but Rehnquist did. The Court was equally divided which meant that the decision of the Fourth Circuit reversing Merhige stood.[25] If the Supreme Court had had the courage at that point to rule in favor of busing across city and county lines as a remedy for desegregating the schools, it is reasonable to believe that most of the white flight would have stopped. There would not have been any place for the white parents to run to avoid having their children go to school with Negro children. At that point some political compromise could have been worked out but instead the Fourth Circuit and the Supreme Court decisions made bad matters worse.

Certainly, inter-district busing was not a novelty during the days of segregation, for Virginia had numerous precedents compelling the busing of Negro students across city and county lines to attend segregated schools. Indeed, Virginia had long-standing legislation providing for regional school boards to facilitate racially segregated public schools.

Ordinarily our office would have handled this civil rights case. However, since Henry Marsh was Vice Mayor of Richmond at the time, our firm couldn't participate in the proceedings. The lawyers who represented plaintiffs were George Little, Louis Lucas, Norman Chachkin, and Bill Taylor.

An analogous contemporary situation involves affirmative action. Had the courts and legislatures been more willing to use stringent measures to remedy past discrimination, by now this society would have adjusted to equal opportunity as the law of the land. Obviously, affirmative action would have been a temporary measure and after the inequalities had been remedied, it would no longer have been necessary.

I make no apologies about advocating affirmative action where necessary because I see how the United States government is willing to send white youngsters as well as black ones to foreign countries to risk injuries and their very lives to fight for democracy. If this country can risk the lives of its young people for democracy on "foreign shores", why can't some white people in America temporarily suffer a little inconvenience or sacrifice a little more economically so that on these shores we can develop a society in which a person's color or ethnic classification becomes immaterial. Why is it that many affirmative action critics are unwilling to give back the considerable material benefits that they have inherited through centuries of discrimination. They want to keep the benefits and privileges of racism, and are unwilling to make some temporary sacrifices or experience some transitory inconvenience for the common good. Where is their patriotism? There ought to be fair opportunities for all, and a sharing of power and resources at all levels of our society.

Moreover, time has shown that affirmative action was and is still needed. Over forty years after <u>Brown </u>and over thirty years after enactment of the Civil Rights Acts, we still do not have a level playing field regarding employment, education, business, social or political opportunities.

182

As I mentioned previously, in our civil rights work, we were simultaneously fighting on a number of different fronts. For example, we were also involved in defending participants in the first sit-in cases. After some Virginia Union University students had been arrested, I immediately asked W. Lester Banks to call a NAACP meeting at the old historic Fifth Street Baptist Church to discuss the sit-in situation. I remember making a speech stating that if necessary we would fill the jails. As folks stood against oppression, and were arrested, we would make the jails "havens for democracy". While I smile now when I think back at my rhetoric then, I am pleased that we were able to establish case law in the U.S. Supreme Court that participating in a sit-in was not a criminal offense.

Before I left for Washington to accept a job in the Kennedy administration, I decided to contact Henry Marsh, who was then working with the Labor Department. I asked Henry to come down, join our office and help Tucker handle some of the civil rights cases that we were working on. Marsh agreed to do so. Not long after that, Tucker and Marsh found out that Prince Edward County was about to use public monies for the white private academies that they were building. Tucker and Marsh went to court and blocked the county from using state funds to subsidize private discrimination. This successful litigation strategy required the white parents to spend their own private dollars to educate their children in the newly built segregated private academy.

In addition, the Prince Edward school system got a new superintendent from Long Island to run the schools for Negroes. For nearly five years there had been no public schools operating at all in Prince Edward County. This situation hurt both whites as well as Negroes. Finally, the large new Negro school building was put to use. The vast majority of white students continued to attend the private academies.

Following my initial participation in the civil rights struggle in the 1960's as a litigator and community activist, I spent a substantial portion of that decade in national governmental service as Assistant to the Commissioner of Federal Housing Administration for Intergroup Relations. My governmental employment responsibilities required me to promote fair housing practices throughout the United States. I made a conscious effort to encourage the development of equitable government housing programs to help disadvantaged groups like Indians.

By joint agreement between the Commissioner and me, my

183

government employment eliminated my private legal practice activities except I continued to help defend my partner, Samuel Tucker, from disbarment proceedings instituted before I accepted the governmental position. (Over a period of six or seven months, I also handled a few other matters to their conclusion.) Under new regulations on client solicitation, the State Bar attempted to disbar Tucker. They argued that he was engaged in unduly influencing lay persons to initiate legal proceedings. The so called "running and capping" regulations were another in a long line of state sponsored strategies to intimidate and silence citizens and advocates who dared to affirm their rights as human beings.

I came back to Richmond near the end of the decade of the 1960s. Upon my return, I rejoined the firm and became involved with Henry Marsh in the landmark employment case known as <u>Quarles v. Phillip Morris.</u>[26] which opened employment opportunities for Phillip Morris workers. After our federal court victories, the company developed some reasonable employment policies. In fact, at one time or another our law firm has filed employment discrimination suits against nearly every major employer in the state of Virginia, including the largest employer, the Newport News Shipyard.

<u>A California Temptation</u>

I attended the NAACP Conference in San Francisco in the late 1950's. Like many folks I was quite impressed. When I returned to Virginia, I told my wife that if I felt like studying for and taking another bar exam, I would suggest that we move to San Francisco. However, the proverbial fly in the ointment was that it had been over twenty-five years since I had taken a bar exam. I was not thinking about taking another one.

It is interesting to speculate on what might have happened had I moved to San Francisco. For example, it is just possible that I might have been offered a position with the NAACP Legal Defense Fund as the Western Regional Counsel. In addition, I could have easily seen myself participating in local political activities and running for public office. There seemed to be less racial bigotry there and better economic opportunities. For example, cases which, at that time, we had to try in a few days in Virginia, often took a week or weeks in California. However, of course, what might have happened is just speculative.

In short, regarding a move to California, nothing happened

because I never felt like taking another doggone bar exam. At that time, California did not have reciprocity for anyone. I don't know whether they do now or not.

A Few Observations on Social Conditions Before the Civil Rights Acts

Up until World War II people bought automobiles and didn't think about changing them every two or three years. In fact Packard advertised the longevity of their automobiles, using the slogan "Ask the man who owns one." As a child I remember aspiring to own a Packard roadster!

Negroes used automobiles in their travels to avoid the indignity of the Jim Crow seating arrangements on trains and buses. Standard Oil's "Esso" gasoline became a favorite among Negroes in the East and South because that company employed a Negro as the company's traveling representative. His popular name was "Billboard Jackson". Jackson formerly worked for the Department of Commerce. He successfully persuaded Standard Oil to initiate a firm policy requiring its dealers to allow Negroes to use male and female restrooms. Prior to that time it was customary for service stations to limit restroom use to white people.

Prior to the mid 1950's, and often until the Civil Rights Acts of the 1960's, hospitals available to Negroes in the South were vastly inferior to those accessible to the non-Negro general public. As a matter of fact, it was a long time before the majority of Negroes developed the practice of going to hospitals in a timely fashion. In earlier days, by the time Negroes decided to enter the hospital, they were frequently in such bad shape that they died. This perpetuated the myth that if you went into the hospital you would not come out alive.

Up until recent years, because of segregation, Negroes were denied admission to most hospitals in the South. Even then, when one was admitted, it was to the colored section of the hospital. Just because a hospital existed in a city, didn't necessarily mean anything to Negroes. It had to have a colored section. Therefore, for instance if a Negro was injured in an automobile accident, she had to be admitted to a segregated ward or hospital. Here in Richmond, Negro patients didn't go to MCV, they went down to St. Phillips which was at the other end of the MCV complex. That's the way things were in most cases, up until the passage of the Civil Rights Act.

185

Money and Fees

During this period of activity, (1939-through the early 1960's), I was working with the NAACP. In Virginia we had the first and strongest NAACP state conference. In Virginia, we were semi-independent in the sense that we handled our own litigation, and much of the financing was done through activities of the Virginia NAACP State Conference.

While the Virginia State NAACP Conference was semi-independent, generally we followed the policies of the National NAACP. National policies were so well coordinated that we functioned within the guidelines of its program.

Among state NAACP organizations, Texas was the nearest competition to Virginia regarding membership and financial strength. Later when I worked at the Federal Housing Administration, I discovered that Maceo Smith, a former president of the Texas Conference, was also an employee of that agency.

While we worked with the NAACP, "employed" is not the right word to describe our civil rights activities. From around 1946 or 1947 until 1955 Spot Robinson's salary stipend as Regional Counsel for the NAACP Legal Defense Fund went into the firm coffers. Occasionally, Spot Robinson and I went to New York to work on briefs and similar activities. The national office paid those expenses. Other than that, however, we were private practitioners. For example, we also received a retainer from a self-insured cab company that kept us active and provided some revenue.

Although we were supposed to be compensated, sometimes, you were lucky to get expenses. So far as payment was concerned, we got very little. Even when we were supposed to be getting paid, the NAACP State Conference constantly owed us several thousand dollars. The situation was complicated. Frequently the National Office would be delinquent in meeting its financial obligations to the State Conference because the branches were often slow in sending money to the National Office. The State Conference hardly had enough to pay the Executive Secretary and his secretary. Therefore, members of the legal staff frequently were the ones who got the short end of the financial stick.

We survived financially on our private practice. However, our client volume was never so high that we could turn away any reasonable employment with a fee attached to it. As a matter of fact if a case

186

presented itself involving race discrimination, we often took it regardless of whether the prospects for fee recovery were good or poor, particularly in cases that had some potential to make a broader impact on the law.

Looking back, it is fair to say that we might have turned away some non paying cases. However, we had families to support, and our firm had always done more than its share of pro bono work.

Fixing and collecting fees has always been my major problem. Maybe we should have run a tighter ship. However, one way or another the money came in. We had to charge fees but the main focus always was on the humanitarian angle of a given situation.

Some Thoughts on Segregation and Human Development

Even though we initially sought enforcement of the separate but equal rule, I once argued before the Court of Appeals that if a school board built two schools from identical plans provided equally qualified teachers, the same curriculum, and furnishings and limited Negro children to attending one school and white children to attending the other, I would still say it was discriminatory against the Negroes. As long as Negroes are excluded from the societal mainstream, they will continue to be relegated to a form of second class citizenship. When the government excludes a person through segregation laws, and the general society by custom, that exclusion places that person in a position where there are too many things that happen that the person doesn't know anything about. White children going to school have parents who are involved in various functions in the political, business and social affairs of the community. Those children bring experiences, perspectives, and other things to the schools that black children have had no opportunity to become familiar with.

An apt analogy was my City Council experience. There were many things I could not identify with when I became a member of the Council. My white colleagues were talking about things with which I had no previous experience or contact in the African American community. Similarly people talk about what a Negro child can learn, and it is true that a Negro child can learn the basic things that you get out of books. But to obtain the intangible things that go along with the culture of the mainstream community from which you are excluded, you need access to information and experience. Opportunity to gain many types of knowledge is important. For instance, whites as well as Negroes need to recognize there are other people of different ethnic groups

187

and colors who have something to contribute. Some of the intangibles flow from sharing educational and other life experiences. It is not all in books.

I never went to school with a white child in my life. Nevertheless, I succeeded in obtaining sufficient knowledge to pass the bar exam on my first try. But I know that I lacked knowledge in many areas that would have made me a more effective contributor to the welfare of my community. Segregation makes one feel excluded. However, not only is one excluded from community life, but one is also excluded from a better appreciation of the culture, worldview, and ideas of other people. Segregation is a narrowing experience both for those who are excluded and for those who are the excluders.

Accordingly, if we are ever going to have better understanding, we must communicate and knock down barriers based on ignorance and fear. We must recognize that evolution is a fact of our collective lives and that change is inevitable. If we are going to direct that change in a positive direction for the commonweal, it must be a cooperative effort on the part of all segments of our society.

In the next two chapters, I will discuss my national government service experiences -- both non military and military.

Chapter V

Military Experience

> *If it hadn't been for that fool chaplain talking about Negroes having tails and being bent on raping English girls, for the past fifty-five years I might have been over there in the bottom of the English channel or buried on one of those beaches like Omaha or Utah. Instead of landing on D-Day, we arrived on the beaches three weeks later.... I was there on the beach and the German planes came over. When the alarm sounded, we immediately took shelter in our previously prepared foxholes. We had the protection of so much anti-aircraft firepower that the Germans had to fly at extremely high levels. Consequently, they did relatively little damage to us still on the beaches. Looking up at the sky from our fox holes it looked like a glorified Fourth of July celebration.*

I was so immersed in preparing for our anticipated attack on segregation laws that at first I didn't pay much attention to increasing American involvement leading up to the Second World War. Of course, everybody had to register for the draft in about 1939 or 1940. I was in my thirties then and married. However, we had no children.

Under threat of a March on Washington by A. Philip Randolph, in 1941 President Roosevelt issued Executive Order No. 8802 creating the Fair Employment Practices Committee (F.E.P.C.). Around this time, William H. Hastie was appointed as a civilian aide to Secretary of the Army, Henry Stimson. As I mentioned, Bill was one of my former professors. We were fraternity brothers and were very close. As a matter of fact, when the NAACP decided to establish its Washington Bureau, Bill recommended me for the position of director of the Bureau. This was the position that Clarence Mitchell later brilliantly and effectively filled.[1]

189

I discussed my draft status with Bill. At that time from his position in the Pentagon, Bill was advocating strenuously that all branches of the military apparatus should be opened to Negroes on the same basis as whites. However, progress occurred so slowly that to bring the military's continuing discriminatory treatment to public attention, he resigned.

I observed many young white lawyers who were getting commissions in the Navy. Until that time, except for the position of mess men, the Navy was closed to Negroes. I decided to apply for a commission in the Navy. I was nearly old enough to be exempted from the draft.

The only apparent governmental response to my application for a naval commission was to hasten my being inducted into the military. This was about the time that the all Negro Tuskeegee Air Corps was being created. The Tuskeegee unit performed heroic and distinguished service in the European Theatre of military operations. While we knew that I was too old to be considered for a position in the Air Corps, one of my State Department contacts thought that it would be a good idea to precisely determine my physical condition.

My State Department contact arranged for me to take a physical examination with some white Air Force applicants at the Armory over the Old Market Place at Sixth and Marshall Streets in Richmond. At the conclusion of the physical examination, my papers were filled out and handed to me.

I was in good physical condition; and the report stated that. However, feeling compelled to make some negative comment, and despite my having a very high arch, there appeared on the report the notation: "racially flat feet."

I was in a very frustrating situation. I had no interest in enlisting in the military service out of any patriotic zeal. In fact, around January or February of 1942, I was interviewed in my Richmond office as part of an FBI investigation. I remember getting into an argument with the F.B.I. agent. He asked me some doggone question. I cannot recall how I worded my response, but I think it was summarized by the fact that I did not favor the English on one island trying to rule the world or the Japanese on another island on the other side of the world attempting to do the same thing. To the agent's disgust, I lumped them together.

On the other hand, the draft board got on me so doggone hard until around December of 1942, the Board was threatening to bring me in at any time! Despite the rampant racism, I was not trying to dodge the military service. At that time I was aware that I could have filed a suit against the government and that might have held up everything. In that case, I might have never gone into the service. What I really wanted to do was break some new ground, as a naval officer.

Finally I went down before the draft board and told them that I could not practice law with the Board's threat of bringing me into the service on short notice. I struck a compromise with the Board. We agreed that the Board would just defer any induction of me until June of 1943. In my protest I was basically volunteering.

In the meantime I had talked with Spotswood Robinson. He had finished law school in 1939 and was teaching at Howard University Law School. However, Spot had never passed the bar. The first time after his graduation that he planned to take the bar, he genuinely got sick and couldn't take it. After that, whenever the bar examination came up he developed a psychosomatic illness.

Earlier I had talked with his Daddy who asked me, "What are we going to do about Spot and the bar examination?" I said, "Well, I just think if we put him under some pressure he will go on and take the exam." We had no concern that he couldn't pass the bar. He had finished Howard with the highest scholastic record anybody's ever made before or since.

At that time, there were some rooms vacant in the old Consolidated Bank Building. Spot used to come home every weekend, and we used to get together. I told him that I was going to have to go in the service. I suggested that we form an association and we could rent some rooms in the bank building over his father's office. He readily agreed to this arrangement.

Spot's father was a practicing attorney specializing in real estate transactions. We worked out an arrangement along these lines: Spot's father would cover legal matters in my office with Spot's assistance in the interim between my induction into the military and the time that Spot received his bar examination results.

Before my induction, I had to get a deferment because my foster mother, Mrs. Lelia Pentecost, died. I attended her funeral in Roanoke.

191

While I was attending the funeral, Spot was also there at the Hotel Roanoke taking the Virginia State Bar Exam. It was a two day exam when he took it and also when I took it nearly ten years earlier in 1933.

Anyway, that's part of the background of my going into the service. I was actually inducted into the military service about 45 days after my thirty-sixth birthday. At age thirty-six, I should have been exempt.

It is an interesting fact of history that in World War I, Negroes had established a brilliant record of valor under fire, principally under French command.[2] Despite this fact, in World War II, there was a determined effort to limit the activities of Negroes as warriors, and to consign Negroes as much as possible to labor and service tasks.

After the establishment of the Tuskeegee Air Corps, the Navy was the most segregated of the armed services. As I mentioned, they would only accept blacks as mess men. The army was not that much better. Negroes were frequently placed in labor battalions or given duties driving heavy trucks. Throughout the military, there were severe limitations on Negroes' opportunities to serve our short-sighted, color-conscious, country.

Upon being drafted, my first cousin, Charlie Pollard, and I passed the physical at Virginia Union University . We were given a choice as to whether we wanted to go into the Navy, Marines or the Army as privates. Well, neither of us gave the Marines the first thought.

We debated whether we wanted to go into the Army or the Navy. We both had the same objection. Present day folks probably do not remember what the old naval uniforms were like. They had the tight tops and pants with bell bottoms. Although I had developed considerable experience as a waiter in earning money to work my way through college, I did not relish the idea of serving as a messman in the Navy. Thus the combination of the uniform and what we believed would be our job assignment helped influence us to decide against going into the Navy. We decided for the Army instead.

From our perspective later, that decision was a big mistake. Had we elected to enter the Navy, I'm sure the same thing would have happened to us that happened to many of my friends similarly situated. We would have been sent to the Great Lakes Naval Station and that would have been the end of it. But we elected to go into the Army. At that time, I also had in mind that I could apply to Officers Candidate

School, and subsequently I did.

The army initially sent us to Camp Meade where we were assigned to the Engineers. Later, they shipped us down to Camp Claiborne in Alexandria, Louisiana where we did our basic training. Of course, when I was in basic training, my wife, Bernie, wanted to come and be closer to where I was. But Camp Claiborne was a real hell hole and I didn't want her down there. I often said that of all the doggone places for the Army to have sent me, this was about the worse. I may as well have been in a foreign country.

As far as I was concerned, if I had been sent anywhere on the East Coast, I was pretty well known and had associates and friends. But I didn't know anybody in Louisiana north of Baton Rouge. I did have several acquaintances down in New Orleans, but, shucks, we were two hundred miles from New Orleans.

It was a segregated Army. We had three Negro officers in our regiment. One officer was named Lt. Collins. He was the special services officer. The other two were, as I recall, each assigned to a different line company.

Starting with my basic training, the Army and I were a problem for each other. They didn't know what to do with me, and I was stymied. I was an experienced trial lawyer and I was older than most of the officers, much less the enlisted men. Nevertheless, like all other draftees, including other lawyers who did not have direct commissions, I started out as a buck private. They put me in Headquarters & Service Company (H & S Company). It was an all-black engineer regiment, with the exception that, other than the three previously mentioned Negroes, all the officers were white.

H & S Company was where the regimental Headquarters was located. H & S Company members were responsible for clerical duties like maintaining personnel files and paying the troops, operating the pool of vehicles, and serving as the nerve center for the regiment. It was not anticipated that we would, in performing our missions, use live ammunition.

The Sergeant Major in our company was an old regular army man. The expectation was that he was going to retire when we completed our basic training and prepared to go overseas. I would then become the Sergeant Major.

However, upon my arrival at Camp Claiborne, I immediately applied for O.C.S. While in the United States, I never received a reply to my application. I raised the issue with my company and regimental officers. They promised to make appropriate inquiries. Nothing, however, was accomplished and I doubt seriously that any help was attempted.

In addition, I hadn't been down at Camp Claiborne more than two or three days when I received a visit from Army Intelligence. These officers questioned me extensively.

I have sometimes reflected on why the F.B.I. may have investigated me and why Army Intelligence continued to monitor my activities. There was no factual evidence to warrant such surveillance. It could have been that when I went back to Washington in 1936 I was involved in the organization I told you about, "The National Negro Congress." The F.B.I. called it a "popular front organization." We marched and we protested in Washington D.C.

Back in those days there was a phrase called "fellow travelers." People in this category weren't communists but they were called "fellow travelers" because they had a lot of association with communists and other "fellow travelers." In those days, quite frequently Negroes were identified with communists because generally the communists supported Negro activities, especially protest marches and similar responses to segregation. In contrast, the majority of white Americans were segregationists, whether anti-communist or not, and were usually hostile, or at the least, aloof to the efforts of Negroes to eliminate racial segregation.

During that period, the communists courted and recruited blacks who showed potential for leadership. They had courted me quite extensively. Accordingly, when I applied for the naval commission, that probably sparked the interest of the military intelligence apparatus. These type associations were probably why the F.B.I. came to interrogate me.

While I was in the military service, Army Intelligence would come by every two or three weeks. After a while, in fact, it became a joke. Upon seeing them on these routine visits, my question to them was, "You back here again?" I knew that I had not done any thing subversive to our democratic form of government. My focus was upon fighting segregation or apartheid prevailing in the United States. To most segregationists, these humane activities were generally considered to be subversive.

As I indicated, I did not have too much use for England, Germany, Russia, Japan or any of the leading nations of the day. For one thing, none of them opposed segregation or apartheid in the United States; and many of them benefitted from it. Like I told the F.B.I., I didn't see any difference among the ruling classes in any of them.

Be it right or wrong, I still believe that one of the reasons that I was drafted was because of my activities in challenging the *status quo* in a state controlled by the infamous political organization known as the Byrd Machine. The Byrd Machine had as a primary objective the preservation of segregation or American apartheid. I had as one of my primary goals, overturning the segregation laws; and I believe that my work as an activist for social change contributed to my being drafted only days before my age would have exempted me from military service.

One day, after being in Camp Claiborne for several weeks, I got a welcomed letter, with an equally welcomed letterhead reading "Hill, Martin and Robinson, Attorneys at Law." Martin had resigned from the Department of Justice and returned to Richmond. Martin and Spot had finished Howard Law School near the same time. I was confident that Martin and Spot would keep up the fight to eliminate legal segregation in Virginia.

Our basic training moved along in an uneventful pattern until near the end of our training at Camp Claiborne we were ordered, in full military gear, to go on a ten mile hike. The temperature was 105 degrees Fahrenheit. I was in excellent physical condition, and along with most of the troops completed the ordeal. However, the trail of our march was peppered with a number of young troops who had fallen along the way, including two or three fatal casualties. Soon thereafter, we left Camp Claiborne via rail transportation and went up to Camp Shanks which is in New York State, not far from New York City. We had only spent a few days there when I received a message from Bernie that her mother had died. I got leave to go to Washington to attend her funeral.

Shortly after I came back, our regiment was loaded aboard a French vessel named the *Normandy*. This was a French luxury liner that had been transformed into a troop carrier and was the fastest ship afloat at the time. Our preparation had been for Europe. It was different from preparation for the Southwest theatre. We didn't really know where we were going. However, we assumed we were going to England.

My little group of buddies in the company consisted of my first cousin, Charlie Pollard, who had worked up to becoming a first sergeant in H & S Company; a soldier from Norfolk named Edney who was the head cook; and a sergeant in the personnel section, from Chicago, named Gonzales.

I was just a sergeant. I hadn't been promoted to Staff Sergeant at that stage. The Sergeant Major also decided he wanted to go to Europe.

Gonzales, Edney, Charlie and I hung out together. We also had an on going partnership pinochle game. Charlie and I played against Edney and Gonzales. At our earliest opportunity, shortly after returning to Shanks, I took them from Camp Shanks to New York City, "The Big Apple." The highlight of the trip was dinner at a "glitzy" restaurant with good food at 42nd Street and Broadway. They were impressed. That was not far from the NAACP Legal Defense Fund office which in those days was on 43rd Street.

Anyway, one day shortly before Christmas 1943, we were loaded on trucks and taken to the docks. This was the area from which the regular transatlantic steamships departed and arrived. There were numerous signs warning and entreating civilians to exercise caution in what they said about troop movements. "A slip of the lip can sink a ship" was one of the quotes.

After boarding, an interesting event occurred as we began to embark on the voyage across the Atlantic to the European theatre. As the ship was pulling out of the harbor, Charlie, Gonzales, Edney and I were sitting there on the ship playing a peaceful game of pinochle. Suddenly, the words came over the loudspeaker loud and clear: "Hear ye, hear ye. Prepare to disembark."

All of a sudden Charlie jumped up and yelled, "You hear what that said? It said disembark. That means to get the hell off this thing." It appeared that the ship had caught on fire and they reversed the movement of the ship and returned to the port in New York.

As soon as we docked, we were loaded on trucks and taken back to Camp Shanks. There the soldiers scattered in different directions. Then another interesting thing happened. I ran to the telephone and called Bernie. I told her to come on up to New York and go to the apartment of my friends, Ed and Ray Dudley. There I would get in touch with her. Ed and Ray were living in New York, and Ed had recently graduated from law school. As children, in Roanoke, Ed and I had lived next door to each other. His daddy was a dentist. (I am four years older than Ed.)

As I walked out of the telephone booth an officer immediately entered it. He soon came out of the booth, cussing profusely. He must have been told no more calls were allowed. Apparently, I was the last one that night to get my calls through on that phone.

Presently, I do not recall how I contacted Ed and Ray to let them know that Bernie was coming. Somehow I also managed to get several consecutive passes. Bernie came up and we had a picnic with Ed and his wife. We stayed for several days during the Christmas holidays. We had a wonderful time as I was familiar with New York. Besides, Ed and Ray were both excellent hosts.

Ed makes an interesting story in himself. He was a lawyer and while we were in Atlanta trying the Atlanta teacher salary case in the late 1940's, Ed was appointed by President Truman as Minister Plenipotentiary to Liberia. During his tenure, his office was elevated to the rank of Ambassador. When he returned to New York City, he became a judge of the Domestic Relations Court. At the time of the Hulan Jack fiasco, Mayor Wagner appointed Ed to the position of borough president of Manhattan. Later he became a judge of the New York Supreme Court where he served for a number of years and later became its Chief Judge.

Getting back to my army days, on January 1, 1944, we were again taken from Camp Shanks and carried to the docks. We were loaded onto the luxury liner, the *Queen Elizabeth*, which had been stripped down to serve as a troop carrier. On January 1, 1944, we shipped out of New York Harbor headed for a destination across the Atlantic. Because of its speed, the *Queen Elizabeth* traveled solo. From the beginning, we were going at high speed and zigzagging. It was too fast for any convoy. In fact, I never traveled in a convoy in crossing and re-crossing the Atlantic or the Pacific.

The ship was divided into three sections designated with the colors red, white and blue. I don't remember which color our unit had. Whatever it was, our color was located in the middle of the ship between the other two colors.

The ship had twenty thousand troops aboard. As you can

197

imagine, it also had a never-ending chow line.

Our colonel had certain ship responsibilities. We had duty for our section and an office in the middle section at the very top of the *Queen Elizabeth.*

After a couple of days it was claimed that a sub had been sighted. From that point on, the speed of the engines was increased even more and we went full speed ahead on a zigzag course until we docked in Scotland. As a consequence, our office was constantly swinging back and forth in a wide arc. It was not long before I got sick and retreated to my bunk in the passenger section of the ship. Some way or other I avoided returning to our office in the sky for the balance of the trip to Scotland.

A few days later, we landed in Scotland and went down to England on a special military transport train. When compared to American trains of that day, the English engines and coaches seemed like miniature trains in an American amusement park.

When we arrived in England, our first billet was in an English school in Hereford, Herefordshire. Our detachment occupied a part of the school. The other part of the school was not in operation. The children had been relocated to a remote place in the countryside.

I remember one day going to the library located in the vacant part of the school and picking up a history book to see what the English reported about the American Revolutionary War. In this history textbook, the Revolutionary War was hardly mentioned.

Speaking of historical perspectives, General Eisenhower was one of those Americans who believed that desegregation was a sociological experiment. It never occurred to him or any of the other segregationists that racial segregation was also a sociological experiment that had never worked successfully. This was true even though the Federal and State governments and the white community organizations put their full power behind segregation laws and practices.

White segregationists not only personally refused to engage in what they regarded as socializing with Negroes, they also disapproved of other whites' involvement in what segregationists perceived as such socializing activities. However, I recall a rather amusing response to the insanity of segregation which occurred in my civilian life. Andy

Ransom's wife, Bill, was a relatively easily identifiable Negro woman who sometimes reacted in an interesting way to white folks who would get up and take another seat when she sat down next to them on the street car or other public transportation in Washington, D.C. When they stood up to find another seat, she would "loud talk them," for example by exclaiming, "You always try to avoid Negroes like you are white! I am going to tell Aunt Lizzie about you the next time I see her!" Sometimes, she would keep up this type of chatter for several minutes as the typically, red-faced embarrassed white person would retreat to a far end of the street car or attempt to get off at the next stop.

Coming back to Eisenhower's solution to the challenge created by segregationists' doctrine, Eisenhower inaugurated a scheme commonly called "white nights" and "colored nights." On colored nights, Negro soldiers could go into town to bars and other public establishments. On white nights, white soldiers were allowed to do likewise.

The idea was to reduce conflict flowing from white soldiers' objections to Negroes socializing with English girls. Indeed, white soldiers tried many ruses to discourage such activities, for example by telling the preposterous lie that Negroes had tails like monkeys.

During the time this policy was implemented I was told that the white nights/colored nights rule was frequently broken by individual soldiers of all shades of the human race.

Within two days after we arrived in England, I received an official letter stating, "Since you are no longer in the continental United States, if you are still interested in attending O.C.S., you should apply to the British Base Section." So I promptly re-applied to the British Base Section for admission to O.C.S. I never heard anything from this application until a few days after landing in France in late June of 1944.

While we were stationed in Hereford, England, we still only had three Negro officers in our whole regiment. As I previously stated one officer was Lt. Collins with whom I developed a close friendship. One of the other officers was named Bianchi, and the third one was named Farrell. Farrell later became a priest. Over the years, I have seen him occasionally; and the last I heard of him, he was still living in Washington, D.C.

Anyway, the officers were just second lieutenants. It was an

199

exceptionally long time before they got their promotions to first lieutenant. Whether any of them received a further promotion I do not presently recall. In recent years, I learned that Colonel Bishop who headed our regiment had said that no Negro second lieutenants would be promoted to first lieutenant until all the white second lieutenants were promoted. Bishop did not want any Negro officers giving orders to white officers. Later after we got to France, one of the Negro N.C.O.'s applied for and received a promotion to warrant officer — a kind of hybrid between an N.C.O. and a commissioned officer.

As I previously stated, I started out as a buck private. One day my name was on the promotion list and I became a private first class. I did not see it or know of the list until I was promoted to corporal. Still later, I was promoted to sergeant.

I was the adjutant's assistant. The adjutant was a kind of general manager of the regiment. All of the correspondence and related matters went through him. We routed communications to the colonel or other appropriate officer.

After being in England for several weeks, I was disgusted with the way things were happening in the regiment. I decided to talk with the adjutant, a man named Captain Gamble who had come up through the National Guard (a military entity from which Negroes were barred throughout the South). I told Captain Gamble I wanted to talk to him after dinner about a regimental problem. We met back at Headquarters and I explained to him the awful conditions and poor troop morale.

One of the things that disturbed the men and me was the officers' appalling lack of concern for the welfare of the troops. This insensitivity was exacerbated by many regimental and company restrictive orders that made some primitive conditions unnecessarily more burdensome. In addition, we experienced the demeaning colored nights and white nights segregation practices. In the face of this degrading treatment of their troops, the white officers seemed to have one overriding concern. That was: when were they going to receive their next promotion. That callous indifference irritated us greatly.

I said to Captain Gamble that one would not have felt worse had he been incarcerated in the jails of Mississippi or Alabama. Initially, Captain Gamble's reaction was to appear incensed that I had the audacity to question the judgment of the regimental officers.

Finally he threatened to have me court-martialed. I told him he could do anything he wanted to. It was just his word against mine. I was not the least bit intimidated; that shook him up.

At that stage I was in fact as angry as he appeared to be. I didn't give a damn. So, it ended without our arriving at a resolution of these problems. However, the discussion or confrontation had some effect. While no immediate change in overall conditions ensued, there was a perceptible change in Captain Gamble, personally. Within a few weeks he was transferred from adjutant to a position in Operations Three. Thereafter, I had very little personal contact with him.

Captain Gamble was replaced by a young lawyer named, as I recall, Stringfellow. We got along quite well.

H and S Company moved from the school we were in to Bullington Convent, on the outskirts of the town of Hereford. This location was right next to a munitions plant. At that time we were on double British daylight savings time. That meant that people who normally went to work at 5:00 a.m. were going to work at 3:00 a.m. Man, one of the eeriest sights you could see was to look out in the morning at 3:00 or 4:00 standard time and see all these little lights coming up the highway. They looked like fire flies or "lightning bugs". It would be people riding bicycles, coming to work in the munitions plant. This particular location was between London and Birmingham.

Due to frequent air raids, as a matter of course, at night, all lights were blacked out. Almost nightly we could see the explosions from the Nazis bombing Birmingham. Our situation was very precarious, and we were constantly sitting on edge during the air raids wondering whether the Germans were going to discover the munitions plant adjacent to our bailiwick. The Germans never did. We could see the glare from air raids on Birmingham. For one reason or another, I never did get to London.

Lt. Collins developed friendly relations with the director of the munitions plant who lived in a nearby village called Home Lacy. On several occasions, he invited Lt. Collins and me to his house to play bridge with him and other members of his family. We became very friendly with him. There was also a community house in the village. On several occasions, Lieutenant Collins and I participated in social gatherings with members of the local village and played bridge there.

201

Speaking of playing bridge, Lt. Collins taught me the one-club system. To my knowledge, at that time, the system had not come into widespread use. Later, the Italians made it famous as the "Italian One Club Bid." Under the system, if you have a strong hand containing seventeen or more points you bid one club. One derived the point total by counting as follows: an ace equals four points; a king, three points; a queen, two points; and a jack, one point.

The immediate response of your partner is an indication of her strength (limited to aces and kings) rather than any valid bid. For instance, if I had one king, I'd bid one heart. For two kings I'd bid one spade. These bids were called "controls." If I had an ace and a king or three kings, I would bid two clubs. An ace and two kings or four kings would require me to bid one no trump. If I had five or more controls, I would bid two diamonds.

My partner would then make a normal bid indicating his or her strong suit or no trump. By then we would know whether the combined hands could or could not make a game, should make a game, or make a slam. The initial artificial bids would make it very easy to get to a game or a slam if you have the cards.

The biggest reason for most of these systems is so that when you have a slam you get to it. And you won't get into unmakeable slams — you try to avoid them as much as possible. We were almost unbeatable - playing our system. Initially, we were a little unfair because we didn't tell our opponents that we were playing a system unless they asked us. Later we corrected this omission. Of course, seasoned bridge players soon realized that we were using a system.

Our system was a big advance in contract bridge at that time. It's a valid strategy but of course bridge players have moved away from that system now and have more complicated systems.

I stayed in touch with the English family for awhile after the war. The plant director's daughter was about eleven or twelve at the time we were in Herefordshire. She used to write to me after the war and tell me about her family and local news, but I am not a good correspondent. Eventually, the letters stopped.

An interesting war-time diversion that I experienced involved our mail courier, Sam Olphin. One day, I joined Sam and rode with him to Chester, England to pick up the mail. On this particular trip, he told me that the top brass finally decided I was not subversive, and they stopped surveilling my incoming mail. This was the first time that I found out that my incoming mail was being censored. The normal practice was to censor the outgoing mail. Whatever came in didn't make any difference. My mail had been censored coming in and going out.

My reason for going to Chester was to purchase a gift for my wife, Bernie. I bought her a beautiful set of green earrings which she kept for many years before she unfortunately lost one of them.

After the war, Sam's brother, James L. Olphin, became a lawyer. For over thirty-five years, until his death in the 1970's, James worked with us in our Richmond offices.

Another thing: during World War II, among the English people with whom I associated in Hereford, the black soldiers were much more highly regarded than the white troops. Reasons for Negro soldiers being held in higher esteem included the fact that many of the white soldiers exhibited condescending and arrogant attitudes in their relationships with British troops, as well as, the general public. The white Americans made fun of the conditions of the lower classes. American soldiers' pay was much higher than that of English soldiers. Petrol there was much more expensive — about fifty cents per gallon as compared with fifteen or twenty cents in the United States. English locomotives looked like toys as compared with our big steam locomotives. Their plumbing and heating systems were antiquated in comparison with our American counterparts. Many other Negro soldiers had positive experiences of English hospitality which were similar to mine.

In essence, the behavior of many white soldiers caused ordinary English folks to resent them. Many of them seemed to look down on the local people. (A series of books called The Ugly American has been published reflecting among other things this condescending American attitude.) In Europe, the situation was a little different because local people viewed American soldiers as liberators, the soldiers had a better perspective of the realities of war, and frankly, they became more mature.

In England and continental Europe, the class distinctions between upper classes and the lower class were very sharp. For example, while we were still in England a situation arose involving a Negro soldier charged with rape of an English girl. I went over to the locality where the alleged rape occurred to investigate. I got the constable's report, and as I started to read it, I could hardly believe my eyes. The report stated that the victim was a poor working class woman and the defendant was a respectable military person. In that sense, it read exactly like a report that a southern sheriff would have written down in Mississippi or Alabama concerning a white man raping a Negro woman.

In one sense the constable was fair about it: at least he didn't refer to the soldier as "a big, black, burly Negro." Prior to World War II, when a crime involved a black man and a white woman, the "big, black, burly Negro" reference was commonplace in southern newspapers.

Nevertheless, the constable's attitude reflected an elitist bias which suggests that some people are intrinsically better than others. Since my unit changed locations, I don't even remember now how the criminal investigation came out. To the best of my recollection, the constable treated the situation very lightly. My mission and primary concern was to ensure that the black soldier was treated fairly.

The thing that struck me was that in most areas of the southern United States, I am sure the situation would have resulted in the soldier's conviction regardless of his innocence or guilt. In contrast, in this foreign country, I felt reasonable assurance that this soldier would get a fair shake.

On the other hand, the British people sometimes seemed a bit unreasonable about some things. For instance, the roads were narrow and winding. Not surprisingly, from time to time an American soldier would unintentionally damage the property of one of the local citizens. Accordingly, if a soldier damaged a landowner's fence or hedgerow, the owner would file a claim against the U.S. Army. At that time, particularly where the amounts of the damage were for small sums, this seemed outrageous to me. I thought that the local people should be more appreciative that we were there to help them save their country. Therefore, they should have been willing to bear minor expenses and damages without complaint.

We moved from the Bullington Convent to a rural mountainous place called Bally over in Northern Wales. We spent several months over there. We were the only troops stationed in that area. Our new location contrasted quite a bit with Hereford which was a relatively good-sized city.

While in Bally for some reason I never did go to the village. I had no personal association with the local people although we were up there two or three months. When we received orders to move down to Carmarthen in South Wales, as we were leaving, some local people who had developed a friendship with some of the Negro troops expressed their surprise and delight regarding how different the troops had been from what they had been told to expect. Interestingly, and not completely surprisingly, our chaplain, who had been a member of the advance party, had told the local people the tales commonly spread by white segregationists. For example, he had told them that Negro troops had tails like monkeys; Negroes were uncouth and had no manners; and Negroes would rape English women.

When this story came out, fortunately for the chaplain, the top brass were able to spirit him away from our camp that night. Somehow Lt. Collins got involved and they got him out of there too. I think that he expressed some strong sentiments about the chaplain.

While I was in South Wales as a member of the advance party, I became aware that D-Day was approaching, in part because our orders were so secret that they were encased in a small safe with armed field grade officers standing guard 24 hours daily. There was a certain tension in the air.

In the meantime, following the chaplain incident, an inspector general came down to investigate the situation. He did his investigation, swore me to secrecy, and I typed his report. The report related all the foregoing facts and expressed the conclusion that the troops' morale had been damaged by learning how the chaplain had denigrated them. He recommended that our regiment be taken off of alert and given three more weeks of orientation before moving out.

We operated from that point forward on a schedule that had us crossing the channel exactly three weeks to the day _after_ D-Day. Obviously, if it hadn't been for that fool chaplain talking about Negroes having tails, etc., I and other members of our regiment might still be over there in the bottom of the channel somewhere or buried on one of those beaches—Omaha or Utah.

When we landed over in France, I, along with three other members of my regiment got separated from the rest of the regiment. We were detained two nights and days on the beach. Each night, some German planes came over. When they did, we jumped in previously prepared foxholes. We had so much anti-aircraft firepower that as we looked up at the sky from our foxholes, it looked like a glorified Fourth of July celebration.

My regiment was about forty or fifty miles from where I was. The German artillery began to shell our troops with one of their "Big Berthas" (big guns on a train). This happened several times and the shellings wounded several men but fortunately there were no fatal casualties.

Shortly, after we landed the Allied troops broke through around St. Lo and then the front just moved away from the beach. I rejoined my outfit.

When I rejoined my outfit, there was a letter waiting for me saying since you are no longer in the British Base Section, if you are still interested in O.C.S. you should apply to the Normandy Base Section. By that time, I was convinced that someone did not intend for me to become an officer. I didn't pursue that any further. I realized they were playing games.

While I was qualified to become an officer, perhaps the institutional racism that blocked my efforts was not a totally negative personal experience. Had I become an officer, like some of my Negro officer friends, I may have been court martialed.

Coming back to the Normandy invasion, after the American troops broke through at St. Lo and began a succession of military advances, naturally I was pleased. Several reasons existed for my being pleased; one of which was perceptible movement towards the day when I would be discharged from the U. S. Army.

Our regimental headquarters settled down in an apple orchard in Normandy. At that time, the line companies of our regiment were scattered around the countryside. As general service engineers, we built field hospitals, operated a quarry, and constructed roads. We also performed diverse other functions, including operating a German prison camp and a small French town. Our regiment was part of the more than fifty thousand Negro engineers who served in the European Theatre between D-Day and the end of the war.[3]

We stayed in the apple orchard until December while the front moved steadily away. To make our lives more tolerable, two soldiers would hollow out a trench several feet deep. They would then use their tents to cover the trench. One tent would be stretched over one end of the trench to be used as a sitting room while the other tent would become the sleeping quarters. We even carved the dirt out of a part of one side of our sitting room and made a fireplace.

The trench/tent innovation reduced the cold air coming in and added a more pleasant touch to a rather difficult condition. In the orchard, I shared a tent with my cousin Charles Pollard. We also hooked up a cord to a generator at the Motor Pool and provided ourselves with electric light.

Our colonel was a regular army officer who was bucking for general. He thought that he could improve his chances for promotion by appearing to be rough and tough as manifested by living in and keeping H & S Company in the woods as much as possible.

As in England, most of our white officers in France were much more interested in promotions than in troop welfare. For example, while our company was still quartered in an apple orchard in Normandy and the battle front continued to move farther from us, the commanding officer of H and S Company, a Captain Olson, frequently paced up and down complaining about when were we going to "see some action"! He believed that if we got to the front lines that he would win a promotion more quickly.

Finally, the men had enough of his "static". I set up an appointment with him one evening at his quarters and told him that the men of the company resented his lack of concern for their welfare. Further, I told him that he should be glad that we had not gone to the front lines because the way the men felt about him, if we went to the front with live ammunition, I believed that his chances of coming back would be very slim. He understood what I meant — that either someone accidentally or intentionally in our unit may well settle a score with him by shooting him.

I suggested to him that for his own safety, he should build a better rapport with the men in our Company. Soon after our talk, he managed to get transferred from our unit.

In addition, soon after we reached France, I began developing a very good system of intelligence stretching through the regiment. Particularly, when disciplinary matters, involving court martials would come up, I had a pretty good grasp of the facts regarding which ones should not be pursued. In such unmeritorious cases, I'd hold them up, find some error in the charging papers, and buck them back. I studied the Army and Normandy Base Regulations and used them to the advantage of the men.

As a result of the cases being bucked back, particular charges could become stale, to the point where I would go to the adjutant and say that to move these stale cases to the Normandy Base Section would subject the regiment to criticism. This usually resulted in the charges being dismissed.

Our company stayed in an apple orchard from July 1944 until December. When the Battle of the Bulge came up, our entire regiment was loaded on French freight cars known as Forty and Eights. (The cars were called Forty and Eights because during World War I they carried forty soldiers and eight mules.)

We moved in the direction of the Bulge. The Battle of the Bulge created such a crisis that some Negro troop units were given live ammunition and pressed into infantry service. Originally, we were headed to the front presumably to participate in the hostilities.

On our first night out while riding on a Forty and Eight, in order to play our continuous pinochle game, we stretched a cord or wire from one side of the car to the other or affixed it to the ceiling of the freight car and hung an English Stilson Lamp from the wire. When the game ended, we put the light out, but failed to take the lamp down. After a period of time, we went to bed and I fell asleep.

Suddenly, something struck me in the head with terrific force. I touched my face and felt blood. Thinking that I had been shot or that perhaps an enemy soldier had struck me and a deadly attack was being launched against us, I reached quietly for my carbine and looked to see if I could discern any movement in our car. There was nothing: only the rolling and rocking of the freight car and the snoring of some of the men in our unit.

After careful observation, I became convinced that no enemy personnel were in the car. I awakened my cousin Charlie, and told him that I had been wounded. After turning on a flashlight, we discovered that the lamp which had a heavy base had fallen from the ceiling and knocked me on the head near my eye. Fortunately, except for a scar that lasted for many years, the wound was more painful than severe.

Later, when the story got out, our colonel made a jesting remark to me to the effect that I would not get a purple heart for the injury that I received. I assured him that I was not the least bit interested in receiving a purple heart.

Some interesting historical facts involve a well known Negro combat unit, the 366th Infantry. That outfit trained at Camp Devon, Massachusetts under the command of Colonel Queen. It was sent to North Africa. This regiment was placed under General Almond's command. The regiment boasted a large complement of Negro officers. One of my former law partners, Samuel W. Tucker, now deceased, held the rank of major in that outfit. He participated in the Howard R.O.T.C. program and received his initial commission through that program.

After the North African campaign, Tucker's unit came up through Italy. They were actually in combat in Africa and Italy.

As I mentioned previously, there were Negro combat troops in World War I but they operated principally under French command. In fact, in every war in which the United States had been involved, from the Revolutionary War down through World War I, the American Negro soldier had exhibited all of the attributes of a true warrior in the military service. When World War II came along, the segregationists tried to restrict, as much as possible, the participation of Negroes in all phases of combat activities. However, eventually some Negroes became combat troops.

During the Battle of the Bulge, Negro truck drivers operated "The Red Ball Express." That was the term used to describe the constant, tireless and efficient stream of military equipment, food, and other logistical support which the drivers furnished the allied combat troops at the front. When the allied forces were confronted with the prospect of defeat, Negro truck drivers were given weapons and live ammunition, and pressed into service as infantry soldiers. They did a marvelous job in helping to thwart the German offensive.

When we started out towards the Bulge, the men were issued their military weapons. I was issued a carbine. In fact, during our training in Camp Claiborne, we had been taught the use and maintenance of rifles and carbines. We practiced on the firing range; and I made sharpshooter. We also went through the orientation course crawling under barbed wire while live ammunition was being used. It did not happen to anyone I knew but I was told that occasionally some frustrated soldier would stick up his head or body, or both, and get wounded or

209

seriously injured while crawling through the live ammunition fire course.

Coming back to our travel in the direction of the Battle of the Bulge, when we got up near Paris, our orders were changed. Instead of going to the battle front, we were sent to a point between Paris and Le Havre. There our mission was to operate what was known as Camp Lucky Strike, a center where the disembarking troops from the States came to receive their orders, and to be reunited with their equipment and receive traveling orders. Camp Lucky Strike was a big old captured German air field. In our working area, there were so many high ranking officers, including colonels and generals, that we were not required to come to attention in the presence of anyone whose rank was not at least that of Major General. We continued to operate the camp there until the war ended in Europe.

In France, we also experienced the effects of color discrimination. For example, for the first several weeks at Camp Lucky Strike, passes were regularly coming in for a small detachment of white troops who were assigned to our regiment. The passes allowed the white troops to go to Paris or Brussels. But none of the passes were assigned to the troops of our regiment.

Several times I raised questions about the pass situation. Each time, I got no results. Finally, one day the colonel was on his way to Normandy Section Base Headquarters. I seized the opportunity to raise the issue with him. The colonel replied that there would probably be so much "star dust" in his eyes that he did not know whether he could do anything about our situation or not. (The star dust would emanate from the light reflecting off the brass of the generals who would interact with the colonel at Normandy Base Headquarters.)

I realized that the colonel could not be counted on to do anything constructive. Accordingly, I got a jeep and driver, went to the Normandy Base Command myself, and looked up and talked with the sergeants who were in charge of issuing the passes in question. I outlined the situation to them and obtained their agreement that matters would be corrected. From that point on, our regiment received the bulk of the passes.

Soon after we arrived at Camp Lucky Strike, while I was in France, I organized the 1310 G.S. regimental chapter of the NAACP. Before organizing the chapter, I cleared it with the regimental executive officer. I collected money for memberships and sent the money to the national

Sergeant and Mrs. Oliver Hill, Sr.
(circa 1945)

NAACP headquarters in New York. As I stated before, although most of the men in our regiment were much younger than I, I had fine rapport with them. Consequently, I had no difficulty persuading the troops throughout the regiment to join the NAACP.

Army intelligence noticed that there was a significant amount of money going from our regiment to the United States. They descended upon me in full force. They were sure that I was engaged in some black market operation. However, I was not worried because I had initially gone through the appropriate channels and obtained the required approval. Thus, nothing really came of their investigation except a few chuckles enjoyed by me and some of the men over the frustration and disappointment of the Army Intelligence Unit.

In the spring of 1945, a general order was issued directing regimental commanders to send in the names of any trial lawyers. In the process of routing the mail and orders, I read the order before the Colonel received it. The Colonel came out of his office and said, "I have good news for you." I replied, "No, you don't either." By that time, I was not interested in a commission. I knew the war would end in Europe soon and I assumed that after the crisis in Paris was resolved, if I were a newly commissioned officer, I would be sent to Japan.

Fortunately, when VE Day occurred my cousin, Charlie Pollard, and I each had received a pass to go to Paris. We arrived the night before and had the good fortune to celebrate VE Day with the French people.

After the war ended in Europe, I felt sure that I, along with some of the other older men, would be sent back to the United States.

Originally, our entire regiment was scheduled to return to the States. To our great dismay, a General Order came down expressing a need for seven additional General Service Engineer regiments. Our regiment was sent to Arles in southern France for further training and reassignment.

In August, we were moved to Marseilles. There we were placed on a U.S. Coast Guard vessel, the *U.S.S. Eberlee,* and headed across the Atlantic to the Panama Canal. We spent a weekend in Panama. We went through the locks of the canal and spent two or three days on the Pacific side. Then we sailed for Manila.

We had crossed the International Date Line and gone through the ceremony characterizing our initial crossing of the Date Line when we learned Japan had surrendered. I found it incomprehensible then and I still fail to understand now why, when Japan surrendered, the orders for our ship were not changed and the ship directed to proceed to sail to the United States. I really should have been released in Europe but I wasn't.

We kept on to Manila; and when we got to Manila the last thing the military officials there wanted was another ship with troops. It took us several days before we received permission to land.

When we landed we were sent to a place called Los Angeles, up in the mountains, about twenty miles from Manila. As soon as we got there and as soon as I could locate a jeep, I hightailed it down to MacArthur's Headquarters and went to the section where I figured I would find the sergeants who would be handling the orders for termination of service. Upon finding this section, I asked what I should do. I was a Staff Sergeant at that time. I was told that they were waiting for some instructions and interpretations of some of the regulations. I said, "Man, that's all I have been thinking about."

We got a copy of the Army regulations. I had a session with the sergeants. I pointed out my interpretation of the regulations to them and what they should expect in the way of an order. At any rate, they appeared sympathetic and cooperative. I do not know whether my actions helped to speed up the process or whether they received orders from higher up sooner than they expected. Two days after my visit to Manila, the first orders for discharge of personnel in my regiment came up the mountains to us: I wasn't on the list. A couple of days later additional orders came through for several other members of my regiment and me.

The orders sent us to the Replacement Depot. We were there three weeks and then were placed on an old liberty ship and returned to San Francisco. (Liberty ships were vessels used to transport troops during the First World War.)

It took us three weeks to come back from Manila to San Francisco. I went across the Atlantic on the *Queen Elizabeth*. I came back from Marseilles on the Coast Guard ship, the *U.S.S. Eberlee*. The speed of each of these vessels was too fast for a convoy.

So this in a nutshell comprises some of my travel and activities in the army in Great Britain, France and the Philippines via the Panama Canal.

Chapter VI

Political Activism

> *To maintain or achieve political domination nationally, both political parties sacrificed Negroes' civil rights on the altar of political expediency so that they could achieve or maintain their legislative objectives. Between Reconstruction and the Roosevelt eras this pattern of political treachery prevailed with particularly harsh consequences to Negroes. In essence, everybody was getting something except Negroes. As in everything else, in politics, generally, it was the Negro against the world.*

At least since I was in college in the late 1920's, I have viewed myself as an agent of social change. For me, that means doing what I can to help ensure that human society progresses in an evolutionary manner to improve conditions for the commonweal. This chapter reviews some of my local, state and national political activities from the time of my return to the state of Virginia in 1939.

In Virginia, from the 1920's through much of the 1960's, the Byrd Organization dominated the Virginia Democratic party. During the Depression and until the late 1960's, the Virginia Republican party was very weak because most of the people who ordinarily would have been classified as Republicans were members of the local Byrd organization. For some elections the Republicans didn't run anybody against the Byrd organization candidate. They had no reason to oppose the organization's candidates because in spirit and deed, although classified as Democrats, Senator Byrd and most people in his inner circle, were top rated Republicans.

In Virginia, an added device of the Byrd organization to ensure

214

organizational loyalty and control involved the State Compensation Board. The Compensation Board was comprised of strong Byrd supporters who fixed the salaries of everyone who had a position in the State Government. All judges, treasurers, county clerks, sheriffs, commissioners of revenue, and local prosecutors had their salaries and budgets determined by individuals intensely loyal to the Byrd machine. The party's control of their income was by itself sufficient to act as a loyalty producing agent.

However, within the Democratic party some opposition existed led by Delegate Robert Whitehead from Nelson County and Frances Pickens Miller of Fairfax, Virginia. These dissident Democrats were found chiefly in the Western part of the state and to a lesser degree in Northern Virginia and in some Tidewater cities. In fact, I remember once in the 1930's that Judge John Hart, a Hustings Court judge in Roanoke, sought re-appointment but I am told that he was considered too liberal by the Byrd dominated state legislature. The legislature refused his reappointment, and elected as Hustings Court judge, J. Lindsay Almond, who was then the Assistant Commonwealth Attorney in Roanoke. However, Judge Hart demonstrated that he was no pushover. In the next election, he ran for a locally elected office (the Commissioner of Revenue) and won.

This is an overview of the situation which prevailed in 1939 when I returned to Virginia. At that time, Negroes had begun to exert greater efforts to participate in the Democratic primary. Normally, a primary win would have been only equivalent to winning a party's nomination. However, the Byrd dominated Virginia Democratic Party was so strong that a primary win was in fact tantamont to winning an election. The Byrd Democratic primary not only excluded Negroes, but it also was for some whites, a closed process. This was consistent with the Byrd organization's policy of discouraging the widespread exercise of voting rights by all Virginians.

One place where Negroes were becoming involved was Greensville County in Southside, Virginia. In those days, I practically lived in my office. I will never forget, late one Friday night about 11:00 or 12:00 o'clock, just before the first Tuesday in August, 1939, Tom Hewin, Jr. came to my law office and said that he had just returned from Emporia where he had met with a local Negro organization called, "The Hundred Men Club." The men said that they wanted Tom to make it possible for them to participate in the Democratic primary in Greensville County, which was to be held in just three days. The white folks down in

215

Greensville County were barring Negroes from voting in the Democratic primary. So Tom and I immediately began drafting a petition and writ of mandamus to file in Emporia, the county seat of Greensville County, to redress this deplorable condition.

The next morning, Saturday, we drove down to the court in Emporia. When we arrived, George Allen, Sr. was representing a client regarding a dispute about a cow which had wandered onto a railway right-a-way and had been struck by a train. George Allen, Sr., founded and provided the longevity going back to 1910 for the now famous law firm of Allen, Allen, Allen, & Allen. He was also the father of George Allen, Jr., who later became a prominent member of the Virginia General Assembly.

E. Ennis Eanes, the lawyer representing the railroad, was also the Commonwealth's Attorney for Greensville County. This situation was common in those days.

I do not remember how Judge Arnold ruled in the civil dispute but after disposing of that case, Judge Arnold asked, "What brings you two young men here this morning?" We told him that we were seeking a preliminary injunction and a writ of mandamus against the Greensville County Electoral Board to remedy the Board's practice of denying Negroes the right to vote in the Democratic primary.

Judge Arnold looked at the papers and turned to George Allen and said, "George, it's two of them and one of Eanes. I am going to appoint you, Counselor, to help Eanes." The Judge marked our petition "Filed", and recessed court until about 2:00 p.m. to give Allen and Eanes time to read our petition.

We came back to court at 2:00 p.m. and presented our argument. George Allen and Ennis Eanes resisted our petition as a matter of law. Judge Arnold said that as a matter of law we were correct; however, he would not assume that as a matter of fact the public officials would disobey the law and deny Negroes the right to vote in the Democratic primary. He stated further that he would be in Emporia on Tuesday and would entertain motions of any qualified voter who was denied the right to vote. Of course, the word got around that the judge intended to enforce the law.

To see if anybody had any problems in voting, Tom and I decided to go back to Emporia on Tuesday, the day of the primary. We rode

216

around the county checking the polling places. On our tour, we came around a sharp turn and started down the grade of a road leading as I recall to the Meherrin River. The road narrowed into just one lane crossing a single lane bridge. As we headed towards the bridge, we saw many white men with poles and ropes. Since we had already begun our descent, and the road was too narrow to turn around, there was nothing for us to do but continue down the narrow road. I don't recall which of us said it, but one of us said, "This looks like this is it!" The other replied, "I believe you are right." While I have been in a lot of tight spots, that one was probably the most harrowing. We thought we might be lynched.

However, when we got closer, we passed the men with poles and ropes, and began crossing the bridge. When we were half way across the bridge, we peered over the side and looked into the water. We saw a car turned over in the river and noticed that they were trying to extract it from the water. We breathed a sigh of relief. When we got to the other side of the river, Tom turned over the car to me saying that he was too weak to drive any farther.

By virtue of this case, in 1939, we reestablished Negroes' right to vote in the Democratic primary in Greensville County. In 1930, in Richmond, a Negro lawyer named Joseph R. Pollard, who was very politically active, and a Jewish lawyer named Alfred E. Cohen had prosecuted a case, West v. Bliley,[1] establishing Negroes' right in Virginia to vote in the Democratic Party primary. Despite that fact, Virginia's Democratic Party officials had paid very little attention to the West case. Thus in 1939, nine years after the Fourth Circuit decided West, we had to go to court to compel the local Democratic County Electoral Committee to allow Negroes in Greensville to do what the Federal Appeals Court had said they could do a decade earlier — namely, vote in the Democratic primary.

In fact, the response of the Greensville County Democratic officials was similar to those of public officials throughout the state who used various means to deprive Negroes of the right to vote. For example, it was the custom in many parts of the state of Virginia for the voting registrars to have their offices in their homes and to largely be absent from their homes during the sporadic, irregular, and often non-existent office hours. In scattered areas across the state, we challenged such practices until passage of the Civil Rights Act in 1964. Indeed, throughout the South, ingenuous means were used to ensure that Negroes would never participate meaningfully in choosing elected

217

representatives.

I really became active in politics during the 1940's before I went to the war. But there wasn't too much we could do in the early phases of this struggle to elect candidates to public office because the elections rarely presented us a choice other than the lesser of two evils. However, we devoted extensive time in arousing Negroes' interest in voting and preparing them to navigate the process of registering to vote.

Speaking of the lesser of evils, Dr. Jesse Tinsley and I went to see Richmond Mayor Ambler whom we had strongly supported in his successful campaign to oust Mayor Bright who had been in office over twenty years.[2] I told Mayor Ambler that we wanted to talk about appointing Negro policemen. He said to us, "So glad you all came in."

The Mayor said, "I have been thinking about how we are going to do this thing and I finally decided what we are going to do is to just put them in uniforms and give them a night stick. They will not carry guns or be able to arrest white people."

The white officers had guns and could arrest any lawbreaker. So Dr. Tinsley and I replied that although a person may be in uniform, he would not be a real police officer if he were not allowed to carry a gun and arrest any law-breaker, be he white or colored. I asserted that we would not accept anything less than full fledged police officers.

Banging on his desk with both fists clinched, Mayor Ambler emphasized that he had decided what he was willing to do. I was seated across the desk from him and while he was banging I began to bang on the desk with both my fists just as emphatically. I asserted that what Ambler was proposing was simply unacceptable. Our banging escapade concluded the session.

In the chapter on Civil Rights, I previously discussed some of my community education and legal work during the period between May 1, 1939 when I returned to Richmond and mid-1943 when I entered the armed services. I also talked about my military career. Accordingly, I will not rehash those events in detail.

Near the end of my military service, President Roosevelt died. I was in the Army with the Allied Forces in France. As I stated before, our regiment was stationed at and operated Camp Lucky Strike, a depot located midway between Le Harvre and Paris. When word came over the wire that Roosevelt had died, I felt so sick that I left Headquarters, went to my quarters, and stretched out on my bunk. I will never forget that experience.

Everyone wanted to know who was this new President Truman. At that time, the only thing that I knew about Truman was that he was a strong senator who chaired the Truman Committee investigating those individuals engaged in fraudulent activities against the government in procuring war material.

Following World War II, things changed and Negroes became more politically active. For instance, in 1947 after returning from the war to make the world safe for democracy for everyone except Negroes in the United States, I ran in the Democratic Primary for a seat in the Virginia House of Delegates. I was sponsored by an organization that I helped to form a few years earlier, called the Richmond Civic Council. The Civic Council was an unincorporated association of Negro individuals, businesses, social groups, and religious bodies seeking to enhance the quality of life of Richmond residents. We employed Reverend Amos Clark as Executive Director of the Civic Council.

I don't remember now all the persons who ran for public office; but I know that in 1945 Reverend W. B. Ball had run for the House of Delegates.[3] He pastored a church in Centrailia, Chesterfield County, Virginia.

In the 1947 race, I ran in coalition with an organized labor group (United Labor Political Action Committee) which was also sponsoring a candidate named W.H.C. Murray. Murray worked as a pressman over at the old Richmond News Leader newspaper. I do not remember who initiated the meeting but Dr. Jesse Tinsley and I met with the labor organization and formed a coalition. It was agreed that the labor group would try to get labor behind me, and we would attempt to galvanize the Negro vote behind Murray.

Until I ran for the House of Delegates, most Negro candidates had just campaigned in predominantly Negro areas. However, this was a city-wide election; and I campaigned all over the city. I went to every meeting where I heard or read that the candidates would speak to voters. If I heard there was going to be a political meeting I went.

Sometimes in white sections of the city voters were cool, but most times I was well received. Typically in white neighborhoods I'd

219

walk into the meeting and I would be the only Negro present. Usually the master of ceremonies and sometimes members of the audience would say, "Why are you here?" I would say, "I came to solicit your support." Then I would make my spiel. I asked the white folks to vote for me just like I asked the Negroes.

Sometimes, I would run into somebody at the candidates' meetings that I knew. Whether or not I met someone that I knew, if there was a social hour I would stay and talk with prospective voters. I was a pretty good campaigner.

Some of these meetings stand out in my mind. One in particular was the first time that I went to the West End Democratic Club to attend a meeting. The West End Democratic Club had a club house and a covered garden. When I walked in everyone was surprised. The master of ceremony inquired regarding my purpose. I said that I heard they were holding a political rally and I requested an opportunity to make a presentation to solicit their support.

In due course, I made my spiel and afterwards was talking to two or three white lawyers in the gathering who recognized me. They invited me into the garden and I sat there and drank beer with the other candidates and white voters.

At that time, the Church Hill citizens also had an East End Democratic Club at 22nd and Venable Streets. I believe but am not sure that the building is still there.

When the election occurred, it appeared that I helped win the Negro vote for Murray who was elected. While I was able to deliver votes for his candidacy, he could not do the same for mine. As a consequence, he beat me out for the last available seat by approximately a hundred and ninety votes. As a matter of fact, had I not gone to my headquarters on the Saturday afternoon before primary day, I would have been elected. Unknown to me, my campaign manager, A. Washington Owens (generally known as "Puss Owens") had prepared a release to the Negro churches and a letter to Negro constituents urging that they "single shot" for me. A number of candidates were running for seven seats. Voters could vote for one or more of the candidates. When a voter casts a single shot vote, she ensures that within a group of candidates for whom she could vote only one actually gets her vote. Thus, a single shot would have ensured that voters who could have voted for both Murray and me would have voted just for me. The single shot would have raised my vote total and suppressed his, rather than increasing both our votes.

The single shot approach would have violated our coalition agreement. Accordingly, when I saw the letters and press notices to the churches, I immediately demanded their destruction. I firmly believed that this was right, and did not regret their destruction for even one moment! Of course, the news got out that I was a person of my word and that I would keep it even though I might be adversely affected.

After his election, Murray did all that he could to keep his part of the general understanding regarding what we intended to do if one or both of us were elected. For example, he introduced bills seeking the repeal of segregation statutes affecting public transportation and seating, as well as sponsoring other progressive measures that I would have pursued had I been elected. Murray was genuine. However, all of this proffered legislation died in committee and his efforts were repudiated by the Richmond Typographical Union. In my mind, no question exists that at that time, had I presented the legislation, it still would have been killed in committee.

Throughout much of my seventy years of political activism, along with other individuals, I have had to battle against the effects of the Virginia Constitution of 1902, as well as similar discriminatory legislation and practices designed to reduce Negro political participation. For instance, as I mentioned, the poll tax was not only a device to frustrate prospective voters, but was also a revenue generator. State law required payment of the poll tax for a number of things including admission to the Virginia bar. While I read of my own bar admission in the newspaper, I was required to present poll tax receipts before receiving official documentation that I had passed the bar. The poll tax suppressed the exercise of voting rights not only of Negroes, most of whom were economically poor, but also of poor whites.

I never seriously considered challenging the poll tax. This was not because I thought the tax was right. I thought the tax was a good rallying point for opposition to the suppression of the rights of Negroes specifically, and other poor people more generally.

Over sixty years after the poll tax was passed to disenfranchise Negroes and poor whites, in Harper v. Virginia Board of Elections, the poll tax was successfully challenged. A Negro lawyer named Joseph A. Jordan, Jr. was one of the lawyers who led the successful fight.

221

An initial consequence of the nefarious 1902 Constitution was passage of legislation which allowed the local registrars in Virginia great flexibility in asking the voter any questions which came to the registrar's mind. Thus obscure, ambiguous and totally irrelevant inquiries were often made of Negro voters to disqualify them from exercising the franchise. For instance, registrars reportedly asked Negroes "What is the ex post facto law?" or "Explain the Shipping Bill of the United States." In contrast, registrars often asked illiterate white voters questions like whether white and Negro children could attend the same schools in Virginia.[4]

Later, another method of obstructing Negroes' exercise of voting rights involved a Virginia statute which provided that in registering to vote, in her own handwriting, the prospective voter had to provide the detailed information including her name, age, place of birth and residence, work history for the two years prior to voting, current occupation, and "any and all questions affecting [her] qualifications as an elector ..." which the registrar might want.[5] While Richmond provided a form so that a prospective voter could fill in the required data, many jurisdictions gave the prospective voter a blank sheet of paper. Since the statute required that applicants had to fill out the paper in the prescribed sequence without assistance from anyone, the process hindered poor writers and those with less information. It was commonly believed among Negroes that the registrars filled out the forms for illiterate white folks.

Incidentally, to address this method of disenfranchisement, the Tuckers (my former law partner S.W. Tucker and his wife, Julia) devised a creative idea for successfully registering prospective Negro electors. The propective voters were encouraged to identify registration questions with the thumbs and fingers of their hands. We furnished diagrams of each hand and on each finger wrote in the information which was required by statute. In this way, the prospective voter knew that each finger and thumb had a special meaning from one through ten.

That's the way we enabled many poor readers and writers to overcome the blank paper problem. In dealing with voting discrimination we had to be as creative as we were in the Alston case where we asked for a special term of the Fourth Circuit Court of Appeals to challenge disparate teacher salaries.

In addition, as I previously mentioned, other means of obstructing Negroes' right to vote included the practices of some local registrars who conducted voter registration at their homes at irregular hours and their propensity to be absent even during the hours which were at best unpredictable. The whole idea was to do as many deceitful, annoying and often intimidating things as possible to ensure that Negroes did not vote. The 1902 Virginia Constitution was one of the devices to effectively bar Negro political participation in Virginia from 1902 until after World War II.

This brings me back to a discussion of Negro political activities after World War II. Shortly after the war ended, the local school electoral board in Roanoke elected a Negro dentist named Dr. Harry Penn to the school board. The local school electoral boards were appointed by local circuit judges and the electoral boards elected all school board members. For many years in Virginia, this practice for electing school board members was common. Only recently have many localities been allowed to elect school boards by their local elected officials like city council and boards of supervisors. Now some school boards are also being elected by popular elections.

In Nansemond County, Virginia in 1947, another Negro, W. A. Lawrence, was elected to the Board of Supervisors by a razor-thin margin: two hundred and ninety two votes to two hundred and ninety.[6] However, at that time few Negroes held elective office anywhere else in the South.

One other example of this rare political phenomenon of Negro elected representatives was an upper classman named Charles W. Anderson, Jr. with whom I attended Howard University. In 1935, he was elected to the Kentucky General Assembly. While we were undergraduates at Howard, this future legislator drove a Ford Roadster with a rumble seat and a big tire on the back along with a banner proclaiming "Phi Beta Sigma fraternity." When I was knocked unconscious in the football game between the Howard University freshmen and sophomore classes, I am told that Anderson drove his car onto the football field, my teammates picked me up, put me in the car, and he roared off to the hospital with me in it. Many observers later informed me that they were more concerned about the injuries that I might receive riding with him to the hospital (at break-neck speed) than with the injuries that I had received on the grid-iron.

Anderson served in the Kentucky state legislature for four terms. In 1936, he was successful in sponsoring legislation to make the state of Kentucky pay for the higher education of Negroes who were barred by the segregation laws from furthering their studies in Kentucky. Anderson

223

also was a leading advocate for civil rights and with Prentice Thomas, in the 1940's, fought to desegregate public education in Kentucky.[7]

An interesting aside is, following World War II, I decided not to join the American Legion because it was segregated. Ed Fleischer and I were members at large of a progressive nonsegregated group called The American Veterans Committee. With Sam and Ann Gellman, we organized a Richmond chapter which included Marvin Caplin, Harry Bernstein, Phil Brenner, and Ernest A. DeBordenave. Caplan later became Director of the Washington Office of The Leadership Council on Civil Rights, Bernstein assumed the position of Labor Editor of the Los Angeles Times, Brenner was a dentist, DeBordenave was a priest, and Fleischer a newspaper deskman.

Early on we had one prominent white veteran from Ashland, Virginia who joined the organization and agreed to serve as President. However, before he could actively participate, he received a job in Washington, D.C. that caused him to relocate there. We also attracted a number of Negro and Jewish former servicemen. However, no other white Gentiles came or joined the American Veterans Committee. In addition, other minority groups which had a non-segregated status like Indians and Hispanics did not attend our meetings.

To help broaden our base of support and participation, we decided to try to get a white protestant to become the president of the local chapter of our organization. In that regard, I approached a young lawyer who was a member of a conservative law firm here in Richmond. I explained our objectives and asked that lawyer whether he would he willing to become president of our group. He said to me that he was very sympathetic to our cause, but that he was married with a wife and a child. He felt that his firm would not favor his taking such a position and he was even afraid to ask them about it because he thought it might have some negative ramifications for his employment at the firm.

I sympathized with his position. As I was getting up from the chair to leave his office, he said to me, "If all Negroes were like Joe Lewis, Marion Anderson, and Paul Robeson, I would have no problem associating with them." At that point I sat back down across from the desk facing him. I leaned forward and said to him, " Did it ever occur to you that if all Negroes were as talented in their respective fields as Joe Lewis, Marion Anderson and Paul Robeson, they would probably be so conceited that that they would not want to associate themselves with the likes of you." He looked at me a bit quizically and said, "You know,

I really hadn't thought about that."

This lawyer later became a very successful business person. However, strange as it may seem, I do not recall our paths crossing from that day forward.

Speaking of Paul Robeson, it is an established fact that in football practice, Robeson's teammates in college broke his shoulder. They were trying to dissuade him from playing on the team. He played, nevertheless, and became an All-American. Had he not been a Negro, this talented man who could sing, act and was a brilliant scholar, as well as human rights activist, would likely have held a much more prominent role in American life and history than has been the case so far.

Coming back to Virginia politics, in the late 1940's the Richmond Citizens' Association was the largest and strongest political organization in the city. The Association had developed a task force headed by Lewis F. Powell, Jr., who later served on the United States Supreme Court. The mission of the task force was to seek a change of the form of the Richmond city government.

Specifically, the Citizens Association advocated abolishing the old strong mayor/weak city council, bicameral legislative system whose members were elected from wards. The two legislative chambers were a Board of Aldermen, corresponding to a senate, and a Common Council, analogous to a House of Delegates. The Citizens Association sought a unitary system in which there would be a ceremonial Mayor (elected by Council from its members), City Council elected at large, and a City Manager who would serve at the will of Council while performing the administrative functions of the executive branch.

Early in this political struggle, Powell and other Richmond Citizens' Association leaders sought out members of the Richmond Civic Council and asked support of the charter change. Under the old ward system, during the 1940's the Negro community was adroitly divided into wards to prevent Negroes from exercising any effective political power. Because of these circumstances, we readily agreed to support the charter change. After agreeing to cooperate with the Citizens' Association, members of the Negro community followed through on our commitment. Working together, the Richmond Civic Council, the Richmond Citizens' Association and other city residents effected a charter change.

In accordance with the new charter provisions, subsequently, a city wide election was scheduled to choose new city council members. You could vote for one candidate or all nine.

At that time I was not on the Citizens' Association Board of Directors but I am told they had an all night session. They agreed on a group of candidates. Despite strenuous efforts to put a Negro on the slate the majority of the board backed off primarily because the majority claimed they believed that presenting a Negro on the slate would undermine the chance of the slate being elected.

It was widely anticipated that Booker T. Bradshaw, a prominent Negro businessman who was president of the Virginia Mutual Benefit Life Insurance Company and board member of the Richmond Citizens' Association would be the Negro candidate on the Citizens Association's slate. After the Citizens Association refused to include Bradshaw on their slate, he and Dr. Jesse Tinsley came to me and asked me if I would run. Part of their reason for asking me to run for City Council was that in my primary campaign for the House of Delegates in the preceding year, I successfully attracted a significant number of white voters. I agreed to run.

As I had done while running for the House of Delegates, when I sought election to City Council, I campaigned all over the city. Of course, I emphasized the negative role that the Richmond Citizens' Association was playing in the councilmanic elections. I contended that the Association was going to control all the political decision making in the city; and we needed a watchdog to keep the public informed. Although we cooperated with the Association in the charter change fight, I did not let that deter me from attacking the Association, too. I used its failure to put a Negro on the slate as further evidence of reasons for suspicion regarding their willingness to fairly represent all of Richmond's residents.

In the councilmanic elections, I got tremendous support from the Negro community including the Phi Phi chapter of Omega Psi Phi, the Richmond Civic Association, a group of black high school children, friends from Washington, D.C., as well as numerous individuals and organizations. In addition, I received a considerable white vote — enough in all to come in ninth. Several of the other Association candidates were sympathetic to me. They knew that we had cooperated with the Richmond Citizens Association and some of them were genuinely concerned about the Citizens' Association's failure to place any Negroes

1948 City Council Election, Campaign Headquarters on Victory Night (Oliver W. Hill, Sr. is seated in the lower middle section of the photo.)

on the slate. Anyway, I got elected.

Of course, after I got elected there were a whole lot of 8-1 or 7-2 votes. During the last year of the term that I served, the newspaper reporters covering City Hall voted that another lawyer named John Davenport and I were the two most effective members of Council.

In those days, we also had a group called the Capital Trade Association. The activities of this group included fostering business opportunities and trade with and among Negro businesses in the Richmond area. To put this issue of economic development in historical context, from the end of the Reconstruction Period through the early 1920's, Richmond was a leading site of Negro business development in the United States.[8] The first Negro bank, the St. Luke's Penny Savings Bank; the first Negro insurance company, The Southern Aid Beneficial Society, and a number of other businesses were started in Richmond. The largest Negro owned financial institution was organized in 1887 by Reverend W.W. Browne and called the Savings Bank of the Grand United Order of True Reformers. It had numerous meeting halls throughout the state of Virginia.

In addition, Maggie Walker served as the Executive Secretary of a benevolent association called the Order of St. Luke. Walker built the Order of St. Luke's membership from seven hundred to over twenty thousand, and helped found the St. Luke's Penny Savings Bank. Because life and other types of insurance for Negroes was often unavailable, such associations collected dues which funded payments made to sick members or to their survivors for funeral expenses. In fact, Madame Maggie Walker was the first female president of any bank in the United States. She also edited a weekly newspaper, the St. Luke Herald.

The St. Luke Penny Savings Bank was a forerunner of Consolidated Bank and Trust Company in Richmond. During the early days of the Great Depression, Consolidated Bank was established by the merger of the Penny Savings Bank, the Second Street Savings Bank and the Mechanics Savings Bank. Consolidated remains the oldest bank owned and operated by Negroes in the United States.

During the period between 1910 and 1920 there appeared to be a modest slowing in the pace of Negro business development in Richmond. However, during the 1920's and leading into the Depression business activity seemed to increase. Despite the Depression, even during the 1930's, a small chain of Negro owned grocery stores called the Red Circle Stores existed in Richmond. I frequently shopped in those stores. Subsequently, however, the competition from large supermarket chains put these small Negro grocery stores out of business.

While this gives you some historical background regarding my election to City Council, on a national level, after Roosevelt's death, Truman issued an Executive Order 9806 on December 5, 1946. Truman's order created a progressive committee to study the areas for constructive change in protecting civil rights, especially of Negroes in American society. The committee included Sadie T. Alexander, wife of Raymond Pace Alexander both of whom were lawyers in Philadelphia. As I stated previously, the committee presented a report entitled, "To Secure These Rights".

Truman endorsed the report's recommendations and stood firm on the recommendations to enhance the civil rights of Negroes and other oppressed groups. He risked the wrath of the segregationists who bolted the Democratic party and worked to defeat him in the 1948 presidential election. In that situation, I said I would stand up for anybody who would vindicate the rights of the oppressed members of our society. Some people said, hell, Truman is not going to win. But I said I was going to support him regardless of whether he won or not.

As a matter of fact because of my support of Truman, I had significant problems from some of my political friends. For example, a number of labor leaders and other liberal minded individuals had organized a progressive party in 1948 supporting the candidacy of Henry Wallace. Wallace was born in Iowa in 1888 and had served in Roosevelt's third term as vice president. However, at the Democratic Convention to nominate Roosevelt for a fourth term, Wallace was bumped in favor of Truman reputedly because many Democrats were afraid that Roosevelt would not live out his fourth term and if he died Wallace would be president. Wallace was considered to be too liberal: that was it, plain and simple.

I was a member of a progressive organization known as the Southern Conference for Human Welfare. Many of the members of that organization supported Wallace. Virginia Durr, who was related to Justice Black, was president of the Virginia branch of this organization. Months before Truman's Committee on Civil Rights made its report, Mrs. Durr and I had discussed at some length what a good president we believed that Henry Wallace would have made had he succeeded Franklin Roosevelt. We talked about who we were going to support in the

229

upcoming presidential campaign and the possibility of working for Wallace because I thought Wallace would have made a wonderful president. However, after Truman stood up like he did in defense of the rights of Negroes and other oppressed people, I was voting for Truman come hell or high water. To my knowledge, this was the first time that a leading white politician had publicly affirmed the rights of Negroes even though he jeopardized his prospects for election.

While the 1948 presidential campaign was in full swing, Alpha Phi Alpha Fraternity held a concert at the Mosque Auditorium in Richmond. To get around our boycott of the Mosque's segregated seating policy, the Alphas adopted a format commonly used now. They sent out invitations soliciting individuals to pay a predetermined price to attend a concert in which Paul Robeson, the renowned Negro singer, actor, and human rights activist was performing. Robeson's appearance produced a sellout crowd; and by this device, the persons who were invited to attend simply showed up and sat anywhere. This led to a non-segregated seating arrangement.

The next day a luncheon was held reputedly honoring Paul Robeson. I was invited to the luncheon and it turned out that everyone there except for me was a Progressive Party member or supporter. Nevertheless, we were all in other organizations together. For instance, most of the people there were active in the NAACP or the Southern Conference on Human Welfare. In addition, Zenora B. Lawson was running for United States Senate and John Drew was running for Congress from the Third District on the Progressive Party ticket. Both Lawson and Drew were strong NAACP workers. I was on City Council at the time and a strong pitch was made for me to come out and support Wallace.

I knew everyone there personally. However, they could not appreciate my point of view and the differences that I had with their position. I was accused of abandoning Wallace which was not true. Paul Robeson and Mrs. Durr were particularly strident in urging me not to abandon Wallace.

I was not abandoning Wallace, I was simply supporting Truman. I could not agree with their position because I thought that all liberals, especially Negro liberals, should support Truman in light of his demonstrated support for the rights of Negroes. Finally, I got very angry and frankly cannot remember how the luncheon ended. However, neither side changed its position and I did not join the Progressive Party.

My election to City Council in 1948 had also attracted national attention. President Truman was in a tight election fight and accordingly Congressman William Dawson, who headed the Negro section of the National Democratic Campaign, contacted me. I had never met Dawson before. Actually, I was campaigning for Truman in Virginia even before Dawson called me. Dawson's campaign headquarters was in New York; and Dawson invited me to come to New York City to campaign for President Truman and Vice President Barkley.

In those days both political parties had Negro sections that were tied to but not fully integrated into the mainstream of party activities. For example, the National Democratic Party had a head of the Negro Division of the Democratic Campaign Committee. The Negro Division was a separate entity within the National Democratic Campaign Committee. The party chairman was James A. Farley and he was also Postmaster General during Roosevelt's first two terms.

As I look back over my political activities, my first experience with a national presidential campaign occurred twenty years before the Truman re-election campaign. In 1928, I was an interested observer of the Al Smith/Herbert Hoover campaign. As I mentioned before, during the summer of 1928 I was a waiter at a hotel in Oswegatchie, about six miles outside New London, Connecticut. That was Al Smith country.

After Hoover's election, a separate inaugural ball for Negroes was held in the Masonic Temple building at Tenth and U Streets, Washington, D.C. I had worked as a waiter at Harvey's Restaurant on Twelfth and Pennsylvania Avenue during Hoover's inaugural parade and I also worked at the Masonic Temple for the Negro Republicans' inaugural party. In these circumstances, it may not surprise you to know that seating was segregated even in the House of Representatives lunch room where I waited tables in law school.

Anyway, returning to the story of my participation in the Truman campaign, when I went to New York I was lodged at the old Taft Hotel near Grand Central Station. Every night we began our campaign activities from the Theresa Hotel where the campaign staff was headquartered. Part of our campaigning involved getting on a flatbed truck with a three piece band. Typically, the truck pulled up to a previously selected corner, the band played, folks assembled, and I would be introduced and then make my spiel. This was a unique way of campaigning in New York City, or the "Big Apple" as they call it.

Each night from about 8:00 p.m. until 10:00 p.m. or later in Harlem, we went around attracting crowds and making our election appeals. Generally, in Harlem, many people were in the streets engaged in various activities. Accordingly, it was easy to get a crowd together. Frequently, the person introducing me would emphasize that I was an example of how if Negroes could win elections in the South it could happen any place. Following that or similar comments, I would make my speech urging the voters to come out and vote for Truman and Barkley. Then we would ride to another section of the neighborhood and repeat the same process.

Congressman Dawson and I became very good friends. I rarely if ever went to Washington without going to Dawson's office, sitting down and talking with him. He encouraged me to stop in and he never was too busy to see me.

After the Democratic Convention and over the objection of General Eisenhower, on July 26, 1948 Truman also issued an Executive Order 9981 to desegregate the American military services.[9] Truman's Executive Order helped stimulate support from Negro voters who ably contributed to making it possible for him to retain his office.

Returning to my local political activities, two years later, in 1950 when I ran for re-election to City Council, I was endorsed and on the slates of the Richmond Citizens' Association and the Richmond Civic Council. In addition, the Richmond Times Dispatch and Richmond News Leader endorsed me as did members of other smaller organizations. I had plenty of support.

However, I had several things that kept me from getting re-elected. For example, one of my chief supporters was a very active dentist, Dr. Leon Reid, Sr. Prior to the campaign, we were in a public meeting of the Richmond Civic Council at the old Fifth Street Baptist Church. Early that evening, the Reverend Vernon Johns from Prince Edward County had everybody all fired up with one of his patented inspirational orations. Following Johns' address, Reverend C. C. Scott decided to take advantage of the crowd's emotions by saying "We ought to announce support for the candidacy of Dr. William Lee Ransome for the House of Delegates." Ransome was an elderly pastor serving the First Baptist Church over in south Richmond. (Delegate Dwight Jones is currently the Pastor of that Church.)

Leon jumped up, went running down the aisle and said, "We

have already agreed on how we are going to handle that nomination." The excitement of the occasion resulted in Leon having a stroke. He lingered two or three months but by the time the campaign occurred, Leon had died.

However, had he remained healthy Leon could have counteracted a man named Ralph Dorsey who operated a real estate business on Adams Street in Richmond. Dorsey was angry at me because he wanted to sell some land to the Virginia Teachers' Association for purposes of constructing a building. That land is where our law office was located until very recently. The property is now part of an enlarged Richmond Center. At that time, the people in the neighborhood didn't want any building in the block. They wanted to keep the neighborhood strictly residential. They came to me to block it: and I did.

As a result, Dorsey campaigned like the devil against me. He was head of an organization known as the Richmond Democratic League. While he identified himself as a Negro, he was as white complexioned as any white person. He and his brother both were supposed to be related to the Harry Byrd family.

During the re-election contest my opponents had local issues to use in their campaign against me. For instance, the big local issue was the question of routing north and south interstate traffic through Richmond. City Council had engaged a firm called SEGOE which came in and made a study known as the SEGOE Plan. The SEGOE Plan recommended that we bring the traffic off of Brook Road (U.S. 1), down to Azalea and on to Chamberlayne Avenue, continue down Chamberlayne Avenue, turn into a newly conceived street to be named Belvidere, and continue through an underpass north of Broad Street. Traffic would then resurface near the old penitentiary area somewhere near Spring Street and cross the James River over the Robert E. Lee Bridge.

Oliver W. Hill, Sr. during the 1950
Campaign for City Council
Re-Election

233

There was no opposition to the SEGOE Plan on the Council. The Richmond Citizens' Association was for it, and the Chamber of Commerce supported it. The Council wanted to and was prepared to pass a resolution adopting the SEGOE Plan. There was only one problem: in researching the matter I discovered a situation in Philadelphia where the City Council had instituted municipal improvements by just doing it themselves without significant citizen participation. The Philadelphia Council ran out of money and the improvements ran into a dead end somewhere near a river in the Philadelphia Metropolitan area — perhaps the Schuykill or the Delaware River. Anyway up until the time I made my research findings, the Philadelphia project had never been completed.

In light of that information, I insisted that we should have a referendum vote by the people. A fellow member of Council named F. Henry Garber of Church Hill joined me. The majority of Council were scared to bring the SEGOE Plan to a vote because they didn't want to appear opposed to submitting the matter to the popular will.

However, Dorsey with whom I had the conflict, circulated the rumor that this was going to take the land of a church and other Negro owned property. The rumor was false and his allegations had nothing to do with the SEGOE Plan. The SEGOE Plan would have affected only a few Negro residents and taken one side street. In fact, SEGOE's plan would have taken much less Negro owned property than any plan that I could foresee being adopted. These facts were not widely understood in the Negro community. Indeed, when the SEGOE Plan was not adopted far more Negro owned property was taken through condemnation proceedings to build the Richmond/ Petersburg Turnpike. That highway was constructed by act of the General Assembly.

Despite the support of the Citizens Association and Chamber of Commerce favoring the SEGOE Plan, the unwise decision was made by these organizations not to have their candidates campaign for it because it was controversial. Former Mayor Bright, a candidate for Council, lead the opposition saying they would dig no ditches through Richmond. As it turned out, I was the only candidate campaigning for the plan.

Notwithstanding this tactical error on the part of the Richmond business community, the crucial factor which caused my defeat in my bid for re-election involved a decision made by the president of the Richmond Citizens' Association. This individual was also a high ranking official of one of the tobacco companies. He called me one day and asked me to stop by because he wanted to read me a letter that he proposed to send to the newspaper. He had written a letter personally attacking a man named Throckmorton who was a former member of the old Board of Aldermen. Throckmorton was running as candidate for City Council as an independent.

I strongly objected to the letter. I told the Citizens' Association president that "We are not concerned about Throckmorton's candidacy. According to our estimation of the situation, Throckmorton is running about 12th or 13th." In my view, no reason existed for sending the inflammatory letter. I added that to attack Throckmorton would make him appear to be a martyr.

I also was convinced and stated that in deciding for whom to vote, many white voters who would otherwise not support Throckmorton might do so in protest of what they perceived as the Citizens' Association's unfair attack on him. I could foresee that they would support Throckmorton at my expense. He simply had no valid reason to attack Throckmorton.

When I told him this, I was on my way to Danville, and when I returned to Richmond the first thing I saw in the paper was that he had sent this daggone letter. And it had just the effects that I knew it would. A lot of white folks rather than support the entire Citizens' Association slate dropped me and supported Throckmorton, who ultimately came in sixth. I came in tenth. I was the odd man out — everybody on the slate got elected except me.

While I had the support of a number of white groups like the Richmond Citizens' Association, the Richmond newspapers, the West End Democratic Club and various other white political clubs, another factor contributed to my defeat. The problem was that some of my white supporters thought, "We don't want him to get too big a vote because then he will be thinking about becoming mayor." The candidate who had come in first in the previous election, was elected the ceremonial mayor by members of Council.

After the election, I must have had four or five hundred white people coming up to me at various times and places saying that they supported me, that had they known I was in any trouble they would have voted for me, and that they were shocked that I lost. How they figured I was going to get elected if they didn't vote for me was more than I could understand. However, even if three fourths of them were just saying those things to make me feel better, had the other one fourth

235

voted for me, I would have won the election.

I lost by forty-four votes. Dorsey probably knocked out fifty or sixty votes. However had Dr. Leon Reid, Sr. been living at the time of the election, I am, confident that he could have counteracted Dorsey's efforts. Despite my defeat, I still received more votes than when I was first elected to Council. However, after we decided to challenge segregation per se, I could not for the next decade, have been elected dog catcher!

Interestingly, Dorsey had all kinds of pull in raising capital to finance his real estate operations. As a matter of fact when I bought a house his brother was the selling agent and I used Dorsey's company to finance the transaction. Later, during the Stevenson campaign we both worked in the campaign and growing out of that experience we became good friends.

Every Christmas Dorsey would send many of his supporters and friends a bottle of Old Forrester or President's Choice whiskey. Typically, the bottle had one's name on it and stated that it was bottled exclusively for him. Sometimes Dorsey sent with or in lieu of the drinks, a Smithfield ham or turkey. I was on his most favored list from the 1952 campaign on. As a matter of fact when he decided to sell his building, although others wanted to buy it, he came to me to solicit my interest in having our law firm buy the building. Although we had not considered it until that time, he let us have it at a good price and we bought that property.

Although the Richmond City Council elections foreclosed one avenue of governmental service for me, as matters evolved another opportunity presented itself. Pursuant to Executive Order 10308 issued December 3, 1951, The President created the President's Committee on Government Contracts Compliance. President Truman appointed me as one of the Committee's public members.

Other members of President Truman's Committee on Government Contracts Compliance included both members of the general public and representatives from five agencies of the federal government. For instance, Truman appointed George Meaney who for many years was head of the A.F.L. as well as James B. Carey, secretary-treasurer of the C.I.O. Truman also appointed someone from the Labor Department; and a young lawyer, Everett L. Hollis, represented the Atomic Energy Commission. A representative from the State Department was also appointed. He and I got to be very good friends. Truman also selected

Irving Engel, Chairman of the Executive Committee of the American Jewish Committee. The only other Negro that Truman appointed was a man named Dowdal Davis. He was editor of the Kansas City Call newspaper. Dwight R.G. Palmer, Chairman of the Board of the General Cable Company, was the chairman of the committee. A prominent New York lawyer who represented circuses and other corporate entities was on it.

After passage of the Thirteenth, Fourteenth, and Fifteenth Amendments and the Civil Rights Act of 1866, other than the Civil Rights Act of 1875, which the Supreme Court gutted in 1883, the only significant subsequent federal measures to enhance the rights of Negroes were Truman's executive orders and Roosevelt's earlier Executive Order 8802. Roosevelt issued his order in response to A. Phillip Randolph's threatened march on Washington in 1941.

Randolph had organized the Brotherhood of Sleeping Car Porters and Maids in 1925 to obtain better wages and working conditions for railroad workers employed by the Pullman Company. A tireless fighter for the rights of workers, and a strong advocate for justice for Negroes, Randolph's call for fifty or a hundred thousand Negroes to come to Washington to focus attention on America's policy of segregation and wage discrimination in employment galvanized widespread Negro support. To help avert the international embarrassment of having attention focused on American racism when the United States was ostensibly supporting democracies like Britain in their battle to overcome the Nazi assault, Roosevelt issued the political "fig leaf" of Executive Order 8802.

Anyway, when Truman appointed the committee on contracts compliance he authorized it to hold hearings, make studies, and report to him with recommendations of how we could enforce non-discrimination in government contracts. Subsequently, we had a series of public hearings in which we attempted to collect information to determine whether or not businesses which were contracting with the government were following a policy of non-discrimination. We questioned how well people handling government contracts were complying with the government's non-discrimination policy.

While there were a number of examples of noncompliance with existing federal regulations, the only instance of blatant recalcitrance that comes to mind was that of the telephone company. In one of those hearings, we received testimony from representatives of the telephone company who took a hard line. In essence the company spokespersons insinuated that the government could not dictate employment policy to the phone company. They as much as said that if the government came down too hard on them, they would discontinue the telephone service to the government.

We considered this type of posturing as essentially a lot of hot air and the Committee was not at all intimidated by it. We were convinced that if matters really dictated, the government could have the telephone company enjoined to maintain telephone service. This is just one example, however, of the intransigent attitude that some private contractors took regarding the government's fair employment practices policies.

At one of the public hearings, counsel appeared reputedly to represent the interests of Native Americans, or Indians. That's when I found out the Indians didn't have a damn thing to say about the Committee's work because they had these white lawyers who wouldn't even let them talk. I was very much concerned. The lawyers or somebody from the Bureau of Indian Affairs did all the talking.

We also had a memorable public hearing with the National Council of Christians and Jews. They prepared quite an excellent set of papers. As I mentioned we had people from various backgrounds coming from all over the country.

While Dwight Palmer, Chairman of the Committee, suggested that we hold hearings in Washington, in retrospect I think that it would have been preferable for us to have had public hearings in a number of different locations around the country. This would have helped in our efforts to familiarize members of the public with our activities.

Later, just before he left office, we made our report to President Truman. The report detailed a number of recommendations including the establishment of a federal department or agency to investigate complaints of non-compliance with the non-discrimination provisions of government contracts. We also contended that the non-discrimination clause was inadequate and suggested a more detailed, specific revision of the clause. Further, we suggested a coordinated federal response to segregation in the economic areas of national life, like employment and business, and ultimately, urged the abolition of segregation in all forms.[10]

Our committee was the predecessor of the Equal Employment

Opportunity Commission (EEOC) established by President Eisenhower.

After the New Hampshire primary in 1952 in which Truman was narrowly defeated in an unexpectedly strong challenge from Senator Estes Kefauver of Tennessee, Truman decided he wasn't going to risk losing in the general election. As I recall, there may have been a minor scandal brewing and Truman was certainly perceived by many white voters as being too favorable in matters affecting Negroes. I recall attending the National Democratic Committee's Jefferson-Jackson Day Dinner, and at that very elaborate affair with lots of fine food and drinks, Truman dropped the bombshell: he announced he wasn't going to run for re-election. A number of people were saying, "No, Mr. President, don't do that. Don't do that." But Truman was adamant and despite our entreaties he decided not to run.[11]

Nationally there was a lot of disarray in the Democratic Party. Further, Eisenhower was a formidable potential opponent and a popular war hero. Truman had tried to get Eisenhower to run as a Democrat. Aside from Kefauver, W. Averell Harriman also challenged Adlai Stevenson for the Democratic presidential nomination. Alben Barkley, Truman's Vice-President, unsuccessfully sought the nomination; however, many political observers and activists thought him too old and frail.

President Harry Truman's Committee on
Government Contract Compliance (Circa 1951)

239

When Eisenhower was nominated I thought that despite Eisenhower's popularity, Stevenson had a very good chance of winning the election. Stevenson was a fine campaigner and I campaigned for him.

When the Democrats lost the election all people in the scheduled jobs, even commissions like ours, turned in their resignations. Davis and I talked and decided that if we resigned, everything would shut down, the staff would be dismantled and the Committee's work would have to be started again from scratch. Consequently, we decided we would not resign but would wait and see what the new administration would do.

Almost two years after the Eisenhower administration came to power, I saw in the newspaper one day that Eisenhower had issued an Executive Order creating a new anti-discrimination commission. Eisenhower changed the name which was no problem because we were only dealing with government agencies and contracts.

I had hoped that the work of the Committee on Government Contracts Compliance would progress much further because the Eisenhower appointed committee had more power. In addition, among the members of the new committee, Eisenhower had appointed James Nabrit, who was then a member of the Howard Law School faculty and later became President of Howard University. Vice President Nixon was named chairman of the committee.

However, during the interim between the Eisenhower administration assuming office and the time that the President appointed a new committee, the administration paid no attention to our committee or its activities. While we lacked a quorum, sometimes when I went up to Washington to visit, and even though I was engaged in other matters, I would nevertheless check on the committee staff. However, as I said, when the appointments to the committee were made, not a word was said to us personally.

By the way, for years I kept my government travel book as a souvenir. To travel by train or plane, all I had to do was fill out a voucher and use it as we now use credit cards or cash. That is, I could use the voucher to purchase a ticket or in lieu of cash on whatever mode of transportation I was using. If as occasionally happened, I caught a train just as it was leaving the station, I gave the conductor a voucher rather than cash. Of course, I never used the travel book after

Eisenhower took office because I didn't know if they had an appropriation to cover it or not, nor was I sure of my legal status to incur expenses. No question of salary was involved because we were paid on a per diem basis. Indeed, after Eisenhower took office, neither Davis nor I submitted further vouchers for reimbursement for any of our activities. We held no hearings and as I mentioned I only checked on the staff to help maintain their morale.

While the Committee existed we went to the Oval Office on two occasions. The first was when the Committee was appointed and the second when we made our report. As I discovered previously, President Truman was a very likeable person.

In the late 1940's, some of my state political activities included another encounter with former Congressman Mitchell. Mitchell was supporting Remmie Arnold, a wealthy businessman from Petersburg as a gubernatorial candidate. During the 1949 gubernatorial campaign I was on the Council. I distinctly remember a meeting at the Moore Street Baptist Church in which Mitchell, Arnold, and an entourage of body guards came striding down the aisle of the church like storm troopers.

In that campaign, John S. Battle was the Byrd organization candidate for governor; former mayor of Richmond, Horace Edwards was an independent; and Francis Pickens Miller was supported by most of the anti-Byrd faction of the Democratic Party. Miller almost defeated Battle in the primary; however, Battle prevailed and won the 1949 gubernatorial election. Incidentally, Miller's son, Andrew, was elected in 1973 and served the state with distinction as Attorney General.

In the early 1950's, I also recall that a civic group over in Church Hill had a public program and Mitchell was invited to be the speaker. This group asked me would I introduce him and in my desire to cooperate with them I agreed to do so.

On the Sunday afternoon in question, I gave Mitchell a very elaborate and favorable introduction, much better than I thought he deserved. However, the program sponsors had posters of Mitchell labeling him an ex-congressman. Mitchell got up and began speaking but instead of carrying out the mission of the meeting, Mitchell launched a tirade about Negroes' inability to comprehend the difference between "former" and "ex." He spent most of the time ranting and raving about the difference between former and ex.

241

I was fuming inside because I knew that the only reason that Mitchell was a former Congressman (as he asserted) and not an ex-Congressman was that Mitchell had not sought re-election in Chicago. Mitchell knew that Congressman Dawson would have defeated him handily and made him an "ex" Congressman. For a number of years until his death, Congressman Dawson had a brilliant career. Further, assuming a valid distinction exists between "former" and "ex", what difference does it make? The majority of the audience lacked the sophistication to grasp the distinction.

More importantly, in my opinion, leaders like Mitchell should be more concerned with what they are going to do to help improve these citizens' living conditions - not to berate them because they might not know the (illusionary?) difference between concepts like former and ex. He was a mess. Super ego. Fortunately, this was my last personal experience with the former congressman.

Under the leadership of Ted Dalton in the early 1950's, the Virginia Republican Party made a semblance of progress in the general election against the Byrd organization. Dalton ran two unsuccessful gubernatorial campaigns against Byrd machine nominees, T.B. Stanley in 1953 and J. Lindsay Almond in 1957. In 1953, some pundits thought that Dalton might have beaten Stanley in the gubernatorial election. However, in a speech before an audience in the Shenandoah Valley, Dalton made some unfortunate statements suggesting that bonds be issued to finance highway construction rather than relying exclusively on Virginia's "pay as you go" plan. Allegedly, those statements cost him the gubernatorial election.

I never was a member of the Byrd organization and I identified strongly with the anti-Byrd opposition. I affiliated with the Richmond Democratic Party also and served on the committee that helped formulate policy positions for the National Democratic Party in 1960.

I have previously stated that the Republicans rarely ran anybody against Byrd and his cohorts because in spirit and action Byrd seemed to be more dedicated to the policies of the Republican Party than the needs of the people of Virginia. He was a Democrat only for purposes of maintaining his seniority and choice of committee chairmanships. For the heck of it, on one occasion I decided to research Byrd's record during that particular term of Congress. All I could find of any significance was that he had proposed legislation to relieve the Duponts of Delaware of a substantial tax burden.

Throughout the South, numerous so-called Democratic politicians took positions more consistent with the National Republican Party objectives than with the objectives of the National Democratic Party. However, for conservative white southern Democrats, membership in the Republican Party was a no-no because the so-called Radical Republican Congress had taken a strong stand against slavery and had instituted legislation (for example, the Civil Rights Acts of 1866 and 1875).[12]

In addition, the Radical Republicans facilitated passage of the Thirteenth, Fourteenth and Fifteenth Amendments providing for equality of civil rights for Negroes. The Southern Democrats united around the objectives of providing a system of little or no education for Negroes, and maintaining political and economic subordination of Negroes. Even in areas where Negroes were the numerical majority, they were excluded from participating in political and economic decision making. At the national level, the Southern Democrats frequently voted with the conservative wing of the Republican Party on most social issues. Accordingly, one reason Negroes were unable to get policy changes regarding segregation was that the Southern Democrats filibustered against civil rights legislation (for example, anti-lynching laws) and large numbers of Republicans refused to help break the filibuster. These Republicans were more concerned with maintaining the fillibuster procedure than protecting the rights of Negroes.

In fact immigrants from all over the world, from the moment that they crossed the street in the United States from the point of embarkation, were accorded a higher social and ultimately political and economic status than Negroes. This was so despite Negroes' presence in America in 1607-- thirteen years before the Pilgrims arrived at Plymouth Rock, Massachusetts.

Furthermore, the great majority of Negroes worked in America without wages for over two hundred and fifty years. While this country evolved through its formative years, Negroes labored, sweated and died, in the tobacco, corn, rice and cotton fields. Their sacrifices gave the American economy a tremendous head start, greatly benefitting the non Negro population (excluding oppressed groups like Indians). Furthermore, through the efforts of Negro brickmasons, carpenters, and metal workers, majestic buildings, mighty railroads, and bridges were built throughout much of the southern part of the United States.

Negroes also fought and died in every military conflict in which

243

the United States was engaged. Nevertheless, they were relegated to the bottom of the American social caste system. Even immigrants who had contributed little to this great land of opportunity, were welcomed with greater social status than were America's Negro citizens.

Regarding political strategies, in many instances, for Negroes to make their votes effective the best that they could do in evaluating candidates was to support the lesser of the two evils. In Virginia, that usually meant voting for the anti-Byrd challenger if there was one in the Democratic primary or the general election. From time to time we endeavored to unseat the incumbent. Thus for example during the late 1940's and early 1950's, some opposition to the Byrd organization occasionally manifested itself in spirited party primary battles. However, I cannot recall any open fights in the legislature regarding the elimination of segregation <u>per se</u>.

Nevertheless, we supported Francis Pickens Miller a couple of times, once for governor and once when he ran against Byrd for the United States Senate. Similarly, the first time A. Willis Robertson ran for the United States Senate, I, along with some others, were urged to support him on the basis that he was going to be a reasonably liberal person. We supported him. Our support didn't make a great deal of difference because Robertson turned out to be basically a Byrd conservative.

After Senator William Spong defeated Robertson in the 1966 Democratic primary for United States Senate, Robertson obtained a position with one of the federal government's foreign aid agencies. Robertson then took an extensive tour of a number of third world countries. When he returned to the United States, he was interviewed by Charlie McDowell, Jr., a *Richmond Times Dispatch* reporter. During the course of the interview, Robertson enunciated a number of positions contrary to his former stances. The contrast was so striking that the news reporter called his attention to the inconsistency of his statements following the trip with his pre-trip positions. Robertson frankly admitted that he had not understood the problems as comprehensively before as he had after leaving the Senate and becoming a consultant to the World Bank.[13]

We consistently urged people to participate in the suffrage process, even when progress seemed hopeless. If we could not do anything else, we urged them to vote against the incumbent. We tried to make the elected officials feel some sense of insecurity in retaining their offices.

I am told that during the period before the 1953 gubernatorial election, Ruth Stanley, wife of T.B. Stanley, whose family was quite wealthy and owned the Stanley Furniture Company in Martinsville, approached Byrd and said that she thought it was time for her husband to be Governor. Because the Stanleys were such heavy contributors to the Byrd organization, despite the organization's previous promise to Attorney General J. Lindsay Almond, Byrd bumped Almond who was one of the poorer members of the organization.

Stanley became the Byrd organization's nominee for Governor. However, many Byrd organization members viewed Stanley as a political lightweight and he had some opposition in the primary.

Despite his limitations and a strong challenge from Ted Dalton, the Byrd organization succeeded in electing him Governor of Virginia. As I stated in a previous chapter, we had a memorable meeting with Governor Stanley on the first Monday following the decision in Brown v. Board of Education.

Byrd and his party controlled Virginia politics but for the most part Byrd and Byrd machine members were Democrats in name only. On the national level in 1952, the members of the Virginia Byrd machine supported Dwight Eisenhower for president. They were "Democrats for Ike". Eisenhower carried Virginia in 1952 and the National Republican Party regained the White House for the first time in twenty years. In situations like this, rather than supporting the party, on election day, Byrd developed the technique of going fishing.

Before and after taking office, Eisenhower took little initiative about desegregating anything. For example, during Truman's second term, Eisenhower expressed his opposition to the President's plan to completely end segregation in the armed services.

As I previously stated, during World War II I had not approved of Eisenhower's way of dealing with segregation. Eisenhower was Commander of the American forces; and there was no segregation in pubs and other places of public assembly in England. Negro soldiers freely associated with and dated white English women. This disturbed white American segregationists who precipitated many antagonistic racial incidents. Eisenhower's solution to this racial problem was to have separate nights for Negroes and white soldiers to go to town. That was supposed to reduce the amount of tension and conflict in the pubs.

If Eisenhower wanted to deal with the matter constructively, in his capacity as Commander in Chief of American forces, Eisenhower could and should have issued a general order stating that while in England American soldiers would abide by English law and custom in public places. This policy would have been no different than the requirement that American service personnel abide by English traffic and other public regulations. Eisenhower's failure to make such an order or take similar measures demonstrated to me that Eisenhower was unquestionably a segregationist.

Although Eisenhower was a segregationist, in his first term as President, some members of his administration were more democratic minded, for instance Attorney General Herbert Brownell. As I mentioned, this was further evidenced by the appointment of an anti-discrimination commission, with James Nabrit, as one of the committee members.

In addition, Eisenhower appointed E. Fred Morrow a former NAACP official, as one of his aides in the White House. Morrow had worked with the NAACP while Walter White was Executive Director. Another Negro appointee during Eisenhower's first term was J. Ernest Wilkins, Sr. (a lawyer out of Chicago) as Assistant Secretary of Labor. Carmel Carrington Marr was appointed as an U.N. adviser.

We regarded these appointments as being made on the strength of the views of progressive members of Eisenhower's administration. Despite these political appointments there was little or no actual movement in the North or the South toward alleviating existing deeply entrenched racial segregation of Negroes.

In fact, Eisenhower reputedly deplored the <u>Brown</u> decision. Indeed, instead of coming forth as head of the Executive Department and supporting the Supreme Court decision, Eisenhower reportedly made some derogatory statements about Chief Justice Warren. He had no idea that Warren would ever come up with a strategy focusing on achieving a unanimous desegregation decision.

After the decision in <u>Brown</u>, the southern congressional group came up with what some people called the "Southern Manifesto" against desegregating the public schools. The congressmen urged their constituents to defy the Supreme Court mandate. Furthermore, the segregationists' disobedience of the law was urged and reflected in a policy of defiance initiated in Virginia and followed throughout the South, known as Massive Resistance.

In the wake of these activities which struck at the heart of the rule of law, instead of being forthright and letting segregationists know that he was going to support the Supreme Court decision, Eisenhower piddled around with them. For example, when Governor Faubus of Arkansas threatened to block Negro children from entering the schools in Little Rock, rather than confront Faubus, Eisenhower invited him to the White House and made a number of weak-kneed vacillating responses. Eisenhower's approach to this situation, instead of preventing Faubus from engaging in a number of stupid actions, emboldened him and other segregationists to act even more outrageously.

In fact, in my mind, it is clear that Eisenhower was forced by the recalcitrant governor Faubus to send troops to Little Rock to maintain national sovereignty rather than to desegregate schools. Had Eisenhower taken a stronger position initially and supported the Supreme Court decision rather than tacitly opposing it, the situation might not have gotten out of hand. Trying to appease southern segregationists was a policy destined for failure, and deeply destructive of community building efforts to bring people of all backgrounds closer together in this country.

Thus, sending the troops to Arkansas made matters worse because it gave the radical segregationists an opportunity to yell, "Here comes another Reconstruction period and they are going to use force to cram stuff down our throats."

The first Civil Rights Act passed following World War II wasn't much more than a study commission. In 1957, in his second term, Eisenhower signed that act. I was cool towards the legislation because I felt the so-called Negro question had been studied enough. My point was, we didn't need more studies. We needed action in eliminating segregation practices.

In that regard, we had a meeting in Washington and a member of the Eisenhower Administration attended. He presented and defended the proposed legislation. We had a serious blowup between Clarence Mitchell of the NAACP and the Eisenhower official whose name I have long since forgotten. The majority of Negroes didn't think too much of the proposed civil rights commission. Everybody who viewed the situation intelligently and objectively knew segregation was wrong and

247

detrimental to American society generally, and more particularly to the Negroes in it.

A further example of what I meant by the need for action involved promotion on federal civil service lists. A Negro employee could work her way to the top of the list. When a position became available, the supervisor could choose among the top three candidates. Typically the supervisor would choose a white employee. After remaining at the top of the list for a certain period of time without being promoted, an employee automatically would be dropped to the bottom of the list. This type of institutional racism ruined the possibilities of success for many Negro employees.[14]

In these circumstances we actively supported Stevenson in both his unsuccessful campaigns against Eisenhower.

On another note, following the <u>Brown</u> decision I spoke with J. Lindsay Almond, Attorney General of Virginia, regarding some of the ridiculous laws which our State Legislature was passing in opposition to <u>Brown</u>. In private discussions with me, he admitted that the laws were ridiculous; nevertheless, when they were passed he embraced and tried to enforce them.

Almond was an interesting figure in Virginia politics. As I have stated, Almond was the first judge I appeared before in the 1930's in Roanoke. In addition, Almond belonged to the Byrd organization. After he became Judge of the Hustings Court for the City of Roanoke, when Cliff Woodrum resigned from Congress to become General Counsel of a major corporation, Almond ran for and won Woodrum's former seat. At that time Almond's support included labor, Negro and some anti-Byrd forces. I was told that later when Staples was elected to the Virginia Supreme Court, the Byrd organization persuaded Almond to accept an appointment to complete Staples' unexpired term as Attorney General with the understanding that in the next election the organization would support Almond for Governor.

After Byrd reputedly reneged on the understanding that he would support Almond for governor, Almond recognized that the organization might support state senator Garland Gray for governor and shunt him aside a second time. To preempt this possibility, long before the end of Stanley's term as governor, Almond declared his candidacy for governor. Before anyone else got in the race, Almond also took a hard stand against desegregation, thereby depriving the organization of any excuse not to support him.

In response to his segregationist stand, I called him one day and said "Judge, I always anticipated that when you ran for Governor, I would campaign for you. You know very well that I cannot support your candidacy now because of your strong pro-segregation platform. That platform makes my support impossible." Almond's only remark was, "All right Oliver. I understand."

In making his early announcement, Almond had a precedent for his political strategy. Governor James H. Price back in the 1937 gubernatorial campaign had done nearly the same thing. He was from the western part of the state. He announced early and got a whole lot of private endorsements. This created a situation in which the party had to support his candidacy. Of course, Price was a strong Byrd organization supporter but I do not recall him being a hard core segregationist.

Many political observers believed that Eisenhower's belated decision to send federal troops to Little Rock helped galvanize the segregationist vote in the 1957 Virginia gubernatorial campaign. Almond captured that vote and defeated Ted Dalton by a large margin.

After his election in 1957, Almond acted consistently with his campaign platform. He defended the Massive Resistance laws and kept Attorney General Albertis Harrison busy.

Following Almond's election, and before his inauguration, a real funny thing happened. Instead of having the usual victory ball, Almond had a public reception in the capitol for all the people of Virginia. About a week before the reception, I was attending a fraternity meeting. I announced that I intended to go to Almond's reception and asked who would like to go with me. Several fraternity members said that they would attend with me. However when the day of the event arrived, the only one who showed up was Rayford Harris, Sr. Harris is presently an activist in the Republican Party. Together, we went to the reception.

As I recall, it was a rainy evening and there was a long line going into the Capitol Rotunda. When we got to Governor Almond he was visibly surprised and said, "Oliver, I'm so glad to see you." Attorney General Harrison was so flustered at our presence that when he turned me over in the receiving line to his wife he stammered, "Mrs. Hill, I want you to meet Oliver Hill." The food and drinks were downstairs. We went down and had a lovely time.

249

It was around this time on the national scene, that prospective Democratic and Republican candidates were scrambling to secure support for the 1960 presidential campaign. One of my fraternity brothers who lived in Boston contacted me; and prearranged for me to meet Senator Jack Kennedy at the old Wardman Park Hotel complex in Washington, D.C. As I said, Chief Justice Vinson formerly lived there, and two of my wife's brothers worked there.

The place of the meeting with Kennedy was determined by the fact that at the same hotel, the National Democratic Women were meeting and my wife was attending this meeting. Senator Kennedy solicited my assistance in getting the support of Negroes in his effort to obtain the Democratic presidential nomination.

Kennedy and I had a pleasant discussion but I made no commitment to support his candidacy. I made it clear that in the event Senator Hubert Humphrey ran for president, I felt obliged to support him. In fact, in 1960, Senator Humphrey entered the race. Nevertheless, the Kennedy supporters continued to press me to join forces with them.

As long as Humphrey had a chance I didn't want to do anything against Humphrey. Kennedy's people made an urgent request for my help in the West Virginia Democratic primary. However, at that stage I refused because Humphrey was still in the race.

In the 1960 Democratic primary campaign, Congressman Dawson was supporting Symington. I was supporting Humphrey. We were up in St. Paul, Minnesota, attending the NAACP National Convention, when Humphrey pulled out of the race. Senators Symington, Johnson and Kennedy were still in it. At that point, I went along with Congressmen Dawson in supporting Senator Stuart Symington of Missouri.

For that summer, my wife and I had planned a long family vacation, which started with St. Paul, where we attended the NAACP Convention. Our party consisted of my wife, Bernie, Oliver, Jr., my son, and William Kindall, Jr., (also known as "Billy Boy") who was company for our son. Billy was the son of a next door neighbor.

Although I was not a delegate, as part of our trip I had included plans to attend the 1960 Democratic National Convention in Los Angeles. George Weaver, a CIO official, and I were good friends. In St. Paul I asked George to arrange some good quarters for us to stay in Los Angeles.

While visiting St. Paul we had a wonderful time. As a part of its recreational activities, the NAACP had a large picnic attended by Congressman William Dawson, Senator Hubert Humphrey, and many other dignitaries. This afforded an opportunity for Oliver and Billy Boy to meet these public figures.

When we left St. Paul, we started the preconvention part of our vacation. This carried us through the South Dakota Badlands on to Yellowstone Park where we spent a couple of days. From Yellowstone, we went on to Mount Rushmore. We continued our journey and arrived in Cody, Wyoming. That afforded me one of the more interesting experiences during the course of the vacation. In Cody, the home of the legendary Buffalo Bill, I went to a barber shop and got my hair cut. This was the first time that this particular barber had cut a Negro's hair. Of course, this provoked a most interesting conversation, and both of us got quite a kick out of it because it was the first time that a white barber had cut my hair. Another interesting experience in Cody was that this furnished our family the first opportunity to observe first hand an Indian ceremonial dance.

Upon leaving Wyoming, we traveled on to Salt Lake City, Utah, where we visited the Cathedral and other local sites. It was in Salt Lake that we first encountered racial segregation on this leg of our trip. Near the motel where we were staying, we entered a Chinese restaurant for dinner. The restaurant was fairly crowded and the waitress took us through several rooms. We went to a room in the rear of the restaurant where, for the first time, I saw a vacant table. Another group was in the room and we ate our meal there.

The next morning for breakfast, we went back to the restaurant and the waitress tried to take us past a number of empty tables back to the back room. When I recognized what she was doing, I refused to be seated in the back of the restaurant and came back to the front and sat down. We were served there without further incident. I found it ironic that we were victims of discrimination by other people of color who were themselves frequently the targets of harassment based on their color, culture and nationality.

We left Salt Lake City, crossed the desert, and went up and over the Great Divide which itself turned out to be a memorable experience. It was a very hot day in July, around the fourth of the month. Many cars and trucks attempting to cross the Great Divide had become overheated and were stalled along the highway. Fortunately we had no

251

problem. We breezed over the Divide and into Sacramento. After an overnight stay there, we proceeded on to San Francisco.

While in San Francisco, Bernie was as fascinated with the city as I had been the first time that I went there. However, I had one near calamity while we were in San Francisco. I had invited a lawyer friend of mine and his wife to come to dinner with us. After a lovely evening at a restaurant on Fisherman's Wharf, the waiter brought us the check. I reached into my pocket for my wallet and my American Express card; and found that I had no wallet, no American Express card, and no money. My friend had to sign for the meal.

I was more frustrated than embarrassed, because I could foresee the trip coming to an abrupt end. I thought that my wallet and card had been lost or stolen. Back in those days they didn't have the nearly instantaneous electronic services they have today to replace lost or stolen credit cards.

Fortunately, when we returned to the hotel, I found my wallet lying on the dresser. I reimbursed my friend from some traveler's cheques that we had. This was also the first time that we had stayed at one of the Great Western Motels.

After spending a week in San Francisco we went on to Yosemite Park. We were awed by the giant Redwoods.

On our way from Yosemite down to Los Angeles the water pump on my automobile broke. A terrific noise emanated from my motor which frightened me terribly. I envisioned a serious automotive problem. However, upon having the matter examined by a mechanic, I was informed that the problem was not such a serious one that it would prevent us from traveling to Los Angeles.

Another factor that disturbed me was that this was Saturday, the first day of the weekend, and while we were in San Francisco I had been unable to carry out our prearranged plan to obtain information on our living accommodations in Los Angeles. Because I had not made contact with George Weaver, or he with me, I was afraid that by the time we got to Los Angeles everyone would have scattered. Thus factors contributing to a frustrating experience for me, included the noise of the car, the unfamiliarity with the geography of the Los Angeles area, and the uncertainty of when we would arrive at the Hotel Biltmore, the Democratic Convention Headquarters. Moreover, on our way to the

Hotel Biltmore, twice other drivers cut me off as I was attempting to exit the freeway. Each time that I missed my exit I had to get off the freeway at the next exit, obtain new directions, and try again. Finally, I just left the freeway. We managed to get into downtown Los Angeles, and simply took our chances. We found our way to the Hotel Biltmore a bit before noon. I was greatly concerned that it would be impossible to find out where George was or anyone else who knew where our housing accommodations were going to be.

I pulled up in front of the hotel, stopped the car, and as I was getting out said to my wife that in case anyone asked her to move the car, to simply say that her husband had to go into the hotel to see Senator Symington who was one of the candidates for president; and that her husband would be right back. An amusing thing happened. While I was in the hotel, sure enough, a policeman came up to the car and asked my wife to please move it. Bernie told him what I had said.

The policeman was very polite and said, "Lady, just move your car up a little bit. Senator Kennedy is coming in and the press wants to take a picture of him entering the hotel."

Meanwhile, as I feared, Dawson and Weaver were nowhere to be found. Accordingly, we drove to the outskirts of the city and found a motel. I checked the family in and went back uptown and ran around unsuccessfully trying to contact Weaver or Congressman Dawson.

When I returned I discovered that my wife had noticed the seat of the toilet had been broken. Someone had simply taped it together. She was very disgusted by this situation. It hardly made matters better when it was suggested by a hotel employee that we put a towel over it and use it anyway.

The next morning I succeeded in contacting George Weaver. He had come through for us wonderfully. George had found a spacious five room furnished apartment on MacArthur Boulevard across the street from MacArthur Park. It was an excellent location with easy access to the freeway to get downtown to the Hotel Biltmore where the convention was being held. In addition, there was a very nice restaurant in the vicinty.

We stayed there the week of the convention and a whole week after the convention to visit friends and see the sights. We entertained a couple of small parties and had a truly enjoyable time and a lot of fun.

253

While I was not a delegate, I had visiting credentials to enter the convention. During the convention, one of the Virginia delegates who happened to be a neighbor recognized us and came into the gallery to greet us.

During the convention, things moved pretty fast. I was down in Congressman Dawson's room on Tuesday night. Dawson had to go out but he told me to wait because he might have some interesting news when he returned.

I never will forget the scene when Dawson came storming back to his room. He exclaimed that Symington had made a stupid mistake. It appeared that Kennedy had offered Symington the vice-presidential nomination and Symington had refused. Symington operated on the assumption that Kennedy and Johnson were going to deadlock the convention. Symington thought that a deadlocked convention would get him the nomination.

However, Dawson had information leading him to conclude that Kennedy would get the nomination and Symington should have followed his advice and accepted the vice-presidential nomination. After Symington declined the vice-presidential nomination, on the following Thursday night Kennedy met with Johnson and offered him the vice-presidency. Johnson was a better vote counter and accepted Kennedy's offer. When Johnson withdrew his candidacy, that assured Kennedy's nomination. As Dawson had predicted, Symington was out.

Johnson's nomination as vice president created a great hullabaloo because a lot of liberal people, particularly a lot of labor folks and some of the Americans for Democratic Action were not happy with Johnson. For various reasons, they didn't want Johnson and perceived him as being unreliable. I wasn't too hot on Johnson myself. Likewise, the NAACP was initially cool towards his nomination. In short, at the end of the convention, there was a big uproar.

As a consequence, Dawson called a meeting to be held in his suite early Sunday morning after the convention concluded. All of the dissident leaders were requested to be present and they attended. Jack Kennedy and Lyndon Johnson came to Dawson's suite together. Dawson made an impassioned speech emphasizing that we elect presidents and not vice presidents. Regardless of who the vice presidential nominee was, the main point was to elect the president.

Dawson introduced Kennedy. Jack made a spiel on Johnson's behalf and then introduced Johnson. When he took the floor, Johnson stood up and shouted, "LBJ stands for Lyndon backs Jack," and with that as a theme, Johnson made a rousing speech. Though there were still rumblings from some of the left wing of the Democratic Party, Johnson's oration salved most of the crowd. However, some folks like my friend, Joe Rauh, were not particularly impressed by Johnson's performance. Nevertheless, Dawson closed the meeting, again emphasizing that we elect presidents regardless of who the running mate of the president may be.

Following this meeting I told Harris Wofford, who graduated from Howard Law School and who was also an important member of the Kennedy entourage, that he could get word to the Johnson people on my behalf that I was willing to be an advance man for Johnson in his campaigns throughout the South. I didn't have to worry about my civil rights credentials being diminished by this activity.

Frank Reeves, a young Negro lawyer and another of my close friends, was an advance man for Kennedy. Frank had held the office of Washington Bureau Chief of the NAACP.

One of my motivations for being at the Democratic Convention was that I did not want Stevenson to get the nomination. He had lost twice. Although I had supported him in his prior campaigns, I believed that he would be desperate, and in any tight political situation the most expendable thing in his political arsenal would be to sacrifice a strong stand on civil rights. It was the fear that he would cave in on civil rights and use it as a bargaining chip that in my view made Stevenson, at that period in time, an unacceptable nominee.

After staying in Los Angeles for another week after the Convention, we continued on to San Diego, California for a couple of days and visited Brown Singleton and Dan Brown, two former Richmonders, who were practicing medicine in San Diego. We also took advantage of the opportunity for the boys to see the famous San Diego zoo.

We left San Diego and went down to Juarez, Mexico for a few days. When we finished visiting Juarez we started our journey back home, crossing Mexico through Mexicala. We proceeded through the Baja region up to Yuma, Arizona.

255

In Yuma there was a fine restaurant across from the motel where we had registered for the night. The motel was a lovely place and the boys wanted to take a dip in the pool before dinner. As a consequence, when they finally got dressed and we started over to the restaurant, the lights went out. Accordingly, we had to make alternative arrangements. We drove a block or two down the street and noticed a place which looked like a proverbial "hole in the wall," but since it was getting late we decided to enter it rather than continue looking.

We sat down at a table and waited for a long time for the waitress to come to serve us. She appeared to be ignoring us. Finally, becoming a bit agitated at the situation, I called the waitress, and she came back stating that, "The manager says we don't serve Negroes." I asked the waitress a lot of questions and gave her a really hard time. I also asked her to get the manager but she said that he was not coming. Finally, we got up and left.

On our way back to the motel from this joint, we heard Barry Goldwater who at that time was a U.S. Senator from Arizona broadcasting a speech from Phoenix saying we didn't need any Fair Employment Practices Committee and other related civil rights initiatives in Arizona. I think if I could have gotten my hands on him at that particular moment, I might have done him some physical damage. In any event, I carried the family back to the motel and we looked in the phone book where we saw a Colonel Sanders advertisement. We went to the restaurant, got a take out order, and brought it back to the motel. We ate there.

The next morning, on the way out of Yuma, we saw a fine eating establishment in the very next block past the place where we were refused service the previous night. I suggested that we stop and get breakfast. My wife was very reluctant because she feared that we would run into the same problem that we had experienced the previous night. However, I insisted that we stop and get something to eat. When we entered that restaurant, you would have thought that the people operating the restaurant had heard about what had happened to us on the previous night and were trying to make amends for the situation. They were very gracious. We had a lovely meal.

Over the years I have noted that it was a common experience to receive unpredictable responses from service establishments. Whether the establishment appeared to be a hole in the wall or an upscale business, as a Negro, one could never forecast by looking at the place whether one would receive or be refused service.

256

I had some interesting experiences starting in 1940 regarding service in businesses opened to the general public. In that year, I had a female friend from college who was doing field work for Gunnar Myrdal, the Swedish social scientist, who produced a classic work on American racism, <u>An American Dilemma</u>. In appearance my friend was as white as any white person. To test the treatment accorded to Negroes and whites in the Richmond area, we spent several days seeking service in local white owned eating establishments. Sometimes when I went into a business alone, seeking service, I received it. Other times I did not. Sometimes the establishments that served me were next door to the ones that did not.

I never received service when my friend and I went into an establishment together. (She did not either.) However, when she went in alone and placed an order it was invariably filled.

From that point forward, I decided to request service at eating establishments which were open to the public unless I knew from previous experience that they practiced segregation.

We left Yuma and went to the Painted Desert in New Mexico. For the first time in the entire trip, I decided that it was best to make advance motel reservations. We determined that we were going to cross the Texas panhandle and go to Dodge City, Kansas. In assessing that trip, it became apparent that it would likely be very late when we arrived in Dodge City. I did not want a repeat of the Yuma experience so advance planning was especially in order.

Our trip across the panhandle necessitated a long, hard drive to arrive in Dodge City by 10:00 p.m. The next day, for the benefit of the boys, we spent the day visiting historic sites. The boys got quite a kick out of reliving the movie version of the "shoot 'em up days" of the wild west, as depicted in western movies. From Dodge, Kansas we went to Wichita and by prearrangement stayed with Alice Christopher and her husband Horace. Horace was a former YMCA Director in Norfolk, Virginia, and served as YMCA Director in Wichita for several years. Alice was a relative of my stepfather.

From Wichita our original plan was to go and visit Denver and Pike's Peak. However, by that time, everyone was "scenic drunk" and the consensus was to go home. Accordingly, we changed our itinerary, made an overnight stop in St. Louis, and stayed several days in Louisville with friends. In Frankfurt, the capital of Kentucky, we were refused service for breakfast because we were Negroes. From there we came back to Richmond.

When I got back to Richmond from this extended work/vacation, I learned that Congressman Dawson had called my office and left a message stating that the Kennedy folks wanted him to take a prominent part in Kennedy's campaign. Due to his health, Dawson wasn't interested in playing an active role. According to his message, however, Dawson had said that he would take part in the campaign if he could have his own lieutenant. I was the one person that he and the Kennedy officials agreed would be a fine lieutenant for him. So that's the way I got involved in the 1960 Kennedy presidential campaign.

We operated out of the headquarters located at Fifteenth and K Streets in Washington, D.C. Sarge Shriver was the nominal head of our group which included Congressman Dawson, Lewis Martin, Marjorie Lawson, Frank Reeves, a gentleman who was Scoop Jackson's legislative assistant, a young Negro lawyer from Michigan who later became solicitor for the Department of Interior, and me.

Our activities were wide-ranging. In the campaign unit and among our contacts, we discussed general issues about the political situation in various states and regions. Our primary focus involved strategies for getting out the Negro vote. My activities centered on the southern United States.

To get a feel for the political situation in Tennessee, my first assignment was to go and see John Seigenthaler who was editor of the Nashville Tennesseean newspaper. After talking with Seigenthaler I then went to Fisk University in Nashville and lined up the support of Professor Vivian Henderson who later became president of one of the Atlanta University colleges.

After these discussions, I left Nashville and went down to Memphis to solicit support of Sugarman and other young lawyers in that city. My objective was to help them to form a working unit for the campaign.

Up until that time, both Democrats and Republicans had separate headquarters to focus on the Negro vote. For example, you will recall that even in the Truman campaign, Congressman Dawson's headquarters were at the Theresa Hotel in New York. (Interestingly, that is the same hotel that Castro stayed in when he visited New York shortly after coming to power in Cuba.) I do not recall where the rest of Truman's national campaign headquarters were.

In the 1960 campaign, Lewis Martin was a member of our working group and later became Deputy Chairman of the National Democratic Committee during Kennedy's administration. Prior to this, Martin had been a publisher and news editor of a paper in Detroit.

I also remember going to New York in 1960 during the Kennedy campaign and having an interesting experience. On my way back to Washington, D.C. I was sitting in a parlor car of a train reading one of the New York newspapers. Normally, I would have taken a day coach. However, none of the regular trains carried a diner that would start serving before we arrived in Washington, DC. For that reason, I caught The Congressional which was all pullman. I was seated with my back to the entrance of the car when a young white woman came into the car and recognized a white woman from her home town. The younger woman spoke with a distinct southern nasal twang and was talking relatively loudly about her two week stay in New York City. She was complaining that the stay had been relatively boring and uneventful until on the Tuesday before she was to leave, she met "Mr. Right." She said that since she was to leave today (Friday), they made a date for Thursday evening for dinner with the expectation that later they would go dancing. He took her to a restaurant that was, at that time, the "in" place.

While they were sitting down to have a wonderful multi-course dinner, everything was going beautifully. Mr. Right had ordered some fine wine and shrimp cocktails. They had finished the first course and the waiter had placed the entree on the table. As they were about to eat dinner, the head waiter had the unmitigated gall to seat a Negro couple at the table next to them. At this point the young southern white woman said to her dinner host that he should insist that the head waiter tell the Negro couple that they had to sit some place else. Her dinner host declined to do so.

According to the narration, the young woman continued to insist that her date intervene in what had become for her an impossible social situation. His persistent refusal to do so led to an impasse between them. Finally, they got up and left their main meal practically untouched. As far as she was concerned, the evening was ruined.

As I sat listening and overhearing this part of her narration, it occurred to me that this was typical segregationist behavior. Not only did the white segregationists insist upon maintaining their view that

259

segregation was the only way to live, they also wanted everyone else to follow their dogma as well. To help ensure compliance from other members of the white community, they were quick to resort to imposing the label, "Nigger Lover" upon anyone who failed to follow their practices. Many whites feared ostracism from this particular label. I sympathized with the plight of those individuals who wanted to do the right thing, but felt fearful that not only they but also their spouses and children would be ostracized if they took a stand in favor of equal rights for all people regardless of color.

The lady to whom this segregationist referred as "Auntie" spoke in modulated terms. I did not hear what she said. I was tempted to turn to see what the younger woman looked like. I resisted the temptation. And when I went to the dining car, I did not return.

The day before the 1960 election, I ended my campaign activities and returned to Richmond to vote and watch the returns. Naturally, we rejoiced the next day at Kennedy's victory. Some of my friends who were Kennedy supporters received positions in the new administration. For instance, George Weaver became assistant secretary in the Labor Department.

Lewis Martin asked me did I have any position in mind that I would like to obtain in the new administration. I told him that I had no office in mind. One reason for my position was that anything that I would have asked for would have also required Senate confirmation. I did not want to chance appearing before the Senate and having Senator Harry Byrd of Virginia blocking my confirmation by declaring that I was personally obnoxious to him. I had no doubt that he was capable of such a tactic.

Besides, I preferred the freedom of action that private law practice and work as a private individual afforded me. However, several months later, Lewis Martin located me in Newark, New Jersey and said they needed somebody with prestige to serve in a position that they wanted to protect from a Republican who desired it. This Republican had long civil service seniority. Martin said to me that it was a Schedule C position and I would not have to go through the confirmation process.

Further, he said that the position was in housing and they wanted someone with experience to help work on the proposed executive order. During the course of the campaign, President Kennedy had focused on housing discrimination and stated that Eisenhower could have ended discrimination in federally insured housing with a stroke of the pen - that is by issuing an executive order. So I agreed to join the Kennedy administration, thinking that while I would be spending most of my time in Washington, I still would be associated with my law firm. Accordingly, I called Henry Marsh who at that time was in the Labor Department, and asked him to come and join Tucker and me in the law office in Richmond.

When I got to Washington to be sworn in, a host of people from Richmond and elsewhere appeared for the swearing in ceremony. I was in an anteroom with the General Counsel and a couple of people from the F.H.A. when for the first time I was informed that I had to resign from the law firm. I said, "Hell no." We sat in the back room for an hour and a half trying to come to an agreeable settlement of the situation. The commissioner, members of my family, other invited guests and dignataries, were out front.

I said I was taking a salary cut to accommodate them. The position paid about five thousand dollars less than I was earning at the time. If this had come up before, I would have told them to go jump in the creek. But everyone was there including my wife and son. So I finally agreed to take the position with some modifications. We worked out an arrangement whereby I remained with the firm for another six months to terminate legal obligations and other professional matters.

As I said, I really didn't want a governmental job, especially a position that required me to take a substantial cut in pay. However, I became assistant to the Commissioner for the Federal Housing Administration. Robert Weaver was the titular head of the whole setup. He was Administrator of the Housing Home Finance Agency. Under that institutional umbrella there were five semi-independent administrations: the Federal Housing Administration, Public Housing Administration, Urban Renewal Administration, the Community Administration and the Home Finance Agency.

After I accepted the position, I was initially very excited by the novelty of many of the experiences associated with being a part of a new governmental administration. In contrast with the Eisenhower administration, the beginning of the Kennedy administration was a breath of fresh air to the federal governmental structure and to the larger American society. We were inspired by the anticipated future changes and the sense of tremendous possibilities.

261

However, after I had worked in the adminstration for a period of time, I became less satisfied with the circumstances there because the administration was moving too slowly to suit me. As I stated, when Kennedy was campaigning he had ridiculed the Eisenhower administration's stand on housing discrimination by arguing that Eisenhower could eliminate that discrimination with the stroke of a pen. It took us about two years for Kennedy to sign the Executive Order. It was a tedious proposition getting the stroke of the pen to become a reality.

The big stumbling block there was Bobby Kennedy. It was not that Bobby Kennedy favored segregation; the problem was that his brother had won the presidential election by the skin of his teeth. Bobby didn't want to do anything that would jeopardize Jack's chances for re-election and non-segregated housing was an extremely controversial topic.

I found that Jack Kennedy was a much more outgoing person than Bobby. I felt that if Bobby hadn't been his Attorney General and chief advisor we would have persuaded Jack to move more forcefully to protect the human rights of Negroes and other oppressed Americans.

Even after Kennedy belatedly issued the Order, I took the position that the main constructive thing that it did was to face the government in the right direction. Starting with the inauguration of federal programs in the mid 1930's, the government had been as insidious in setting up discrimination in housing as any segregationist could desire. For example, the federal government had established separate public housing for whites and Negroes. In addition, the government gave priority for insuring FHA loans to so-called homogeneous neighborhoods. In essence, that meant that federal financing was used to maintain Negro neighborhoods for Negroes and white neighborhoods for white folks.

Further, during the Eisenhower administration, urban renewal focused on obtaining the cheapest land for urban development. Frequently, that meant properties belonging to Negroes in desirable neighborhoods were purchased at inexpensive prices. During the clearance period, the Negroes would be removed. After the renewal period ended, Negroes would seldom be allowed to move back into the neighborhoods from which they were removed unless they returned as tenants in segregated public housing. The bottom line was that in many instances they were paid less than the property was worth and lost their neighborhoods because they were unable to move back into the new housing.

In addition, there was little financing at the federal level to assist Negroes in making home purchases in segregated neighborhoods. These were some of the many gimmicks that were used to maintain and guarantee segregated communities. In fact, during that period the government was not alone in aiding and abetting segregationists. Lending institutions and developers also willingly and eagerly participated in these reprehensible activities.

While the new Executive Order had very little enforcement power, it was better than nothing. However, we should have been farther along at that stage of the game. I never really became enthused over the Order.

Looking back on the situation, when I first went to Washington, D.C. it seemed that I became involved with nearly everything other than the Executive Order. In fact, I had little impact in the creation of the Executive Order.

The only housing related matter that I had a substantial impact on was the inclusion of Indians in federal housing programs. Early on, I realized that no one in the bureaucracy was paying any attention to the needs of the Indians. This reminded me of my experiences working with Indian affairs issues on Truman's Contract Compliance Committee. Accordingly, I set up a visit to the Seattle, Washington area to see what was the status of housing for Negroes and Indians in that area.

When I went to the Seattle area, I started out in some outlying communities to get a view of the situation and a feel for what was happening. After several days, I contacted the Federal Housing Director in the District Office in Seattle.

Upon my initial arrival at the Director's office, I received a tremendous shock. As you entered his office, you confronted a huge grizzly bear rug with a correspondingly gigantic grizzly bear's head and teeth. I was startled. In my opinion, this was certainly not the situation that members of the general public should confront as they entered a federal official's offices. He had made his office appear to be a private hunting lodge.

Two things were obvious to me. First, he was not too hot on Negroes and second, he knew nothing at all about Indians and cared

263

less.

This turned out to be a most unsatisfactory visit for both of us. When I returned to Washington, D.C. to talk with the Commissioner about my findings and experiences, I recommended that we find some way of getting rid of this director in the Seattle office. His lack of sensitivity vis à vis members of the general public and his hostile attitude towards Negroes and Indians convinced me that his removal was required to alleviate the situation. The Seattle director was in the civil service and we could not fire him. However, by death or retirement a vacancy appeared in the Philadelphia District Office and we decided that the Seattle director needed a change of scenery. He was offered the District Director job in Philadelphia. It was a promotion for him. However, he did what we hoped he would do - he resigned.

To get the Indians involved in the benefits furnished by the federal housing programs, I had to deal with the Bureau of Indian Affairs. I managed to hammer out an agreement between the Federal Housing Administration and the Bureau of Indian Affairs to allow the Indians to participate in the opportunities afforded by the Federal Housing Administration's programs.

I quickly obtained the signature of the Commissioner of the Federal Housing Administration. However, obtaining the final approval of the Bureau of Indian Affairs took months. The persons with whom I was dealing gave me the impression that the matter was on the Commissioner's desk. However, no one in the Bureau would push the Commissioner to sign. I felt that this behavior indicated they were afraid to bring the matter to the attention of the Commissioner.

After many months, I made an appointment with the head of the Bureau of Indian Affairs and went to his office. I told him that we were waiting for his signature on the agreement. He soon signed the agreement. I suspect that had he been presented the document earlier he would have signed it earlier.

Much later, in working out practical details to facilitate Indian participation in the programs, an Indian tribal custom raised somewhat novel concerns. In at least one Indian group when the chief died, the custom was to burn down his wigwam. What was one to do if the chief or other official applied for a mortgage to live in federally insured housing? Anyway, the agreement between the Bureau of Indian Affairs and the Federal Housing Administration was the first one developed to

264

include Indians' particpation in these federally insured housing programs.

When I first went to Washington, Neal Hardy was the F.H.A. Commissioner. He later resigned and Phillip Brownstein became commissioner. Following Kennedy's assassination, Johnson created HUD. That was a great advance for Robert Weaver who became HUD's secretary. Phil Brownstein, who was the Commissioner, became Assistant Secretary for Mortgage Credit and Commissioner of FHA. This dual title came at the behest of people in the housing industry and realtors who desired to retain as much of the title of FHA as before HUD was created.

When the FHA was an independent agency, I felt that I had a great deal of freedom. As far as I was concerned that was fine. Following the creation of HUD instead of being an independent agency we were part of a huge bureaucracy.

I had spent five years working for the government in Washington during the early and mid-1960's. That was longer than I had anticipated remaining in D.C. Two things made me decide that I had worked in the federal government long enough. First, I wanted to return to Richmond and spend some time with my son before he finished high school and went off to college. Secondly, I was becoming increasingly dissatisfied with the work itself. In federally assisted housing programs there was too much congressional sentiment for regarding as frills and amenities - programs that I viewed as necessities. For example, in the Section 221(d)(3) Housing Program, the units lacked air conditioning. A number of congressional people thought that air conditioning for low and moderate income people was a frill. I disagreed. Of course, to get its appropriation, our agency had to accommodate the congressional views. Anyway, I left federal government service.

In 1966, when I came back to Richmond, Virginia, from Washington, Mills Godwin had been elected governor with some Negro support. He and other membeers of the old Byrd Machine promised a new day in Virginia politics. Discussions were held between Negro leaders and purported moderate Democrats. Negro suffrage was one issue of special concern. Governor Godwin created the Commission to recommend revisions to the Virginia State Constitution and appointed me to serve on it.

In 1969, for the first time, Negroes actively supported candidates,

265

in both parties in the gubernatorial race in Virginia. A big issue that political organizations, the NAACP and others were pushing was the appointment of a Negro as a circuit court judge. Linwood Holton succeeded Godwin, and during the early part of Holton's administration, a vacancy came up for a circuit judgeship in Richmond. I was never really interested in a judicial position because I viewed judicial life as being too restrictive for me. However, I have consistently been an advocate for social change. Someone needed to try and break the glacial ice of the then existing segregated judiciary. I permitted my name to be placed in nomination for endorsement of the Richmond Bar Association. At that time the Bar Association endorsed the two candidates with the highest number of votes for a particular judicial vacancy. A white Republican lawyer named James M. Lumpkin received a majority vote; and I came in second. Pursuant to the rules, both of our names were forwarded to Governor Holton with the Bar Association's endorsement.

Governor Holton invited me to the Governor's office, interviewed me and stated that he would love to have the honor and pleasure of making the first judicial appointment of a Negro person to a court of record in Virginia. He said, however, this was the first time since Reconstruction that they had had a Republican governor. Since this was the Republicans' first chance in such a long time to make an appointment, Holton felt he just had to appoint a Republican. Holton also reminded me, "Besides you know you campaigned like hell against me." That was true. I was campaigning for Bill Battle, a Democrat. Well, I told him that I understood and said I had no problem with his reasoning. Holton gave Lumpkin a recess appointment until the General Assembly could consider the matter.

At the next session of the state legislature, Judge Lumpkin went before the Judiciary Committee in the House. I am told that the committee, which was comprised primarily of Democrats, gave him a severe cross examination. The committee had little difficulty concluding that he was too inexperienced in trial practice to receive a permanent appointment as a circuit court judge.

Promptly following the hearing of the judiciary committee, that evening I received a call from an emissary from the committee. In essence, he said that "We don't have a problem at all bumping this guy because he has very little trial experience. So far as the committee was concerned, Holton has made such a bad choice, that all you have to do is say the word and the committee will appoint you." I said, "Let me think about it. I'll call you back first thing in the morning." I thought about several things. For instance, one factor was after his election, Holton carried his children to the predominantly Negro public schools located in the Negro neighborhoods in Richmond that they would have normally attended had they been children of ordinary citizens. That didn't sit too well with the segregationists of both political parties. But as far as I was concerned it was a good symbolic example of progressive leadership.

Governor Holton also brought a Negro into the Governor's office for the first time as a member of his staff. In fact, starting with Holton's inaugural address, he indicated that he planned to be the type of governor of whom all Virginians, Negro and white, could be proud.

As I weighed matters, it occurred to me that if I accepted the circuit court judgeship under these circumstances, it wasn't going to improve race relations in the progressive manner that I was seeking. After careful thought, the next morning I called my contact and told him that I thought it best to tell the committee to confirm Judge Lumpkin and let the matter rest.

I never personally observed Judge Lumpkin on the bench with any idea of critically examining him. I am told that early in his judicial term it took him a long time to make decisions on some issues involving matters of law. Although Judge Lumpkin started slowly, he improved steadily and as far as I am advised his judicial career was successful.

I only tried one case in his court. That was an appeal from the traffic court and I had a jury which acquitted my client. After about twenty years on the bench, Judge Lumpkin retired.

As is usual in such situations, Judge Lumpkin obtained his judicial appointment because he was a Republican. In all probability, if Bill Battle had been elected governor I would have gotten the nomination for the circuit judgeship and would have accepted it. I would have done so not because I wanted to become a judge, but to break the segregated judicial ice. I could have been the first black judge of a court of record in the state of Virginia. I turned it down because of the way the thing came up.

Incidently, since the early years of his governorship, Holton and I have been very good friends. However, Holton was too liberal not only for the Byrd machine but also for the Virginia Republican party. Accordingly, despite his important contributions to state politics in being a governor responsive to and representative of all Virginians, Holton did not receive substantial Republican Party support for further elective office. Holton's gubernatorial win turned out to represent a personal victory for Holton rather than a lasting change in the ideology of the Virginia Republican Party.

To put in perspective this issue of a possible judgeship for me, during the 1950's when we were engaged in the fight against massive resistance, from time to time, people would ask me whether I wanted to become a judge. I told them No. I said, however that I thought Spotswood Robinson would be an excellent Judge. Spot was later appointed to the United States District Court for the District of Columbia.

The funny part was that Spot became an excellent judge on the Court of Appeals but according to some members of the District of Columbia bar, he was a pain in the neck as a district judge. Spot was one of these people who looked at both sides of the issue to the Nth degree. That meant that matters piled up while he was thoroughly examining both sides of the issue . The Washington bar was tickled to death to boost Spot to the Court of Appeals to get him off the District Court. The rationale was not because he was not fair or smart or well versed in the law. He was all that and much more. Rather he was so very cautious that other people felt this caused unnecessary delays.

Later I touted my former partner, S. W. Tucker. Both Spot and Tucker had the temperament and love for the law necessary to make excellent jurists.

A number of individuals from my firm have become judges. Whenever members of the firm were interested in seeking judgeships, the members of our firm actively supported them. However, the only person that I actually tried to get to apply for a judicial position was James Benton. During the Carter administration a vacancy came up and I knew we had a chance to obtain an appointment in the Federal District Court. I tried to get Benton to apply for it. At that time, he felt that he had not had enough trial experience in federal court.

After I took the initiative on Benton, and Benton declined to apply, it came to my attention that Judge James Sheffield of the Circuit Court for the City of Richmond had expressed an interest in a federal appointment. We then decided to support Judge Sheffield. Henry Marsh and I made an appointment to meet with the member of the Justice Department in charge of judicial appointments and we conferred with him on behalf of Judge Sheffield. In my presence, the official said to Henry that if Henry wanted the judgeship, the official would send Henry's name to the White House that day. Henry declined because he was not interested in a judgeship; moreover, he was supporting Sheffield. Several years later, we supported Benton for the Virginia Court of Appeals.

Some years later, when the legislature instituted the State Bar Disciplinary Board, the Chief Justice of the Virginia Supreme Court didn't ask me, he just appointed me to a three year term. When my first term expired the Chief Justice appointed me for another three year term.

So I served the maximum six years in a quasi-judicial capacity. We tried, disciplined or dismissed charges against lawyers. Our workload was limited to members of the Bar. Thus I ended up receiving some judicial experience, and confirming the fact that I did not want to be a judge.

A number of lawyers have ascended to the bench from our firm. They include federal district judge Raymond Jackson, his wife, state trial judge, Gwendolyn Jackson, state circuit judge Randall Johnson, Sr., state circuit judge John Scott, state circuit judge, Margaret P. Spencer, and state circuit judge Gary Hicks. D. Eugene Cheek is a general district judge and Richard D. Taylor, Jr. serves as a state juvenile and domestic relations judge. Judges Spencer, Scott and Hicks were general district judges before being elevated to the circuit court. Spot Robinson always took pride in having been the first member of the firm to become a judge.

Following the Reconstruction Period, the first black to serve in the Virginia judiciary was Willard Douglas. Douglas had worked for our firm in the 1960's. After leaving our firm, he later served as an Assistant City Attorney. Douglas was appointed as a judge in the Juvenile and Domestic Relations Court and served in this capacity several terms until he retired.

I also had an interesting experience involving Negro economic development opportunities during the early years of the Nixon administration. A statute was enacted allowing the government to subsidize some Negro and other minority businesses. The law furnished substantial tax incentives to major corporations to fund such minority business organizations. President Nixon held a conference at the White House to promote the objectives of this statute. The conference was attended by a number of major corporate officials. A high ranking official in a major corporation who had attended this conference at the White House said to me that he was interested in having his corporation participate in this particular program. He suggested that I investigate it and submit a proposal to him.

I researched the matter and made contact with a local minority business which had developed a basic baseboard heating device which they were seeking to market. We prepared a detailed written analysis of the proposal and the legal procedures. We presented our recommendation to this corporate executive. The proposal included a provision whereby, pursuant to statute, the donor corporation could invest three hundred thousand dollars in the capital structure of the minority business to carry out the objectives of the particular project.

The executive who originally contacted me hit the ceiling. He said that wasn't what he had in mind. He was talking about an article that he had read in a local newspaper regarding Waller, a jeweler, who used to be located on First Street in downtown Richmond. Waller had been burglarized several times and he wanted to help Waller or someone similarly situated.

The thing that disturbed me greatly was that while I was working in Washington I had information that the same company had willingly participated in another speculative business venture in which they invested a similar amount of money in a project sponsored by a developer from a neighboring state. Further, this situation had occurred a number of years before the statute was enacted, and the corporate leadership willingly invested in the project despite the absence of any governmental financial safeguards to protect the company in the event that the venture failed. In fact, when the developer presented the corporation with a proposal and the proposal was costed out, it became evident that the developer's plan required an initial outlay of nearly three hundred thousand dollars. The white developer told me that his heart sank because he knew that he would be unable to raise that kind of money. He then asked the corporate officials what could be done about the insufficiency of funding for the proposal. He was told not to worry, that it could be "taken out of petty cash". Earlier this same developer had been extended similar favorable treatment by the Veterans Administration which had granted him an extension of time to complete a project. The net result was that at that time this white developer was telling me this story, he had become a millionaire. Of course neither public officials nor ardent segregationists ever complained about this type of affirmative action.

In any event, it became clear to me that this corporate executive leadership was uninterested in this project. Even though it was suggested that I meet with other people in the corporation, and we did, nothing ever came of it.

This is an example of the type of problems we have confronted for a long time. This particular corporate executive was interested in doing something for a single Negro, but was not interested in supporting a Negro initiated project that would help Negroes enter the economic mainstream as entrepreneurs.

On a related topic, people talk negatively about the Great Society. The Great Society never had a chance because President Johnson, its sponsor, was distracted by the Vietnam War; and funds which would have been utilized to carry out the programs of the Great Society were spent on that war.

Most of the projects that were financed by the Nixon and other administrations were too often gimmicks which had no great hope for success. It also should be noted that initially court action was required to compel the Nixon Administration to implement the Great Society programs to the extent that they did. However, it must be admitted that once he got started, Nixon made reasonable efforts to implement affirmative action programs. Nevertheless, too many governmental programs only gave participants something to do. If you came up with a real good proposition to develop some industry and provide significant employment opportunities, your chances of getting any help were very slim. Programs for political and economic freedom must be crafted to reinforce each other — voting, jobs and lawful behavior go together.

Evaluating Presidential Performance

In leading our country on issues involving civil rights, I list Presidents Truman and Johnson tied for first place as the best presidents. My reason is that with Truman, for the first time, there was a president who was involved with an issue that directly affected his prospects for re-election and the civil rights of Negroes. Truman elected not to abandon Negroes as had usually been the case by other white political leaders similarly situated. Instead Truman stood firm. He did what he knew was right despite the warnings of Strom Thurmond and other segregationists who threatened to bolt the Democratic party. They carried out the threat and formed the Dixiecrat Party in an unsuccessful bid to defeat Truman in the 1948 presidential election.

271

As far as Johnson is concerned, for years he had been a wheeler and dealer, and generally supported fillibusters of the segregationists on issues important to Negroes. However, Johnson had refused to sign the Southern Manifesto criticizing the <u>Brown</u> decision, and advocating massive resistance to the Court's mandate to desegregate. After Johnson became vice president, Kennedy sent Johnson on a tour to visit many underdeveloped countries. According to Johnson, that tour opened Johnson's eyes to many deplorable conditions of people in the third world.

Johnson also developed heightened sensitivity to the wretched conditions of Negroes in this country. While I was working for the Kennedy Administration, I vividly recall on one occasion that Johnson conferred with a group of us at the conclusion of a meeting on inter-group relations at the State Department. Johnson voluntarily stated that if he ever had an opportunity, he would do something to correct the prevailing catastrophic conditions affecting Negroes and poor people. Johnson's statement left no doubt in my mind that he had a true change of heart. This was evident in his zeal in supporting passage of the Civil Rights Acts of 1964 and the Voting Rights Act of 1965 as well as other features of the program known as the "Great Society".

An interesting anecdote involves the fact that when Johnson was delivering his speech to Congress regarding passage of the 1964 Civil Rights Act, a group of us were holding a meeting of the Pigskin Club at the old Statler Hotel at 16th and K Streets in Washington, D.C. As Johnson began speaking we broke up our meeting and gathered around televisions to listen. After Johnson had made several excellent statements, in the room where I was, the crowd was buoyed and excited. I spoke up and said, "You haven't heard nothing yet. Wait until he gets to the part where he says, 'And we shall overcome'". When Johnson actually said, "We shall overcome", I could not convince anyone that I had no part in writing the speech. But I just knew from previous conversations with Johnson and the tone of this speech, that that expression was inevitable.

Since then, appearing on the highly regarded network, C-Span, on separate occasions, both Jack Valenti and Bill Moyers related similar stories demonstrating Johnson's sincerity. Johnson followed through on his earlier assertions that given an opportunity he would do something about the problems of poverty and the discrimination against Negroes and other minorities in this country.

272

Continuing with my list of best presidents, there would be a tossup between Carter and Kennedy. Roosevelt would come next in that although earlier progressive things happened in his administration, Roosevelt had to be pushed to do what was needed. My sense is that his wife, Eleanor, played a more important part than we will ever know.

We will have to wait until the end of President Clinton's second term to evaluate where he would rank on my list.

A Brief Retrospective

During my long career in the law, I have been involved with a treasure trove of brilliant lawyers and activists. Most of these individuals I met while working with the NAACP and the NAACP Legal Defense and Educational Fund, Incorporated which later became known as the Legal Defense Fund. In addition to the people I have previously mentioned, these dedicated individuals include William Coleman, James Nabrit, III, Judge Constance Motley, Elaine R. Jones, Judge Louis Pollak, Professor Charlie Black, Judge Jack Weinstein, Franklin Williams and Louis Redding. Constance Motley was an excellent trial lawyer and is an exceptional judge. Jack Greenberg followed Justice Marshall as Director of the Legal Defense Fund and did an excellent job. Julius Chambers succeeded Jack and also did an excellent job; Elaine Jones is now the Director of the Legal Defense Fund. Elaine continues the legacy of extraordinary service and dedication associated with that office.

Louis Pollak, the former dean of Yale and the University of Pennsylvania Law Schools, presently serves as senior district judge for the eastern district of Pennsylvania, and performed yeoman service in the preparation of the arguments and briefs of Brown v. Board of Education, as did Charlie Black and Jack Weinstein. James Nabrit, III followed in the outstanding footsteps of his father. Franklin Williams later became western regional counsel for the Legal Defense Fund. Louis Redding was another gifted Negro lawyer who, with Jack Greenberg, brought the Wilmington public school desegregation case that was consolidated as part of Brown v. Board of Education. William Coleman is an excellent lawyer, former law clerk for Justice Frankurter, former secretary of transportation for the Ford administration and served for many years as President of the Legal Defense Fund.

While I was in law school, Samuel Leibowitz who worked with the International Labor Defense, served as a lawyer in the celebrated Scottsboro Boys case. Leibowitz was a guest lecturer for our law school class. He later became a New York Supreme Court judge.

William Henry Lewis, Sr., the first Negro appointed to a position requiring Senate confirmation in the federal government, also lectured to our law school class. Lewis graduated from Amherst and Harvard Law School. In 1911, President Taft appointed him as an assistant attorney general in the Justice Department.

When I returned to Washington in 1936, through a fellow Roanoker, John Whitten, I had the good fortune of meeting and having some continuing association with Ms. Mary McLeod-Bethune. Whitten was a lieutenant of Ms. McLeod-Bethune.

In those days, seeking to find an excuse for not calling Negro ladies "Mrs.", some white folks called them "auntie." Ms. Bethune had an interesting response when a white stranger called her "Auntie." She often said, "Lord child, you children sure grow up fast. Which of my brother's children are you?"

Ms. Bethune also had a marvelous vocabulary, speaking voice and intellect. One day she came to Richmond and spoke at the historic Fifth Street Baptist Church. I went into the balcony and sat near the front of it so that I was nearly directly over her. As she spoke, I leaned over to the person next to me and said, "Isn't she beautiful?" Even though she was the antithesis of the traditional Atlantic City beauty contestant, to me she was a black beauty ...

Another spell binder who spoke eloquently was Dr. Mordecai Johnson. I often wish that he and Dr. Bethune had come along at the time when the masses of people would have had access to the media to hear these individuals.

I also worked with Ella Bauer, the national membership director of the NAACP for many years, as well as Ms. Daisy Bates, a fearless activist and mentor for the "Little Rock Nine" students.

In the 1940's and 1950's, A.P. Tureaud, a courageous Negro lawyer in Baton Rouge, Louisiana worked with us on a number of matters including the fight to desegregate Louisiana State University. I also met and worked with Ed Morial, Sr. who later became Mayor of New Orleans.

I also knew Zephaniah Alexander Looby who at one time was

Grand Basilus of my undergraduate fraternity, Omega Psi Phi. Looby was a lawyer, social activist and dean of an accredited evening law school in Nashville, Tennessee. Looby served for a number of years on Nashville City Council. Another great Omega man was J. B. Blayton who practiced his profession as a certified public accountant in Atlanta and gave a number of Negroes an opportunity to do their field work so that they could become CPAs.

Arthur Davis Shores of Birmingham was a pioneering civil rights lawyer under adverse circumstances. His house was firebombed, but despite the constant threat of a grisly death he persevered.

Colonel Austin Thomas Walden of Atlanta was a very progressive Negro lawyer, NAACP leader, and advocate for human rights for Negroes. Earl Dickerson was president of the Supreme Liberty Life Insurance Company in Chicago, an attorney, and active NAACP member. President Roosevelt appointed him to the Fair Employment Practice Committee.

Bob Ming was another brilliant lawyer, member of the Illinois Utilities Board, and law teacher at Howard and the University of Chicago. I tried to recruit him as head of the President's Committee on Contract Compliance. At that time, however, the salary level for the directorship was $10,000 which was too much of a cut in income for Bob to accept the position.

Bob Ming also led our legal team in defending my partner, S.W. Tucker, from disbarment proceedings. The Virginia State Bar Association brought trumped up charges against Tucker under the massive resistance statutes on "running and capping" in effect in the late 1950's. The State Bar charged Tucker with improper solicitation of clients.

In addition, I developed good working relationships and friendships with Walter White and Roy Wilkins who were National Executive Secretaries of the NAACP. Similarly, I had a very positive relationship with Whitney Young, Executive Director of the National Urban League. (Lester Granger was the Executive Director of the Urban League before Young assumed office.) Because of my long standing membership on the Board of the Richmond Urban League, when Young was first appointed as Executive Director, he outlined to me his vision for a more aggressive national organization. I promised to help as much as I could.

I also met Vernon Jordan who did an outstanding job in

275

succeeding Young. While I have never been associated with him I would like to state that the present director of the Urban League, Hugh Price is doing a superb job. I also had a long and strong friendship with Judge A. Leon Higginbotham, Jr. Our friendship commenced in the early 1950's while he was president of the Philadelphia chapter of the NAACP and he invited me to speak at one of the chapter's public meetings. Leon was a man of many talents - an excellent lawyer, judge, law professor and social activist. One of Leon's many important contributions was a documentary on civil rights lawyers which he produced with Dr. William Elwood, an administrator of the graduate school at the University of Virginia.

I have also enjoyed a close and longstanding friendship with Judge Damon Keith of the United States Court of Appeals for the Sixth Circuit. For example, one of his early judicial opinions which was affirmed by the court of appeals and the U.S. Supreme Court contributed to Nixon's exit from the Presidency. In 1998, Damon won the prestigious DeWitt award conferred by federal judges upon their colleagues. His forceful, thoughtful and direct approach to legal issues confronting him as a jurist has made him one of the greatest judges of this century.

Similarly, Nat Jones, former national general counsel for the NAACP, and also a judge on the Sixth Circuit, has been one of my long time companions. Another leading civil rights activist and tireless worker is Ms. Dorothy Height, former president of the National Council of Negro Women. In addition, Loren Miller of Los Angeles was a brilliant lawyer, legal theorist and marvelous brief writer. Another extraordinarily gifted lawyer and scholar is Professor Charles Ogletree of the Harvard University Law School. Two other pioneering political activists are L. Douglas Wilder, Jr., and Henry Marsh, who were law school roommates. Douglas Wilder was the first and only Negro elected to serve as governor of a state in the United States. Henry Marsh was one of my law partners, the first black mayor of Richmond, and is presently a state senator. In this regard a major political challenge for the twenty-first century is for the American electorate to elect Negro, Latino and other people of color to governorships, the U.S. Senate and the Presidency. Wilder, my long time bridge partner, followed Charles Robb and Gerald Balilles, two of the most progressive governors Virginia has had in the past two decades. Chuck Robb currently serves as one of Virginia's United States senators.

Matthew J. Perry (South Carolina), James R. Spencer (Virginia), Gabrielle MacDonald (Texas) and Richard Erwin (North Carolina) have served on the federal district court bench with great distinction, and

276

James R. Spencer, Raymond Jackson and Gerald Lee, all of Virginia are currently doing so. Gabrielle is presently a judge for the United Nations War Crimes Tribunal for the former Yugoslavia.

When I look back on my activities from World War II onward, my primary objectives focused on making this a more interesting, enjoyable and fulfilling planet on which to live through evolutionary progressive social change. For example, I sought election to the legislature on two separate occasions. In 1947 I ran because no Negroes were in the legislature and I thought Negroes should have a voice in the public policy making of the state of Virginia. On the second occasion, I ran in 1955 seeking to lend a progressive legislative voice to the discussion on what Virginia's public policy should be in the aftermath of the Supreme Court's unanimous decision in <u>Brown v. Board of Education</u>.

I also sought and won election to City Council; particpated in the Truman, Kennedy and Johnson administrations; and tried to do my part to enhance, through the political process, the quality of life of all human earthlings.

Henry L. Marsh, III, Samuel W. Tucker and Oliver W. Hill, Sr.,
Senior lawyers in the firm of Hill, Tucker and Marsh

Chapter VII

Family Life

Bernie and I were both born in Richmond. Her father was Andrew Walker. Andrew and Maggie Walker's husband, Armistead, were brothers who were partners in a contracting firm and built several buildings in Richmond. Armistead Walker, Bernie's uncle, was shot and killed by his own son. He was up on the roof of his home at night for some unknown reason.

It appears to have been one of those ugly family messes and I am uncertain of what was the real story. However, whatever happened, it created a family rift. This resulted in Andrew Walker leaving Richmond and taking his family to Youngstown, Ohio. Mr. Walker obtained employment there working in the steel mills.

In the 1920's, Bernie had a brother (Richard "Dick" Walker) in Washington. Her sister, Evalyn, also came to Washington in the mid-1920's to work in the Howard University registrar's office and to attend the University. Later when the whole family moved to Washington, D.C., Bernie matriculated at Minor Normal School.

When I was attending Howard University's undergraduate college, Bernie was attending Minor Normal School right across Sixth Street from Howard. During the spring quarter, it was a favorite past time for Howard University boys to congregate at the corner of Sixth and Euclid Streets and watch the Minor Normal School girls walk by. Generally, Bernie took another route home and was not in the group of young women who routinely passed by each afternoon after school. These young ladies appeared to enjoy the "ahs and ooohs" of the college boys. In those days Washington, D.C. was noted for having beautiful Negro women.

278

Minor was a training school for Division Thirteen, the Negro division of the Washington, D.C. public school system. The top Minor Normal graduates automatically obtained teaching positions in the Washington, D.C. schools. Upon graduation from Minor Normal, Bernie received an appointment to teach in the Washington public schools. Minor Normal evolved into Minor's Teaching College and has now become a part of the University of the District of Columbia.

Some of the Minor women's students had a little club, and a young woman named Grace Evans who lived next door to me on Gresham Place invited me to a party which the club was giving. Back in those days, quite frequently, there were a number of unescorted women at such parties. I was out with three or four of my friends when I decided that I would take Grace up on her invitation to attend the party. I extended my invitation to my friends.

We went to the party and Bernie was on the door. She knew I was supposed to be there but she didn't know about the others. Consequently, she wouldn't let my friends in. I took the absurd position that since my uninvited friends could not enter I wouldn't come in either. That's when I first saw her. I did not see her again for some time.

During the spring of 1930, Bernie and I were both present at a party given by a friend of mine named Jack Young. I recognized her and she recognized me. We both got a big kick out of the confrontation at the Minor Normal girls' club party. Anyway, I wound up making a date with her. From that point forward, we saw each other from time to time. The first time I ever carried her to a social affair was the day after Thanksgiving. That year the Howard/Lincoln football game was played on Thanksgiving in Washington. The Howard/Lincoln game was the biggest social event in the Fall on the East Coast, and was played alternately in Philadelphia and Washington, D.C. In Washington, there were certain traditional dances associated with the event. For example, the day following Thanksgiving, the Kappa Alpha Psi Fraternity had a dance down at the Dunbar High School Armory in the afternoon. On the same day, the Omegas had a supper dance at the Lincoln colonnade.

I carried Bernie to the Kappa's dance. When that was over, we went to the Omega's supper dance at the Colonnade. This affair was called a supper dance because it occurred in the evening hours, not because of food being served. (There was no food.) After the supper dance, I carried her home to meet my mother.

279

By this time we were both hungry. There was a famous restaurant on Florida Avenue, named "Harrison's." To use a well known radio expression which subsequently developed, Harrison's was considered a place where "the elite meet to eat." I carried Bernie to Harrison's for dinner. To start the meal, I ordered Brandy Alexanders. Oh boy, she later claimed that she thought I was the sharpest thing in town.

From that point on, we started going steady and continued to do so until we got married. We didn't get married until after I finished law school. If I had any sense, I probably would have married her while I was in law school. It would have eliminated the long courtship.

Bernie's parents were cordial. Her father was a fine old man. Her mother just couldn't understand me; but she tolerated me. I was too wild for her.

One reason that Bernie's mother thought I was too wild was the first time I took Bernie out to a social affair, in addition to the dances I just described and following dinner at Harrisons, I carried Bernie to a late night party. Finally, at Bernie's insistence, in the wee hours of the morning I carried her home. When we arrived at her home, we found her mother sitting up waiting for us. As you may imagine, that was not the most auspicious start. While I had come by Bernie's house to see her before, I had never taken her out. At this time in my academic career, I studied in the afternoon after law school classes were finished, and in the evenings, I had a job. Therefore, rarely was I able to see Bernie until after 9:00 p.m.

Even after Bernie and I had been dating for a couple of years, my stock with her mother had not significantly improved. For example, Andy Ransom, one of my law professors at Howard, and his wife Willa (whom we called Bill), lived very close to my future wife. We would get together and by my senior year in law school, we had established a pattern of playing bridge on Sunday afternoons. One time Bill called Bernie's home. Bernie happened to be out when the call came and her mother answered the telephone. Bill told Bernie's mother to tell Bernie that we would be unable to play bridge on the coming Sunday. Bernie's mother was a very religious person, and when she found out that Bernie was playing cards on Sunday, she had a fit. Of course, this did nothing at all to raise my stock with her mother.

Bernie's father and I got along fine. Her old man was a nice sort of guy. When I started courting Bernie, he had retired.

In addition, he liked to nip. However, I don't remember nipping with him at that stage - until after I got married. When I was a child, in my family it had been a big problem as to how they were going to deal with me because my father had been an alcoholic. They were worried about how I would turn out. To resolve this dilemma, on festive occasions, my family would sometimes give me a taste of toddy. As I grew older, I had my supply of home made wine which Mrs. Pentecost produced from the grape arbors in the backyard.

Incidentally, when I was in college, one of my friends would go with me to the nip joints. I would go in and get the whiskey and he would stay outside in the car. Later, he turned out to be an alcoholic and I didn't.

Other than being a lovely person, some of the attributes that attracted me to Bernie were that she was "a long, tall, brown-skinned gal": and she had long hair way down her back. Her long hair created a problem one day. In fact, I almost threatened to quit her. We had been going together for a year or two by this time, and I was working at the Manor Country Club, located in Maryland outside of Washington, D.C. I came in town during the middle of the week one summer day, and she had cut her hair. She had a stylish, boyish bob. She was not expecting me because if I was coming to town, I usually came on a Monday or a Tuesday. She had made a date to go out with an old friend that evening. That did not disturb me because I lacked a reason to do anything but trust her. However, I had fits about her cutting her hair.

Bernie thought that I was upset because she had made the date; and she was going to break it. I urged her not to, because as I said, I felt I could trust her. In addition, I was returning to the country club that evening. Nevertheless, I was very upset about the new haircut; and it took me several days to get over it.

During my high school and college days before I met Bernie, I dated a wide assortment of girls - all sizes, shapes and colors. This was not because I dated so many girls, rather I had no inflexible criteria for dating. However, at that time, I was not interested in getting married.

During my freshman year, I was going with a sharp, coal black complexioned girl named Thelma Stafford. She had big, beautiful eyes and long black hair. In my college days, even in the Negro community, Washington, D.C. was color conscious. At that time, I was a member of a six man pledge club and I heard one of the big brothers boast that

281

no black complexioned girl had ever been allowed to come into the frat house. This unwritten rule had an important personal impact on me later.

During my senior year in high school, Percy Newby, who was the Basilus of the Alpha Chapter of the Omega Psi Phi fraternity, and I were dating two sisters who lived in the city. One was in college and one in high school. Accordingly, from time to time I was seen in his company, as I frequently walked across campus. The Omegas assumed that since I was in Percy Newby's circle of associates, I had been at Howard longer than, in fact, I had. Incidentally, Percy was also the president of the Howard University student council and had been leader of a student strike the year before.

Having a student enter school in the spring quarter was, for this Omega Chapter, probably an unprecedented experience. However, since I entered college during the spring, that's when I pledged, even though I should not have been pledged at that time because I had not been in school long enough. This situation occurred because the fraternity was blinded by the prestige of Percy, and my ignorance regarding the pledge process.

As I stated, the club consisted of five other members and me. We were all high spirited and active. During the following fall, one of the things that our pledge club decided to do was to have a party at the fraternity house. We got permission to have the party, but we did not advise the big brothers in the fraternity that it was to be a closed party. The party was only for us and our escorts. We had a three piece band and to make sure that there were no problems with uninvited guests, we hired a bouncer. The bouncer kept all of the big brothers of the fraternity out of our party.

It never occurred to me not to take Thelma to our closed party and thereby break the color barrier if it in fact existed. I paid for it though. When I was going through initiation into the fraternity, breaking the unwritten rule and bringing Thelma into the house was one of the things somebody beat the hell out of me about. "You so damn smart, you have a party and wouldn't let the Brothers come in. You broke the barrier on bringing a black gal in here." They beat me so bad I was black and blue for three or four weeks. I swore I would never join another organization. For many years I didn't.

I broke up with Thelma long before I even knew anything about

282

Bernie. It was obvious that Thelma wanted to get married. I was not ready for marriage and knew it. I didn't want to get involved and I didn't want to hurt her either. So I thought the simplest thing to do would be just to break off with her.

On the other hand, while Bernie and I hadn't talked about marriage, we both knew that we would eventually get married. When I asked Bernie to marry me it was about two years before we actually got married. We were in a cab going to a dance and I pulled out an engagement ring and put it on her finger.

After law school, I realized that if I started circulating in Roanoke as a single person, then came back to Washington, D.C. and married Bernie, and subsequently relocated from Washington to Roanoke, this might create a problem for Bernie. In my judgment, the best thing to do was to get married before I returned to Roanoke. So I married her and came back to Roanoke with a wife.

Bernie had three brothers who were named Richard (Dick), Sam and Armistead Walker. The oldest brother, Dick, worked for the United States government; however, I do not presently recall with which agency. In addition to his government job, Dick Walker and a friend of his, Freck Boone, had an organization named "The Smarter Set". They gave dances periodically at Murray's Casino on U Street. When I was in high school, The Smarter Set would sponsor afternoon dances; and to make it appear that the event was exclusive, some individuals would be sent an invitation. Sometimes there was quite a scramble to get tickets which typically cost about twenty-five cents.

Bernie's youngest brother, Sam Walker, worked at what was then called the Wardman Park Hotel which advertised itself as being the largest apartment hotel in the world. Sam was a doorman at the Wardman Park and later became superintendent of service.

Bernie's middle brother, Armistead, also worked at the Wardman Park. During the Truman Administration, Senator Vinson was also living at the Wardman Park when Truman appointed him as Secretary of the Treasury. Vinson got Armistead to quit the hotel job and come work with him. When Truman appointed Secretary Vinson as a judge of the United States Court of Appeals for the District of Columbia Circuit, Armistead went along with the now Judge Vinson as his bailiff. Later when Truman appointed Vinson as Chief Justice of the United States, Armistead went with him to the Supreme Court. One time when my son was about two or three years old, Armistead, Bernie, he and I went back to the Chief Justice's chambers for a visit with the Chief Justice. Afterwards, Armistead carried Oliver back into the courtroom and put him in the Chief Justice's chair. We were trying to inspire him to become the first black chief justice. However, Oliver got sidetracked along the way; and never even went to law school.

After Bernie finished Minor Normal School, she continued her education by attending evening school at Howard University. There she successfully completed the program and obtained her undergraduate degree.

Later Bernie obtained her masters from Howard. After World War II, Bernie moved with me to Richmond, and she was appointed as an elementary school teacher in the public school system. Subsequently, in her professional career, she became an elementary school supervisor in the school system, and for several years before retiring, Bernie was Director of the Remedial Reading program for the Richmond Public School System.

As I have explained in earlier chapters, I was quite active in legal and political affairs while Bernie and I were married. Occasionally, this affected my dealings with the Richmond School Board, but never seemed to have much negative impact on Bernie. For example, back in the 1940's, the Capital Trade Association, a business oriented Negro organization, used to give an annual bazaar at Maggie Walker High School. The bazaar ran three or four nights. After I had returned to Richmond and been here for three or four years, I was asked to head up the bazaar committee. When I became chairman, I followed the custom and applied to have the bazaar at Maggie Walker High school.

Mr. & Mrs. Oliver W. Hill, Sr.
(Circa 1948)

However, earlier in the 1940's, I had sued the City School Board to equalize teachers' salaries between Negro and white teachers. When I applied on behalf of the Capital Trade Association to use the school for a bazaar, the School Board refused to grant us permission to use the high school where the affair had been held for years. Accordingly, I had to get another hall in which to have the affair.

Only once did I sense that my legal and political activities may have adversely affected the way that the school administration treated Bernie. The particular situation involved attending the 1963 March on Washington. Bernie was refused permission to attend the March. Aside from this action on the part of the School Board, I do not believe they ever bothered Bernie.

In the 1960's when the sit-ins began, Bernie and I also picketed. She got the members of a couple of social clubs to which she belonged to picket as well. Many of the teachers in the school system were intimidated by the prospect of becoming involved in civil rights activity but Bernie was able to persuade a number of them to get involved in some level of the civil rights struggle. For instance, in Richmond, we picketed two large department stores, Thalhimers and Miller & Rhoads. The restaurants in the department stores had refused to serve blacks. For the most part, the picketing was peaceful except for one occasion in which the police dragged Mrs. Jesse Tinsley, the wife of Dr. Jesse Tinsley, across the street with the police dogs growling and snapping at her. This incident was pictured in Life Magazine.

1960 was also a presidential election year, and Senator Kennedy and Vice President Nixon were the primary political contenders. While others have taken the credit, it is my recollection that when Martin Luther King was arrested, Marjorie Lawson who was working in our unit of the Democratic campaign had the idea of having Senator Kennedy call Mrs. King to express his sympathy and support. We later learned that someone in the Republican campaign had the same idea; however, Nixon did not call Mrs. King because he was afraid that if he did so he would have alienated white southern voters.

Interestingly, Nixon's dilemma is not uncommon. I leave for others the evaluation of whether Nixon's record demonstrates that he was racist in his thought and action. The fact remains that for many white people, regardless of whether they were liberal minded or at least not blatantly racist, they all faced this dilemma: if they were perceived as being too friendly with Negroes or aligning themselves with Negroes on issues of public policy, they would be labeled by segregationists as "Nigger lovers." To use a cowboy expression in Western movies, this was considered "a fate worse than death!" Of course, in the movies, the white cowboys were referring to Indians attacking white women.

Although in some respects my wife and I were partially opposites and partially compatible, as far as my civil rights and political activities were concerned, she was totally devoted. A few memorable examples of that devotion include the following.

In 1947, Bernie and I moved into a four apartment building owned by one of my cousins, Edna Armistead Green, and her husband, Dr. Green. One night while I was out of town, in the space of thirty-five to forty-five minutes several related incidents occurred. First, the police came and said that it had been reported that I had been killed. Bernie informed the police that she knew nothing about the reported killing; however within minutes of her conversation with the police, the fire department came and asked her where was the fire. Bernie replied there was no fire. Approximately fifteen minutes later the mortician came (prematurely) to pick up my body. This was purely part of a plan of racial harassment.

In 1949, after our son was born, we moved to a home on Overbrook Road (a previously white neighborhood in Richmond). Shortly afterwards, Bernie received a call one night from someone stating that they were going to "get his ass" that night. Bernie concluded that they would try to kill me as I drove through the dark alley into the garage. Accordingly, Bernie stretched an extension cord about seventy-five feet from the back porch to the garage and installed a flood light.

When I returned, Bernie, who had been watching from the window, ran out of the house to warn me of the impending danger. However, that night nothing happened. Thereafter, when I returned home late at night, to ease Bernie's mind, I no longer parked in the two car garage.

Around the same time as the garage incident, on another occasion I came home and found Bernie sitting on the front porch with a pistol in her hand. She had received a telephone call stating that they were going to "get his hind parts" that night. Bernie called two of my friends, Tom Henderson and Lester Banks, who came and began riding back and forth in our block to provide protection for me. At that time, Tom Henderson was dean of Virginia Union University and one of my closest pals. He also appeared as an expert witness in a number of our school cases. Lester Banks was another very good friend who served as Executive Director of the Virginia State NAACP.

On this occasion, I had been out of town and expected to return later that night. I was more alarmed to find Bernie with a pistol in her hand than to discover the threats against me: I knew that she knew very little about shooting a pistol.

The incident that got into the newspapers occurred when the segregationists placed a cross in our yard and set it afire. This event attracted the fire department, police department, and the newspapers. When one person learned that this was not the first threatening incident, he asked why I had not reported similar episodes before. I asked, "What for?". I stated that reporting the incidents would only encourage some other nuts to copy cat these activities with increasing frequency.

Furthermore, before our son was born, we had been getting harrassing phone calls. Consequently, until our son became a teenager, we would not allow him to answer the telephone. We received all types of calls, sometimes ranging from cursing, lewd threatening calls, to calls in which the caller said nothing. A somewhat amusing call started out, "I want to speak to the HNIC ("head nigger in charge"). Other calls were simply vicious.

To get a full night's sleep, before going to bed, my wife or I took the phone off the hook. The phone company raised hell about that; however, I told them if they would cooperate and trace the abusive calls, the problem would cease.

Sometimes after six or seven months of taking the phone off the hook each night, we would put the phone on the hook to see if we could sleep through the night peacefully. It never worked. The abusive calls continued from 1947 until I went to Washington in 1961.

During our married life together, Bernie was always supportive of me in numerous other ways. For example, she frequently went with me to various functions. When I was on the City Council I never missed an opportunity to go anywhere that we were invited regardless of whether we wanted to go or not. We went principally because we knew that if we did not attend, there would be no Negroes there. In addition, sometimes we went because we wanted to ensure that segregationists knew that we believed that we had the right to be there. Many times attending

287

these functions was the last thing either of us wanted to do.

In looking back on it now, it may have been that Bernie and I were amiss in not putting forth more effort to develop a larger number of white friends.

As far as children were concerned, Bernie and I were married about fifteen years before our only child, Oliver, Jr., was born. After we had been married about two years, Bernie became pregnant. Unfortunately, she became so desperately ill, that to save her life, the doctors aborted the baby. We were disappointed by this development and by the medical advice that we received which was that we would not be able to have children. At that time, we accepted this news. However, we were not worried.

After I returned from the army following World War II, Bernie and I started talking about the possibility of having a child or adopting one or two children. Then, as happens so often with many couples in that type of situation, Bernie became pregnant, but that pregnancy ended in a miscarriage. The next year, she became pregnant again. To prevent her from losing the child, we elevated the bed so high that she was practically standing on her head. However, despite our best efforts, that pregnancy still ended with a miscarriage.

Bernie became pregnant the following year, and she got so large that the doctors put her on a strict diet. When Bernie delivered on September 19, 1949, we discovered that she had twins, but this had not shown up on X-rays. One of the twins was stillborn; he died of malnutrition. However, Oliver, Jr. survived.

By the time my son was ready to attend junior high school, we had finally overcome some of the legal barriers to desegregating the public school system. The year before Oliver began junior high school, two Negro girls had attended the previously all white Chandler Junior High School on Brookland Park Boulevard. Oliver was one of the first Negro children to attend Chandler and also to attend John Marshall High School in Richmond.

Interestingly, I noticed that while Oliver was a lad in elementary school, that he liked to ride with me to the James River and some of the local canals and then sit quietly watching the water. His quiet, reflective spirit would later emerge as an important part of his life's activities.

288

Oliver was also involved in several other extra curricular activities while receiving his secondary education. For instance, he was an excellent swimmer and became a lifeguard. In addition, in high school Oliver played tackle on the football team, and was an excellent bowler. In fact, in bowling Oliver won a number of tournament trophies. During most of Oliver's time in high school, I was working in Washington, D.C. On many weekends I came down to Richmond and unless he had a tournament, we would go bowling. Oliver often bowled two hundred thirty and higher; I was lucky to bowl two hundred.

When the time came for him to start thinking of which college he would like to attend, I said to him, "Make a list of schools you think you want to go to. We'll carry you around to visit them." Accordingly, Oliver made a list with six or seven schools on it. The top one was Howard. Bernie and I did not think anything about that because both of us were graduates of Howard University. However, all of the schools on Oliver's list were predominantly black schools. I showed the list to Bernie and said, "Look at this thing. What do you think it is saying?" She replied, "I do not know what you mean. What do you think?" I stated, "To me, it reads loud and clear! 'All I want to do is get the hell away from white folks'."

Oliver attended Howard as an undergraduate. Throughout high school in the summers, he had worked at my former law office. This was during the 1960's and it was almost a foregone conclusion that he was going to be a lawyer. I never pushed him as to which profession to choose. I always told Oliver to seek the profession that he desired most. Had he elected to become a lawyer, I believe that Oliver would have been an excellent one. Subsequent events intervened and shaped his career a different way.

Mr. & Mrs. Oliver W. Hill, Sr. (Circa 1960)

I know several people who insisted that their sons follow in the father's footsteps and those children became unhappy persons.

If Oliver hadn't gotten involved in sit-ins and other related activities, he probably would have gone to law school. After those school related difficulties, Oliver had to turn himself around. The thing that helped turn him around was that he attended a lecture on Transcendental Meditation given by Maharishi Maheshyogi. Oliver got involved with Transcendental Meditation and decided that he wanted to teach it.

Four Generations of the Hill Family
(December, 1973)
Seated left to right: Olivia Hill (Holding
Great Granddaughter, Jananda Hill),
and Oliver W. Hill, Sr. Standing: Oliver W. Hill, Jr.

After graduating from Howard, Oliver attended summer school at the University of Massachusetts for advanced studies in Transcendental Meditation. He studied under Maharishi on the island of Mallorca off the coast of Spain. After teaching Transcendental Meditation for a year or so, Oliver and his first wife, Sharon, traveled to Switzerland to study with Maharishi.

During the early years, Oliver operated Ashrams in Washington, D.C. and in Richmond, Virginia. When he and Sharon returned from Switzerland, he was sent to Boston and later transferred to Detroit. While working in Detroit, I raised the issue with Oliver of obtaining the proper academic credentials if he was going to be a teacher. He then decided to go to the University of Michigan where he received both his masters degree and doctorate in experimental psychology.

While in Michigan, his advisor was involved in SIDHA Yoga; and he persuaded Oliver to switch from Transcendental Meditation to SIDHA Yoga. He is heavily committed to his SIDHA Yoga Foundation work and is among the leaders of that organization. Periodically the Foundation has him come up to their headquarters in South Fallsberg, New York to conduct seminars. Not only does he conduct seminars at the headquarters, but also at other locations. His work has encompassed international satellite hook-ups and other advanced media. Oliver's second wife, Renee, is deeply interested in it.

Bernie, my wife, (during her lifetime) was interested in SIDHA Yoga too. I had no problem with Bernie participating. While I was the only family member not involved in the SIDHA Yoga activities - except occasionally - that did not create a problem for them or me. In early years, I practiced both Transcendental Meditation and SIDHA Yoga forms of meditation.

Since 1981, Oliver has been a professor of psychology at Virginia State University. Oliver has written numerous articles in psychology journals and serves as a consultant for the National Institutes of Health. He has also lectured widely on psychology-related matters.

Mr. & Mrs. Oliver W. Hill, Sr.
(Circa 1981)

While Sharon and Oliver were in Richmond, Sharon conceived and their daughter, Jananda, was born. Later, after Oliver and Sharon divorced, Jananda moved with her mother to Atlanta and attended Montesorri schools there.

Subsequently, in a class of three hundred and ninety-eight students, Jananda graduated from David Mays School as class valedictorian. With a grade point average of 4.35, she completed her studies in computer technology at Massachusetts Institute of Technology. Currently, Jananda works for the Lucent

291

Corporation and has started her Ph.D. studies (via computer) at Stanford University.

As I previously mentioned, Bernie also had a sister, Evalyn Shaed, who was so brilliant that she was a registered genius. Evalyn graduated at the head of her high school class in Youngstown, Ohio, excelled in mathematics and English at Howard University, and also testified as an expert witness regarding statistical data in some of our school cases.

In addition, even though ostensibly Puss Owens and Tom Henderson were my official campaign managers, in each of my political campaigns, Evalyn ran the campaign office. Along with many volunteers in Richmond and some of my old friends from Washington, D.C., Evalyn helped prepare campaign material. In my political campaigns, we did not spend much money because we had so many volunteers. Like her sister, Bernie, Evalyn was very supportive of all of my civic and political activities. She also served as manager of our law firm.

I had tremendous support from members of my family, the NAACP and numerous other individuals throughout the state and nation. However, because I have lost many of the records over the years, and my memory is not what it once was, I will not endeavor to mention more names.

Oliver W. Hill, Sr. and Family in Front of the Oliver Hill Courts Building, Richmond, Virginia (August 1996) Standing left to Right:
Renee A. Hill (Daughter-in-law), Jamaa M. Bickley-King (Step-grandson), Maia M. King (Step-granddaughter), Oliver W. Hill, Sr., Jananda I. Hill (Granddaughter), Oliver W. Hill, Jr., and Judge Richard D. Taylor, Jr.

Chapter VIII

The Big Bang and Beyond

As societies progress and become more civilized and experienced in dealing with technological and mechanical advances, society ought to strive to benefit all people. Some would say that's utopian. I admit it and suggest from the perspective of those who lived a thousand, five hundred or even a hundred years ago, our scientific, technological and potential societal advances would, viewed from that perspective, also have appeared to be utopian. I believe that human earthlings should dream of and work to produce a more utopian society.

In this chapter, I will focus on one of my overriding concerns, namely the need for human earthlings to recognize that change is inevitable, and that we need to guide change in a constructive, progressive, evolutionary manner. I plan to touch on a number of issues involving evolutionary change, including the creation of the universe, family relationships, the church, government, economy, and race and gender relations. As I have previously emphasized, I hope to provoke discussion among human earthlings on evolution and the inevitability of change. For human beings to direct change that will enure to the common good of human earthlings, we must understand how societies evolve and envision better ways for them to evolve.

In this context, it seems wise to go back and rethink a lot of our ideas. Let's start at the beginning with the "Big Bang."

Creation and "The Big Bang" Evolutionary Theory

There appear to be at least three principal theories on evolution of the universe. One perspective is the Judean/Christian/Muslim view that a God created the universe in seven days.[1] A second theory is that the universe always existed.[2] A third theory, and the one I accept is the "Big Bang". No one really knows whether some evolutionary process caused the Big Bang or vice versus. From my perspective, the beginning of the universe involves evolution. For millions of years before man even appeared, the universe and our world were evolving. The planets cooled, life forms eventually evolved and progressively changed from simpler to more complex forms.

As far as our planet is concerned, frequently evolutionary changes resulted in the better adapted forms of life advancing. Human technology is an example of adaptation. Nature's evolutionary processes as influenced by human technology and scientific progress have culminated in our contemporary world. So far as we can understand, human earthlings have had a greater impact on the world than any other animal or life form. When I use the term "human earthlings," I am simply referring to human beings here on earth.[3] As far as I am concerned, I am willing to allow others to obtain their technical, biological knowledge about evolution from scientists. Though I am not a natural scientist, scientists tell us that more than eighty percent of the human body is water. The rest of our bodies consists of other compounds. There is a little variation in the make-up of some of the genes which gives you different skin colors, eyes and similar attributes, but basically we each have the same requirements. If human earthlings are essentially the same, why should we compete for all the essentials of life? We ought to work on overcoming destructive competition.

Since human beings have the same basic needs, in a civilized society, processes should exist that help provide the essentials of life through non-competitive interaction. For example, work furnishes opportunities to obtain life's necessities like food, shelter, clothes, education and health care. In addition, and equally important, work facilitates the ability of individuals to develop proper self-esteem.

However, a non-competitive perspective of the workplace differs from the present one that human earthlings in the United States and other parts of the world have. Too frequently, and with some justification, human earthlings view their places of employment as a jungle.

In contrast to the present competitive model, a cooperative format would afford an opportunity for a more civilized existence and individualistic variety in nonessential matters. For instance, if you want

295

to play basketball until midnight, or as I did, read at 2:00 a.m. or get up to play tennis at 4:00 a.m., wonderful. However, we must all cooperate to meet everyone's essential needs like an adequate diet, employment, health care, education, lodging and recreation. For instance, job sharing, a shorter work week and more time for educational and recreational activities may be partial responses to the problem of unemployment and underemployment. We should think in terms of cooperation as well as competition and provide for the needs of human earthlings irrespective of where they live on planet earth.

I am more interested in human earthlings learning to understand evolutionary processes and living together in a nonconfrontational manner on planet earth. Accordingly, when speaking of evolutionary processes, the development of the human body is just a minute part of life as we think we know it. My focus is the development of human societies. All things presently existing will change. Since change is inevitable, we should strive to influence change so that society will move forward progressively and orderly in a way that enures to the benefit of those at the bottom of the economic ladder as well as those at the top. That type of change will afford human earthlings the best opportunity to achieve the greatest joy and fulfillment possible.

One way to help achieve the objective of progressive evolutionary change would be to develop among the general public a better understanding of evolution. For instance, if you ask a real fundamentalist religious person, "Do you believe in evolution?", in all probability the person will say, "No" because most fundamentalists have been taught to accept the literal biblical description of the origin of the universe including the human species. Religious fundamentalists usually compare the literal text of the Bible to the scientist's evolutionary description of our origins. Such individuals often believe that when the Bible says that God created the heavens and the earth in six days, that the Bible is talking about six days of relatively twenty-four hours each. In a general sense evolutionary theory and biblical teaching have some areas of agreement and some well known areas of disagreement. For instance, evolutionary theory and Biblical teaching agree that the universe and the planet earth were created over a period of time. In fact, I agree with some religious folks that God exists in the sense that God is the Creator of the universe. I accept the idea of a Creator as a starting point primarily because I cannot conceive of the universe materializing from nothing or by happenstance.

However, from that point on my ideas of the beginning of the universe vary from that of most Christian fundamentalists. While I agree, on faith, that the universe including the earth was formulated by the Creator, I do not know nor do I believe that anyone else can furnish the form and content of the Creator. Obviously, I disagree with some religious people who believe that God is an anthropomorphic kind of being sitting somewhere on a throne who for centuries pulled puppet strings but who now I assume sits before a giant console pressing computer buttons and influencing billions of people's lives.

As I view it, evolution affects everything whether animate or inanimate and regardless of whether we can perceive the evolutionary process. Accepting this as a fact, it behooves human earthlings to guide the inevitable changes in a manner that redounds to the benefit of the commonweal.

As societies progress and become more civilized and experienced in dealing with technological and mechanical advances, society ought to strive to benefit all people. Some would say that's utopian thinking. I believe that we should do more utopian thinking and less mean-spirited thinking. I was always taught to avoid the kind of thinking expressed in the story of a man whose prayer went like this:

> *"Heavenly Father, bless me and my wife,*
> *Our son, John, and his wife,*
> *Us fo', and no mo."*

From the perspective of those who lived a thousand, five hundred, or even a hundred years ago, many of our contemporary scientific, technological and material advantages would be regarded as utopian. Our potential as human earthlings is nearly limitless. Therefore, we should work towards creating a utopian society. I will explain my reasoning by discussing some aspects of human history and by addressing some possible criticisms of my views.

Cooperation in Early Human Societies and Utopia's Modern Critics

Again, putting these matters in historical context, in the early days of the hunter/gatherer societies, substantial evidence points to human cooperation. Admittedly, long ago there were smaller groups. However, those groups established what we now regard as old-fashioned customs, namely, everybody in the community cared for the community, especially the children. Despite some present day nay-sayers, the village did participate in raising its children. (Even when I was a child,

297

individuals living in my neighborhood viewed it as a part of their civic responsibility to participate in the raising of neighborhood children.) Cooperation made living easier. As the groups got bigger, other things interfered. That's when we got male domination with the emphasis being placed on competition rather than cooperation.

From that point on we were off on the wrong track. Maybe in the days to come we will recognize the fact that important life decisions do not have to be male or female dominated.

Although written from a western societal perspective, some of my thoughts are reflected in a book called *The Chalice and the Blade.*[4] It shows how once the society became male dominated, we began to have more conflict. In the early days when explorations discovered caves in Europe with paintings and pictures, some earlier researchers thought that they were depicting soldiers in warlike situations. Now a more careful review demonstrates some drawings that were originally thought to be militaristic merely depict fields, grass and nonmilitary scenes.

Unlike the cooperative model of the hunter/gatherer societies, today we must overcome the notion that our first obligation is to make it possible for somebody to get rich. We must eliminate exploitation, that is the idea that some people exist to make it easy for the smarter or more ruthless ones to get rich. In our society, to exploit the poor, uneducated and unknowing, some multinational corporations and big time operators have moved to the southern United States and beyond our borders to Asia, Africa, and Latin America. Exploitation assumes some people are unintelligent and ignorant and that justifies their being abused and oppressed.

However, today if we can train people to go kill and exploit other people whom they have never seen or been personally offended by, we can train them to cooperate and to act constructively. The acceptance of a more cooperative worldview is the big hurdle.

I contend that we need to evolve towards an egalitarian society. Of course, news media, particularly those with so-called conservative authors, editors and publishers, ridicule egalitarian thinking. However, egalitarian thinking does not necessarily mean that everybody must have the same thoughts, or live on the same economic or social plane, or have the same religious affiliation. For example, the unique perspectives of various denominations and faiths are essentially irrelevant when we consider basic civic obligations of human earthlings to protect human life from unjustified physical violence, abuse and neglect. Thus, it matters not whether one is a Christian, Muslim, Jew, or agnostic when the issue is protecting children from starvation, prostitution, and preventable diseases. Nevertheless, there can be great diversity while maintaining respect for human dignity and individuality.

As a starter, we must insist that the segments of our population known as the lower middle class and the poor receive a larger share of the income from various forms of societal production. We must distribute income in this manner for at least three reasons. First, a society with extremes between rich and poor leads to unnecessary suffering on the part of the lower middle classes and the poor during their daily lives as well as during periods of economic recession and depression. In fact such disparity may even play a major role in producing such societal catastrophes.

Second, such suffering may also lead to violent forms of revolutionary activities like terrorism and wars.

Third, an impartial market does not exist. Human earthlings, corporations, and governments influence market forces: and natural events impact supply. That is why I say that no impartial market exists. Furthermore, human beings decide to change prices and often determine whether supply (for example, oil) will be ample or spare.

The bottom line is that the necessities of civilization must be accorded to all human earthlings.

I know that some of my positions will draw criticism and be unpopular. However, I challenge critics and skeptics to assume for a moment that we never had another war. If we continued our same ideas about maintaining military preparedness, we would still have all this military hardware, numerous battleships and military missiles. Now imagine that the material resources consumed in keeping all these navies and armies doing nothing constructive were used to provide essential needs to the people. In those circumstances society could and would constructively allocate resources to make it possible for every human being to live a productive, useful, pleasant and joyful life.

We presently waste a tremendous amount of resources on the military. Bottom line: If you don't use military hardware it becomes obsolete and it's no good; and if you use it, you destroy it and a lot of other resources. If these resources were used for more constructive purposes like housing, education and jobs, we would probably have few, if any, homeless or unemployed people.

We've never had a utopian society or nation; nevertheless that does not mean that it is impossible to achieve. The situation is analogous to earlier days when many people believed human beings would never be transported long distances through the air. Now air travel is routine. Long ago, we had more cooperative societies — sometimes little colonies with utopian characteristics. The notion that a utopia does not work is for the birds. No one knows.

We do know that when human earthlings put their minds to it, they can make tremendous strides like building satellites which can take pictures of a person from space. With similar determination and sufficient funding we can create a global society without significant poverty.

In short, if we have the vision and the will, we can have what would now be termed a utopian society. I have a suggestion of one way we can make a small start in this direction. As part of their national defenses, the U.S. and other nations should create within their borders one or more institutions of higher learning focused upon teaching people to live and work together under diverse conditions, to value one another's differences, and to resolve conflicts through non-military means. In America, the student population of these institutions would consist of forty to sixty per cent Americans and the balance would come from other countries on the planet.

To initiate such a program globally, we must work assiduously in the U.S. and in other nations to persuade each country to create similar institutions. In the nations participating in this program, national agencies of non-violent conflict resolution could be located within their Departments of Defense. In part, program funding would come from the savings engendered from reduced military expenditures on armaments and war. Hopefully nations would join the effort of reducing their military forces to the minimum needed for maintaining domestic peace, and seek to transfer these activities to a local police constabulary. This transformation will take time and obviously could not be effectuated unilaterally.

This idea is not new, for the eighteenth century abolitionist, Benjamin Rush, urged the creation of a "Secretary of Peace" cabinet

300

position in the new American government. Rush's idea was warmly endorsed by the Negro mathematician, surveyor, and astronomer, Benjamin Banneker. Banneker published the Peace Proposal in Banneker's Almanac in 1793.[5]

President Franklin Roosevelt had a similar vision in his famous "Four Freedoms" State of the Union message in 1941:

[W]e look forward to a world founded upon four essential human freedoms ....
The Fourth is Freedom from fear - which, translated into world terms, means a world-wide reduction of armaments to such a point and in such a thorough fashion that no nation will be in a position to commit an act of physical aggression against any neighbor - anywhere in the world.[6]

Progressive Evolutionary Change and the Family

My thoughts on the relationship of progressive evolutionary change to the family are as follows. I believe that the family and other social institutions should have a strong role in many important areas. For example, in my view, moral instructions should be taught in the home. However, if the home is not instructing the child in moral development, then the next level of moral education would be the child's school. If school is not providing such education, then the government should make some provision to supply these needs. In other words, some branch of our society should be doing it.

Right now we have several problems which exemplify the need for moral instruction. For instance, we have a large number of young children having babies. We need to break that negative societal pattern of behavior. We know that a woman should have prenatal care to ensure that she and the baby are healthy. After delivery, the mother and child should have post-natal care. We also know that if the child is exposed to a stimulating environment during the first three years, the child is going to be far more active and intelligent than a child who lacks such stimulation. Some interesting thoughts along these lines were presented to the 1997 National Governor's Conference.[7]

My ambition, if I could accomplish it, would be for every human earthling to be born under circumstances where the mother had benefit of fine prenatal care and the child was provided a stimulating living situation. In addition, starting with this generation, children should be taught the use of their various organs.

For instance, when the child is young, teach the child what the various human bodily functions are. Tell the child that the mouth receives food which provides energy to enable them to live. The nose takes in air which helps oxygenate the blood. One of the penis's purposes is to eliminate the urine; and the anus provides the means to eliminate the body's other wastes. The child should be taught waste is poisonous to the body. It is essential that children recognize and respect bodily functions to maintain good health. Accordingly, children should be instructed to utilize these bodily processes to get rid of bodily waste as quickly as possible.

By the time children get to the point where they begin to feel sexual urges, they could be taught another important lesson. They live in two evolutionary environments. One stage is called civilization which human earthlings made. The other stage involves a natural evolutionary process, namely perpetuating the human species. Human sexuality helps to ensure the continuation of the human species. What we call civilization developed in a complex relationship with the evolutionary process of perpetuating the species.

Therefore, in this context, the child should learn that sexual urges are a part of a natural function. However, the child should also be taught that the child doesn't need to succumb to the natural urge to engage in sexual relations so early because through medical science, humans have made it possible for people to live much longer provided they take advantage of this new scientific knowledge. Accordingly, we don't need to use sex so early to perpetuate the species. We should teach the kids to refrain from sex not because it is morally wrong but for health reasons.

Thus, children should refrain from sexual activity until the female is fully developed as that will help eliminate a number of what formerly were called "female ailments," and will enhance the probability of prolonging her life as well as producing healthy offspring. Boys should be taught to cooperate in avoiding early sexual experiences so that girls will have a better opportunity to attain physical maturity in good physical health. Aside from protecting their physical health, girls and boys should refrain from having promiscuous sex because promiscuity undermines development of a sense of long term commitment.

This type of education should help young people have a better

302

appreciation of and respect for the sexual experience. Our aim is a society of physically and mentally healthy parents and children.

In addition, we should give young people a wider range of other constructive physical and emotional activities. An excellent example of what I am speaking of is athletic events for children. We need diverse activities to divert their attention so that everything will not be riding on sex. Exercise can release a whole lot of energy. Everybody should have homes and showers, too. Showers help you out a whole lot of times!

If you encourage people to participate in constructive activities, such activities tend to reinforce each other. Therefore we should have as much emphasis on intellectual activities as on athletic ones. Thus, music, art, literary and scientific studies should be encouraged and awards given for outstanding performance.

As I say, if you present rules of conduct to children based on some intelligent reason, I believe that you will have a better chance of getting them to adopt the rules. In my case, I know that sex education obtained in public school classes had a highly beneficial impact on me, for example, illustrations of the use of condoms and pictures of the effects of venereal diseases. In addition, when I was coming up, extended family networks among parents kept many young people from doing a whole lot of things which they might have otherwise gotten into trouble doing.

To reach consensus on what to teach the children, we are going to have to get people to have a better awareness and understanding of evolution and the evolutionary process. By elevating the public's consciousness in these areas, it will become easier to demonstrate to the general public, the fallacy of the argument that evolution is invalid because it is contrary to biblical teaching. People will see that millions of years before man or religion came on the scene, evolution and evolutionary processes existed.

Where the family and related institutions have failed to provide adequate moral instruction, I don't have problems with calling upon government (or some agency of the government) to lead in forging consensus on what constitutes good moral development for all human earthlings. I view schools and similar institutions as agencies of the government.

303

These are the kinds of things we have to think about.

Religion

I also have some thoughts on religion and progressive evolutionary change. I was baptized in Roanoke, Virginia when I was thirteen. Prior to that time, I believed in the total inerrancy of the *Bible* and the power of the Baptist faith. When I was fourteen I remember one night going with some of my peers to see and hear an evangelist at a camp meeting under a big tent. This particular evangelist came up with a long tale of how he was on his way to a little town out west to catch a train and saw a bank robber leaving the bank after holding it up. Instead of going to catch his train the evangelist joined the sheriff and a quickly formed posse. They went after the bank robber. In the meantime the train that he was going to catch arrived and departed. It appeared that the train made connections in another town with a ship on which the evangelist anticipated traveling.

Because he missed the train, that made him miss the connection with the ship to cross a lake. According to his narration, a storm came up on the lake and capsized the ship he would have taken but for the intervention of the bank robber episode. The evangelist said everybody on the ship perished. The evangelist also stated he recognized that God must have saved him for some purpose. Therefore, he interpreted these events as a calling from God to become God's disciple and an evangelist dedicated to saving souls for God.

You've probably heard this kind of tale before. Frankly, I believe the Creator possessing the power to create what we now call the universe could find a far more humane way to convince this human earthling to become an evangelist than the convoluted process expounded by this evangelist. In the first place, when I was a child, to be sent to prison was a disgrace to the person and his whole family. So now according to this evangelist, God ruined this robber's life, disgraced his family, deprived the robber's children of his presence, and on top of all that, killed all those other innocent people on the travelers' capsized ship, just to convince one person to be an evangelist. It did not make sense to me as a fourteen year old youth. It still does not make sense to me today. It is this type of glorified nonsense that detracts from many people's understanding of how religious faith can enhance our lives.

As a consequence of this evangelist's narration, I started critically listening to what preachers said. In the majority of situations, I discovered that the content of the message was what I considered to be "glorified nonsense." In fact, once a prominent religious leader and I were having a discussion during the course of which I said, "You know, Bishop it has occurred to me that about seventy-five percent of what preachers speak of in their sermons is nothing more than glorified nonsense." He replied, "If you would raise your percentage, I would agree with you."

Regarding the *Bible*, many people are turned off by the ridiculous and extravagant statements of some preachers. My point of view about the *Bible* is that in the first place I am positive that the books of the *Bible* were written by men — and maybe occasionally a woman. The *Bible* contains some historical facts, some ancient myths, some good prose, some beautiful poetry, some sound moral principles, some useful law and commandments — and some glorified nonsense.

The people who wrote the *Bible* thought that heaven was an overnight journey by wing power from the earth. Today, scientists estimate that if one flew from earth to the nearest planet outside our solar system, it would take eight thousand years traveling at the speed of twenty-four thousand miles per hour.

I know of no country, developed or undeveloped, in which the prevailing religions have been adequate to inspire people to actually create a moral society. One of the reasons there isn't any adequate religion in any society is because religions have premises that we now know are contrary to fact. We have moved in an evolutionary fashion; everything continues to evolve, expand or deteriorate.

As I said previously, I personally believe there is a Creator. I so believe not because I have any proof other than the fact that I can't conceive of everything happening in such an orderly fashion. As most natural things do, it couldn't be just happenstance. However, I think it is ridiculous to say that we can define God. Whatever the Creator was or is, I am sure it wasn't and isn't a superman sitting on a throne.

Having said that, I have a number of questions. For instance, the first commandment says that we shall have no other gods before the biblical God because God is "a jealous God". What has man got for God to be jealous of?

I have heard it argued that God made humans in God's image and that we should not focus our lives on acquiring material wealth.

305

Taken to extremes, materialism can be a form of idolatry; however, it seems to me if one wants to convince somebody that he should be more altruistic than materialistic, one can express that more sensibly than saying God is jealous of man.

Moreover, why would God be worried about what some man feels or does? Of course there is the age old question about free will and faith. How is it that God has all this power, yet human beings choose to do wrong things? If God can guide everybody why not just guide them in the right way? To me it seems that if God was making the determination for human earthlings of whether we would do right or wrong, all God would have to do is figuratively lift God's finger and guide them in the right way.

Another question that comes up is what is the nature of God? Is God really a foreign power far away, removed, who doesn't care; or is God the Christian concept of a personal God? Christians' concept of God has gone through an evolutionary process. For example, in the first five books of the *Bible*, God was described as a tyrannical, jealous, vain God. But Jesus came along a number of centuries later and declared that God was a God of love, forgiveness and compassion. These perceptions reflect differing understandings of God, and an evolution in human thought regarding the nature of God.

Many of us consider ourselves Christians. Jesus obviously believed in a communal type of living. According to the *Bible*, while they were following Jesus, it appears that Jesus' immediate disciples abandoned their established homes.[8] Instead, they did everything in a group situation.

On the issue of Christian beliefs about non-violence, it has been two thousand years since the doctrine was announced by Jesus, and many centuries earlier by Confucius, the Chinese philosopher. Yet, few people have bought the idea of turning the other cheek or walking the extra mile.

While we supported the sit ins and picketing of large department stores in Richmond in the early 1960's, I never considered marching with Martin Luther King and others further south. Several considerations influenced me. First, I was a federal official. Second, in the 1960's, I was in my fifties; and thirdly, I had been involved in civil rights activities for over thirty years. More importantly, I wasn't going to have some prejudiced whites physically abusing my body. As I mentioned previously, when I was in the service I was stationed in Alexandria, Louisiana. I didn't go into Alexandria except on a few occasions. When I did go I had an open knife in my pocket and my hand on it. The MPs in Alexandria had a reputation for beating up people and I had predetermined that if some MP, white or Negro, started beating on me, we were both going to hell together. My regard for my own physical being and self respect did not permit me to voluntarily submit to desecrating acts of violence merely to give satisfaction to some ignorant prejudiced person.

An interesting incident occurred while I was stationed in Louisiana in the military. Curfew was 10:00 p.m. and I got caught out one night. I was in a residential area, so I went up on a porch, sat down in a chair and stayed off the street. Whoever lived there didn't come out and the MP's didn't know I didn't live there. Regardless of what you believed, you had to use common sense. I tried to do that at all times. I didn't look for trouble and sought positive responses or actions for avoiding it.

One additional point about non violence: from its creation to promote and protect civil rights of Negroes until this day, despite a number of brutal assassinations, assaults, and other violent acts, individuals acting under the auspices of the NAACP have never initiated similar types of physical violence. Where violence has ensued in response to Negroes attempting to obtain their civil rights, it has invariably been precipitated by the police or others acting under color of law, the Ku Klux Klan, the White Citizens' Councils or organizations of that ilk.

On a slightly different note, down through the years, people have always talked about being God-fearing people. Well, if one accepts the concept of God as portrayed by Jesus, why should one need to fear God? My objection to the idea of fearing God goes beyond that. In the first place I don't think as yet we have become sufficiently civilized, knowledgeable or intelligent to define the dimensions of the Creator. I still believe that is beyond human comprehension. This idea of a superman sitting up there somewhere on a throne is a primitive notion. Although we can't define the Creator, we can infer that the Creator exists just as we can infer that there are different types of nuclei even though we can't see them. That's my conception of the Creator unburdened by a lot of human vices.

I don't run around fearing God because I don't think the Creator, who is capable of making something as vast and complex as the universe,

307

is worried about what Oliver Hill thinks or doesn't think about anything. That doesn't stop me from saying that I ought to try to bring myself into harmony with what I perceive to be the Creator's view of creation and try to make not only my life enjoyable but also try to help to do what I can to make everybody else's life a pleasant experience. Accordingly, I do think that we ought to try — if the Creator has a general plan — to live a decent life and try to make this a joyful experience for everybody else. We should seek out certain principles, rules and facts which in light of our best knowledge and experience are calculated to provide the best opportunity for human earthlings to live peacefully on planet Earth comfortably and joyfully. I don't know about belief in a personal relationship with God. I think if you do what is conceived as and can be defended rationally as right, you improve your chances of a healthy, fulfilling and enjoyable life. Thus, if you protect your health by practicing preventive medicine (like eating properly), exercising, and exhibiting moderation in most of one's activities, you may live longer. Of course, by doing otherwise, you can hasten your demise. Unfortunately, however, you can just be plain unlucky.

On another somewhat related subject, I believe that the concept of reincarnation is nonsense. In the first place, by the time you go through life here whatever composed your body would be so scattered after your death that you could never get it all together again in some other form. I guess those who believe in reincarnation proclaim that the soul is the thing that continues to exist. I have read some concepts that people have been on earth three or four times. Maybe. But what good does it do if he or she does not have any consciousness of previous lives and cannot use the previous reincarnation experiences beneficially? How are you going to put a human soul in a cow or vice versa? It is nonsense as far as I am concerned.

When I reflect on my experiences with religion, I recall that one thing that disturbed me when I was in high school involved my Catholic friends. Catholicism had many more restrictions then than now. For instance, Catholics couldn't eat meat on Friday and all that sort of stuff. However, the really big issues were marriage, divorce and childbirth. Some bishops wouldn't let a Catholic marry a non-Catholic even though the Catholic was a pregnant female. For example, when I was in high school a very attractive Catholic girl became pregnant, and the father of the child, a divorced man, wished to marry her. However, the church refused permission for them to marry. The young girl became so depressed that she committed suicide. Even when they did not lead to such tragic conclusions, in my opinion such rules were ridiculous.

For many years, the Roman Catholic Church and other hierarchical religions covered up the activities of priests who sexually abused and took advantage of young parishioners. In recent years, the Roman Catholic Church has confronted revelations that sexually abusive priests have assaulted parishioners. Contemporary human earthlings have become more willing to expose the inappropriate activities of priests and other officials.

I thought that one of the most unfortunate things that happened so far as modern day Catholics were concerned was the death of Pope John XXIII in 1963. Although he was an elderly man when he became Pope, he started thinking of new approaches to living. He was not in office long. Nevertheless, he did a tremendous amount of good. Along with other people of a variety of religious faiths, I was saddened by his death.

Many practices of Baptists and other Protestant denominations were just as horrendous as the Catholics. As I said, when I was coming along as a kid my granddaddy was one of those fire and brimstone Baptist ministers. I didn't have any opportunity to evaluate him because he died when I was about six years of age. However, that was my concept of him confirmed by others after I grew up.

When I was a child the various Protestant churches forbad their members from playing cards, dancing or going to the movies. For teenagers, many recreational activities were maligned as sins. On Sundays you were expected to be sanctified.

Fortunately for me, I was reared by people who didn't believe in many of those restrictions. It got to be a hangup with kids. They would come to my house to engage in innocent things they couldn't do anywhere else. They weren't things one would consider immoral or anything like that. When I was coming along, I had a lot of friends who drank liquor and did many other foolish things. Then they would go to church and put on a big act. Well, I might have been a minister if I wanted to be hypocritical about it. For example, some churches had rules about putting people out of church because they went to a dance and all that sort of stuff. If we had had a more open society — less hypocritical and not having all these simple-minded restrictions I could have seen entering the ministry. Anyway, I passed up the ministry.

I knew Howard Thurman, who was a mystic. I also have known some Baptist preachers who were reasonably decent people and by their living and conduct earned the respect of all facets of society.

Back in the 1950s the *Richmond Times-Dispatch* ran a series of articles in which several people were asked to write an article on their religion. I was one of them. I still have it.

Some argue and I agree that we ought to have a reasonable code of conduct. The trouble is most religions add so many unnecessary restrictions to what I would regard as a reasonable code of conduct. For many years, I used to affiliate with the church on my terms. From the time of my arrival in Washington in 1923, I attended the Berean Baptist Church. We had a very good minister, Dr. Rivers, whom I respected. I organized a young peoples' forum while attending college, and during the group's existence (several years) we usually met three or four times per year. We invited prominent people, (often government officials) to come in and speak to us.

It was real funny. I was everything as far as officiating was concerned. We would take little collections and I used to dump the money in a drawer. Finally it occurred to me that I better put this money in the bank. So I gathered it up and put it in the Prudential Bank which was down on Florida Avenue between Georgia Avenue and Eighth Street. The cashier who was one of the founders was from Richmond. Shortly after depositing the funds, the bank failed. I thought, hell, I should have kept it in my drawer. This was early in the Depression. Several years after the bank collapsed, we received a small fraction of our deposit.

My mother was very active in Berean Baptist Church where she sang in the choir. As I told you, in Richmond my grandfather had built the Mount Carmel Baptist Church which came out of Ebenezer Baptist Church on Leigh Street. In the 1950's, Mount Carmel moved from First Street over to Thirty-second and Broad Streets in Church Hill. In those years, it was more of a Pentecostal church. Later I joined Ebenezer which was more sedate.

Thus, my family ties reached into two churches —Mount Carmel, founded by my paternal grandfather, and attended by some of my paternal relatives, and Ebenezer, the church of my mother and some of her relatives.

When I first moved back to Richmond, I did not attend either church with any degree of regularity. One reason was that on Sundays

Dr. Jesse Tinsley and I would go to churches in outlying counties promoting activities of the NAACP. As I mentioned previously, Dr. Tinsley was president of the Richmond branch and the Virginia State Conference of NAACP branches.

After World War II, when my wife, Bernie, became a permanent Richmond resident, things changed. Bernie was more religious than I was. When she was young, her father was a deacon in a Baptist church in Youngstown, Ohio. They lived next door to the church and spent all day Sunday as well as several other nights in church. She enjoyed attending church immensely. Her sister, Evalyn, was just the opposite. She was more like I am.

I also had a memorable experience involving the vexed issue of the church and politics. In 1947, I invited Raymond Pace Alexander to come and speak at Ebenezer Baptist Church. Raymond was an outstanding Philadelphia lawyer, and in his day, one of the leading civil rights and human rights advocates in the United States. At no expense to the church, Alexander was scheduled to speak on a Sunday afternoon on civic matters. The event had been well publicized and preparations were being finalized when on Saturday afternoon, less than twenty-four hours before the program, Mr. Chris Foster, who was the church treasurer, a member of the Deacon Board and a staunch member of the NAACP called. Mr. Foster apologetically stated that the chairman of the Deacon Board had decided that we could not have the program at the church. The stated reason was that we were allegedly bringing politics into the church.

I called the chairman of the Deacon Board. I asserted that we were only trying to elevate people's consciousness of their civic responsibility. A vociferous argument ensued (at that time I had a short fuse). Finally I called him all kinds of sons of God and I hung up.

I immediately rushed around and contacted the church clerk . I made arrangements to have the event held at Fifth Street Baptist Church. (Its pastor, Rev. C.C. Scott, and the pastor of Ebenezer were attending a convention in Texas.) I then contacted and obtained a commitment from the Times Dispatch to put a front page notice in the Sunday edition of the change of location of the meeting.

Later that evening, a couple of blocks from his house, I literally ran into Jeep Smith, the son of our pastor. When he asked why was I so agitated, I explained my problem to him. He suggested that we should

311

go and speak to his mother who was an influential Ebenezer member. We did that and I explained the whole situation to her. She called the chairman of the Deacon Board and prevailed on him to allow us to have the program as planned. Of course, I had to undo the alternative plans that had been made.

The Deacon's attitude at that time exemplified some church leaders' fear and ignorance regarding the role of the church and the need to address the whole person's needs — spiritual, emotional, physical, and societal. In my work in those days, I often encountered people who were fearful of antagonizing the established order by having programs associated in some way with civil rights, the NAACP, and freedom for the oppressed.

Despite such obstacles, finally, under pressure from Bernie and my mother, in the 1950's I joined Ebenezer Baptist Church where Dr. E.E. Smith, a very good Baptist minister, was pastor. When Dr. Smith died he was succeeded by Reverend David Shannon. When I returned to Richmond in the late 1960's, at the suggestion of Rev. David Shannon, I was elected to the Trustee Board of Ebenezer and ultimately became chairman. During the tenures of Rev. Smith and Rev. David Shannon, Ebenezer Sunday services were well attended.

Ebenezer had a sabbatical program. However, while I was there it never produced the intended results. For example, Dr. Shannon went away to get his doctorate but never came back to Ebenezer. When he did come back to Richmond, he came to Virginia Union as its president.

The present pastor, Reverend Cook, used the program to pursue advanced or further training in dentistry. This caused significant disaffection among some congregants. The disaffection caused a reduction of membership. My wife and I were among those who found the situation there untenable. What really caused me to leave the church was the convening of a church meeting at which it was determined that Reverend Cook could use sabbatical time and funds for further study in dentistry. In that meeting, his supporters claimed that they were on God's side, to which I respectfully disagreed.

Up until that time, in so far as I could determine, Reverend Cook had not been active in any community activities. I felt that he was taking advantage of and misleading the people by persuading them to believe that God sanctioned his actions.

I was chairman of the Trustee Board at that time but I just dropped out. Bernie was just as disgusted with our minister as I was.

He's been there close to twenty years now. I haven't been there since I left over ten years ago. On occasion, I have gone to Ebenezer for other activities. For example, once, the local Howard Alumni Chapter had the Howard University choir there in concert and I went to support the program and hear them sing. I have attended a couple of funerals, and one year I participated in a fund-raising program for the church.

I dropped out of Ebenezer and generally I decided not to get emotionally involved with any other church. For one thing, I did not previously nor do I now believe that I needed somebody to stand between me and the Creator. I think I can relate to the Creator just as well as anybody else. I think you ought to have some standards of conduct and I have no difficulty with Christ's concept of doing unto others as you would have them do unto you. You should treat other people as you want them to treat you. Be considerate of other people and think in terms of working in cooperation with people. Although I am sure that some people find church attendance helpful, you don't need to go to church to act considerately and cooperatively.

However, I am not anti-church. I believe that the church is a useful institution and highly beneficial to many of its congregations. I respect ministers whom I am convinced are positive forces in the community. I cannot tolerate ministers who are taking advantage of people for their own selfish financial advantages by playing on the emotions and attitudes of church members. My problem is usually with church leaders. This applies to big names as well as little ones. For example, I remember going to hear the Reverend Billy Graham in the 1950s. At that time he was a rising star in the religious world; and he appeared at the Belgian Building on Virginia Union campus. This was also a period in which we were fighting hard to eliminate de facto and de jure racial segregation. I remember coming out of the meeting after Dr. Graham's speech and a student came running up to me. He said, "What do you think about the Reverend's speech?" I replied spontaneously that "never before have I heard nothing expressed so eloquently."

I expected Dr. Graham to say something about racism. But later I read an article where he said he avoided controversial issues because he didn't want to do anything to interfere with his saving souls for God. To me, that sounded like a whole lot of baloney. The only times I have

313

ever listened to him since then were when he was on TV and I got trapped because nearly everyone else there wanted to listen to him and I had no feasible exit.

My problem with Dr. Graham was and still is that I consider him as possessing a tremendous talent, and he could have been a great force for the improvement of the conditions affecting the common man or woman. Instead, he catered to the rich and powerful and settled for becoming a super entertainer. For example, he was a big factor in the White House of all Republican administrations from Eisenhower to Bush (with the possible exception of the brief Ford administration). While I have no doubt that with his religious extravaganza he attracted crowds of thousands of people, the attendees of his religious services were not all different people. I am certain that the repeaters were numerous. Accordingly, it is difficult to believe that the United States would have been any worse morally had Dr. Graham devoted more time to "controversial issues."

I am not picking on Dr. Graham. In my opinion, for the majority of church services the best thing you can say for them, considering what happens in some of them, is that it is a form of non-obscene family entertainment. It's better than a whole lot of things that people could be doing. Consequently, I wouldn't oppose it. So far as its having any lasting effect on human beings, I see people who never go to church and they have just as good Christian ideals as people who go to church every day.

When you look at people who get wrapped up in what we regard as fundamentalism, many times they are actually a detriment to human society. Fundamentalists of all kinds (religious, economic or social) must face reality and avoid all obsolete practices. Fundamentalists should stop obstructing change directed at improving the general condition of human earthlings.

For example, there is now a surge on behalf of those labeled the "Religious Right" which is going to make it difficult to improve the lot of human earthlings, particularly those of the lower economic brackets. But if we get an effective organization promoting sound thought on evolution, I think we can overcome these obstacles to progress. My point is, you can develop an organization to do what needs to be done. We have got to enlighten people.

The *Bible* tells you the Lord created the heavens and the earth.

However, as I understand it, according to some scientists, creation of the universe is still going on. If you consider reality, everything moves, everything changes and new things emerge and most old things pass on unless through the years they are capable of demonstrating their validity. For example, one constructive societal expectation is that parents should nurture, love and educate their children to become useful members of society. In this regard, when I read the Ten commandments, I do not believe that if God had written the Ten Commandments that God would have left out the requirement that parents love, nurture and teach their children to be useful members of society, thus laying the foundation for children to love, honor, and respect their parents.

I am not anti-religious, and do not oppose people assembling in ritualistic observance of the Creator of the Universe. I merely seek to help human earthlings to make changes where circumstances require.

As I bring these thoughts on religion and related activities to a close for now, I will state that I disagree strongly with many church officers on the issue of tithing. In earlier days when the tithing idea was more prominent, the church performed social services that government and other independent agencies now perform. For a long time I believe that the church has called on people to tithe more than they should because the church doesn't perform anything like the number of activities they used to in Biblical and earlier times. It just does not add up and some people don't bother with any of it. If the government and the society did what it should do, there would be no need for the church to have the burden of any social services and churches would have more time to devote to true moral instruction.

For many years I have believed that societal problems should be addressed through the government because the government represents all the people, not just those who belong to a particular church. I now turn to a few additional thoughts about government in a progressively evolving society.

Government

We have come to the point that we need to revise our concept of our function on earth and how to conduct ourselves. Presently, all around the planet we seem to have adopted the notion that we need to construct economic systems that allow some people to become rich and powerful. However, a better concept is to set up an economic and social system to make it possible for all human earthlings to live in a useful and peaceful manner as they pass through their life spans. This can only be accomplished by establishing a societal instrument that deals fairly with and for all the people.

For these reasons, I believe government should be regarded not as a big brother or uncle, rather government should be regarded as a tool that people use just as you use a lever. For instance, if you are going to move a heavy object a lever makes it possible and simpler. We will have to use government as a tool to handle problems properly to become a truly civilized society. We must find a way to move in an evolutionary manner from individual, fragmented, and hostile sovereign states to a unified, cooperating global governmental system. Such a cooperative system must have mechanisms to allow a culturally diversified people to provide for their own needs in a fair and equitable manner. In other words, we must learn to deal creatively, constructively and efficiently with the needs of all human earthlings. To more closely approximate a utopian situation, in the transitional period as we move from many governments to a unified global government, national government should deal with mass accumulation and distribution of wealth issues, national defense, manufacturing, technological innovation, and establishing and maintaining peaceful ties with other human earthlings. At the same time nation states must ensure creation and expansion of democratic governmental systems.

Government and other entities must put a limit on the acquisition and control of individual property. There isn't any reason in the world why some individual human earthlings operating under a corporate structure, and others acting without that legal cover, should do anything they want to do without regard for the widespread effects on the general public. For example, large corporate type entities lay off thousands of people just to make more money. It has got nothing to do with the well-being of people. Problems affecting the masses of people ought to be handled by the representatives of the masses of people. Nevertheless, I am not opposed to people who work harder receiving greater material fruits of their labors than those who do not work as hard or as well. In a civilized society, everyone should have a right to a job that pays an adequate wage for themselves and their dependents. The person should also have access to training to competently prepare themselves for such jobs.

Many discoveries, scientific and otherwise, that affect the masses of people, have been the result of public funding. However, after the discovery is made with public funds, the private individuals start talking

316

about "getting the government off our backs. Let us make the money off of our discoveries."

Notwithstanding these prevailing ideas, I am all for the super conductor and building satellites in the sky because I think that Planet Earth is eventually going to become overcrowded. What are we going to do? We already know how to live underground and are capable, for limited time periods, of living under water. We can live in space for varying durations. For a long time human earthlings will have to come back to earth periodically; but eventually people will be able to live in space for longer and longer intervals and will live on other planets.

If scientists are even partially right, there are billions of galaxies and there is bound to be some similar life form in some of those galaxies. I believe that when we finally learn how to extend our travel beyond our solar system, we will connect with such life forms. Even if we don't, so what? Eventually, we will end up populating another planet somewhere. I don't know how long it will be, it might be a century or more, but it is going to be the next step. During the twenty-first century I believe human earthlings will likely develop the capability to live in space and under water for extended periods of time. Just recently, scientists confirmed the existence of another solar system other than our own; and they are even more certain now that other stars exist with planets like our own.

Given this historical context, it is of utmost importance to get the general public to understand evolution, that inevitably things change, and how they change. The more advanced technologically we become, the faster changes will take place. Once upon a time you could go away and stay fifty years and come back and the general scene would be about the same. Now, that is not true. If we transfer societal resources away from armaments and into technological advances, we can enhance the quality of life for all human earthlings. For instance, if we shift resources from making guns and missiles to educating our children, we could have top rated computers in every classroom and, even more importantly, we could have smaller classes and thus more individual attention as is provided in private schools. In addition, we could pay educators' salaries consistent with the invaluable work that they do, their formal education, and with compensation of their compatriots in other professions.

Similarly, government should step in to deal with compelling societal problems when individuals cannot or will not do so. An example involves often predictable massive floods that happen annually in many parts of the world including the United States. Since these natural catastrophes are foreseeable, in the United States, why don't we have a piping or other irrigation system to divert the water from flooded areas to arid places, other waterways which are not near flood stage or to the oceans?

I repeat: I look upon government not as an uncle, big brother or tyrant but as an instrument or tool which people can and should use to further the opportunities for helping to obtain the necessities and enjoyments of life. If you view government as a tool rather than as a sovereign separate and apart from people, that's a better concept. All human earthlings have the same basic needs. One essential instrument devised to provide these needs is a democratic government.

Democracy involves people making decisions affecting how society is governed. People have to use government and participate. In a democratic society, I'm for limited terms for legislators and high ranking officials in the executive branch of government for two reasons. First, limited terms would provide opportunity for wider participation by more people in the governing process. Second, when persons occupy a privileged position such as a legislative or executive office in government, then within a limited time period they should return to civilian life and live under the laws and rules which they created. If people had to live with the consequences of their legislative or administrative behavior more quickly than they do now, they would have a different attitude towards passing laws, issuing administrative rules and regulations, and making policies.

I do not advocate limited terms based on the argument that we should throw the incumbent "Bums" out. Besides, I have had sufficient association with government officials in high echelons and in the more permanent civil service level to know that while occasionally there are some bums, generally contemporary public officials are of just as high caliber and dedicated in performing their duties as people in other segments of society.

Another concept which is sometimes contrasted with government is the market. Here are some of my thoughts on the market.

The Market?

In discussions about appropriate public policies, sometimes folks talk about the alternative of "letting the market decide". Well, hell, what's the market? The market is a materialistic thing. It symbolizes the golden calf that the early people were warned against worshiping. A number of factors affect market activity - acquisition of profits, meeting perceived societal needs for goods and services, developing better products, catastrophic natural events, greed and fear. While many influences affect the market, greed and fear stand out.

Those who are afraid believe they will lose money and will sell irrespective of whether the financial condition of a company justifies sale or not. If they think they are going to make a whole lot of profit, often times they buy and raise the price regardless of whether the company's fiscal condition justifies purchase of its stock. These emotions and perceptions are the biggest motivation.

Nobody goes into the market just to provide an equitable means of distributing societal benefits and luxuries. Investors invest to make money. Investors hold on to various types of property, and if they fear they are going to lose money, they sell. It is like a big lottery, particularly the new practice of day trading.

Speaking of fear, whether it rains on a particular Thursday usually doesn't matter a lot. It might be bad if you plan to go to a picnic or something. However, if for some personal reason we wagered our considerable wealth on whether it is going to rain on that particular Thursday, most persons would try any and all feasible means to make it rain or prevent it from raining. Fear of losing their material possessions would impel them to take definite steps.

Similarly, greed as reflected in the attempt to take advantage of other people's difficulties would have the same effect. Indeed, fear and greed not only make a difference in people's thinking, those emotions also lead them to anti-social behavior. Fear and greed often seem to drive market activity. A typical example involves whether interest rates will rise or fall.

Let's put the argument about the wonders of the market in our twentieth century context. When I was growing up, a working man actually had very few rights. The foreman or the proprietor could fire him for no reason. The law called that at-will employment. Now, in some instances, the law protects workers from that kind of human behavior.

Similarly, I remember during the 1930's an economist wrote a book saying that a three-percent unemployment rate was essential to maintain a smooth operating economy.[9] Well, for that population in those days, even three per cent unemployment was bad. With the population expanding more and more, even if the percentage of the unemployed remained constant, the pool of unemployed people would get bigger and bigger.

However today, some policy makers are talking about five percent as being an acceptable unemployment rate. I do not believe this is all right even with those who are employed, much less with those who are out of work. The higher the rate of unemployed persons, the more workers' wages are depressed.

I have no problem acknowledging that the American form of economic enterprise has proven superior to the totalitarian dominated economic systems, be they capitalist or communist. However, I also believe American economic superiority does not mean that we have reached the epitome of economic systems. Such an argument would be as illogical as it would have been for someone living in the Middle Ages to have argued that because the stage coach was superior transportation to the chariot, that the coach epitomized (and would always epitomize) the best in public transportation. The conclusion does not necessarily follow from the premise. Many different transportation developments occurred since the times of the chariot and stage coach. Now both the chariot and the stage coach have become obsolete.

Similarly, once upon a time a poor person would lay on a bed or on the side of the road and starve to death. People don't think that way now. If they can't get necessities legally, they start thinking of ways to obtain them illegally. The type of economy we have, our so-called free enterprise, is not free. There is no economy that is not partially governmentally controlled, even ours. However, some economies are more stringently controlled than others.

What else has the market produced: a black market functioning in an underworld economy.

On a somewhat different topic, I think from a very early age children should be taught the work ethic. For instance, when I was a kid, you had to work at a very early age. As a matter of fact, as I previously mentioned, some of the things I did would be regarded now as child abuse. For example, during World War I when I was ten years old, I used to get up at 3:00 a.m. and go down to the newspaper printing press and get my papers fresh off the press. I would then go and sell my papers on my route. I got up at 3:00 a.m. so that after selling and distributing my papers I could get back home in time to dress and go to Sunday School.

But, today parents and guardians would be soundly criticized if they allowed a ten year old child to go out in the street at that time of morning particularly in the bitter cold winter weather such as we had in Roanoke. Even though I was well wrapped from head to toe - complete with hat, gloves, shoes and other cold weather gear, changes in the prevailing societal circumstances, for example escalating crime rates would make this work activity too dangerous today as compared to my childhood. Now a parent would have all kinds of protective services on his back. There is no place for a small child to work alone on the city streets - particularly at ungodly hours. Things have changed.

It is true that at one time if you gave a person a fish, you fed the person for a day, whereas if you taught the person to fish, she could feed herself for an indefinite period. Nevertheless, today things are not so simple as literally teaching a person to fish in an urban setting where no places to fish exist. Such instruction would not provide her the means of survival or a decent standard of living. Furthermore, where fish habitats exist, many of the streams are so polluted, that fishing is prohibited.

People must obtain education to absorb the training necessary to utilize complex technology and machinery. Moreover, even though one may succeed in obtaining the knowledge, the question remains how to procure capital for business development and training. The point is often overlooked that all people do not have the capabilities to become entrepreneurs. Entrepreneurship is a special talent like athleticism or musical genius. Since we can not all become entrepreneurs, by some means jobs with reasonable pay and benefits must be provided.

However, until we get to the point where we develop an economic system that provides everybody the opportunity for sufficient educational training so that he can work and make his maximum contribution, be it as an employee or entrepreneur, I can't conceive of all humans sharing equitably. I don't think this requires us to reach a point where everyone

321

would receive a government mandated and regulated diet, for instance, sixty pounds of flour, three pounds of sugar, two pounds of potatoes, a pound of meat and several fish occasionally thrown in. While government should be free to recommend what would constitute a nutritionally correct diet, everyone should have sufficient capital and choice to select such a diet. The same would be true with respect to adequate housing, health care, recreation, and even religious freedom. The ways and means of obtaining these important human rights must be created and assured by individuals and the government.

Our civilization and our machinations including the market were created and are shaped by human earthlings. Most of our concepts, in fact nearly everything we do, is created by human earthlings. Since humanity made much of what exists, and human conditions are influenced by human creations, we confront this question: how do we get rid of some of these evils that plague human earthlings today?

We think in terms of capitalism as if it was "it" — that is "The Ideal." However, we confront differences in conditions of people: on one hand, extreme poverty, on the other, the super rich. Obviously, this is not a satisfactory economic system for a civilized society. In other words, we have got to improve the situation so we don't have people living below the poverty level. We don't have to have a society in which people are not trained to do anything to help themselves.

There are so many things that need to be done. The only way we can change them is to have an understanding of what options exist for making progressive change and recognize the fact that anything man has made man may be able to improve. This does not mean that we should waste our time on a scheme seeking redistribution of existing capital. Rather we should seek new and unique ways of helping human earthlings starting with those below the poverty level and moving upward, at least through the lower middle class. In an evolutionary fashion, we must find ways through economic development — for example labor, industry and discovery — to help those at the bottom to receive a larger share of the economic wealth derived from labor, technology and natural resources.

Business is no more important than technology, health services, or recreation. We need all these things. Consequently, people ought to be trained to do whatever their talents enable them to do; and then work cooperatively to utilize these talents for the benefit of all people.

I do not consider myself as being a socialist or a communist. Nevertheless, there are elements of capitalism, socialism and communism that, if properly practiced, could uplift the human population. We must learn to cooperate more and compete less. While I am not a socialist, I also recognize that if you look at the biblical Jesus and claim to be Christian, Jesus preached a communal form of life. He wasn't a capitalist. He was concerned about doing what he could to help human earthlings. However, Jesus apparently had good connections with people with material wealth because, as one line of thought suggests, he was the leader of the zealot organization. The zealots were dedicated to driving the Romans from Judea.

On a somewhat different topic, we have gotten to the point now where we have some workaholics and we have some people who don't want to do any work. So far as the workaholics are concerned, I have no problem with them. If that's what they want to do, let them do it. Back at the other end, if you don't produce at least enough to take care of yourself, and you are physically and mentally able, then there will have to be some requirements placed upon you to induce you to produce adequately and responsibly as required by your situation. Through experience we ought to develop the best ways of getting voluntary cooperation from those who refuse to produce. Maybe the best way would be to isolate them. I don't know. That's too far down the line for me to worry about. Now we need to get the process working right so that every human earthling obtains the necessities of life and conforms his behavior to a standard that ensures that he does his part towards providing for his necessities.

However, before we start talking too much about restrictions, we should ask: "Have we brought the people up right?" Human beings are very pliable. For example, in some societies, people thought the finest thing they could do was to die for the king. There is a lot of leeway between dying for something and teaching human earthlings that for the civilization to move forward collectively we have to produce more than we consume. Otherwise we run into stagnation. Now is the time for a new idea: <u>Live for the people as well as for yourself.</u>

I am convinced we should start by looking at ourselves as human earthlings and recognizing the fact that we all have the same primary needs. We should develop an economic system that will provide for our needs as human earthlings rather than Americans, Chinese, or English or what not. We need to get over these cultural, nationalist, and color "humps". That is not to say that people in different societies have failed to develop different ethnic usages. They have, but such things are incidental. One should not dislike other human earthlings because they have developed different cultural practices regarding food, dress, and social interactions. Rather we should do one of two things. One approach would be to respect their customs unless the traditions were a health hazard. Second, we should evaluate their ways to see whether their practices might be superior to our current ways of doing things.

Further, we must continue to bear in mind our common need for equal access to health care, diet, recreational resources, and religious observance if so desired. Above all, human earthlings deserve access to training to prepare them to make their contribution in society.

Somewhere early in human civilization we got off on the wrong road and have never been able to get back on the correct path. At least during the hunter/gatherer period everyone shared. Now we have enough resources so that everyone can live well, yet some people are starving.

From the early stages of their development, we need to insure that all human earthlings recognize that for civilization to progress, we've collectively got to produce more than we consume. In discussing a market driven society, the preceding illustrations exemplify what I am talking about. I now turn to a discussion of other practical aspects of evolutionary thinking.

Practical Applications of Evolutionary Thinking

Another reason why we need to understand progressive evolutionary change is evolution affects everything — even your thinking. For example, one of my favorite stories in the early 1960's involved a jurist of a juvenile court in a Scarsdale type community in New York. When a juvenile delinquent's case warranted it, the judge developed the practice of drawing the defendant's attention to a big picture of George Washington hanging over his head. The judge would ask the defendant to look at the picture and tell him what he saw. Typically, the boy would tell the judge he saw our first president or one of the varying facts or myths you hear about George Washington. Then the judge would take off from what the boy said and give him a little lecture, dismiss his case and tell him to go home and emulate the virtues of George Washington that had been discussed.

Finally, along came a little Negro boy. The same situation developed. The judge was fair minded and thought the Negro boy was entitled to the same treatment he had been giving all the white kids. He asked him the same question. The boy was standing in front of him with his head held down. So the judge asked him to look at the picture and tell him what he saw. The boy did not raise his head, he just lifted his eyes and said laconically, "A slaveholder." That upset the judge. Naturally, the child didn't get the usual lecture although the judge was fair minded enough to grant the child the same clemency that he had given to white children.

In the 1960's, when this story was told, the unexpected answer of "slaveholder" generated some laughs among the audience. I used it to warm up the audience before moving on to discuss other matters. However, over the years, my thinking has <u>evolved</u>. Rather than poking fun at the bewildered judge and ridiculing George Washington, today in the 1990's I would portray that judge as typical of our keen minded judges of our Richmond Juvenile and Domestic Relations Court. In today's rendition of the story, the judge would not be bewildered; instead our quick thinking jurist would come back with remarks such as these: "Son, that's a very perceptive and courageous statement that you made. Stand up. Raise your head up. You show great intelligence and courage."

The judge could take off from that and say, "Yes, he was a slaveholder which of course was one of his negative qualities. But he also had some positive qualities. So now you want to look at both Washington's negative and positive traits. Take advantage of your perception of both. Emulate the positive qualities of George Washington and avoid the negative thoughts and behavior. I am going to dismiss the case against you. You go forward and follow George Washington's finer qualities."

By taking this more flexible approach today, we can use the same illustration, but modify it to give a different emphasis depending on the circumstances. In the 1960's, the story served the objective of providing some humor and loosening up the audience by poking fun at the judge and critically evaluating George Washington. In the 1990's version, the modification in the story demonstrates a greater sensitivity to the feelings of different audiences — some of whom may identify more positively with the judge or with George Washington. The 1990's story would be designed to promote positive evolutionary change in the individual context.

325

Adapting stories and strategies to confront and overcome new challenges like everything else is influenced by the evolutionary process. The law does it all the time. For example, we take principles from one case and apply them by analogy to a different type case.

In fact, our approach to the <u>Brown</u> litigation was evolutionary. Charlie Houston realized that to challenge segregation head on in the early 1930's would result in our running into a legal stone wall. That would have accomplished nothing constructive. Accordingly, it was decided to challenge <u>inequality</u> which was the practical result flowing from <u>Plessy's</u> separate but equal doctrine. We started with the teacher salary cases and also challenged the abominable facilities that many Negro children were obliged to attend.

Our legal strategy afforded us an opportunity to carefully educate the public and the courts regarding the moral evils and social and economic detriments of segregation. We also chose good cases, developed the records, and recognized that initially we would likely obtain relief primarily from appellate courts, not courts of first instance.

I, too, exemplify evolutionary change. For example, I studied law specifically to train myself to challenge segregation. Of course, I had to live, so I had to use my legal talents to survive economically.

Nevertheless, I regard myself as an advocate for social change. When I started law school, I was thinking in terms of civil rights for Negroes. From my point of view, in the United States, it was the Negro against the world. All other ethnic groups, nationalities and "races" could and in most instances did have their social and civil rights. Negroes were the only people in the United States who were automatically restricted and excluded. For example, even immigrants coming out of Ellis Island or wherever the port of entry was, as soon as they crossed the street, were automatically granted a superior status to Negroes in practically every aspect of social, economic, political, educational and religious life.

In a somewhat different vein, telecommunications is yet another example of the evolutionary process. We could today have a conference and deal with a written document, agree to and make our changes, fax it on to someone in Sacramento, California. They could read it, and fax it back with their changes or signature as the case required. This process would result in a document agreed to by any number of people without anybody leaving their habitat. On top of that, if you want to go to the expense, we could all hear each other discussing it, and see each other, too.

The potential for a real gorgeous existence on planet earth is within our grasp. Accordingly, a critical question is how can we make this a wonderful existence for all human earthlings. One way is to critically analyze the existing opportunities and seek to develop those that furnish the greatest likelihood for human earthlings to reach our optimal potential.

The most modern view of evolution is that the universe has never stopped evolving. Everything is in motion. It is still expanding. I think it is inevitable that we will have to learn how to live in a cooperative fashion or else we are going to end up destroying ourselves.

I'm interested in evolution in the broad sense that things develop and change. I am finding that there are authorities who have a wider concept of physics and chemistry who have come to the same conclusion. Scientists speak in terms of a unified theory or a "unification of physics."[10] Scientists point out that evolution affects everything - from a loaf of bread to extra terrestrial bodies like meteors, planets and the stars. Because you can't get around it, I find it surprising that some people don't believe in a concept like evolutionary change. Change is inevitable. In cooperation with other human earthlings, we need to analyze and attempt to channel it with wisdom and compassion. I now turn to a major human challenge:

Racism and Evolutionary Change

My life experience has been such that, I have some thoughts on the evolutionary process and the human conflict which revolves around how people deal with skin color and other physical differences. For instance some people argue you are always going to have racism because you have always had racism. We haven't always had racism. I don't care even if as long as the memory of man goes you can find racism, there must have been a time when there wasn't any racism. In fact, some scholars identify the rise of racism with the growth of the African slave trade and slavery.[11]

Jim Crow was a blot on the American government's human rights record. You have to recognize, however, that there never was any universal determination that we in the United States were going to have a free and democratic society. For example, even when they were fighting

327

for their freedom, Washington and many of the American colonists opposed the use of Negro troops. The American colonists would have continued to exclude Negroes had it not been for the fact that the British offered them freedom. Negroes responded by joining up with the British.[12] So the American colonists had to change their practice, and permit the Africans, slave and free, to fight for their freedom. It wasn't any big democratic or altruistic decision that made them do it. These decisions were made for practical, self interest reasons.

Incidentally, it appears to me that as many or more decisions are made for ulterior reasons as are made for altruistic ones. This situation exists in many areas of human life and many times we do not worry whether the motive for doing a thing is ulterior or practical. If it is thought necessary, we do it.

After the <u>Brown</u> decision, I expressed some thoughts on the issue of racism and progressive change in Petersburg, Virginia. I pointed out to an audience that the <u>Brown</u> ruling was probably as much as we were going to get from the courts for a very long time. I was convinced that what we had to do was to try and devote more time to developing political strength. That's where ultimately we should expect to get our rights. I still think that. At that time, I did not expect to get the results that we succeeded in obtaining through enactment and implementation of the Civil Rights Acts of 1964 and the Voting Rights Act of 1965. A great contribution to that legislation becoming a reality was our increased political participation.

Prior to and after <u>Brown</u>, menial jobs, nasty jobs, anything that was and is undesirable were jobs for black people. When we started breaking open segregation practices, we knew that we were not automatically going to have change. Consequently there had to be some affirmative approach to cover this period. We called this approach "affirmative action". We assumed that once employment opened up and schools became desegregated there would be no need for affirmative action. But until you could break the ice, a program was needed that would sustain the desegregation process and help Negroes through the transition period.

The best proof that we needed and still need affirmative action was that the segregationists were and still are resisting desegregation. If there were no authoritative pressure segregationists would never change their discriminatory practices. Initially, affirmative action was not considered a permanent tool in achieving justice in America. We have not yet reached the point where we can say that affirmative action is unnecessary, or that this country is colorblind.

Some pessimists argue that people of color must accept a permanent status at the bottom of American society. I don't buy the idea that we should accept a subordinate status. During the transitional period back in the 1950's and early 1960's, we recognized that we might have to abide by and conform temporarily to continued exclusion and subordination in various aspects of American life, like employment. However, we did not willingly accept it. Every chance we had to terminate and change these conditions we sought to do so. My idea of accepting oppression involves recognizing opportunities to do something about it and failing to do anything constructive to alleviate or remove the oppression.

Today we hear a lot about opposition to affirmative action. Many opponents of affirmative action fail to acknowledge that they are beneficiaries of affirmative action. In colonial times, the founding great-grandfathers came to this country and set up a system designed to benefit themselves and their progeny, including some present day affirmative action opponents. For example, the founders came to America, and made the Indians offers that they could not refuse at the point of a gun. The colonists told the Indians, in effect, move into the hills or move to lands further west until we get ready to take them, or die.

While the Colonists were subjugating Indians, they also reaped tremendous fortunes through the trans-atlantic slave trade and establishing slavery on the land taken from Indians. The founding great-grandfathers excluded Negroes and Indians from participation in most aspects of political, religious and economic life. Following the issuance of the Declaration of Independence in 1776, the founding fathers continued this pattern resulting in a social structure that put white people of varying descriptions at the top. It is no accident that white folks, especially white men, take for granted that they will lead this society. Their great-grandfathers by hook and crook created a massive system in which their successors feel that they have built-in equity or ownership. This causes resentment when democratic ideals of sharing power and wealth are proposed.

I would like affirmative action opponents to recognize that over the centuries, white folks have developed many structures to benefit whites, at the expense of Negroes, Latinos and Native Americans. A few examples: 1) free land for whites (forcibly taken from Indians); 2) all

329

white professions and occupations in much of this country for decades; 3) superior education for whites; and 4) political decisions like disenfranchisement laws to put Negroes and other people of color at the bottom of the social hierarchy.

Societal punishment in the criminal law was evident from early colonial days where sanctions for Negroes who committed the same offense were greater than for whites. As early as 1650, three indentured servants escaped and when captured, two of them, a Scot and an Irish person were placed in the stocks for two or three hours. The Negro, convicted of the same crime was stripped to the waist and given fifty lashes with a cat-o-nine tails. Similar disparate treatment of Negro criminal defendants continues to this day. In some states even poll taxes for free Negroes were greater than for whites. Whites paid four dollars and Negroes paid five dollars. These patterns of oppressive thought and action were heartily endorsed by nearly all segments of society, including government, the business community, many religious, and civic institutions, and the overwhelming majority of white private individuals. Of course, some exceptions existed too, like various groups of Quakers.

I raise these issues not because I want segregationists or other affirmative action opponents to don sack cloth and ashes or to devise individual reparations. Nevertheless, we must keep up the struggle if we hope to change things. I have a supreme faith in our having the means to achieve positive change. I think there are a combination of reasons which will produce change. One reason for my belief in the inevitability of change is I see the way things were when I was a kid. Later, I thought that I could do something about segregation, and many of us joined together and made a difference.

In addition, the evolutionary process affords the opportunity to produce change for better or worse depending on the human reaction to the changes. However, if you are going to develop change along a particular line, you must do something to direct that change. In fact, you can direct it in a way that is satisfactory to you personally but is destructive to society. For example, General Schwartzkopf made a foolish statement when he said that the Army would never accept homosexuals. The same was said about Negroes in the military. For a long time, some people argued that white military personnel were not going to accept Negroes in higher military echelons. Despite these dire predictions, more and more of them accept Negroes in such positions, and as time passes, more and more of them will accept an increased Negro leadership role in the military and civilian employment.

I don't see why many individuals fail to perceive that the same kind of arguments used to defend racial segregation are being utilized to maintain segregation on the basis of sexual orientation. For a while they were running to campuses and military installations asking ROTC members and enlisted personnel whether they wanted gay and lesbian soldiers in the military. What did they think the soldiers were going to say? Many soldiers seem to be using arguments like the segregationists during the days of Massive Resistance. In fact, when Massive Resistance was at its height, every time a dozen white folks got together in the southern states and had a little convention or meeting they would come up with a resolution. "We believe segregation is in the best interest of the races. God made the races separate and they should stay that way."

Back then we questioned whether God created races geographically separate. For example, it appears true that in early times, people used to be scared to go too far from where they lived and worked. When the existing source(s) of food ran out they did what came naturally: they moved on. It seems to me if God had intended people to be separated, why did He give them the foresight, tenacity, endurance and everything else to overcome the natural boundaries that made it possible for them to develop into ethnic groups. Furthermore, if God wanted white people to remain white, black people to remain black, etc., why did God create humans so that fertile males and females of any hue can procreate with one another, even though they come from opposite "ends" of the earth. Thus, people of differing colors can have children who are genetically members of the same family. Now we question whether human beings can be validly categorized as belonging to separate races.[13]

For people who think as I do, that the sexual orientation of the vast majority of people is genetic, it makes discrimination on the basis of sexual orientation both cruel and stupid. Hopefully rapid progress to eliminate such discrimination will be made, and in the foreseeable future discrimination based on sexual orientation will no longer be an issue.

When I look back on it, I see a development of my thinking in the area of so-called race relations. As I mentioned before, when I was a youngster we had stereotypical sayings like - "you could always tell a good white person from a bad one because the good ones were all buried at least six feet deep." "Never trust a white person because he is so crooked he would steal the pennies off his dead mother's eyes." At that time, I thoroughly believed those ideas.

331

Oliver W. Hill, Sr. next to his bust in the Black History Museum,
Richmond, VA., that was sculpted by Paul DePasquale (1997)
for the Virginia Historical Society

However, finally when I became a young man I thought more deeply about these matters and I arrived at the conclusion it was just as simple and stupid for me to hate people because they are white as it was for them to hate me because I am not white. I had started to work and deal with some decent white people. I recognized that there was just as much diversity among white folks as there was among Negroes. Some Negroes you got along with and some you didn't. Similarly some white folks you got along with and others you didn't.

I concluded that it should not matter if a person is white. I subjected him to the same scrutiny as I did anyone else. Then I made a determination based on that scrutiny. I am convinced that human beings are one race with many traits in common as well as some differences.

I gained many good insights on human beings from reading O'Henry's stories. Many of these stories illustrated examples of how to determine human character from observation. The author stated for instance that you could always determine the type of person you were dealing with by watching how he treats his children and his wife or acts in unguarded moments with respect to those holding so called menial positions. You also could learn about a person by observing how children and pets related to him.

I studiously applied those observations. Particularly I was very conscious of how people treated the humans who worked under them as servants. It made it easy to determine if this was a good white person or not.

Of course, just because a guy was good did not necessarily pay the bills. When I was a waiter trying to make some money, I wasn't interested in his goodness. I was interested in the gratuity. A lot of times the worst racists would be the one who gave the biggest tip. Unless some basic principle was involved, you put up with it.

As I close these thoughts on race and evolutionary change, I wish to emphasize that our understanding of race relations in the United States must change as more historical facts come to light. For instance, in 1969, many of us believed that in 1619, Negroes first came to Jamestown, Virginia. Accordingly, to commemorate the three hundred and fiftieth anniversary of the landing of Negroes at Jamestown, I invited a number of distinguished individuals to participate on a program in Jamestown. The principal speakers were Dr. Charles Wesley (a renowned Negro historian), and Dr. Samuel Proctor (a leading Negro pastor, preacher, university president and civil rights activist). Drs. Wesley and Proctor were introduced by Dr. Edgar Toppings, a well respected historian at Virginia State University and Dr. J. Rupert Picott, an educator, activist and Executive Director of the Virginia Teachers Association. Other invitees included a number of ambassadors and representatives of African countries. Lt. Governor Fred Pollard represented the Commonwealth of Virginia.

In planning and implementing this program, I received tremendous support from the leadership and members of the Virginia State conference of NAACP branches. In addition, the Alpha Beta Boule of the Sigma Pi Phi Fraternity furnished financial support for the celebration. Furthermore, I obtained excellent cooperation from the Director of the Jamestown Foundation. Together, these dedicated individuals and other similar minded persons made it possible for us to have a fine program which was attended by approximately five thousand persons on a dreary, overcast day in September, 1969.

333

Nevertheless, more recent scholarship has indicated one important reason that John Rolfe, Secretary and Recorder for the colony of Virginia, did not emphasize the novelty of the arrival of "twenty Negers" via a Dutch ship. **In 1619, Negroes were already in Jamestown.** They had come over with the original settlers in 1607. It remains to be seen how this new information will affect our understanding of race in this nation.

Gender Roles and the Evolutionary Process

When the controversy involving admitting women to Virginia Military Institute first came about, I wrote a letter to the Trustees many of whom I knew from my service as a member of the Board of the George C. Marshall Foundation. I urged the VMI trustees not to waste funds, time and energy in fighting admission of women. I pointed out that it was a normal evolutionary process in action, that they should apply to the court for time to formulate a plan, and that they should implement the necessary physical changes to make buildings female friendly.

Further, I argued that they should take the money they were going to waste fighting gender desegregation and launch a national campaign to recruit a number of female applicants. In that way, when women started attending, there would have been a reasonable number of female cadets and this would help make the women cadets feel comfortable. In addition, I urged some type of training to prepare the males for the transition. The recent U.S. Supreme Court decision in that case (<u>U.S. v. Virginia</u>) suggests that my approach was legally and morally defensible.[14]

Admittedly, many years ago, in the old days, when the all-male Virginia Military Institute was established, the popular stereotype was that a gentle lady's first line of defense was to faint, and presumably she would be of no use in a professional military situation. However, when you got down to just an ordinary woman and an ordinary man, in most situations the women worked just as hard and were just as reliable as the men. This was demonstrated repeatedly on the frontier in North America. More recently, women in the military served with distinction in the Persian Gulf War.

I cite the V.M.I case not to boast but to point out that if my advice had been followed, the entry of women into V.M.I. would have reflected great credit upon that institution. In addition, I hope that as other individuals, institutions, and agencies confront similar types of situations, instead of digging in and resisting the evolutionary change, those involved will seek experienced advice: and follow the advice when the suggestions clearly show that the change inures to the best interests of the commonweal.

Regarding leadership in society, government, business, and the family, the ideal situation would be men and women working in pairs. Sometimes a woman might have more talent in some things, and men in others. We are evolving all the time. For example, you have home fathers doing domestic work. Where a man's ability is to manage a home or rear the children, he is going to and should be doing it. Incidentally, in the commercial world, as strange as it may seem, so far as numbers are concerned, men have always out-cooked women.

I think we would be much better off with male/female partnerships based on equality. One is just as responsible for making things function properly as the other. For the type of relationship that we heterosexuals have, a woman is just as important as a man. You used to say you couldn't have a child without a woman, but, hell, for centuries, a woman couldn't have a child without a man.[15]

Speaking of human reproduction, there is talk about putting fertilized embryos in incubators, and cloning humans. Whether they would be human beings in the sense that we know is questionable. But that's it! We always talk about things as we know them; however, things change. We must have vision to see beyond our present circumstances.

In that regard, a modified version of the well known "Serenity Prayer" is relevant:

> *God grant me the serenity to temporarily accept things I cannot change, the courage to change things I can change, the wisdom to know the difference, and above all, the vision to see the things that need to be changed.*

The Way It Always Has Been

So far as I am able to ascertain, all human cultures tend to resist change. I think it stems from lack of understanding of evolution. I'm a strong believer in effectively motivating and guiding people in how they should act and react by relying on reason rather than blindly relying on custom or emotion.

The Big Bang, <u>Brown vs Board of Education</u> and Beyond

Accepting and adapting to change did not come easy to me. For example, when I was a child my foster mother belonged to a couple of whist clubs. The club members regularly entertained in their homes. They played in ten minute frames. Every ten minutes the bell would ring and they would jump up and run from one table to another - creating a whole lot of confusion. When I was nine years old I started playing with them. I became a regular substitute. I enjoyed playing cards and all the confusion. The emphasis was on playing as many hands as possible in the ten minute period, without any regard to the quality of play.

When I was in the sixth grade I went to Washington, D.C. to live for a while. The family next door was having a whist party. I heard them talking about playing four rounds and the winning couple would move to the next table. I thought that was so ridiculous. They lost all the excitement. I was trying to tell the hostess how they should play ten minutes and then run to the next table. However, she had sense enough not to pay any attention to me. I later learned it makes far more sense to play the four rounds and move than the old ten minute frames that I was trying to preserve. It makes for a much better quality of play and a more relaxed game. There wasn't anything more stupid than the process that we were using in Roanoke. The only thing is now I think they give the players too much time to play four hands.

But I strongly supported the Roanoke method not because I reasoned it out but because that's the way we did it. Most people think the way they do things is the best, and that's the way it ought to be.

In promoting evolutionary change, the other thing you can't hammer too much is a sad old idea: "This is the way it has always been." While it may be true that folks did the same things for centuries, if you stop to think about it, there isn't anything that has always been on planet earth.

Another example of resistance to societal change is the existence of racial prejudice. Bigotry against Negroes was more firmly ingrained among members of the American public than we ever thought. When I was coming along, the general concept was that a child was born with a brain like a smooth billiard ball. The brain was principally changed by two processes — environment and training. We know now that while environment and training are important, certain inheritable traits influenced by DNA processes also play a significant role. Heredity seems a stronger force than we thought it was. It seems genes might be

336

pre-programmed and move in a certain direction. I do not know if they are programmed to make people think that they should hate something. I do not believe that prejudice is inherited. Whatever it is, we know that segregation is more deeply ingrained in people than we thought it was.

Just like religious concepts. A few summers ago, when we were working on a commission, one of my fellow commission members was a strong anti-abortion advocate. We rode along together two or three times going to sites for the hearings. My colleague was good company and I was able to keep the conversation in a humorous vein. Nevertheless, this commissioner spent much of our travel time trying to convince me that my religious concepts were wrong. My colleague admitted at one time having beliefs similar to mine but now claimed to see the light and was born again. Now my colleague believes the Bible is the inerrant word of God, and everything can be explained through properly understanding biblical passages. Things are just not that narrow. I hate for people to say they are conservative because I know that generally means that they are more resistant to change in matters affecting human relations.

I guess fear has a lot to do with people's opposition to change.

You have to bear in mind things have different rates of change. Since change is inevitable things will either get worse or get better. My favorite example is the fruit fly that has several generations in a very short period of time as compared with the redwood tree which takes thousands of years to go through the same process. Both life forms evolved in the evolutionary process. But their rates of growth and spans of life are different.

Speaking of evolutionary changes in politics and society, we often talk about the brilliance of the founding fathers. At one time, I thought the founding fathers were complete geniuses — all of them. Everything they did was right. In some respects, the founding fathers were rebels leading a movement against the prevailing status quo.

However, now we know that while they did some right things, they also did many wrong things, and some of the right things could have been just plain luck. We know for sure that they were a long way from thinking about genuine democracy.

Another factor that is often overlooked is the stupidity of King George III and his advisers including the London Board of Trade. Had

337

they recognized the evolutionary process and the inevitability of change, at least they probably could have taken effective steps to maintain English sovereignty over the American colonies for a longer period. For instance, rather than seeking to exploit the colonies, they could have made a few judicious appointments of dukes and lords from among the colonists.

Moreover, if the Colonists and Indians had been more cognizant of principles of progressive evolutionary change, it is possible that they could have jointly developed a richer and more civilized American culture, including both groups.

It is important to put things in an historical perspective. For instance, once in many feudal societies, it was considered a badge of honor when the poor peasant's daughter went to spend the night at the lord's manor. If they had a child, well and good. Similarly, at one time a whole lot of people thought that the finest thing that could happen would be to sacrifice their lives for the king.

Today, we recognize that type of thinking as narrow and provincial. Nevertheless, if those kinds of cultures can develop despite such limited vision, we can progress even more. We need a more sensible approach to dealing with social change and working to promote a cooperative society.

In contrast to European cultures, for numerous reasons, we do not know as much about African societies. Some of the things that we think we know about Africa have proven inaccurate. For example, at one time it was thought that the "dark continent" was inhabited by folks who were and always had been "savages." That view has been proven parochial by scholars in various fields. Scholarly research demonstrates that Africa is central to human civilization as reflected in the culture of Ethiopia and her daughter, Egypt.[16] According to some scholars some African societies had developed trial by jury while the English were still settling civil disputes by mortal combat.[17]

As one considers progressive evolutionary change, we need to evaluate which path we should take that would be beneficial to all human earthlings. In that regard, I don't know how communists ever figured that the government would wither and pass away. I have never been able to conceive of that. To be perfectly frank I was always too mentally lazy to read <u>Capital</u> in its original form.

338

One day a young man asked what would I say if I imagined myself writing a letter to people alive now and to future generations. I would say:

> "Things have changed. Opportunities have opened up. The best thing you can do is prepare and train yourself to do something constructive that applies to the present and to the future. We must recognize the inevitability of change, prepare for change and adapt accordingly."

That's a short letter.

Evolution and Death

I have no fear of death at all because I know that it is just a natural part of the evolutionary process. Everyone is going to die one of these days. Sometimes there is nothing you can do about it, for instance, when a responsible citizen is killed by a random bullet fired by one thug shooting at another. Similarly one may have a genetic defect that causes an early death.

On the other hand, when people use moderation and follow the latest knowledge in prevention and treatment of illnesses, including diet, exercises, recreation and rest, they may prolong human life to the proverbial one hundred and twenty years.[18] Regardless of how long we live, eventually we will die. I don't know whether we would want to do anything about dying. Suppose nobody died. There would probably be some other means of removing human earthlings from this scene.

I remember when I was a kid I had a terrible fear of dying. As my understanding of evolution improved and I recognized that death is just a process that everything goes through, the less fear of death I have. Death is just the beginning of something else. We might change from one form to another. I have no recollection of experiencing life activity before birth in 1907. I do not believe that I will have any knowledge of what will happen after I die. They say, "Matter is neither created nor destroyed." I don't know if they know what they are talking about or not.

While I have a great regard for faith and don't believe that you can live without it, it seems to me that the ramifications of faith are very limited. We exercise faith when using the electric razor, traveling by auto, bus or plane, or eating in a restaurant or at home. If you

339

lacked faith that people would drive like they had some sense you would be scared to walk on the street. As a matter of fact, in earlier days some people didn't ride elevators and airplanes because they lacked faith in the ability of the equipment to function properly, and accordingly believed that the equipment would fail and injure them.

I don't believe people now have the fear of death that they once had. I can remember when I was a kid there was a common saying that people were "getting too damn smart and the Lord is going to smack them down. If the Lord intended man to fly he would have given him wings." Presuming the God as perceived by such people exists, we now know that God didn't have to give man wings. He gave man a mind and ingenuity which enabled man to make his own wings.

The other thing, during Biblical times, people thought that the angels had wings and that the distance to Heaven was just an overnight journey by wing power. In those days nobody had the faintest notion that the universe was as vast as it is or that relative to that vastness the earth was as insignificant as it is.

When I was a kid we used to sing, "Twinkle, twinkle little star, how I wonder what you are, up in the air so high, like a diamond in the sky." It never occurred to me that that little star up there twinkling might be several times bigger than this whole earth or our sun! Nor did it occur to me that what I saw twinkling had occurred many light years previously. On a starlit night, the whole sky would be adorned with stars, comets and the moon. Think how far they are away and how many of them there are. In addition, it was not unusual to see meteors or shooting stars as we called them. It was a beautiful sight that those of us who live in the city no longer have the opportunity to enjoy.

Concluding Comments on Evolutionary Change

I do not see evolutionary change as primarily biological. People don't realize that evolution is all pervasive. As human beings, we produce things. But everything we produce, technology or any other thing, goes through an evolutionary process. It doesn't make any difference what you do, creation is still evolving. Therefore, we have to constantly look at all institutions that affect the human being and try to see how we can improve conditions for the commonweal.

In his book, <u>Cosmos</u>, the late Carl Sagan stated that the theory that the earth was the center of the universe was accepted by the medieval European church.[19] As a consequence, according to Sagan, scientific progress in this area was hindered for nearly a thousand years. While some scientists disagreed with Ptolemy's position, they were unwilling to challenge the prevailing orthodox views.

Similarly, an area in which Aristotle, Plato and Socrates, and other great classical Greek philosophers were wrong involved the nature of matter. These great thinkers ridiculed Democritus because he believed matter consisted of atoms that were indivisible, infinite in number and shape, and widely scattered.[20]

If we had a panorama of the history of the universe, two things would stand out: first, change is inevitable. Second, if we start with the Big Bang and come to the present, the human era would seem like a little dot on the historical scene. You would have a hard time seeing it. From this perspective, history extends over billions of years. On the other hand, viewing planet earth from a creationist standpoint, may lead to the conclusion that the history of the planet earth and human beings is less than ten thousand years.

Implementing Education on Evolutionary Change

We need to develop a variety of programs to help the general public realize that evolution is all pervasive, and not just limited to Darwin's Origin of the Species. People often talk about things evolving. We need to consciously and conscientiously apply this insight to our daily lives, individually and for the commonweal.

Things must change. Just like we don't know when we are going to die, no one knows what is really the end of the situation. For instance, consider the difference between contemporary humans and the first set that evolved sufficiently beyond the monkeys and apes to be considered human.

Many of our problems stem from several inadequacies. One is a lack of understanding of evolution and the inevitability of change. Instead of opposing change we should try to direct the change into a constructive direction. The second is lack of a model of the type of environment needed for a truly civilized society. We need to work assiduously to correct this defect. One way to do that is to promote in the twenty-first century a renaissance in human relationships. That's where I am now.

341

THE SECRET JOURNAL OF SISTER JESS:
A TRUE (?) STORY IN HONOR OF
OLIVER W. HILL, SR., ESQ.

Jonathan K. Stubbs

INTRODUCTION

> "I am convinced that human beings are one race with many traits in common as well as some differences."
> *Oliver W. Hill, Sr., Esq.*

Oliver Hill places his finger squarely on a modern struggle, namely, the idea that human beings can be both one and many. Many humans seem to think that it is impossible to have more than one identity. For example, suppose a black person says "I am a human being first and my color is secondary." Some people hearing this statement would interpret it as a (foolish) repudiation of one's "racial" identity. To some the statement means "He wants to be a human being rather than a black person. This definition of being human means being bleached of his blackness. To be bleached of one's blackness leaves one colorless. Perhaps he is too naive to realize that; or maybe he is running from his blackness and subconsciously wants to be white."

However one can view the statement that "I am a human being first and my color is secondary" another way. You can recognize that the speaker has embraced two identities — her humanity first and her color second. If you recognize that the speaker's gender, age, nationality, culture, and religious beliefs are also significant aspects of her humanity, you can see that she fits Mr. Hill's description of humans, namely:

"one race with many traits in common as well as some differences."

I agree that we are one race with many common traits as well as some variations. The following story addresses reasons for humans to embrace the truth within Mr. Hill's statement: and conscientiously apply it.

PROLOGUE:

Let's use a bit of imagination. Suppose the proverbial woman from another planet landed on earth and assumed the guise of a human earthling. What would she find? Hear the story of Sister Jess.

THE SECRET JOURNAL OF SISTER JESS

Some time ago I set out on an expedition to carefully explore the beautiful, blue-green planet called earth for the primary purposes of evaluating how we could best develop its mineral, animal and plant resources.

I landed about three o'clock a.m. on a moonless night in a deserted area of a large land mass on the western half of the planet. I later discovered that the land mass is called North America and more specifically, the United States.

My first task was to assume the guise of a human earthling. With a little difficulty (because too much sun is bad for one's health) I succeeded. You should see me now! Taking on the identity of the local population, I generated something called "hair", which was long, black and straight and covered the top of my body. I look somewhat like many of the inhabitants here in New Mexico (a subdivision of the United States). Because of my aversion to sunlight, the covering of my body, which human earthlings refer to as "skin" is quite dark. In addition, to remind myself of the beauty of our home planet and the gorgeous green skies there, I decided to make the color of my visual organs (eyes), green.

My second challenge was to conceal the space craft. (I did so) in a cave, deep in a large secluded ditch, called a canyon.

I had landed not too far from a place (a "motel") which is a kind of residence for human earthlings who are seeking shelter on a temporary

343

basis. Unlike our own planet where we would gladly accommodate individuals without requesting anything in return, on planet Earth a major source of commercial revenue involves charging one's fellow earthlings a fee for necessities like food and shelter. Fortunately, I had studied this peculiar earthling custom and had a credit card (a rectangular one by two inch piece of plastic with strange notations on it) which allowed me to obtain shelter for the rest of the night. The person managing the motel looked at me rather quizzically and since mental telepathy is one of our primary senses, I read his mind. I do not care to recount all of the rather coarse (especially sex related) thoughts of this human earthling. However, the gist of it was "What in the heck have we here? Straight hair like an Indian, green eyes like a white woman, skin like one of those African Negroes! I wonder what her parents looked like?"

When the manager asked me to sign my name to the motel credit card papers, for a moment I did not know what to write: however, the phrase "Sister Jess" popped into my head so that's what I wrote down. The manager looked at me in disbelief because this name was not the one which was originally on the credit card. However, while he was still staring at me I used a short burst of thought energy to change all of the computer records to make them conform with my new name. As he looked at me, again through thought power, I changed the names on the original credit card receipt which was on a desk behind him. When he turned around and re-examined the receipt, you should have seen his face! He was dumbfounded. I asked him was there a problem. He muttered something about having been up too long, and gave me my key.

I went to my room which was a rectangular ten-by-fifteen foot dwelling with some furnishings on which human earthlings recline and sleep. While we have found it much more efficient to sleep standing, they lie down. I sought local information by turning on a gadget called a television. One fact that especially captured my attention was the pervasive nature of conflicts among human earthlings. In this country called the United States, there are certain groups that believe in a doctrine of "white supremacy" which means that human earthlings who have lighter anatomical coverings called skin, relatively straight hair, and varying eye colors, are said to be intellectually and morally superior to all other human earthlings. Accordingly, I decided to investigate some of the manifestations of white supremacy, and the nature of this thing called race. Based on these investigations I have made some preliminary conclusions about this "higher life form" called human earthlings. I will outline those thoughts at the end of this first report.

344

I use the terms human earthlings, humans, and people, interchangeably. (Some of my data sources are attached to the end of this journal.)

I discovered that white supremacist groups in nations like the United States, the United Kingdom, France, Germany, the Czech Republic and Canada are preparing to physically annihilate people of color. In the United States, a series of brutal acts have unnerved many members of the general public. These incidents often involve attacks upon people who are perceived as different and therefore inferior because of variations in the hue of the skin, texture of the hair, architecture of the nose, as well as beliefs about the Creator. For instance, recently a gunman walked into a Jewish community center and gunned down five persons, four of whom were children. The would be murderer was reported to have desired to spark a "race war" by his actions.

Parenthetically I should say that human earthlings have a number of ways of classifying themselves. One classification involves how they relate to the Creator and to each other. For some human earthlings these beliefs and relationships constitute religion. There are numerous religions on this planet and innumerable subdivisions within each religion. The Jewish religion is one of those religions on the planet which has a long and interesting history involving some great achievements as well as great tragedies. Periodically, it seems that Jewish people on planet Earth get what human earthlings call the "short end of the stick" and are often blamed for circumstances for which they have no responsibility. For example, several hundred earth years ago the Jews were accused of spreading an epidemic, referred to as the "bubonic plague" and more recently many of them were brutally murdered by a white supremacist group called the "Nazis".

I probably need to say something about other terms that I will use occasionally in this report, for example, the phrases "African American", "Filipino-American" and "Korean American". African Americans, Filipino-Americans and Korean Americans are referred to as people of color, meaning that they are groups of people who have a darker tint to their skin color than most white people. (Some people of color would describe the situation the other way around - that white people are human earthlings who have a lighter skin hue than people of color.)

This gets kind of confusing and crazy. Europeans are often thought of as white people but on the European continent many white people are of differing complexions, getting progressively darker as one travels toward the Equator. So what does it mean to be "white"? Whatever it means, my research suggests that Europe is a kind of cultural and (recent) historical home of many white people.

"African American" refers to human earthlings who come from the second largest land mass on the planet, the continent called Africa. Human scientific discoveries suggest that humans originated in Africa and spread across planet Earth from there. Without going into great detail about many disputed aspects of human history, suffice it to say that several hundred years ago Africans were forcibly removed from the African continent by Europeans (with the assistance of some Africans) and brought to North and South America. In North America, in the English colonies, after about fifty or sixty years, the social system called slavery took shape. Many slaves were treated no better than less exalted earthlings like cattle, horses, and dogs. This treatment lasted for over two hundred years and was followed in large portions of the United States by a similar social system called segregation. Like slavery, it was premised on the notion of white supremacy, and gave African Americans the lowest social, legal, and economic status possible in the United States, with the exception (perhaps) of Indians.

Incidentally, I forgot to mention that Indians were the original inhabitants of the North American continent. They immigrated from Asia thousands of years ago. Over a period of several centuries, they were dispossessed by Europeans whom they had often befriended. While I cannot give you a complete social history of all of the cultures and groups on the planet in this short journal, I wanted to give you a feel for some of the groups that are involved in this evolving understanding of what constitutes race.

With this background information (which is what humans call the "tip of the iceberg") I will resume my earlier discussion on human conflict along the color line. Shortly after the attempted murders at the synagogue, the gunman who had just shot five Jewish people, shot and killed Joseph Ileto, a Filipino-American postal employee. Published reports said that the killer's primary reason for slaying Ileto was that Ileto was a person of color.

A quick bit of research on the Philippines where Ileto's recent ancestors originated reveals that the Philippines constitutes a large group of islands off the southeast coast of the largest land mass on earth, namely

Asia. In addition to a long, rich and fascinating history, the Philippines shares complicated political, economic, cultural and military relations with the United States. While the historical context may give you some insight into this situation, Ileto's alleged killer seemed to view Ileto as just another colored "beast" who was part of a vast conspiracy to take over a country that belonged to white people.

Approximately a month before the synagogue shootings, another member of a white supremacist organization shot and fatally wounded an African American former athletic instructor and a Korean American graduate student. The Korean American who was shot was a member of a cultural group which for centuries has lived on a peninsula in Northeast Asia called Korea. Like the Filipino-Americans, Korean Americans are more recent immigrants to the United States than the African Americans and for the most part have come voluntarily. Many of the Korean-Americans are becoming, or have become, American citizens, however, they also suffer from the negative bias which flows from attitudes of human earthlings who believe in white supremacy. I should mention that the gunman who killed both the African American and the Korean American wounded a number of Jewish people near a synagogue.

Not long before these shootings, James Byrd, an African American man in Jasper, Texas, was shackled to the back of a pick up truck by three white men and dragged at high speed along the highway until his head and one of his arms were ripped from his body. Byrd's killers have been adjudged guilty of this crime and two were sentenced to death and the other to incarceration for life. This crime was especially horrible; nevertheless, I am struck by human earthlings' lust for blood. One would think that the horror of permanently ending a person's life would be so great that the survivors, in a moment of sober reflection, would resolve to break the cycle of pain and destruction. In much of the United States human earthlings have failed to learn that killing a killer as a means of punishment only fuels more feelings of pain, anger and alienation. As you know, on our planet we use severe punishment with some rehabilitation. However, human earthlings believe in revenge. They act like the killer, and hide behind the legal system to obliterate the Creator's precious gift of life. On this planet, I ask myself, when does the shedding of blood end?

Sadly, I must say I do not know. For instance, just in examining this one area (race), I discovered that in the past several years, racist murders include the beheading and burning of another African-American

347

man by two of his European-American associates in Virginia, the murder of an African man by an European-American identified with a Nazi-like group called "Skinheads" at a bus stop in Colorado, and the vicious butchering of an Asian-American in California. A startling thing about these atrocities is that they have occurred contemporaneously with the burning of scores of isolated, rural houses of worship in which people of color gather to pay homage to the Creator. An increasing number of people in this society seem to be moving to an incessant drum beat of white supremacist propaganda by all white militias preparing for what they view as the inevitable "race war".

When I look at the United States of America, I must conclude that the societal waters involving race are troubled.

As I examined data from other nations of the West I discovered that they, too, are experiencing similar social disintegration. For instance, in London, England (a place near and dear to many human earthlings), in January, 1998, Muhammed Rafique Khan, an Asian shopkeeper, was attacked and brutally murdered by a young white man in a section of the city which has "one of the highest rates of racial attacks in Britain." Khan's slaying occurred not too far from the site of a well publicized murder of a black teenager, Stephen Lawrence. Though he was slain several years ago, Lawrence's murder continues to draw attention not only because of the brutality of the attack of a gang of hooligans, but also because of the documented failure of the local police to competently prosecute Lawrence's killers. (The police are humans responsible for facilitating the enjoyment of the rights that human earthlings possess.)

Similarly, a recent public inquest was held into the killing of a black musician who allegedly was burned to death by four white assailants in London in February, 1998. The inquest jury concluded that the death was a homicide but that the police's failure to properly conduct the investigation made the likelihood of successful prosecution remote. Although the victim told an officer the identity of one of the assailants who had set him ablaze, the police allegedly failed to write down the name of the attacker. Further, the police secured the scene many hours after the incident occurred. That made it more likely that evidence would be corrupted.

I also briefly surveyed news reports coming from the European continent. To my dismay, I learned that in November, 1997, a Sudanese student, Hassian Elamin Abdelradi, was stabbed to death by members of a (Nazi) skinhead group in the Czech Republic. And not long ago in Germany, the government commissioner for foreign persons asserted in her annual report that Neo-Nazis have set up "liberated zones" in more than twenty-five towns and cities throughout the country. Foreigners most of whom are people of darker skin tones are forbidden to enter the liberated zones. Such zones include cafes, discos, clubs, and "even whole streets". The commissioner for foreigners concluded that this was an "alarming, apparently wide-spread and growing phenomenon".

I do not wish to give the impression that all the victims of racist hate crimes are people of color. A significant portion of such crime involves incidents in which white people have been victimized. For instance, in the United States the California Attorney General's report regarding hate crimes in California in 1996 suggests that, second to African Americans, white people were the most likely group to suffer racist crimes.

In all candor, I must tell you that the rise of racist attacks in the United States, the United Kingdom, Germany, the Czech Republic, and other nations has not confined itself to violence between people of different hues (inter-color conflict). Some devastating and deadly attacks have involved human earthlings of the same color but different nationalities. The most recent well known outrage involved the nearly successful extermination of Albanians in Kosovo by the Yugoslav government and its militia. As with many human conflicts that I have studied (the list is too long to discuss), retaliatory atrocities are occurring following the Yugoslav conflict. Other examples of intra-color conflict include violence by Nazi-type groups in the Czech Republic and in Slovakia against so called "Gypsies"; inter-group conflict in Bosnia-Hertzegonivia (human earthlings call it ethnic cleansing), and the genocide of nearly a million Tutsi people in Rwanda. My conclusion: on this planet intolerance of difference has become an equal opportunity destroyer.

Before reaching even tentative conclusions about how we should deal with human earthlings, I thought it wise to do more research. Many human earthlings are obsessed with race, so I researched background data on that controversial word.

I discovered that the Oxford English Dictionary defines race as involving at least two major classifications. First, race encompasses rapid or continuous movement: "The act of running"; "Onward movement of a thing, as the heavenly bodies, a vehicle . . . running or rush of water".

349

Humans sometimes use race as an action verb. An example of this use of race is: "I'll **race** you to the house".

Similarly, race may mean: "[A] portion of time or space"; "The act of running, riding, sailing . . . in competition with one or more rivals". In this context race is used as a noun, for example, as in the statement, "The older I get, the harder it is to keep up in the race".

The second major meaning of race revolves around groups of persons, animals, or plants with common characteristics. Thus, the Oxford English Dictionary states that a race is: "A group of persons, animals, or plants, connected by common descent or origin", "A limited group of persons descended from a common ancestor; a house, family, kindred", "A group or class of persons, animals or things having some common feature or features".

I was utterly amazed to find that the Oxford English Dictionary contains nearly a half dozen pages single spaced, triple columned (in small type!), of definitions and illustrations of race. Etymological studies suggest that race became a part of European languages sometime during the period 1200-1500 C.E. For purposes of making my report, I will focus attention on the second major classification of race, namely concerns about humans who are perceived as constituting groups of individuals "having some common features."

Earlier I mentioned that human scientists have made some findings on race. The scholarship is vast, though of varying quality. I will not try to summarize all of it but merely give you a sense of some of the material that seems reasonable, reliable, and useful. I recently read a significant social science article entitled "On the Non-Existence of Human Races" by Dr. Frank B. Livingstone, a noted anthropologist. Livingstone stated that "the term, race, has had a long history of anthropological uses and it can be generally defined as referring to a group of local or breeding populations within a species." Livingstone noted that this definition of race failed to take into consideration the societal structure and movements of many early human populations. This description of race did not account for the impact of "the basic cause of biological variation, natural selection". Livingstone suggested that the concept of race should be abandoned in favor of "cline", a term proposed by Dr. Julian Huxley. Cline refers to a "gradation in measurable characters". For instance, over a particular geographical area, one can observe variations in human characteristics like the skin color of northern and southern Europeans.

I was especially struck by Livingstone's conclusion that the variability of genes is almost infinite; and accordingly if one classified individuals into distinct races based on whether they had different genes, there would be innumerable races. "With this definition there is also a high sickle cell gene frequency race consisting of some Greeks, Italians, Turks, Arabs, Africans and Indians, and low sickle cell race consisting of the rest of humanity. One could also speak of a high color blind and a low color blind race."

Among human earthlings, the notion that a race is a "single breeding population that varies in definable ways from other human sub populations" continues to have some modern followers. However, Dr. Audrey Smedley, a respected anthropologist, has pointed out that:

> Among the problems with the concept of races as breeding populations that [scientists] have recognized is the question of what constitutes a breeding population. What level of fertile endogamous marriage (or matings) must be maintained [to constitute] a breeding population? Should it be expressed in terms of percentage of all actual fertile matings? If so, what percentage should be definitive: 90 percent, 60 percent, or a simple majority (51 percent)? If, in a long-stable community, most people marry within a twenty-block area of their homes, is this population a race? If it were shown that over several generations, 70 percent of all marriages took place among people who attended the same high school, does the high school constitute a racial population? How does one ascertain breeding populations when social barriers prevent intermarriage, but not intermating? ... How long a period of time, or how many generations of intramating, does it take to produce a race? Underlying these questions is a more fundamental one: If races are breeding populations, are all breeding populations races?

Some scientists have noted that "in practice . . . the common designation of race is based on socially defined phenotypic traits, usually skin color and facial features, as they are seen through the filter of individual as well as social prejudice". One significant work involving genes and race noted that:

> The change of gene frequencies from one population to another is generally clinal rather than discrete. . . . [O]ur judgment about the

grouping of human races is quite subjective and dependent on the availability of gene frequency data. (We shall use the word <u>race</u> and <u>population</u> interchangeably without any social implication.)

Professor Ashley Montagu, a physical anthropologist, and a leading twentieth century thinker on race has argued that many physical anthropologists have assumed that races exist meaning that "in nature there exist groups of human beings comprised of individuals each of whom possesses a certain aggregate of characters which individually and collectively serve to distinguish them from the individuals in all other groups." Some scientists have called these groups races. However, Montagu contends that the existence of human races ought not to be assumed, rather it must be proved.

In a similar vein, Professor Jonathan Marks has argued that:

Human races, whatever they are conceived to be, cannot be objectively limited in space; to a large extent membership within them is culturally rather than biologically defined. We don't know how many there are, where to draw the boundaries between them, or what those boundaries and the people or places they enclose would represent. Human biological variation, instead, is gradual and continuous. Populations from different parts of the world are obviously often distinguishable from one another as they represent end points of a continuum. Given that race has little biological meaning for humans, we are left with populations.

Human populations differ, and often differ from one another on the average in some particular biological characteristics. In some cases the differences are constitutional and genetic; in others they are not. The social differences that often exist between human groups have served to exaggerate their biological differences.

In other words, race does not refer to groups of people classified solely on scientific information. Human earthlings are too similar to make such a system work. In fact, racial classifications tend to be subjective and arbitrary. For example, in a well known American legal decision, <u>Plessy v. Ferguson</u>, Homer Plessy was classified as a member of the Negro race even though "the mixture of colored blood was not discernible in him." The Supreme Court of the United States upheld a local law which forced Plessy to ride in a separate railway carriage from white persons. The <u>Plessy</u> case was used by white supremacists to justify segregating people of color in the worst public schools, transportation, accommodations and jobs. In short, I am tempted to say that among human earthlings race is such an elastic word that depending on how you categorize people, every family could be a "race".

Many natural scientists have abandoned the use of race as a concept for classifying human beings in any significant way. Nevertheless, strident dissenting voices exist. For example, in a recent controversial work, J. Philippe Ruston, contended that his research demonstrates that:

> On more than 60 variables, people of east Asian ancestry (Mongoloids, Orientals) and people of African ancestry (Negroids, blacks) define opposite ends of the spectrum, with people of European ancestry (Caucasoids, whites) falling intermediately, and with much variability within each broad grouping. This racial matrix emerges with measures of brain size, intelligence, reproductive behavior, sex hormones, twinning rate, speed of physical maturation, personality, family stability, law-abidingness, and social organization.

Ruston's studies have convinced him that despite initial misgivings, "the races do differ genetically, in the mechanisms underlying their behavior."

As I mentioned, I am not attempting to resolve these controversies; rather I merely outline a few of the ways in which "race" has been used by human earthlings. As I said, we can evaluate how to deal with human earthlings, later.

Let me tell you briefly about the use of race by other members of the general public.

It is not uncommon in twentieth century American conversation to hear terms such as the following used: "white race", "black race", "brown race", "yellow race", and "red race". In contexts where words denoting skin hue are used with the term race (for example "white race"), race serves as a proxy for color.

Similarly, some people use the term "African American race" or "Hispanic race" as a way to describe individuals who are classified as belonging to certain groups. When human earthlings use the words African

American or Hispanic in connection with "race", these words attempt among other things, to identify something about people's culture. Culture involves patterns and peculiarities of individual and group life and perceptions of reality.

For example, in his seminal work on the concept of race, Ashley Montagu states that:

> If you or I, with our present genetic background, had been born and brought up among a group of Australian Aborigines, we should be, culturally, behaviorally Australian Aborigines though physically we should remain members of our own ethnic group... Why? Because -- and by "culture" is ... the way of life of a people; cultures are people's ideas, sentiments, religious and secular beliefs, its language, tools and other material products, its institutions, customs, and ideals - because culture is something that one acquires by experience, unlike one's physical appearance, which one acquires through the action, for the most part, of inherited genes, but which under the influence of culturalizing factors is subject to considerable modification. The culture of persons, as of groups, will differ according to the kinds of experience they have undergone.

In addition, though less common now than in the past, the phrases "Jewish race" and even "Mohammedan race" are not foreign to the contemporary American lexicon. Here race is associated with terms that address individuals' religious and theological beliefs and practices. Similarly, phrases like "Mexican race" still occasionally find their way into contemporary conversation. It seems that in using words like "Mexican" in conjunction with race the speaker is attempting to identify people of a common nationality. Furthermore, race is sometimes identified even with people's language - the "Spanish race" or "the English race".

Similar terminology has long infiltrated the United States Supreme Court decisions. For example, <u>Ozawa v. U.S.</u> involved the denial of a citizenship application of a person who was born in Japan, lived in the United States for twenty years, raised his children in the United States, and received most of his own education in the U.S., too. Justice Sutherland wrote for a unanimous United States Supreme Court and said that Ozawa was "a person of the <u>Japanese race</u> born in Japan", that Ozawa was "clearly of a race which is not Caucasian," and that "a large number of the Federal and State courts have so decided and we find no reported case definitely

354

to the contrary." Sutherland stated, "These decisions are sustained by numerous scientific authorities. We think these decisions are right and so hold." During the course of the opinion, Justice Sutherland also said that the authors of the original Immigration Statute of 1790 intended to:

> confer the privilege of citizenship upon that class of persons who the fathers knew as white, and to deny to all who could not be so classified. It is not enough to say that the framers did not have in mind the <u>brown</u> or <u>yellow</u> <u>races</u> of Asia. It is necessary to go further and be able to say that had these particular races been suggested, the language of the Act would have been so varied as to include them within its privileges.

More recently, in <u>St. Francis College v. Al-Khazraji</u>, the United States Supreme Court noted that the Congressional debates leading to the passage of the Civil Rights Act of 1866 were "replete with references to the Scandinavian races . . . as well as the Chinese . . . Latin Spanish . . . and Anglo-Saxon races . . . Jews . . . Mexican . . . blacks . . . and Mongolians were similarly categorized." The Court said that:

> based on the history of ' 1981, we have little trouble in concluding that Congress intended ' to protect from discrimination identifiable classes of persons who are subjected to intentional discrimination solely because of their ancestry or ethnic characteristics. Such discrimination is racial discrimination that Congress intended ' 1981 to forbid, whether or not it would be classified as racial in terms of modern scientific theory.

In a remarkable footnote, the <u>St. Francis College</u> court stated that: There is a common popular understanding that there are three major human races - Caucasoid, Mongoloid, and Negroid. Many modern biologists and anthropologists, however, criticize racial classifications as arbitrary and of little use in understanding the variability of human beings . . . These observations and others have led some, but not all, scientists to conclude that racial classifications are for the most part socio-political, rather than biological, in nature.

The Court concluded that the United States' Civil Rights Act of 1866 authorized a citizen of the United States who had been born in Iraq to sue based upon racial discrimination.

355

The Big Bang, <u>Brown vs Board of Education</u> and Beyond

Very recently, United States Supreme Court Justice Antonin Scalia in a brief concurring opinion suggested that "In the eyes of government we are just one race here. It is American."

By simply listing these examples, one is struck by the way in which race serves as a proxy for a number of inter-related concepts: for example, color ("brown race"), culture ("African American race"), religion ("Jewish race"), nationality ("Mexican race"), and language ("Japanese race"). To state the matter differently using the Supreme Court's language in <u>St. Francis College</u>: race embraces "ancestry or ethnic characteristics." In other words, in contemporary American society, race refers to an individual's color, culture, religion, nationality, and language. The bottom line: race has become mixed up with a number of fundamental attributes associated with one's human identity.

Bear with me; I am trying to make sense of this (apparent) nonsense. I make the following preliminary observations. First, human earthlings have a complex organized way of making sense of reality. We can call this human earthlings' worldview or earthview. Second, based on my observations I believe that most human earthlings have a multi-racial worldview. In other words, many humans believe that the human race consists of a number of different races. Third, humans are convinced that these so-called races are identifiable based on color, culture, religion, nationality, and even language. Fourth, a careful analysis of past and present circumstances suggests that each of these attributes of human identity fits into a hierarchy.

In these circumstances, I propose to carry out further research on some of human earthlings' thought patterns (worldviews or earthviews) on race. That way I can better advise on the type of contact (if any) that we should have with these fascinating and strange life forms on this strange and fascinating planet.

I must say I am skeptical. Human earthlings are reputedly the highest life form on the planet and they butcher and exploit each other because of their skin colors, religious beliefs, and place of birth. I wonder whether we should have anything to do with them. If we leave them to themselves, perhaps in as little as fifty earth years we may be able to have the planet without bargaining or fighting. For example, in the United States, Americans seem to teach their children to disrespect human life early, as reflected in the recent murder of twelve children and a teacher by their classmates at Columbine High School in the nearby state of Colorado which is not too far from where I landed. The child killers then turned their weapons on themselves and destroyed their own lives .

On the other hand, I sense a genuine desire within the core of many human earthlings. They really want to experience what Oliver Hill, Sr., a far sighted human earthling, calls "a renaissance in human relations." Perhaps Dr. Martin Luther King, Jr., a visionary leader in the 1950's and 1960's expressed human earthlings' dilemma best:

> *[I]f we are to have peace on earth, our loyalties must ... transcend our race, our tribe, our class, and our nation; and this means we must develop a world perspective. No individual can live alone; no nation can live alone ... [W]e must either learn to live together as brothers or we are all going to perish together as fools.*

I will write again soon about my findings on the way human earthlings think, feel and act.

ENDNOTES

Introduction
Endnotes

1. Andrew Buni, The Negro in Virginia Politics: 1902-1965, 17 (1967).
2. Virginia Writers' Project, The Negro in Virginia, 239 (1940).
3. 194 U.S. 147 (1904).
4. Buni, supra note 1 at 24.
5. Id. at 27; Virginia Writers Project, supra note 2 at 240.
6. 281 U.S. 704 (1930) (per curiam).
7. 245 U.S. 60, 70-72 (1917).
8. Slaughter-House Cases, 83 U.S. 36 (1873); Strauder v. West Virginia, 100 U.S. 303 (1879); Ex Parte Virginia, 100 U.S. 339 (1979).
9. Luther P. Jackson, Negro Office Holders in Virginia, 1865-1895, passim (1946); Virginia Writers Project, supra note 2 at 233-234.
10. Jackson, supra note 9 at 69; Buni, supra note 1 at 1.
11. Jackson, supra note 9 at 69-74.
12. Id. at 80.
13. See, e.g., John Hope Franklin and Alfred A. Moss, Jr., From Slavery to Freedom: A History of African Americans, 249-254 (7th ed. 1994).

Chapter I- The Early Years
Endnotes

1. Alston v. School Board of Norfolk, 112 F.2d 992 (1940), cert. denied, 311 U.S. 693 (1940).

Chapter II - High School and College Days
Endnotes

1. Arthur R. Ashe, Jr., A Hard Road to Glory: A History of the African-American Athlete 1919-1945, 45 (1988).

2. Id. at 46.
3. J. Clay Smith, Jr., Emancipation: The Making of the Black Lawyer, 1844-1944, p. 390 (1993).
4. United States Constitution, Article 1, Section 2.
5. United States Constitution, Article 1, Section 9.
6. United States Constitution, Article 4, Section 2; United States Constitution, Article 1, Section 8, Clause 15.

Chapter III - Civil Rights and Human Rights Activity
Endnotes

1. Sometimes people think of civil rights as including the liberties and duties set out under the Constitution and laws of this country. In contrast, human rights embrace rights which come with being a human being on the planet earth. We fought initially for civil rights; but we soon recognized the need for both kinds of rights. For example, we sought to achieve the civil right to vote and the human right in a civilized society of an opportunity for employment. International instruments which seek to promote and protect human rights include the International Covenant on Civil and Political Rights, the International Covenant on Economic, Social, and Cultural Rights, The Second Optional Protocol to the International Covenant on Civil and Political Rights, The International Convention on the Elimination of All Forms of Racial Discrimination, and The International Convention on the Elimination of All Forms of Discrimination against Women.
2. See, John Hope Franklin & Alfred A. Moss, Jr., From Slavery to Freedom: A History of African-Americans, 261 (7th ed. 1994).
3. See, The Negro in Virginia, (Virginia Writers Project of the W.P.A.) 242 (1940); Andrew Buni, The Negro in Virginia Politics, 73 (1967).
4. See, e.g., Genna Rae McNeil, Groundwork: Charles Hamilton Houston and the Struggle for Civil Rights 70-72 (1983).
5. Id. at 33-45.
6. Id. at 53-56.
7. 271 U.S. 323 (1926).
8. Gilbert Ware, William Hastie: Grace Under Pressure 48-49 (1984).
9. Richard Kluger, Simple Justice: The History of Brown v. Board of Education and Black America's Struggle for Equality, 127 (1975).
10. 303 U.S. 613 (1938).
11. 309 U.S. 227 (1940).
12. McNeil, supra note 4 at 75.
13. Franklin and Moss, supra note 2 at 352.

14. <u>New Negro Alliance v. Sanitary Grocery Co.</u>, 303 U.S. 552 (1938), <u>amended</u> 303 U.S. 592 (1938). See also, Franklin and Moss, <u>supra</u> note 2 at 400-401.

15. J. Clay Smith, Jr., <u>Emancipation: The Making of the Black Lawyer 1844-1944</u>, 241 (1993).

16. Thomas Calhoun Walker, <u>The Honeypod Tree: The Life Story of Thomas Calhoun Walker</u>, 119-138 (1958).

17. Buni, <u>supra</u>, note 3 at 101; Herbert Aptheker, <u>A Documentary History of the Negro People in the United States</u>, 801 (Volume II, 1951).

18. McNeil, <u>supra</u> note 4 at 114-115.

19. <u>See also</u>, A. Leon Higginbotham, Jr. <u>Shades of Freedom</u>, 139-43 (1996) discussing the not uncommon American legal reality of prosecutors and judges making racist comments in the courts.

20. See, Arthur R. Ashe, Jr., <u>A Hard Road to Glory: A History of the African-American Athlete 1919-1945</u>, 54 (1988).

21. <u>See</u>, Pauli Murray, <u>Song in a Weary Throat: An American Pilgrimage</u>, 169-75 (1987); <u>Waller v. Commonwealth of Va.</u>, 178 Va. 294 (1941), 316 U.S. 679 (1942), 316 U.S. 712.

22. <u>Bradshaw v. Commonwealth</u>, 174 Va 391 (1939).

23. <u>Legions v. Commonwealth</u>, 23 S.E.2d 764, 765 (1943).

24. <u>Hampton v. Commonwealth</u>, 190 Va. 531, 537 (1950).

25. <u>Mills v. Bd. of Educ. of Anne Arundel County</u>, 30 F. Supp. 245(1939).

26. <u>Chambers v. Florida</u>, 309 U.S. 227 (1940). For further discussion of this all too common example of police abuse of Negro citizens, <u>see</u>, Higginbotham, <u>supra</u> note 19 at 162-163.

27. <u>Loving v. Virginia</u>, 147 S.E.2d 78 (1966), <u>rev*d</u>, 388 U.S. 1 (1967).

28. Rona Hirsch Mendelsohn, <u>Senate Confirmation of Supreme Court Appointments: The Nomination and Rejection of John J. Parker</u>,

29. <u>Roles v. School Board of Newport News</u>, 61 F. Supp. 395 (1945) (discussing the background of this lawsuit which was instituted in 1942). <u>Id.</u> at 396-98.

30. <u>Freeman v. County School Board of Chesterfield County</u>, 82 F. Supp. 167 (D. Va. 1948), <u>aff'd</u>, 171 F.2d 702 (4th Cir. 1948).

31. See, Higginbotham, <u>supra</u> note 19 at 154, 122-23; <u>Mitchell v. Chicago, R.I. & Pac. Ry.</u>, 229 I.C.C. 703 (1938), <u>Mitchell v. U.S.</u>, 313 U.S. 80 (1941).

32. Luther P. Jackson, <u>Negro Office Holders in Virginia, 1865-1895</u>, 46 (1946); <u>The Negro in Virginia</u>, <u>supra</u> note 3 at 236. William Cheek and Aimee Lee Cheek, <u>John Mercer Langston and the Fight for Black Freedom</u> 456 (1989).

33. Franklin and Moss, <u>supra</u> note 2 at 328-330, 445-48.

34. <u>Chance v. Lambeth</u>, 186 F.2d 879 (4th Cir. 1951), <u>cert. denied</u>, 341

U.S. 941 (1950); <u>sub nom</u>, <u>Atlantic Coast Line R.R. v. Chance</u>, 198 F.2d 549 (4th Cir. 1952), <u>cert. denied</u>, 344 U.S. 877 (1952).

35. Smith, <u>supra</u> note 15 at 236-37. <u>See also</u>, Okianer C. Dark and Allen Moye, <u>L. Marian Poe: A Model of Public Service</u>, 32, 38, Virginia Lawyer (1990).

36. Thomas Calhoun Walker, <u>supra</u> note 16 at 170-175, 212.

37. <u>Missouri ex rel. Gaines v. Canada</u>, 305 U.S. 337 (1938); <u>Sipuel v. Board of Regents</u>, 332 U.S. 631 (1948); <u>McLaurin v. Oklahoma State Regents</u>, 339 U.S. 637 (1950).

38. <u>Morgan v. Virginia</u>, 328 U.S. 373 (1946).

39. <u>Steele v. Louisville & Nashville R.R.</u>, 323 U.S. 192 (1944); <u>Tunstall v. Brotherhood of Locomotive Firemen</u>, 323 U.S. 210 (1944).

Chapter IV - Working Towards <u>Brown</u> and Beyond
Endnotes

1. <u>Corbin v. County School Board of Pulaski</u>, 177 F.2d 924 (4th Cir. 1949).

2. Genna Rae McNeil, <u>Groundwork: Charles Hamilton Houston and the Struggle for Civil Rights</u>, 113-15 (1983).

3. <u>Id</u>. at 277-78, note 33.

4. 182 A. 590 (Md. 1936).

5. 305 U.S. 337 (1938).

6. <u>Id</u>. at 351.

7. <u>To Secure These Rights: The Report of the President's Committee on Civil Rights</u> (1947).

8. <u>Id</u>. at 151-173.

9. 322 U.S. 631 (1948); 339 U.S. 637 (1950), respectively.

10. 323 U.S. 192 (1944); 323 U.S. 210 (1944), respectively.

11. 339 U.S. 629 (1950).

12. <u>Sweatt v. Painter</u>, 339 U.S. at 633-34.

13. <u>McLaurin v. Oklahoma State Regents</u>, 339 U.S. 637, 640 (1950).

14. <u>Blue v. Durham Public School District</u>, 95 F. Supp. 441 (D.N.C. 1951).

15. <u>Carter v. School Board of Arlington County</u>, 182 F.2d 531 (4th Cir. 1950).

16. 345 U.S. 972 (1953).

17. Bernard Schwartz, <u>Decisions: How the Supreme Court Decides Cases</u>, 96 (1996).

18. <u>R.R. Commonwealth v. Pullman Co.</u>, 312 U.S. 496 (1941).

19. <u>Hill v. School Board of Norfolk</u>, 282 F.2d 473 (4th Cir. 1960).

20. <u>School Board of Warren County v. Kilby</u>, 259 F.2d 497 (4th Cir. 1958).

21. <u>Allen v. School Board of Charlottesville</u>, 240 F.2d 59 (4th Cir. 1956),

<u>cert.denied</u>,, 353 U.S. 910 (1957).

22. <u>See</u>, <u>Harrison v. Day</u>, 106 S.E.2d 636 (Va. 1959).
23. <u>See</u>, <u>James v. Almond</u>, 170 F.Supp 331 (D. Va. 1959) <u>appealed dismissed</u> 359 U.S. 1006 (1959).
24. <u>NAACP v. Button</u>, 371 U.S. 415 (1963).
25. 412 U.S. 92 (1973).
26. <u>Quarles v. Phillip Morris</u>, 279 F.Supp. 505 (E.D.Va.1968).

Chapter V - Military Experience
Endnotes

1. Genna Rae McNeil, <u>Groundwork: Charles Hamilton Houston and the Struggle for Civil Rights</u>, 163-64 (1983); Richard Kluger, <u>Simple Justice: The History of Brown v. Board of Education and Black America's Struggle for Equality</u>, 219-26 (1976).
2. John Hope Franklin and Alfred A. Moss, Jr., <u>From Slavery to Freedom: A History of African Americans</u>, 331-35 (7th ed. 1994); Kelly Miller, <u>The World War for Human Rights,</u> 540-712 (1919).
3. Franklin and Moss, <u>supra</u> note 2 at 391.

Chapter VI - Political Activism
Endnotes

1. 33 F.2d 177 (4th Cir. 1930).
2. Andrew Buni, <u>The Negro in Virginia Politics: 1902-1965</u>, 122-23 (1907).
3. <u>Id</u>. at 151.
4. Thomas C. Walker, <u>The Honeypod Tree: The Life Story of Thomas C. Walker, "Lawyer Walker of Gloucester,"</u> 177 (1958).
5. See Va. Code of 1924, Section 93.
6. Buni, <u>supra</u> note 2 at 156.
7. J.Clay Smith, Jr., <u>Emancipation: The Making of the Black Lawyer 1844-1944</u>, 330 (1983).
8. See, The Virginia Writers Project, <u>The Negro in Virginia</u>, 292-300 (1940).
9. Executive Order Number 9981 issued July 26, 1948. See, Jack Foner, <u>Blacks and the Military in American History</u>, 181-183 (1974); Richard M. Dalfiume, <u>Desegregation of the Armed Forces: Fighting on Two Fronts 1939-1953</u>, 170-174 (1968).
10. The President's Committee on Government Contract Compliance, Equal Economic Opportunity 63-77 (1953).
11. Alonzo B. Hamby, <u>Man of the People: A Life of Harry S. Truman</u>,

585-604 (1995).

12. John Hope Franklin and Alfred A. Moss, Jr., From Slavery to Freedom: A History of African Americans, 225-27 (7ᵗʰ ed. 1994).

13. Charles McDowell, Jr., Richmond Times Dispatch, February 18, 1968.

14. See also, Franklin and Moss, supra note 12 at 394.

Chapter VIII - The Big Bang and Beyond
Endnotes

1. Genesis 1-2:1.

2. See, Stephen Hawking, A Brief History of Time, 46-51 (1988). Hawking discusses a number of theories of the creation of the universe including the Big Bang and the steady state theories.

3. I do not remember the name of the first person ever to use the term human earthling. I think Buckminister Fuller first used the term.

4. Raine Eisler, The Chalice and the Blade (1987).

5. John Hope Franklin and Alfred A. Moss, Jr., From Slavery to Freedom: A History of African Americans, 97 (7ᵗʰ ed. 1994).

6. Franklin D. Roosevelt, State of the Union Message 87 I Cong. Rec. 44, 46-47 (1941).

7. See also, the report of the Carnegie Corporation, Stating Points: Meeting the Needs of our Youngest Children, passim (1994).

8. Mark 4:16-20; Matthew 4:18-32; Luke 5:1-11.

9. I believe it was John Kenneth Galbraith.

10. Hawking, supra note 2 at 155-169.

11. See, Ashley Montagu, Man's Most Dangerous Myth: The Fallacy of Race (5ᵗʰ ed. 1974) 2242, especially 22-24, n.50, 35-40; Ivan Hannaford, Race: An Idea in the West (1996).

12. Franklin and Moss, supra note 5 at 74-76; Benjamin Quarles, The Negro in the American Revolution, 19-32, 119-157 (1961); Jack Foner, Blacks and the Military in American History, 8-18 (1974).

13. See, Montagu, supra note 11 especially 74-101.

14. 116 S.Ct. 2264 (1996).

15. Some years ago I was reading a book entitled, Milk Ain't Good for Nothing But a Cow. The text discussed how detrimental milk is to a lot of people. In fact, once I went to my doctor for treatment of a medical condition and asked why I had trouble with gas following consuming milk or milk products. He said, "Because you are a Negro." I said, "What in the hell do you mean by that?" He replied that the darker one's complexion, the more difficult it is to digest the lactose in milk.

16. <u>See</u>, Ali Mazrui, <u>Africa Since 1935</u> (UNESCO); Ali Mazrui,
      <u>The Africans</u>; Cain Hope Felder, <u>Troubling Biblical Waters</u> (1989).
17. Franklin and Moss, <u>supra</u> note 5 at 8. (See Joel Roger's works, too.)
18. Genesis 6:3.
19. Carl Sagan, <u>Cosmos</u>, 53 (1980).
20. G.S. Kirk and J.E. Raven, <u>The Presocratic Philosophers</u>, 406-408
      (1971).

SELECTED BIBLIOGRAPHY

Books and Articles

A Documentary History of the Negro People in the United States (Aptheker ed.), New York: Citadel Press 1951.

Adjusted Payment Compensation Act of 1936, 74 Cong. Sess. 2, Ch. 32 (January 27, 1936).

Ashe, Jr., Arthur R., A Hard Road to Glory: A History of the African-American Athlete 1919-1945, New York: Warner Books 1988.

Berry, Mary Frances, Black Resistance, White Law: a History of Constitutional Racism in America, Englewood Cliffs: Prentice Hall (2nd ed. 1994) 1971.

Bruce, John E., The Blood Red Record: A Review of the Horrible Lynchings and Burning of Negroes by Civilized White Men in the United States, as Taken from the Records, Albany [NY]: Argus Company 1901.

Buni, Andrew, The Negro in Virginia Politics: 1902-1965, Charlottesville: University of Virginia Press 1967.

Carnegie Task Force on Meeting the Needs of Young Children, Starting points : meeting the needs of our youngest children : the report of the Carnegie Task Force on Meeting the Needs of Young Children, New York: Carnegie Corporation of New York 1994.

Chace, James, Horatio Alger With Deep Pockets, New York Times, July 26, 1992, Section 7, page 11.

Cheek, William and Cheek, Aimee Lee, John Mercer Langston and the Fight for Black Freedom 1829-1865, Urbana: University of Illinois Press 1989.

Dalfiume, Richard M., Desegregation of the U.S. Armed Forces: Fighting on Two Fronts 1939-1953, Columbia: University of Missouri Press 1969.

Dark, Okianer C. and Moye, Allen, Lavinia Marian Poe: A Model of Public Service, 38 Va. Law. 32 (1990).

DuBois, W.E.B., The Souls of Black Folk: Essay and Sketches, Essays and Sketches Chicago : A. C. McClurg 1903.

Durham, William H., Coevolution: Genes, Culture and Human Diversity, Stanford: Stanford University Press 1991.

Eisler, Riane, The Chalice and the Blade: Our History, Our Future, Cambridge [Mass]: Harper & Row 1987.

Felder, Cain Hope, Troubling Biblical Waters: Race, Class, and Family, Maryknoll [NY]: Orbis Books 1989.

Foner, Jack, Blacks and the Military in American History: A New Perspective, New York: Praeger 1974.

Franklin, John Hope and Moss, Jr., Alfred A., From Slavery to Freedom: A History of African Americans, New Delhi: Amerind (7th ed. 1994) 1967.

Grubstein, Clifford, Fowler, Michael and Mendeloff, John, *External Human Fertilization: An Evaluation of Policy*, Science (1983).

Garonzik, Joseph, The Department of Housing and Urban Development: A Chronology, Washington, D.C.: U.S. Dept. of Housing and Urban Development, Office of Public Affairs(1977).

Hamby, Alonzo A., Man of the People: A Life of Harry S. Truman, New York: Oxford University Press 1995.

Hannaford, Ivan, Race: The History of an Idea in the West, Washington, D.C. : Woodrow Wilson Center Press 1996.

Hawking, Stephen, A Brief History of Time: From the Big Bang to Black Holes, New York: Bantam Books 1988.

Higginbotham, Jr., Leon A., Shades of Freedom: Racial Politics and Presumptions of the American Legal Process, New York: Oxford University Press 1996.

Holy Bible, *Deuteronomy* 5:7-8 (King James Version).

Holy Bible, *Exodus* 32 (King James Version).

Holy Bible, *Genesis* 1-2:1 (King James Version).

Holy Bible, *Genesis* 6:3 (King James Version).

Holy Bible, *Luke* 5:1-11 (King James Version).

Holy Bible, *Mark* 4:16-20 (King James Version).

Holy Bible, *Matthew* 4:18-21 (King James Version).

Jackson, Luther P., Negro Office-Holders in Virginia, 1865-1895, Norfolk: Guide Quality Press 1946.

Jackson, Luther P., Negro Office-Holders in Virginia 1865-1895, Ann Harbor [MI]: University Microfilms 1945.

Judge Dalton Dies; Guided Virginia G.O.P., Washington Post, November 1, 1989, B9.

Kelly, Tom, *Bonus Army's Tense Standoff, Vets '32 Protest Had U.S. on Edge*, Washington Times, Aug. 1, 1992 at C-1.

Kirk, Geoffrey S. and Raven, John E., The Pre-socratic Philosophers:a Critical History with a Selection of Texts, Cambridge [England]: University Press (2nd ed.) 1963.

Kluger, Richard, Simple Justice: The History of Brown v. Board of Education and Black America's Struggle for Equality, New York: Knopt 1976.

McDowell, Charles, Jr., *Printers Union Drops Murray From Two Post,* Richmond Times Dispatch, February 18, 1948.

McNeil, Genna Rae, Groundwork: Charles Hamilton Houston and the Struggle for Civil Rights, Philadelphia: University of Pennsylvania Press 1983.

Mendelsohn, Rona Hirsch, *Senate Confirmation of Supreme Court Appointments: The Nomination and Rejection of John J. Parker*, 14 Howard L. J. 105 (1968).

Miller, Kelly, Kelly Miller's History of the World War for Human Rights, Marietta

[OH]: S.A. Mullikin 1919.

Montagu, Ashley, <u>Man's Most Dangerous Myth: The Fallacy of Race</u>, New York: Oxford University Press (5th ed.) 1974.

President's Committee on Government Contract Compliance, <u>Equal Economic Opportunity: A Report</u>, Washington 1953.

President's Committee on Civil Rights, <u>To Secure These Rights: An Editorial Comment on the President's Civil Rights Committee Report</u>, Norfolk 1947.

Quarles, Benjamin, <u>The Negro in the American Revolution</u>, Chapel Hill: University of North Carolina Press 1961.

Roosevelt, Franklin D., The State of the Union Message, 87 I Congressional Record (1941).

Sagan, Carl, <u>Cosmos</u>, Tokyo: Asahi Shinbunsha 1980.

Schwartz, Bernard, <u>Decision: How the Supreme Court Decides Cases</u>, New York: Oxford University Press 1996.

Sherman, Richard B., <u>The Case of Odell Waller and Virginia Justice, 1940-1942</u> Knoxville: University of Tennessee Press 1992.

Smith, J. Clay, <u>Emancipation: The Making of the Black Lawyer 1844-1944</u>, Philadelphia: University of Pennsylvania Press 1993.

UNESCO International Scientific Committee for the Drafting of a General History of Africa, <u>Africa Since 1935</u>, (foreward by Ali Mazrui) Berkeley: University of California Press (2nd ed. 1999) 1993.

United States Senate Committee on Armed Services. <u>Universal Military Training, Hearings Before the Committee on Armed Services, United States Senate</u>, 80th Congress, 2d session- 82d Congress, 1st session 996, Washington, D.C.:The Committee (1948).

Walker, Thomas Calhoun, <u>The Honey-pod Tree: The Life Story of Thomas Calhoun Walker</u>, New York: J. Day Co. 1958.

Writers' Program of the Works Project's Administration In the State of Virginia, <u>The Negro in Virginia</u> New York: Hastings House 1940.

Others

42 United States Code Sections, 1981 and 1983
Constitution of the United States of America.
Virginia Constitution

TABLE OF CASES

369

LIST OF PHOTOGRAPHS

INDEX